SUCCESSFUL PROJECT MANAGEMENT

SUCCESSFUL PROJECT MANAGEMENT

Jack Gido

Penn State University

James P. Clements

Towson University

SOUTH-WESTERN College Publishing

An International Thomson Publishing Company

Publishing Team Director: John Szilagy
Acquisitions Editor: Charles McCormick
Developmental Editors: Sara Schroeder, Judith O'Neill
Production Editor: Amy C. Hanson
Production House: Lifland et al., Bookmakers
Internal Design: Craig Ramsdell
Cover Design: Jennifer Lynne Martin
Cover Photo: Mitchell Funk/Image Bank
Photo Research: Cary Benbow
Marketing Manager: Steve Scoble
Manufacturing Coordinator: Sue Kirven

Library of Congress Cataloging-in-Publication Data

Gido, Jack, 1945–
    Successful project management/Jack Gido, James P. Clements.
      p. cm.
    Includes bibliographical references and index.
    ISBN 0-538-88152-6
    1. Industrial project management.   I. Clements, James P.
  II. Title.
  HD69.P75G53   1999
  658.5--dc21   97-35412
                                                    CIP

5 6 7 8 9 C5 5 4 3 2 1 0

Printed in the United States of America

International Thomson Publishing
South-Western College Publishing is an ITP Company.
The ITP trademark is used under license.

To Rosemary, Steve, Jeff, Katie, and Wendy
for all the joy that you bring

J.G.

To my beautiful wife, Beth
and three wonderful children, Tyler, Hannah, and Maggie

J.P.C.

BRIEF CONTENTS

CONTENTS

PREFACE

We'll start digging from this side of the mountain. You and your gang start digging from the other side. When we meet in the middle, we will have made a tunnel. And if we don't meet, we will have made two tunnels!

OUR APPROACH

Project management is more than merely parceling out work assignments to individuals and vainly hoping that they will accomplish a desired result. In fact, projects that could have been successful often fail because of such take-it-for-granted approaches. Individuals need hard knowledge and real skills to work successfully in a project environment and to accomplish project objectives. *Successful Project Management* was written to equip its users with both. How? By explaining concepts and techniques and by illustrating through numerous examples how they are skillfully applied.

Although the focus of the book is squarely on the practical—the things readers absolutely need to know to thrive in project environments—the book does not forsake objective learning; it simply challenges readers to think critically about project management principles and to apply them within the context of the real world. We capture lessons learned from years of managing projects, teaching project management, and writing extensively about it.

Successful Project Management is intended for students as well as for working professionals and volunteers. The book is designed to outfit them with the essential skills they need to make effective contributions and to have immediate impact on the accomplishment of projects in which they are involved. Thus, it supports business and industry's life-long learning programs, which develop and train employees to succeed on interdisciplinary and cross-functional teams, and sends students into the workforce with marketable skills.

Successful Project Management is written for everyone involved in projects, not only for project managers. Projects with good or even great project managers still may not succeed, as the best efforts of all involved are essential. All of the many people who contribute to a project—the project team—must have the knowledge and skills to work effectively together in a project environment. People do not become project managers by reading books; they become project managers by first being effective project team members. This book provides the foundation individuals need to be effective members of project teams and thereby boosts everyone's potential to rise to the challenge of managing teams and projects.

Our book is written in an easy-to-understand, straightforward style and contains a minimum number of technical terms. Readers acquire project management terminology gradually as they read the text. The text does not use complex mathematical theories or algorithms to describe scheduling techniques nor does it include highly technical projects as examples. An overtly technical approach can create a barrier to learning for those individuals who lack deep understanding of advanced mathematics or technical backgrounds. Our book includes a broad range of easily understood examples based on projects encountered in everyday situations. For example, real-world applications include conducting a market survey, building an information system, and organizing a town festival. The mathematics used in this book is purposely kept simple. Separate appendixes are provided for readers who want in-depth coverage of probability considerations and time–cost trade-offs.

DISTINCTIVE FEATURES

Successful Project Management has many distinctive features to enhance learning and build skills.

Real-World Vignettes Each chapter opens with two real-world vignettes that set the stage for the topics to be presented in the chapter. These vignettes not only reinforce chapter concepts but also draw readers into the discussion and pique their interest in what is to come.

Chapter Outlines Each chapter opens with an outline of the key topics that will be covered. These outlines clarify expectations and allow you to see the flow of information at a glance.

Examples and Applications Real-world examples and applications—conducting a market survey, building an information system, and organizing a town festival—are diffused throughout this text, ensuring that specific, relevant, and compelling illustrations are never far from view.

Graphics and Figures Over 130 exhibits appear in the text to illustrate important points and project management tools.

Reinforce Your Learning Questions Brief questions appear alongside the text to ensure that readers retain key concepts and that the fundamentals are not ignored. These in-the-margin questions "pop up" throughout the text to provide positive reinforcement and serve as an in-text study guide.

Chapter Summaries At the end of each chapter you'll find a concise summary of the material presented in the chapter—a final distillation of core concepts.

Review Questions and Problems Each chapter has a set of questions and problems that first test and then apply chapter concepts.

World Wide Web Exercises Each chapter has a set of exercises that ask readers to search World Wide Web sites for information on various project management topics. These exercises invite learners to explore real-world applications of project management in an online, hands-on manner. An end-of-book appendix provides Web addresses of all the project management sites mentioned in this text.

Case Studies End-of-chapter case studies provide critical-thinking scenarios for either individual or group analysis. Variety in case format ensures that all learners can relate to the problems presented. Our cases are fun and will spark interesting debates. By fostering discussion of various viewpoints, the cases provide opportunities for participants to expand their thinking about how to operate successfully when differing views arise in the work environment. Thus students gain valuable insight into what teamwork is all about.

Project Management Software An appendix discusses the use of personal computer–based project management software as a tool in the planning and control of projects. Common features of project management software packages are discussed, along with criteria for selecting among them. A review of a few popular software packages is also included, and an extensive list of vendors offering project management software has been compiled for you.

Project Management Organizations A list of project management organizations worldwide is provided in an appendix for those individuals who want to contact these organizations about professional development, access to periodicals and other publications, or career opportunities.

ORGANIZATION

Successful Project Management is divided into three parts:

- Part 1, *The Life of a Project,* covers project management concepts, needs identification, proposed solutions, and implementing the project.

- Part 2, *People: The Key to Project Success,* discusses the project manager, the project team, types of project organizations, and project communication and documentation.
- Part 3, *Project Planning and Control,* covers planning, scheduling, schedule control, resource considerations, and cost planning and performance.

Part 1 consists of four chapters. Chapter 1, *Project Management Concepts,* covers the definition of a project and its attributes, the key constraints within which a project must be managed, how a project is "born," the life of a project, the steps in the project management process, examples of projects, and the benefits of project management. Chapter 2, *Needs Identification,* includes identifying needs and selecting projects, developing a Request for Proposal, and the proposal solicitation process. Chapter 3, *Proposed Solutions,* deals with proposal marketing strategies, the bid/no-bid decision, development of winning proposals, the proposal preparation process, pricing considerations, evaluation of proposals, and types of contracts. Chapter 4, *The Project,* discusses the elements involved in establishing a project plan, the steps in the project control process, and actions that should be taken when a project is terminated.

Part 2 includes four chapters. Chapter 5, *The Project Manager,* discusses the responsibilities of the project manager, the skills needed to successfully manage projects and ways to develop those skills, approaches to effective delegation, and how the project manager can manage and control changes to the project. Chapter 6, *The Project Team,* covers the development and growth of teams, characteristics of effective project teams and barriers to effectiveness, team building, sources of conflict during the project and approaches to handling conflict, problem solving, and effective time management. Chapter 7, *Types of Project Organizations,* deals with the characteristics, advantages, and disadvantages of the functional, project, and matrix organization structures. Chapter 8, *Project Communication and Documentation,* includes personal communications, effective listening, types of project meetings and suggestions for effective meetings, formal project presentations and suggestions for effective presentations, project reports and suggestions for preparing useful reports, and project documentation and keeping track of changes.

Part 3 contains five chapters. Chapter 9, *Planning,* discusses clearly defining the project objective, developing a work breakdown structure, assigning responsibilities and defining detailed activities, developing a network diagram, and utilizing the systems development life cycle for information system development projects. Chapter 10, *Scheduling,* covers estimating activity durations, calculating earliest and latest start and finish times for each activity, determining slack, and identifying the critical path of activities. This chapter also includes a special appendix on probability considerations. Chapter 11, *Schedule Control,* deals with the steps in the project control process, the effects of actual schedule performance on the project schedule, incorporating project changes into the schedule, calculating an updated project schedule, and approaches to controlling the project schedule. This chapter also includes a special appendix on the time–cost trade-off. Chapter 12, *Resource Considerations,* includes taking resource constraints into account when developing a project plan, determining the planned resource utilization for a project, leveling the use of resources within the required time frame for a project, and determining the shortest project schedule when the number of resources available is limited. Chapter 13, *Cost Planning and Performance,* covers items to be considered when estimating the project cost, preparation of a baseline budget, cumulating actual costs, determining the earned value of work actually performed, analyzing cost performance, calculating a forecast for the project cost at completion, approaches to controlling costs, and managing cash flow.

The book includes a special appendix devoted to project management software, which discusses the common features available in most project management software packages, sample printouts, a review of a few popular software packages, criteria for selecting a software package, advantages of and concerns about using project management software, and a list of vendors offering project management software. Other appendixes provide a list of project management organizations, project management World Wide Web sites, and project management acronyms. Finally, the book includes references for each chapter, answers to the Reinforce Your Learning questions, and a glossary of terms.

SUPPORT MATERIALS

A comprehensive set of support materials is available for *Successful Project Management.* These materials are designed to guide the instructor and to minimize class preparation time. The supplements include the following.

An *Instructor's Manual with Test Bank* includes

- sample syllabi
- a set of learning objectives for each chapter
- suggested teaching methods for each chapter
- lecture outlines for each chapter
- answers to the end-of-chapter questions
- a comprehensive test bank of true/false, multiple-choice, and problem-solving exercises for each chapter
- transparency masters of key figures from the text
- a hard copy of the PowerPoint slides for each chapter

Westest 3.2 for Windows, a computerized test bank, makes questions and problems from the printed test bank available on disk. Westest allows instructors to create exams by selecting among provided questions, modifying existing questions, or adding questions.

PowerPoint Slides give the instructor a complete set of slides, on disk, for use during class lectures and discussions. All you need is Windows to run the PowerPoint viewer and an LCD panel for classroom displays.

ACKNOWLEDGMENTS

We would like to acknowledge the individuals who helped with the publication of this book. Jason Oakman did a meticulous job in preparing the graphics, Glenn Fueston carefully checked the Web sites, and Joan Lang and Robert Lentz put in long hours typing. We want to thank all the members of the project team at South-Western College Publishing, who helped turn our vision into reality and contributed to the successful completion of this project. Special recognition goes to Developmental Editors Sara Schroeder and Judy O'Neill, Production Editor Amy Hanson, and all the folks at Lifland et al., Bookmakers. We would also like to recognize the important contributions of the reviewers of this book:

Charles Bilbrey
James Madison University

Tim Butler
Wayne State University

Sam DeWald
Penn State University

Ike Ehie
Southeast Missouri State University

James Ford
Ford Consulting Associates

Laurie J. Kirsch
University of Pittsburgh

Richard E. Kust
California State University, Fullerton

Mary Jo Maffei
MQ Associates

Jeffrey Pinto
Penn State University

H. Dan Reid
University of New Hampshire

Carl R. Schultz
University of New Mexico

William Sherrard
San Diego State University

Christy Strbiak
New Mexico State University

We would like to acknowledge all the individuals with whom we worked on projects and all the people who participated in our many project management seminars. They provided a learning environment for testing the practical lessons included in this book.

There are those who make things happen,
those who let things happen, and
those who wonder what happened.

We hope that *Successful Project Management* will help the readers/ learners have an enjoyable, exciting, and successful experience as they grow through their future project endeavors—and be the catalyst for helping them make things happen.

Jack Gido
James P. Clements

ABOUT THE AUTHORS

Jack Gido is Director of PENNTAP, the Pennsylvania Technical Assistance Program, at Penn State University. He previously held dual positions as Manager of the Industrial Technology Extension Service of the New York Science and Technology Foundation and as Deputy Director of the Industrial Effectiveness Program at the New York State Department of Economic Development. His 20 years of industrial management experience includes management of productivity improvement and manufacturing technology programs. He received a B.S. in electrical engineering from Penn State University and an M.B.A. from the University of Pittsburgh. He has authored two other books on project management and has taught workshops on project management.

James P. Clements is Chairperson of the Department of Computer and Information Sciences at Towson University and serves as Adjunct Professor of Information Systems and Technology for the Whiting School of Engineering at The Johns Hopkins University. He earned a Ph.D. at the University of Maryland Baltimore County and dual master's degrees in operations analysis and computer science at the University of Maryland Baltimore County and The Johns Hopkins University, respectively. An active promoter of collaborative learning in core computer and information science courses, Dr. Clements is a four-time winner of the Faculty Member of the Year Award given by students at TU. His research and consulting interests have led to associations with a variety of business and industry groups, including Applied Physics Lab at The Johns Hopkins University, Bell Atlantic Corp., Chesapeake Directory Sales Corporation, General Physics Corp., G.P. Taurio, Inc., UPS/Roadnet Technologies, and USF&G.

The Life of a Project

The chapters in Part 1 introduce the concepts of project management and the project life cycle. A project is an endeavor to accomplish a specific objective through a unique set of interrelated tasks and the effective utilization of resources. It has a well-defined objective stated in terms of scope, schedule, and cost. Projects are "born" when a need is identified by the customer—the people or organization willing to provide funds to have the need satisfied.

The first phase of the project life cycle involves the identification of a need, problem, or opportunity and can result in the customer's requesting proposals from individuals, a project team, or organizations (contractors) to address the identified need or solve the problem. The second phase of the project life cycle is the development of a proposed solution to the need or problem. This phase results in the submission of a proposal to the customer by one or more individuals or organizations. The third phase of the project life cycle is the implementation of the proposed solution. This phase, which is referred to as performing the project, results in accomplishment of the project objective, leaving the customer satisfied that the full scope of work was completed in a quality manner, within budget, and on time. The final phase of the project life cycle is terminating the project.

Project management involves a process of first establishing a plan and then implementing that plan to accomplish the project objective. Taking the time to develop a well-thought-out plan is critical to the successful accomplishment of any project. Once the project starts, the project management process involves monitoring progress to ensure that everything is going according to plan. The key to effective project control is measuring actual progress and comparing it to planned progress on a timely and regular basis and taking corrective action immediately, if necessary.

The ultimate benefit of implementing project management techniques is having a satisfied customer—whether you are the customer of your own project or a business (contractor) being paid by a customer to perform a project. Completing the full scope of work of the project in a quality manner, on time, and within budget provides a great feeling of satisfaction. When projects are successful, everybody wins!

Project Management Concepts

Musical Superstars Put on Projects for Charity

Over the last decade or so, numerous musical projects have raised millions of dollars for charity. The one that seems to have initiated this trend is Live Aid, which was put together in the 1980s by rock musician Bob Geldof. This massive musical undertaking, which involved dozens of top musical acts, harnessed the strong, affective component of music and created a solidarity between American and British youth and the starving people of Ethiopia. Geldof's successful planning and organization of this monumental famine relief effort created awareness and helped initiate global action for starvation relief. Since that very successful project, numerous other musical superstars have stepped forward and joined in helping charitable causes.

In October of 1996, the Farm Aid IX mega concert was held at Williams-Brice Stadium on the University of South Carolina campus. This event featured Willie Nelson, Jewel, John Mellencamp, Neil Young (with Crazy Horse), hometown rockers Hootie & The Blowfish, and over fifty other musical acts. "Both musically and financially this project was a resounding success," said Glenda Yoder, associate director of Farm Aid. "It's a real challenge to pull off a project like this with so many bands and long hours," Yoder said. "I give a lot of credit to the team of people who organized, planned, and orchestrated this event."

The Farm Aid projects have netted over $12 million over the past ten years, with the money going to food and emergency relief, education and scholarships, land stewardship, technical assistance, churches, and service organizations.

In September of 1992, Hurricane Relief, an evening of music and comedy at Joe Robbie Stadium in Miami, Florida, raised over $1.3 million for victims of Hurricane Andrew. Gloria Estefan, Whoopi Goldberg, Jimmy Buffett, Paul Simon, the Bee Gees, Rosie O'Donnell, Sinbad, and numerous others entertained a sellout crowd of 53,000 in the nine-hour benefit event. The Hurricane Relief project came about just after Hurricane Andrew struck on August 24, creating the worst natural disaster in U.S. history. Gloria and Emilio Estefan initiated the idea and pulled the whole project together in just three weeks.

Each of these projects required serious planning, scheduling, organization, teamwork, communications, and leadership—all of which will be discussed in detail in this book.

Sources: C. Flippo, "Seventh Farm Aid Benefit," *Billboard,* September 30, 1995; R. Waddell, "Another Farm Aid Hit," *Amusement Business,* October 21, 1996; F. Westley, "Bob Geldof and Live Aid: The Affective Side of Global Social Innovation," *Human Relations,* October 1991; and D. Wilker, "Hurriedly Arranged Hurricane Event Is a Hit," *Billboard,* October 12, 1992.

The Department of Labor and Industries

The State of Washington's Department of Labor and Industries (DLI) decided the department could save time and money by developing a computerized system that would scan, index, and retrieve documents for processing all Worker's Compensation claims. However, soon after the project was initiated, the situation became anything but promising. The first project manager had come and gone, and the second quickly did the same. In addition, the state's top executives were already upset over the failure of another major project in the state. The $20 million imaging systems project was off to a troubled start.

In order to avert the potential failure, DLI assigned Tom Carroll to the position of project director. Carroll was a seasoned project manager who saw this as an excellent opportunity to use some of the management and leadership skills he had acquired as an intelligence officer in the Navy. He immediately formed a team of core people who worked with a major consulting firm to plan, design, develop, and implement one of the largest imaging systems in state government. By the end of the year, the project team had fully implemented the system, ahead of schedule and under budget.

More important, the system met all expectations. Workers could now scan, index, and retrieve documents for processing all Worker's Compensation claims at a savings of tens of millions of dollars.

Behind the achievements of this story and numerous others lies a critical component—project management. By thoroughly studying and understanding the material discussed in this text, you can greatly improve your chances of one day contributing to a similar success story.

Source: T. Newcombe, "Project Management at Ground Zero," *Government Technology,* March 1996.

This chapter presents an overview of project management concepts. You will become familiar with

- the definition of a project and its attributes
- the key constraints within which a project must be managed
- how a project is "born"
- the life of a project
- the steps involved in the project management process
- the benefits of project management

ATTRIBUTES OF A PROJECT

A **project** is an endeavor to accomplish a specific objective through a unique set of interrelated tasks and the effective utilization of resources. The following attributes help define a project:

- A project has a well-defined **objective**—an expected result or product. The objective of a project is usually defined in terms of *scope, schedule,* and *cost.* For example, the objective of a project might be to introduce to the market—in 10 months and within a budget of $500,000—a new food preparation appliance that meets certain predefined performance specifications. Furthermore, it is expected that the work scope will be accomplished in a *quality manner* and to the *customer's satisfaction.*
- A project is carried out through a series of *interdependent tasks*—that is, a number of nonrepetitive tasks that need to be accomplished in a certain sequence in order to achieve the project objective.
- A project utilizes various *resources* to carry out the tasks. Such resources can include different people, organizations, equipment, materials, and facilities. For example, a wedding is a project that may involve resources such as a caterer, a florist, a limousine, and a reception hall.
- A project has a *specific time frame,* or finite life span. It has a start time and a date by which the objective must be accomplished. For example, the refurbishing of an elementary school might have to be completed between June 20 and August 20.
- A project may be a *unique* or *one-time endeavor.* Some projects—like designing and building a space station—are unique because they have never before been attempted. Other projects, such as developing a new product, building a house, or planning a wedding, are unique because of the customization required. For

example, a wedding can be a simple informal occasion, with a few friends in a chapel, or a spectacular event staged for a prince.

- A project has a customer. The **customer** is the entity that provides the funds necessary to accomplish the project—it can be a person, an organization, or a group of two or more people or organizations. When a contractor builds a customized home for a couple, the couple is the customer funding the project. When a company receives funds from the government to develop a robotic device for handling radioactive material, the customer is the government agency. When a company provides funds for a team of its employees to upgrade the firm's management information system, the term *customer* takes on a broader definition, including not only the project funder (the company's management) but also other stakeholders, such as the people who will be the end users of the information system. The person managing the project and the project team must successfully accomplish the project objective to satisfy the customer(s).

- Finally, a project involves a *degree of uncertainty*. Before a project is started, a plan is prepared based on certain assumptions and estimates. It is important to document these assumptions, since they will influence the development of the project budget, schedule, and work scope. A project is based on a unique set of tasks and estimates of how long each task should take, various resources and assumptions about the availability and capability of those resources, and estimates of the costs associated with the resources. This combination of assumptions and estimates causes a degree of uncertainty that the project objective will be completely accomplished. For example, the project scope may be accomplished by the target date, but the final cost may be much higher than anticipated because of low initial estimates for the cost of certain resources. As the project proceeds, some of the assumptions will be refined or replaced with factual information. For example, once the conceptual design of a company's annual report is finalized, the amount of time and effort needed to complete the detailed design and printing can be better estimated.

REINFORCE YOUR LEARNING
1. *What are some attributes of a project?*

The following are some examples of projects:

Staging a theatrical production
Developing and introducing a new product
Planning a wedding
Designing and implementing a computer system
Issuing a new $1.00 coin
Modernizing a factory
Consolidating two manufacturing plants
Converting a basement to a family room
Hosting a conference
Designing and producing a brochure
Executing an environmental clean-up of a contaminated site
Holding a high school reunion
Building a shopping mall

REINFORCE YOUR LEARNING
2. *Identify five projects in which you were involved during your lifetime.*

Performing a series of surgeries on an accident victim
Putting on a centennial celebration
Rebuilding a town after a natural disaster
Hosting a dinner for twenty relatives
Designing a business internship program for high school students
Building a tree house

The successful accomplishment of the project objective is usually constrained by four factors: *scope, cost, schedule,* and *customer satisfaction.* See Figure 1.1.

The scope of a project—also known as the **project scope** or the work scope—is all the work that must be done in order to satisfy the customer that the deliverables (the tangible product or items to be provided) *meet the requirements or acceptance criteria agreed upon at the onset of the project.* For example, the project scope might be all of the work involved in clearing the land, building a house, and landscaping to the specifications agreed upon by the contractor and the buyer. The customer expects the work scope to be accomplished in a quality manner. For example, in a house-building project, the customer expects the workmanship to be of the highest quality. Completing the work scope but leaving windows that are difficult to open and close, faucets that leak, or a landscape full of rocks will result in an unsatisfied customer.

The **cost** of a project is the amount the customer has agreed to pay for acceptable project deliverables. The project cost is based on a budget that includes an estimate of the costs associated with the various resources that will be used to accomplish the project. It might include the salaries of people who will work on the project, materials and supplies, rental of equipment or facilities, and the fees of subcontractors or consultants who will perform some of the project tasks. For example, if the project is a wedding, budgeted items might include flowers, gown, tuxedo, caterer, cake, limousine rental, photographer, and so on.

The **schedule** for a project is the timetable that specifies when each activity should start and finish. The project objective usually states the time by which the project scope must be completed in terms of a specific date agreed upon by the customer and the individual or organization performing the work. It might be the date when a town's centennial celebration will take place or the date by which you want to complete the addition of a family room to your home.

The objective of any project is to complete the scope within budget by a certain time to the customer's satisfaction. To help assure the achievement of this objective, *it is important to develop a plan before the start of the project; this plan should include all the work tasks, associated costs, and estimates of the time necessary to complete them.* The lack of such a plan increases the risk of failing to accomplish the full project scope within budget and on schedule.

Once a project is started, unforeseen circumstances may occur that jeopardize the achievement of the project objective with respect to scope, cost, or schedule.

- The cost of some of the materials may be higher than originally estimated.

FIGURE 1.1 Factors Constraining Project Success

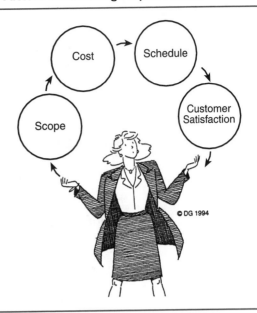

Courtesy of Dynamic Graphics, Inc.

- Inclement weather may cause a delay.
- Additional redesign and modifications to a sophisticated piece of automated machinery may be required to get it to meet the performance specifications.

The challenge to the project manager is to prevent, anticipate, and/or overcome such circumstances in order to complete the project scope on schedule, within budget, and to the customer's satisfaction. *Good planning and communication* are essential to prevent problems from occurring and to minimize their impact on the achievement of the project objective when they do occur. The project manager needs to be proactive in planning and communicating and provide leadership to the project team to accomplish the project objective.

Ultimately, the responsibility of the project manager is to make sure the customer is satisfied. This goes beyond just completing the project scope within budget and on schedule or asking the customer at the end of the project if he or she is satisfied. It requires ongoing communication with the customer to keep the customer informed and to determine whether expectations have changed. Regularly scheduled meetings or progress reports, frequent phone discussions, and email are examples of ways to accomplish such communications. Customer satisfaction means involving the customer as a partner in the successful outcome of the project through active participation during the project. The project manager must be aware of the degree of customer satisfaction throughout the project. By maintaining regular communication with the customer, the project manager demonstrates to the customer that he or she is genuinely concerned with the expectations of the customer and prevents unpleasant surprises later.

REINFORCE YOUR LEARNING

3. What are four factors that constrain the achievement of a project objective?

PROJECT LIFE CYCLE

Figure 1.2 shows the four phases of the **project life cycle** and the relative amount of effort and time devoted to each phase. As the project moves through its life cycle, different organizations, individuals, and resources play dominant roles.

Projects are "born" when a need is identified by the *customer*—the people or the organization willing to provide funds to have the need satisfied. For example, for a growing family, the need may be for a larger house, whereas for a company the problem may be a high scrap rate from its manufacturing process that makes its costs higher and production times longer than those of its competitors. The customer first must identify the need or problem. Sometimes the problem is identified quickly, as in the case of a disaster such as an earthquake or explosion. In other situations, it may take months for a customer to clearly identify a need, gather data on the problem, and define certain requirements that must be met by the person, project team, or contractor who will solve the problem.

This *first phase* of the project life cycle involves the identification of a need, problem, or opportunity and can result in the customer's requesting proposals from individuals, a project team, or organizations (contractors) to address the identified need or solve the problem. The need and requirements are usually written up by the customer in a document called a **request for proposal (RFP).** Through the RFP, the customer then asks individuals or contractors to submit proposals on how they might solve the problem, along with the associated cost and schedule. A couple who need a new house may spend time identifying requirements for the house—size, style, number of rooms, location, maximum amount they want to spend, and date by which they would like to move in. They may then write down these requirements and ask several contractors to provide house plans and cost estimates. A company that has identified a need to upgrade its computer system might document its requirements in an RFP and send it to several computer consulting firms. Not all situations involve a formal RFP, however. Needs often are defined informally during a meeting or discussion among a group of individuals. Some of the individuals may then volunteer or be requested to prepare a proposal to determine whether a project should be undertaken to address the need. Such a scenario might be played out when the management of a hospital wants to establish an on-site day care center for the children of its employees. The management team or a specific manager may write down the requirements in a document and give it to an internal project team, which in turn will submit a proposal for how to establish the center. In this case, the contractor is the hospital's own internal project team, and the customer is the hospital's manager or, possibly, board of directors. It is important to define the right need. For example, is the need to provide an on-site day care center, or is it to provide child care for the children of the hospital's employees? Is "on-site" necessarily part of the need?

FIGURE 1.2 Project Life Cycle

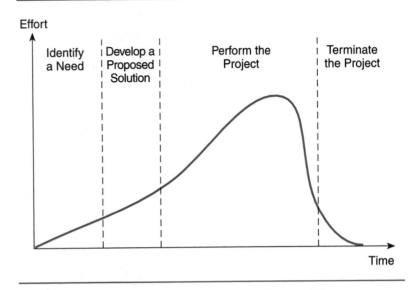

The *second phase* of the project life cycle is the development of a proposed solution to the need or problem. This phase results in the submission of a **proposal** to the customer by one or more individuals or organizations (contractors) who would like to have the customer pay them to subsequently implement the proposed solution. In this phase, the contractor effort becomes dominant. Contractors interested in responding to the RFP may spend several weeks developing approaches to solving the problem, estimating the types and amounts of resources that would be needed, and estimating the time it would take to design and implement the proposed solution. Each contractor documents this information in a written proposal. All of the contractors submit their proposals to the customer. For example, several contractors may submit proposals to a customer to develop and implement an automated invoicing and collection system. After the customer evaluates the submissions and selects the winning proposal, the customer and the winning contractor negotiate and sign a **contract** (agreement). In many situations, a request for proposal may not involve soliciting competitive proposals from external contractors. A company's own internal project team may develop a proposal in response to a management-defined need or request. In this case, the project would be performed by the company's own employees rather than an external contractor.

The *third phase* of the project life cycle is the implementation of the proposed solution. This phase begins after the customer decides which of the proposed solutions will best fulfill the need and an agreement is reached between the customer and the individual or contractor who submitted the proposal. This phase, referred to as performing the project, involves doing the detailed planning for the project and then implementing that plan to accomplish the project objective. During the course of performing the project, different types of resources will be utilized. For example, if the project is to design and construct an office building, the project effort might first involve a few architects and engineers in developing the building plans. Then, as construction gets under way, the resources needed will substantially increase to include steelworkers, carpenters, electricians, painters, and the like. The project will wind down after the building is finished, and a smaller number of different workers will finish up the landscaping and final interior touches. This phase results in the accomplishment of the project objective, leaving the customer satisfied that the full scope of the work was completed in a quality manner, within budget, and on time. For example, the third phase is complete when a contractor has completed the design and installation of a customized automation system that satisfactorily passes performance tests and is accepted by the customer or when an internal project team within a company has completed a project, in response to a management request, that consolidated two of its facilities into one.

The *final phase* of the project life cycle is terminating the project. When a project is completed, certain close-out activities need to be performed, such as confirming that all deliverables have been provided to and accepted by the customer, that all payments have been collected, and that all invoices have been paid. An important task during this phase is evaluating performance of the project in order to learn what could be improved if a similar project were to be carried out in the future. This phase should include obtaining feedback from the customer to determine the level of the customer's satisfaction and whether the project met the customer's expectations. Also, feedback should be obtained from the project team in the form of recommendations for improving performance of projects in the future.

Project life cycles vary in length from a few weeks to several years, depending on the content, complexity, and magnitude of the project. What's more, not all projects formally go through all four phases of the project life cycle. If a group of community volunteers decide that they want to use their own time, talents, and resources to organize a food drive for the homeless, they may get right into phase three—planning the event and carrying it out. The first two phases of the life cycle would not be relevant to such a project. Likewise, if a company's general manager determines that changing the layout of equipment in the factory will increase efficiency, she might simply instruct the manufacturing manager to initiate such a project and to implement it using the company's own people. In this case, there would be no written request for proposal from external contractors.

In other situations, such as a home remodeling project for which a contractor will likely be hired, a customer may go through the first two phases of the project life cycle in a less structured, more informal manner. He may not write down all of the requirements and ask several contractors for estimates. Rather, he may call a contractor who has done satisfactory work for him or a neighbor in the past, explain what he wants done, and ask the contractor to provide some sketches and a cost estimate.

REINFORCE YOUR LEARNING

4. *Match the phases of the project life cycle, in the column on the left, with the descriptions, in the column on the right:*

C First phase   A. *Developing the proposed solution*

A Second phase   B. *Implementing the proposed solution*

B Third phase   C. *Identifying the need or problem*

D Fourth phase   D. *Terminating the project*

In general, the project life cycle is followed in a more formal and structured manner when a project is conducted in a business setting. It tends to be less formal when a project is carried out by a private individual or volunteers.

THE PROJECT MANAGEMENT PROCESS

Succinctly, the project management process means *planning the work and then working the plan*. A coaching staff may spend hours preparing unique plans for a game; then the team executes the plans to try to meet the objective—victory. Similarly, project management involves a process of first *establishing a plan* and then *implementing that plan* to accomplish the project objective.

The front-end effort in managing a project must be focused on establishing a baseline plan that provides a roadmap for how the project scope will be accomplished on time and within budget. This planning effort includes the following steps:

1. *Clearly define the project objective.* The definition must be agreed upon by the customer and the individual or organization who will perform the project.
2. *Divide and subdivide the project scope into major "pieces," or* **work packages.** Although major projects may seem overwhelming when viewed as a whole, one way to conquer even the most monumental endeavor is to break it down. A **work breakdown structure (WBS)** is a hierarchical tree of work elements or items accomplished or produced by the project team during the project. The work breakdown structure usually identifies the organization or individual responsible for each work package. Figure 1.3 is an example of a work breakdown structure. (Work breakdown structures will be discussed further in Chapter 9.)
3. *Define the specific activities that need to be performed for each work package in order to accomplish the project objective.*
4. *Graphically portray the activities in the form of a* **network diagram.** This diagram shows the necessary sequence and interdependencies of activities to achieve the project objective. Figure 1.4 is an example of a network diagram. (Network diagrams will be discussed further in Chapter 9.)
5. *Make a* **time estimate** *for how long it will take to complete each activity.* It is also necessary to determine which types of resources and how many of each resource are needed for each activity to be completed within the estimated duration.
6. *Make a* **cost estimate** *for each activity.* The cost is based on the types and quantities of resources required for each activity.
7. *Calculate a project schedule and budget to determine whether the project can be completed within the required time, with the allotted funds, and with the available resources.* If not, adjustments must be made to the project scope, activity time estimates, or resource assignments until an achievable, realistic **baseline plan** (a roadmap for accomplishing the project scope on time and within budget) can be established. Figure 1.5 shows an example of a project schedule,

FIGURE 1.3   Work Breakdown Structure

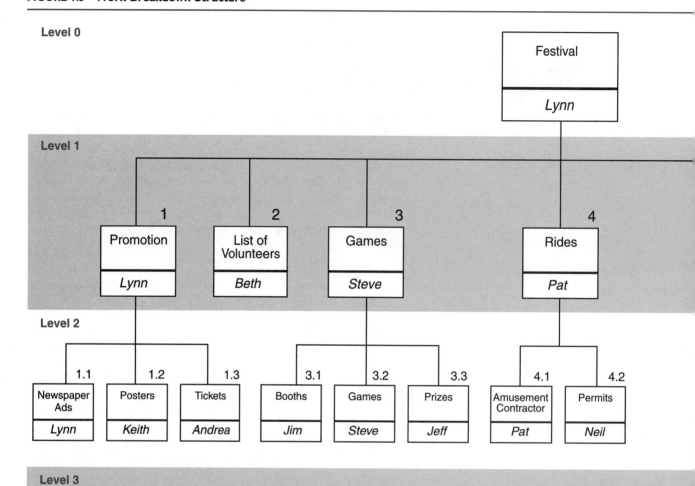

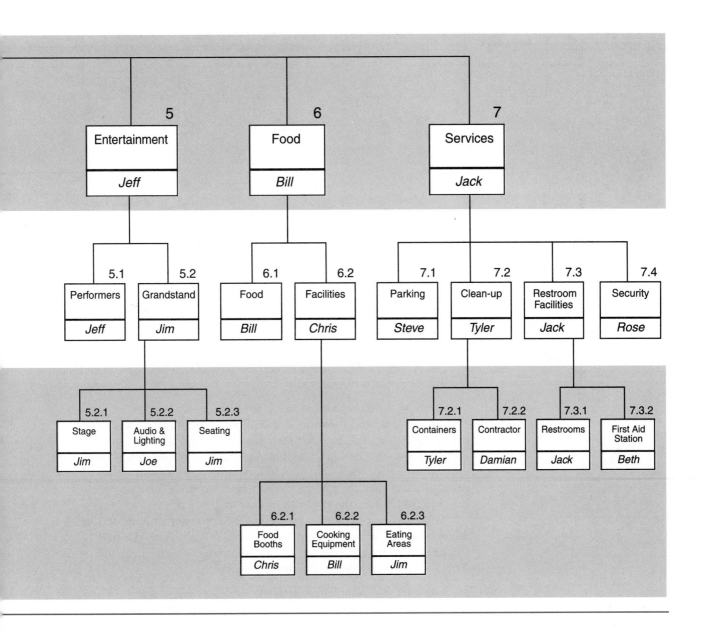

FIGURE 1.4   Network Diagram

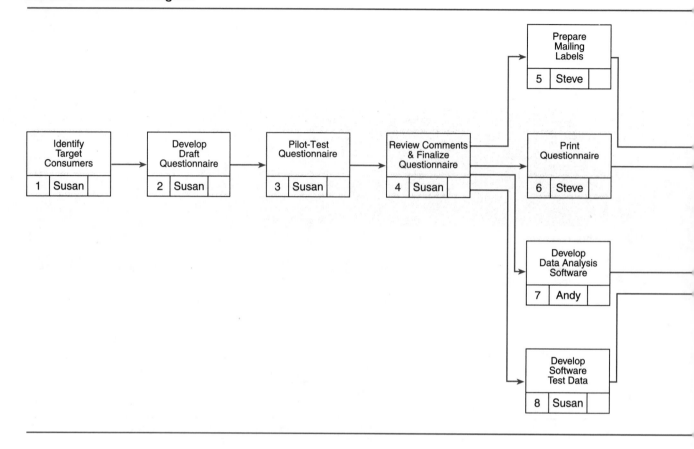

and Figure 1.6 illustrates a project budget. (These will be covered in Chapters 10 through 13.)

Planning determines what needs to be done, who will do it, how long it will take, and how much it will cost. The result of this effort is a baseline plan. Taking the time to develop a well-thought-out plan is critical to the successful accomplishment of any project. Many projects have overrun their budgets, missed their completion dates, or only partially met their requirements because there was no viable baseline plan before the project was started.

The baseline plan for a project can be displayed in graphical or tabular format for each time period (week, month) from the start of the project to its completion. (Plans are discussed and illustrated in Part 3.) Information should include

- The start and completion dates for each activity
- The amounts of the various resources that will be needed during each time period
- The budget for each time period, as well as the cumulative budget from the start of the project through each time period

Once a baseline plan has been established, it must be implemented. This involves performing the work according to the plan and

REINFORCE YOUR LEARNING
5. *The front-end effort of managing a project involves establishing a* baseline   plan   *.*

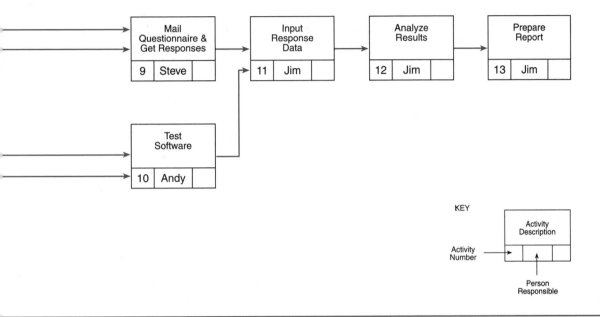

KEY

Activity
Description

Activity
Number

Person
Responsible

controlling the work so that the project scope is achieved within the budget and schedule, to the customer's satisfaction.

Once the project starts, it is necessary to monitor progress to ensure that everything is going according to plan. At this stage, the project management process involves measuring actual progress and comparing it to planned progress. To measure actual progress, it is important to keep track of which activities have actually been started and/or completed, when they were started and/or completed, and how much money has been spent or committed. If, at any time during the project, comparison of actual progress to planned progress reveals that the project is behind schedule, overrunning the budget, or not meeting the technical specifications, corrective action must be taken to get the project back on track.

Before a decision is made to implement corrective action, it may be necessary to evaluate several alternative actions to make sure the corrective action will bring the project back within the scope, time, and budget constraints of the objective. Be aware, for instance, that adding resources to make up time and get back on schedule may result in overrunning the planned budget. If a project gets too far out of control, it may be difficult to achieve the project objective without sacrificing the scope, budget, schedule, or quality.

FIGURE 1.5   Project Schedule

CONSUMER MARKET STUDY PROJECT

	ACTIVITY	RESPON.	DUR. ESTIM.	EARLIEST		LATEST		TOTAL SLACK	
				START	FINISH	START	FINISH		
1	Identify Target Consumers	Susan	3	0	3	–8	–5	–8	
2	Develop Draft Questionnaire	Susan	10	3	13	–5	5	–8	
3	Pilot-Test Questionnaire	Susan	20	13	33	5	25	–8	
4	Review Comments & Finalize Questionnaire	Susan	5	33	38	25	30	–8	
5	Prepare Mailing Labels	Steve	2	38	40	38	40	0	
6	Print Questionnaire	Steve	10	38	48	30	40	–8	
7	Develop Data Analysis Software	Andy	12	38	50	88	100	50	
8	Develop Software Test Data	Susan	2	38	40	98	100	60	
9	Mail Questionnaire & Get Responses	Steve	65	48	113	40	105	–8	
10	Test Software	Andy	5	50	55	100	105	50	
11	Input Response Data	Jim	7	113	120	105	112	–8	
12	Analyze Results	Jim	8	120	128	112	120	–8	
13	Prepare Report	Jim	10	128	138	120	130	–8	

REINFORCE YOUR LEARNING

6. *Implementing the baseline plan for a project involves* <u>performing</u> *the work according to the plan and* <u>controlling</u> *the work so that the project scope is achieved within the* <u>budget</u> *and* <u>schedule</u>.

The key to effective project control is measuring actual progress and comparing it to planned progress on a timely and regular basis and taking corrective action immediately, if necessary. Hoping that a problem will go away without corrective intervention is naive. Based on actual progress, it is possible to forecast a schedule and budget for completion of the project. If these parameters are beyond the limits of the project objective, corrective actions need to be implemented at once.

Attempting to perform a project without first establishing a baseline plan is foolhardy. It is like starting a vacation without a roadmap, itinerary, and budget. You may land up in the middle of nowhere—out of money and out of time!

BENEFITS OF PROJECT MANAGEMENT

The ultimate benefit of implementing project management techniques is having a *satisfied customer*—whether you are the customer of your own project, such as remodeling your basement, or a business (con-

FIGURE 1.6   Cumulative Budgeted Cost Curve

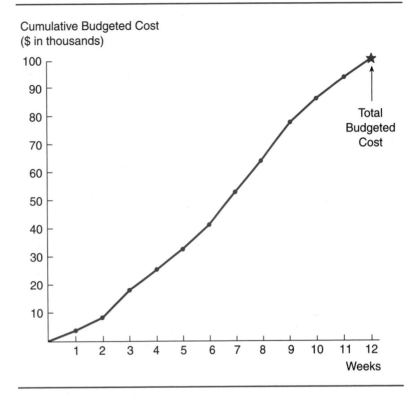

tractor) being paid by a customer to perform a project. Completing the full project scope in a quality manner, on time, and within budget provides a great feeling of satisfaction. For a contractor, it could lead to additional business from the same customer in the future or to business from new customers referred by previously satisfied customers.

"Hey! Great for the customer, but what about me? What's in it for me?" If you are the project manager, you have the satisfaction of knowing you led a successful project effort. You also have enhanced your reputation as a project manager and positioned yourself for expanded career opportunities. If you are a member of a project team that successfully accomplished a project, you feel the satisfaction of being on a winning team. You not only contributed to the project's success, but also probably expanded your knowledge and enhanced your skills along the way. If you choose to remain an individual contributor, you will be able to make a greater contribution to future, more complicated projects. If you are interested in eventually managing projects, you will be in a position to take on additional project responsibilities.

When projects are successful, everybody wins!

SUMMARY

A project is an endeavor to accomplish a specific objective through a unique set of interrelated tasks and the effective utilization of resources. It has a clearly defined objective stated in terms of scope, schedule, and cost. The responsibility of the project manager is to make sure that the project objective is accomplished and that the work scope is completed in a quality manner, within budget, and on time, to the customer's satisfaction.

The first phase of the project life cycle involves the identification of a need, problem, or opportunity and can result in the customer's requesting proposals from individuals, a project team, or organizations (contractors) to address an identified need or solve a problem. The second phase of the project life cycle is the development of a proposed solution to the need or problem. This phase results in the submission of a proposal to the customer by one or more individuals or contractors or the project team. The third phase of the project life cycle is the implementation of the proposed solution. This phase, which is referred to as performing the project, results in accomplishment of the project objective, leaving the customer satisfied that the work scope was completed in a quality manner, within budget, and on time. The final phase of the project life cycle is terminating the project, which includes evaluating the execution of the project in order to enhance future projects.

Project management involves a process of first establishing a plan and then implementing that plan to accomplish the project objective. This planning effort includes clearly defining objectives, dividing and subdividing the project scope into major "pieces" called work packages, defining the specific activities that need to be performed for each work package, graphically portraying the activities in the form of a network diagram, estimating how long each activity will take to complete, defining the types of resources and how many of each resource are needed for each activity, estimating the cost of each activity, and calculating a project schedule and budget.

Taking the time to develop a well-thought-out plan is critical to the successful accomplishment of any project. Once the project starts, project management involves monitoring the progress to ensure that everything is going according to plan. The key to effective project control is measuring actual progress and comparing it to planned progress on a timely and regular basis and taking corrective action immediately, if necessary.

The ultimate benefit of implementing project management techniques is having a satisfied customer—whether you are the customer of your own project or a business (contractor) being paid by a customer to perform a project. Completing the full project scope in a quality manner, on time, and within budget provides a great feeling of satisfaction for everyone involved in the project.

QUESTIONS

1. Define *project*.
2. Define the term *project objective* and give some examples.
3. List some examples of resources that are used on a project.
4. What role does a customer have during the project life cycle?

5. What aspects of a project might involve some degree of uncertainty? Why?
6. Define *scope, schedule, cost,* and *customer satisfaction.* Why are these considered to be constraints?
7. Why is it important to satisfy the customer?
8. List and describe the main phases of the project life cycle.
9. List and describe the steps required to develop a baseline plan.
10. Why must a manager monitor the progress of a project? What can be done if a project is not proceeding according to plan?
11. List some benefits of using project management techniques.
12. Consider a project in which you are currently involved or in which you have recently been involved.
    a. Describe the objectives, scope, schedule, cost, and any assumptions made.
    b. Where are you in the project life cycle?
    c. Does this project have a baseline plan? If yes, describe it. If not, create it.
    d. Are you or is anyone else monitoring the progress of the project? If so, how? If not, how could you do so?
    e. Describe some unexpected circumstances that could jeopardize the success of the project.
    f. Describe the anticipated benefits of the project.

WORLD WIDE WEB EXERCISES

If you have difficulty accessing any of the Web addresses listed here, you can find these exercises (with up-to-date addresses) on the home page of Dr. James P. Clements, co-author of this book, at

www.towson.edu/~clements

1. Using your favorite Web search engine (Infoseek, Lycos, Yahoo, Excite, Magellan, etc.), do a search for "project management." How many sites did you find?
2. Explore at least five of the links that your search produced. Give the Web address for each of those sites.
3. Describe, in general, what each of those five sites contained.
4. Do several additional Web searches by adding, after the words "project management," some of the key words listed in this chapter. For example, search for "project management objectives," "project management life cycle," "project management process," "project management work breakdown structures," and so on.
5. Visit the Web site of James P. Clements, co-author of this book, at

www.towson.edu/~clements

Explore some of the links, including the project management links.

CASE STUDY

The Board of Directors of a local not-for-profit organization that collects and buys food and distributes it to people in need is having its

February board meeting. Sitting in a conference room are Beth Smith, the board chairperson, and two board members, Rosemary Olsen and Steve Andrews. Beth announces, "Our funds are almost exhausted. The demands on the food bank and soup kitchen have been increasing. We need to figure out how to get more funds."

"We have to have a fund-raising project," responds Rosemary.

Steve suggests, "Can't we ask the county government if they can increase their allocation to us?"

"They're strained. They may even cut our allocation next year," replies Beth.

"How much do we need to get us through this year?" asks Rosemary.

"About ten thousand dollars," answers Beth, "and we are going to start needing that money in about two months."

"We need a lot of things besides money. We need more volunteers, more space for storage, and another refrigerator for the kitchen," says Steve.

"Well, I guess we can make that all part of the fund-raising project. This is going to be fun!" says Rosemary excitedly.

"This project is growing. We'll never get it done in time," Beth says.

Rosemary responds, "We'll figure it out and get it done. We always do."

"Is a project what we need? What are we going to do next year—another project?" asks Steve. "Besides, we're having a hard time getting volunteers anyway. Maybe we need to think about how we can operate with less funds. For example, how can we get more food donations on a regular basis so we won't have to buy as much food?"

Rosemary jumps in, "Great idea, you can work on that while we also try to raise funds. We can't leave any stone unturned."

"Time out," says Beth. "These are all very good ideas, but we have limited funds and volunteers and a growing demand. We need to do something now to make sure we don't have to close our doors in two months. I think we all agree we need to undertake some type of initiative. But I'm not sure we all agree on the objective."

Case Questions

1. What are the needs that have been identified?
2. What is the project objective?
3. What assumptions, if any, should be made regarding the project to be undertaken?
4. What are the risks involved in the project?

Group Activity

Contact a local not-for-profit organization in your community. Tell them that you are interested in learning about their operations. Ask them to describe a project that they are currently working on. What are the objectives? The constraints? The resources?

If possible, have your team contribute a few hours to the project. Through this process you will be helping someone in need and learning about a real-world project at the same time. Prepare a report summarizing the project and what you learned from this experience.

2

Needs Identification

The Minnesota State Fair

Jim Sinclair, who led the effort to line up the 1995 independent midway at the Minnesota State Fair, had heard it said repeatedly that a large fair over Labor Day weekend would never work because just about every good piece of equipment was already booked for that week. Sinclair paid no attention to those predictions and had no problems in getting the equipment he wanted. He developed a comprehensive request for proposal (RFP) that described exactly what he wanted. Some of the rules specified in the RFP were that each piece of equipment had to be wholly owned by the person bringing it in, no space could be subcontracted, no more than six rides or six games could be supplied by one individual, and no one could have both food and games. Some of these rules were established to make the fair unique and to ensure that participants didn't steal rides or an entire show from another fair.

The response to the RFP was overwhelming—in quantity and quality. In fact, Sinclair said that the response to his RFP was much greater than anticipated, and he was extremely happy with the quality and selection. Specifically, he received 156 responses, offering a total of 530 rides, 470 games, and 150 food and beverage concessions. Each of the responses was evaluated, and the suppliers were chosen.

The final lineup for the independent "Mighty Midway" at the Minnesota State Fair featured 66 rides, 62 games, and 14 food facilities, and it was a major success. Attendance at the two-week event reached 1,673,312, which broke the previous attendance record by 52,000, and gross revenue totaled over $4.4 million. All of this was achieved because the project leader didn't listen to naysayers and went ahead and developed a top-notch RFP.

Sources: T. O'Brien, "'Everything in Place' for Minnesota Indy Midway," *Amusement Business,* May 15, 1995; R. Waddell, "Minnesota Midway Grosses $4.4 Million," *Amusement Business,* September 18, 1995.

The Bank of Boston

Officials from the Bank of Boston recently discussed how the firm created an effective, all-encompassing request for proposal. Kevin Roden, director of consumer banking systems, and George Swick, project manager of the retail workstation infrastructure, indicated that their focus is on business requirements. They conduct a cost-benefit analysis and examine available products and services only after they ensure that a project will meet business requirements. If the project does not directly support the business, it is not pursued.

The Bank of Boston had a goal: improve sales and customer service and increase the range of products, such as mutual funds and small business loans, in the bank's branches. Given their resources and the availability of resources, they found that it would be more cost-effective to outsource much of the work. So they developed two comprehensive requests for proposal (RFPs). The first was for procurement, deployment, and installation of the system. The second was for support and maintenance.

There were eleven responses to the two RFPs, which were reviewed by more than twenty representatives of various technology and business committees within the bank. IBM and Anderson Consulting were chosen to help with the procurement, deployment, and installation, and IBM was chosen to help with the support and maintenance. The Bank of Boston branches will be getting a complete facelift: new client/server-based local area networks, new customer service and sales applications software, electronic mail, and remote software distribution, as well as automated data backup and recovery systems.

The bank reports numerous benefits from developing an RFP using a disciplined approach similar to the one discussed in this chapter. According to the author of the article in which this project was reported, the major lesson to be learned from the Bank of Boston's success is that applying project management discipline and techniques to a proposal beforehand results in a more comprehensive RFP.

Source: L. Goff, "Method to Madness: Developing Request for Proposals," *Computerworld,* January 16, 1995.

R ecall that the project life cycle consists of four phases: identifying needs, proposing a solution, performing the project, and terminating the project. This chapter focuses on needs identification, the first phase of the project life cycle (see Figure 2.1). You will become familiar with

- identifying needs and selecting projects
- developing requests for proposal
- the proposal solicitation process

IDENTIFYING NEEDS, PROBLEMS, OR OPPORTUNITIES

Needs identification is the initial phase of the project life cycle. It starts with the recognition of a need, problem, or opportunity and ends with the issuance of a request for proposal (RFP). The customer identifies a need, a problem, or an opportunity for a better way of doing something and therefore sees some benefit to undertaking a project that will result in an improvement or advantage over the existing condition.

For example, suppose a company's management recognizes that the time the company takes to issue invoices and collect payments from its customers is too long. Furthermore, the fact that company payment records are not up to date has caused second invoices to be sent to customers who have already paid, thus upsetting some good customers. Also, as business increases, more clerical staff must be added to process the additional invoices and payments, and more file cabinets must be purchased to store the increased paperwork. Management recognizes several problems and opportunities for improvement, so it develops an RFP asking contractors to submit proposals for implementing an automated billing and collection system. In a different scenario, the company's management might request a proposal from an individual or a project team within its own company rather than from an external contractor.

Before a request for proposal is prepared, the customer must clearly define the problem or need. This may mean gathering data about the magnitude of the problem. For example, if a business thinks the scrap rate or reject rate from one of its manufacturing processes is too high, it may need to gather data regarding the actual rate and its impact on costs and cycle times. It is important to try to quantify the problem so as to determine whether the expected benefits from implementing a solution outweigh the costs of conducting the project and, if so, by how much.

Once the magnitude of the benefit or improvement has been estimated, the customer can determine the budget for a project to implement an improvement. For example, if a business estimates that it could save $100,000 a year by reducing its scrap rate from 5 percent to 1 percent, it might be willing to pay a one-time cost of $200,000 for new automated production equipment, thus breaking even after two years of operation. However, the business may not be willing to spend $500,000 for a solution. Businesses have a limited amount of funds

FIGURE 2.1   Project Life Cycle

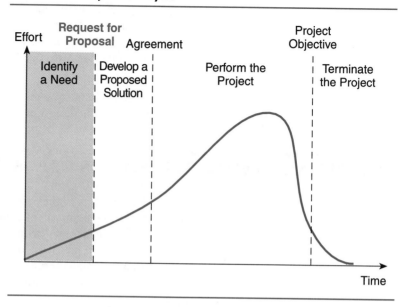

REINFORCE YOUR LEARNING

1. *The initial phase of the project life cycle is* ~~needs ID~~ *. It starts with the recognition of a need or opportunity and ends with the issuance of a* ~~request for proposal~~ *RFP* .

available and, therefore, usually want to spend those funds on projects that will provide the greatest return on investment. Even in a nonbusiness example, such as staging a town's Fourth of July celebration, there is usually a budget within which the project must be accomplished.

Once it has been determined that there is an overall benefit to be achieved by addressing the problem, need, or opportunity, the customer prepares a request for proposal.

There are often situations where a company has identified several needs but has limited funds and people available to pursue projects to address all of those needs. In such cases, the company must go through a decision-making process to select those needs that, when met, will result in the greatest benefit for the cost expended.

PREPARING A REQUEST FOR PROPOSAL

The purpose of preparing a request for proposal is to state, comprehensively and in detail, what is required, from the customer's point of view, to address the identified need. A good RFP allows contractors or a project team to understand what the customer expects so that they can prepare a thorough proposal that will satisfy the customer's requirements at a realistic price. For example, an RFP that simply requests contractors to submit a proposal for building a house is not specific enough. Contractors could not even begin to prepare proposals without information about the kind of house that is wanted. An RFP should be comprehensive and provide sufficiently detailed information so that a contractor or project team can prepare an intelligent proposal that is responsive to the customer's needs. A sample RFP is shown in Figure 2.2.

FIGURE 2.2   Request for Proposal

February 1st

To Whom It May Concern:

AJACKS Information Services Company is seeking proposals from contractors with relevant experience to conduct a market survey of the technical information needs of manufacturing firms nationwide. The objectives of this project are

1. To determine the technical information needs of manufacturing firms nationwide, and
2. To recommend approaches to promote the purchase and utilization of AJACKS Information Services by such firms.

This project must provide adequate information for AJACKS Information Services Company to determine

- Future information products or services, and
- The best methods for delivering these products or services to its customers

The contents of this Request for Proposal are to be considered confidential information.

1. **Statement of Work**

   The contractor will perform the following tasks:

   Task 1: Identify Technical Information Needs of Manufacturing Firms

   Conduct a survey of manufacturing firms nationwide to determine their specific needs for external (to their firms) technical information. The assessment should determine the various specific types of technical information needed and the frequency with which each type of information is needed.

   Task 2: Determine the Best Approaches to Promote the Purchase and Utilization of AJACKS Information Services by Businesses

   The survey should include an identification of the firms' perceptions of the most effective direct and indirect marketing approaches that influence the firms' decisions to both purchase and utilize specific services or products, in particular information services.

2. **Requirements**

   The survey should determine the various specific types of technical information needed and the frequency with which each type of information is needed.

   The survey should identify the current sources for the various types of technical information that are used by manufacturing firms, their frequency of use, and the firms' perception of the value (benefit, cost, accuracy, timeliness) of each source. It should determine the various methods the firms currently use to access these sources of information. The survey should determine the average and range of funds (both internal to the firm and external fees) that firms currently expend for obtaining the various types of technical information.

   The assessment must provide sufficient detail to permit demand-driven product planning by AJACKS Information Services Company. Therefore, it must include: (1) the information content most frequently needed by firms; (2) the applications for which the firms use the information; (3) the persons (title, skill level) responsible for both accessing and utilizing the information; and (4) the channels that firms use to access the various types of information.

   AJACKS Information Services Company is interested in developing and delivering products and services that are valued by the users (manufacturing firms). With these interests in mind, the contractor must generate information about which firms (as distinguished by size, sector, location, or other important factors) may benefit most from information products and services or represent the most appropriate markets for such products and services.

   The contractor should determine the size of the market for the various types of technical information and determine the market sensitivity to price, timeliness, accuracy, and delivery mechanisms for such information.

   The survey methodology should include both focus groups and mail surveys.

   The focus groups should be categorized by major manufacturing sectors and by multi-sector firm size (large, medium, small).

FIGURE 2.2   Request for Proposal (continued)

Based on the results from the focus groups, a draft mail survey questionnaire should be developed and pretested on representative firms. This survey instrument should be finalized after sufficient pretesting.

The contractor should provide a sampling design for the mail survey that is stratified by sector and firm size, is representative of the entire population of manufacturing firms, and that is sufficiently large to present the survey results for each stratum at the ninety percent confidence level.

3. **Deliverables**
   A. A detailed report of the results of Task 1 must be prepared that identifies and analyzes the results for all respondents and also provides detailed analyses (1) for each sector and (2) by firm size. The contractor must provide twenty (20) copies of the report. The database of the survey responses used in the analysis must be delivered in a format suitable for further analysis by AJACKS Information Services Company.
   B. Based on the analysis of Tasks 1 and 2, provide a detailed report of recommendations of the most effective approaches, and associated costs, to promoting technical information services to manufacturing firms with the objective of getting such firms to purchase and use such services. Discuss any differences in approaches based on sector or size of business. The contractor must provide twenty (20) copies of the report.
   C. Written reports on project progress must be faxed to AJACKS Information Services Company on the 15th and 30th of each month. Reports should be brief and focus on progress compared to the contractor's original plan and schedule. These reports should cover activities, milestones achieved, plans for the next month, obstacles encountered or anticipated, and hours and dollars expended. For any work items where progress is behind schedule, a plan must be proposed to complete the project within the original schedule and budget.

4. **Items Supplied by AJACKS Information Services Company**
   AJACKS will provide the contractor with detailed information about its current information services and products as well as statistical information regarding its current customer base.

5. **Approvals Required**
   The contractor must obtain the approval of AJACKS for the final version of the survey instrument before it is implemented.

6. **Type of Contract**
   The contract will be for a fixed price for all of the work the contractor proposes to meet all the requirements of this Request for Proposal.

7. **Due Date**
   The contractor must submit five (5) copies of the proposal to AJACKS Information Services Company on or before February 28th.

8. **Schedule**
   AJACKS Information Services Company expects to select a contractor by March 30th. The required period of performance of this project is six months, from May 1st to October 30th. All deliverables must be provided to AJACKS on or before October 30th.

9. **Payment Terms**
   AJACKS Information Services Company will make payments to the contractor according to the following schedule:
   - One-third of total amount when project is shown to be one-third complete
   - One-third of total amount when project is shown to be two-thirds complete
   - One-third of total amount when AJACKS Information Services Company is satisfied that the project is 100% complete and that the contractor has fulfilled all contractual obligations

10. **Proposal Contents**
    As a minimum, the contractor's proposal must include the following:
    A. **Approach**
       A discussion that indicates the contractor clearly understands the Request for Proposal and what is expected. Also, a detailed discussion of the contractor's approach to conducting the project and a detailed description of each task and how it will be accomplished.
    B. **Deliverables**
       A description of each deliverable the contractor will provide.

FIGURE 2.2   Request for Proposal (continued)

C. **Schedule**

A bar chart or network diagram showing the weekly schedule of the detailed tasks to be performed in order to complete the project by the required project finish date.

D. **Experience**

A discussion of recent similar projects the contractor has performed, including customer names, addresses, and phone numbers.

E. **Staffing**

The names and detailed resumes of the specific individuals who will be assigned to work on the project and highlights of their experience on similar projects.

F. **Costs**

The total fixed price must be stated and supported by a detailed breakdown of hours and an hourly cost rate for each person who will be assigned to the project. Additionally, an itemized list of all direct expenses must be included.

11. **Proposal Evaluation Criteria**

AJACKS Information Services Company will evaluate all contractor proposals according to the following criteria:

A. **Approach (30%)**

The approach and methodology the contractor proposes to conduct the survey and analyze the results.

B. **Experience (30%)**

The experience of the contractor and the staff assigned to the project in performing similar projects.

C. **Price (30%)**

The fixed price of the contractor's proposal.

D. **Schedule (10%)**

The detail and overall duration of the contractor's proposed schedule to complete the project on or before the required project finish date.

REINFORCE YOUR LEARNING

2. *What is the purpose of a request for proposal?*

It should be noted that in many situations a formal RFP may not be prepared; instead, the need is communicated informally—and sometimes orally rather than in writing. This is often the case when the project will be implemented by a firm's internal staff rather than by an external contractor. For example, if a company needs to change the layout of its manufacturing facility to make room for new production equipment that has to be incorporated into the production flow, the manufacturing manager may simply ask one of the supervisors to put together a proposal for "what it's going to take to reconfigure the production line."

Following are some guidelines for drafting a formal request for proposal to external contractors:

1. *An RFP must provide a **statement of work (SOW).*** An SOW deals with the scope of the project, outlining the tasks or work elements the customer wants the contractor or project team to perform. For example, if the RFP is for a house, the contractor needs to know whether he should design and build the entire house, build it according to the customer's design, or include finishing the basement and installing the carpeting. If a customer needs a marketing brochure, the RFP must state whether the contractor is just to design the brochure or to design and print and mail it.

2. *The RFP must include the* **customer requirements,** *which define specifications and attributes.* Requirements cover size, quantity, color, weight, speed, and other physical or operational parameters the contractor's proposed solution must satisfy. For the marketing brochure, the requirements might be for a trifold self-mailer, printed on card stock in two colors, with a print run of 10,000. Requirements for the house might include an overall size of 3,000 square feet with four bedrooms, two baths, a two-car garage, central air conditioning, and a fireplace.

   Some requirements address performance. If the RFP is for an automated billing and collection system, performance requirements might include the capacity to process 12,000 transactions a day and provisions for special functions such as consolidated multiple invoices for individual customers and automatically generated second invoices for payments not received within thirty days of the initial invoice.

   Such performance requirements may also be used as acceptance criteria by the customer. For example, the project contractor will have to run tests on the automated billing and collection system to prove to the customer that it meets the performance requirements before the customer accepts the system and makes the final payment to the contractor.

3. *The RFP should state what* **deliverables** *the customer expects the contractor or project team to provide.* Deliverables are the tangible items that the contractor is to supply. With the brochure example, the only deliverable might be 10,000 copies of the brochure. With the billing and collection system, the contractor may be expected to supply the hardware (computers), software (disks, as well as certain printouts), operator manuals, and training sessions. Deliverables could also include periodic progress reports or a final report that the customer requires the contractor to provide.

4. *The RFP should list any customer-supplied items.* For example, the RFP might state that the customer will supply a copy of its logo for use on the brochure. If the RFP is for a piece of automated equipment for testing electronic circuit boards, it may state that the customer will provide a certain quantity of the boards for the contractor to use during factory testing of the equipment before it is shipped to the customer.

5. *The RFP might state the approvals required by the customer.* For example, the housing customer may want to review and approve the plans before construction is started. The brochure customer may want to review and approve the brochure's layout before printing is started.

6. *Some RFPs mention the type of contract the customer intends to use.* It could be fixed price, in which case the customer will pay the contractor a fixed amount regardless of how much the work actually costs the contractor. (The contractor accepts the risk of taking a loss.) Or the contract might be for time and materials. In this case, the customer will pay the contractor whatever the actual costs are. For example, if the RFP is to remodel a base-

ment, the RFP might state that the contractor will be paid for the hours expended and the cost of materials.

7. *An RFP might state the payment terms the customer intends to use.* For example, the brochure customer may intend to make one payment at the end of the project. On the other hand, the customer for the house may specify progress payments, based on a percentage of the total price, that are made as certain milestones are accomplished—25 percent when the foundation is complete, another 25 percent when the framing is complete, and so on, until the entire project is finished.

8. *The RFP should state the required schedule for completion of the project.* It might state simply that the house must be completed within six months, or it might include a more detailed schedule. For example, the billing and collection system must be designed and developed and a design review meeting conducted within four months of the start of the project; then, the system must be installed and tested within four months of the design review; and, finally, the contractor must provide all system documentation and operator training within one month of the system's installation.

9. *The RFP should provide instructions for the format and content of the contractor proposals.* If the customer is going to compare and evaluate proposals from several contractors, it is important that they be consistent in format and content so that a fair evaluation can be made. Instructions might state the maximum number of pages, the number of details the customer wants the contractor to show regarding the costs, and other specifications.

10. *The RFP should indicate the **due date** by which the customer expects potential contractors to submit proposals.* Customers want to receive all proposals by a certain date so that they can compare and evaluate them at the same time. For example, a customer may give potential contractors thirty calendar days from the time the RFP is formally issued to submit a proposal. Customers usually state in the RFP that any proposals submitted after the due date will not be accepted for consideration, since it would be unfair to give some contractors extra time.

11. *An RFP may include the **evaluation criteria**.* These are the criteria that the customer will use to evaluate proposals from competing contractors in order to select the one to perform the project. Criteria might include the following:

    a. The contractor's *experience with similar projects.* How recently has the contractor completed similar projects? Were they completed within budget and on schedule? Were the customers satisfied?

    b. The *technical approach* proposed by the contractor. What type and configuration of computer hardware will be used? What is the design approach for the data base? Which software language will be used for developing the management information system?

    c. The *schedule.* Will the contractor be able to meet or beat the required schedule?

REINFORCE YOUR LEARNING

3. What are some elements that may be included in a request for proposal?

d. The *costs*. If the estimate is based on time and materials, are the costs reasonable? Have any items been left out? Does it appear that the contractor has submitted a low cost estimate but will add costs after the project is under way, resulting in final costs that are much higher than the original estimate?

12. *In rare cases an RFP will indicate the funds the customer has available to spend on the project.* Usually, the customer expects contractors to submit a proposal that meets the requirements in the RFP at the most reasonable cost. In some situations, however, it may be helpful for the customer to indicate a "ballpark" amount to be spent. For example, stating in the RFP that the cost of building the house should be about $300,000 would be helpful. Contractors can then submit proposals that are appropriate to that level of funding, rather than submitting proposals for houses that cost far more than the customer has available. Otherwise, all the contractors might submit proposals with prices much higher than the available funding, and the disappointed customer will have to ask all the contractors to resubmit proposals for a less expensive house.

SOLICITING PROPOSALS

Once the RFP has been prepared, the customer solicits proposals by notifying potential contractors that the RFP is available. One way for customers to do this is by identifying a selected group of contractors in advance and sending each of them a copy of the RFP. For example, a customer who has prepared an RFP for designing and building a customized piece of automated testing equipment might send it to several well-known companies (contractors) that specialize in producing such equipment. Another approach to soliciting potential contractors is for the customer to advertise in certain business newspapers that the RFP is available and give instructions on how interested contractors can obtain a copy. For example, federal government organizations advertise their RFPs in *Commerce Business Daily.*

Business customers and contractors consider the RFP/proposal process to be a competitive situation. Customers should be careful not to provide to one or more of the contractors information that is not provided to all interested contractors. Therefore, during the proposal development phase, customers may not want to answer questions from individual contractors who are preparing proposals for fear of giving those contractors an unfair competitive advantage over other contractors who do not have the same information. Business or government customers may hold a bidders' meeting to explain the RFP and answer questions from interested contractors.

As a final note, we should repeat that *not all project life cycles include the preparation of a written request for proposal and subsequent proposals from contractors.* Some endeavors move right from defining what needs to be done into the project phase of the life cycle, where the project is planned and performed to satisfy the need. This process bypasses the RFP and proposal steps. For instance, when a company decides to initiate and implement a project to meet a certain need or solve a particular problem, it may use its own staff and project team rather than external contractors. Or when a group of volunteers decides to put on a countywide week-long arts festival, the volunteers may elect to do all the work themselves. When an accident victim requires a series of reconstructive surgeries, a team of surgeons may determine what needs to be done and then plan and perform a series of operations spanning several years. In all these examples, requests for proposal or proposals from contractors would not be appropriate.

There are other projects in which requirements are not written down in a formal RFP, but are communicated to several providers or suppliers (contractors). For example, in planning a wedding, the bride and groom may define their requirements for the reception, dinner, flowers, and other items and then shop around to select the suppliers that most closely match their requirements and budget.

Although projects can be businesslike or informal, they all start with the identification of a need, problem, or opportunity and then proceed to the customer's defining (in writing or orally) the scope, requirements, budget, and schedule for what is to be accomplished.

SUMMARY

Needs identification is the initial phase of the project life cycle. The customer identifies a need, a problem, or an opportunity for a better way of doing something. The need and associated requirements are usually written down by the customer in a document called a request for proposal (RFP).

Before a request for proposal is prepared, the customer must clearly define the problem or need. This may mean gathering data about the magnitude of the problem. It is important that the customer try to quantify the problem so as to determine whether the expected benefits from implementing a solution outweigh the costs of conducting the project.

The purpose of preparing a request for proposal is to state, comprehensively and in detail, what is required, from the customer's point of view, to address the identified need. A good RFP allows contractors or a project team to understand what the customer expects so that they can prepare a thorough proposal that will satisfy the customer's requirements at a realistic price.

RFPs may contain a statement of work; customer requirements for physical or operational parameters such as size, quantity, color, weight, and speed; deliverables the customer expects the contractor to provide; and a list of any customer-supplied items; any approvals required by the customer; the type of contract the customer intends to use; the payment terms; the required schedule for completion of the project; instructions for the format and content of the contractor proposals; the due date by which the customer expects potential contractors to submit proposals; and criteria by which the proposals will be evaluated.

Once the RFP has been prepared, the customer solicits proposals by notifying potential contractors that the RFP is available. Business customers and contractors consider the RFP/proposal process to be a competitive situation. Customers should be careful not to provide to one or more contractors information that is not provided to all interested contractors.

Not all project life cycles include the preparation of a written request for proposal and subsequent proposals from contractors. Some endeavors move right from defining the need into the project phase of the life cycle.

QUESTIONS

1. Why is it important to do a thorough and detailed job of needs identification?
2. Describe a situation in your life in which you performed needs identification.
3. Give examples of situations in which a business might develop a request for proposal.
4. Give examples of situations in which an individual might develop a request for proposal.
5. Why is it important for a business to try to quantify the expected benefits of implementing a solution to a problem?
6. What should be contained in a statement of work?
7. What is meant by customer requirements? Why must they be precise?
8. Why would an RFP state the approvals that will be required during the project? Give some examples.
9. Why would a customer give contractors instructions in the RFP to submit their proposals according to a standard format?
10. Develop an RFP for a real-world project such as landscaping the grounds surrounding a nearby business office, building a deck for your house, or holding a big graduation celebration. Be creative in specifying your needs. Feel free to come up with unique ideas for the RFP.

WORLD WIDE WEB EXERCISES

If you have difficulty accessing any of the Web addresses listed here, you can find these exercises (with up-to-date addresses) on the home page of Dr. James P. Clements, co-author of this book, at

www.towson.edu/~clements

1. Since it was founded in 1969, the Project Management Institute (PMI) has grown to nearly 25,000 members worldwide, and it has a goal to reach 100,000 members by the year 2002. Pennsylvania-based PMI is, by far, the leading nonprofit professional association in the area of project management. It establishes standards, spon-

sors seminars, develops educational programs, has a professional certification program, and publishes *Project Management Journal* and *PM Network*. It also has an excellent Web site for project management. Check out its home page at

www.pmi.org

2. Locate general information about PMI, as well as membership information.
3. Check to see if there is a PMI chapter in your state. If not, where is the closest one?
4. Check out the details on PMI's upcoming annual seminar/symposium. Where is this event going to take place? When?
5. Check out information on *Project Management Journal,* either by linking to it from PMI's home page or going directly to it at

www.pmi.org/publictn/pmj.htm

Describe some of the articles recently published in this journal. Can you find any articles on requests for proposal?
6. Check out the link for "What's New." Describe some of the most recent news listed.
7. From the news link, check out information in PMI's *Project Management Body of Knowledge (PMBOK),* or go directly to it at

www.pmi.org/publictn/pmboktoc.htm

What is *PMBOK*?
8. *PM Network* is PMI's monthly professional magazine. Check out the on-line site from the publications link, or go directly to it at

www.pmi.org/publictn/pmnet.htm

Print out the editorial calendar for the year. Do any of these articles relate to the information in this or the previous chapter?
9. Explore some of the other links that PMI provides.

CASE STUDY

Jennifer Childs is the owner and president of a midsize pharmaceutical company. At an October staff meeting she tells her managers that company profits for the year are expected to be $200,000 more than anticipated. She tells them she would like to reinvest this additional profit by funding projects within the company that will either increase sales or reduce costs. She asks her three key managers to get together to develop a prioritized list of potential projects and then to meet with her to "sell" her on their ideas. She mentions that they should not assume the funds will be divided equally among the three of them. She also mentions that she is willing to put all of the funds into just one project if it seems appropriate.

Julie Chen, Manager of Product Development, has had a team of scientists working on a new prescription drug. This effort has been taking much longer than expected. She is worried that larger firms are working on a similar prescription drug and that those firms might get it to the marketplace first. Her team has not made any major break-throughs yet, and some tests are not producing the expected results. She knows this is a risky project but feels that she can't stop it now. Julie believes the company's long-term growth depends on this new drug, which can be sold worldwide. She has tried to be optimistic at staff meetings about progress on this development project, but she knows that Jennifer is growing impatient and that her peers believe she should have terminated the project after the initial tests were negative. Julie would like to use the additional funds to accelerate the develop-ment project. She would hire a highly respected scientist from a larger firm and buy more sophisticated laboratory equipment.

Tyler Ripken, Manager of Production, has been with the company only six months. His early observation is that the production flow is very inefficient. He believes this is the result of poor planning when additions were made to the plant over the years as the company grew. Tyler would like to form several employee teams to implement a bet-ter layout of the equipment in the plant. He thinks this would increase plant capacity while reducing costs. When Tyler mentions this idea to some of his supervisors, they remind him that when Jennifer's father ran the business, Jennifer was in charge of production, and she was responsible for the design of the current plant layout. They also remind Tyler that Jennifer is not a fan of using employee teams. She believes production employees are paid to do their jobs, and she expects her managers to be the ones to come up with and implement new ideas.

Jeff Matthews, Manager of Operations, is responsible for the com-pany's computers and information systems as well as its accounting operations. Jeff believes that the company's computer systems are outdated, and as the business has grown, the older computer equip-ment has been unable to handle the volume of transactions. He thinks that a new computer system could keep better track of customer orders, reduce customer complaints, and issue more timely invoices, thus improving cash flow. The employees in Jeff's operation joke about their outdated computers and put pressure on Jeff to buy newer equipment. Jennifer has told Jeff in the past that she is not interested in spending money on new computers just for the sake of having the latest equipment, especially if the current system is working all right. She had suggested that Jeff look into hiring an outside service to do the accounting operations and reduce his own staff. Jeff would like to use this year's excess profits to buy new computers and to hire a com-puter programmer to upgrade the software to run on the new com-puters. He feels that this would be cost-effective.

After Jennifer's October staff meeting, Joe Sanchez, Manager of Marketing, stops in Jennifer's office. He says that although he has not been asked to come up with project ideas for the extra profits, his feeling is that she should forget this project nonsense and just give him a larger budget to hire a few more sales representatives. "That would increase sales faster than anything else," Joe tells her. And besides, that's what your father would have done!" Joe is counting on disagreements among the other three managers in establishing priorities. He hopes that if Jennifer sees a lack of consensus, she might give him funds to hire the additional sales representatives.

Case Questions

1. How should Jennifer go about making her decision?
2. What exactly should Jennifer require the others to submit in the way of proposals?
3. What do you think Jennifer should do with the $200,000? In explaining your answer, address the concerns and positions of Julie, Tyler, Jeff, and Joe.

Group Activity

Select five course participants to play the roles of Jennifer, Julie, Tyler, Jeff, and Joe. While Jennifer and Joe leave the room, have Julie, Tyler, and Jeff role-play (preferably in front of the remaining course participants) a meeting in which they discuss their proposed projects and develop a prioritized list to "sell" to Jennifer.

After Jennifer and Joe re-enter the room, have all five participants role-play (preferably in front of the class) a meeting with Jennifer in which Julie, Tyler, and Jeff try to sell her on the prioritized list of projects and Joe promotes his agenda.

Discuss what took place. What positions did the players take? How was the final decision made? What was the final decision?

3 Proposed Solutions

The Florida Department of Transportation

The Florida Department of Transportation's High-Speed Rail Office received five very different proposals in response to an RFP (request for proposal) to finance, build, and operate a high-speed rail system linking Orlando, Tampa, and Miami. Three steel-wheel and two magnetic levitation proposals, all varying widely in approach and cost, were submitted.

The proposals, which took months to develop, ranged in estimated cost from $740 million to $5 billion. Each proposal included the average expected travel time between the cities and the projected number of riders each year. The average trip time from Miami to Orlando was as low as forty-nine minutes in one proposal and as high as two and a half hours in another. The projected number of riders for the year 2010 also varied, from six million in one proposal to thirty million in another.

As you can imagine, putting together a proposal of this magnitude takes a huge number of hours and is by no means an easy task. Once you have a clear understanding of the topics discussed in this chapter, you should be ready to start developing winning proposals!

Source: The Florida High-Speed Rail Office, "Five Bidders, Five Contrasting Scenarios," *Railway Age,* December 1995.

Effective Bidding

Submitting a competitive bid for production of a specific product or performance of a particular job is a task required of organizations in many different types of industries, such as construction, manufacturing, and government contracting. In their paper "Effective Bid Pricing for Unit Price Contracts," John Burnett and J. Howard Finch explore the process of setting the price of a bid. They stress that a firm must set a price that will be profitable for the firm, yet competitive with other bids. A higher-priced bid will increase the firm's rate of return, but it may take the firm out of the competition. A lower-priced bid will certainly increase the firm's chances of winning the contract, but it may also render the project unprofitable. Therefore, great care must be taken when setting the price. This chapter will introduce you to various types of contracts and pricing considerations that are addressed during this bidding process.

Source: J. Burnett and J. Finch, "Effective Bid Pricing for Unit Price Contracts," *Engineering Economist,* Summer 1994.

The development of proposed solutions by interested contractors or by the customer's internal project team in response to a customer's request for proposal is the second phase of the project life cycle. This chapter covers this phase, which starts when the RFP becomes available at the conclusion of the needs identification phase and ends when an agreement is reached with the person, organization, or contractor selected to implement the proposed solution (see Figure 3.1). You will become familiar with

- proposal marketing strategies and the bid/no-bid decision
- the development of winning proposals
- the proposal preparation process and the elements that may be included in a proposal
- pricing considerations
- the evaluation of proposals
- types of contracts between the customer and the contractor

In many situations a request for proposal does not involve soliciting competitive proposals from external contractors. For example, suppose company management sees a need to develop new marketing materials (brochures, videotapes, sample diskettes of software) or to reconfigure the office layout. Management may ask an individual or team to prepare a proposal that defines what should be done, what company resources would be needed, how much it would cost, and how long it would take. Once the individual or team has prepared the proposal, management can decide whether or not to go forward with the project, maybe modifying it in the process. Once a decision is made to go forward, the project proceeds directly to the third phase of the project life cycle—creating a detailed plan for the project and then implementing that plan to accomplish the project objective.

FIGURE 3.1   Project Life Cycle

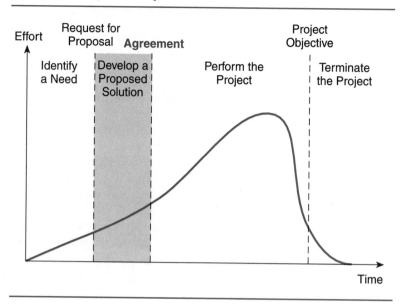

The second phase of the project life cycle may be completely bypassed for certain endeavors. Examples would include a project that one or two individuals do by themselves, such as building a swing set, or a project carried out by a volunteer group, such as organizing a charity event. In such situations, there is neither a request for proposal nor an actual proposal; rather, after the need is identified, the project moves right into the planning and implementation phase of the project life cycle.

PRE-RFP/PROPOSAL MARKETING

Contractors whose business depends on creating winning proposals in response to business or government RFPs should not wait until formal RFP solicitations are announced by customers before starting to develop proposals. Rather, such contractors need to develop relationships with potential customers long before the customers prepare requests for proposal.

Contractors should maintain frequent contacts with past customers and current customers and initiate contacts with potential new customers. During these contacts, contractors should help customers identify areas in which the customers might benefit from the implementation of projects that address needs, problems, or opportunities. Working closely with a potential customer puts a contractor in a better position to be selected eventually as the winning contractor when the customer does issue an RFP. A contractor who is familiar with a customer's needs, requirements, and expectations can prepare a more clearly focused proposal in response to the customer's RFP.

These pre-RFP or pre-proposal efforts by a contractor are considered marketing or business development and are performed without any cost to the customer. The payoff to the contractor for these efforts is expected to come later—when the contractor is selected as the winning contractor in response to the customer's RFP.

During this pre-RFP/proposal activity, the contractor should learn as much as possible about the customer's needs, problems, and decision-making process. The contractor should ask the customer for information, data, and documentation about the identified need or problem. The contractor may then develop some pre-proposal concepts or approaches and present them to or review them with the customer. By getting the customer's reactions to such concepts, the contractor can begin to understand and clarify what the customer expects, as well as develop a responsive and favorable image in the eyes of the customer. The contractor may invite the customer to visit another of the contractor's customers who had a similar need or problem for which the contractor proposed and implemented a successful solution. Such a visit can enhance the contractor's reputation with the customer.

In some cases, the contractor may prepare an *unsolicited proposal* and present it to the customer. If the customer is confident that the proposal will solve the problem at a reasonable cost, the customer may simply negotiate a contract with the contractor to implement the proposal, thus eliminating the preparation of an RFP and the subsequent competitive proposal process. By doing a good job in pre-RFP/proposal marketing, the contractor may obtain a contract from a customer without having to compete with other contractors.

Whether the goal is winning a competitive RFP or obtaining a noncompetitive contract from a customer, *a contractor's pre-RFP/proposal efforts are crucial to establishing the foundation for eventually winning a contract from the customer to perform the project.*

REINFORCE YOUR LEARNING

1. *What is the outcome of a successful pre-RFP/proposal marketing effort?*

BID/NO-BID DECISION

Because the development and preparation of a proposal takes time and can be costly, contractors interested in submitting a proposal in response to an RFP must be realistic about the probability of being selected as the winning contractor. Evaluating whether or not to go forward with the preparation of a proposal is sometimes referred to as the **bid/no-bid decision.** Some factors that a contractor might consider in making a bid/no-bid decision are the following:

1. *Competition.* Which other contractors might also submit a proposal in response to the RFP? Do any of these contractors have a competitive advantage, because of either pre-RFP marketing efforts or their previous work for or reputation with the customer?

2. *Risk.* Is there a risk that the project will be unsuccessful—technically or financially? For example, are there too many uncertainties regarding the technological feasibility of developing an integrated elec-

tronic circuit that will meet the customer's requirements? Or, does the customer want contractors to submit a proposal based on a fixed-price contract for a project that involves a research and development effort with only a 50-percent chance of technical success?

3. *Mission.* Is the proposed project consistent with the contractor's business mission? For example, if a contractor's business is to develop and implement automated systems for business-oriented applications, such as accounting, order tracking, or financial reporting, developing an automated system for monitoring, testing, and controlling a chemical process for a pharmaceutical company would not be within this contractor's business mission.

4. *Extension of capabilities.* Would the proposed project provide the contractor with an opportunity to extend and enhance its capabilities? For example, if a contractor has been providing automated inventory control systems to individual food markets, an RFP to provide an integrated inventory control system for a supermarket chain of ten stores might provide the contractor with an opportunity to extend its capabilities and expand its business to a larger customer base.

5. *Reputation.* Has the contractor successfully completed projects for the same customer in the past, or were there problems that left the customer dissatisfied? Has the contractor unsuccessfully bid on RFPs from the customer in the past?

6. *Customer funds.* Does the customer really have funds available to go forward with the project? Or is the customer on a "fishing expedition"—issuing an RFP although unsure whether the project will ever be funded? A customer may issue an RFP with the best of intentions but do so prematurely, anticipating that the board of directors will approve funding. However, if the company is having financial difficulties, the board may decide to postpone the project indefinitely, even after proposals have been received from interested contractors. Good pre-RFP marketing by the contractor will help to determine the viability of a project. Contractors should not spend time responding to RFPs by developing proposals that probably will not be funded.

7. *Proposal resources.* Are appropriate resources available to prepare a quality proposal? It is not enough for a contractor to just prepare a proposal. It is imperative that the proposal be of sufficient quality to have a good chance of winning. To prepare a quality proposal, a contractor must have the appropriate people—that is, resources—to work on it. If the contractor's organization does not have the right resources available to prepare a quality proposal, the contractor should make arrangements to secure other resources so as to ensure the best possible proposal. A contractor should not use inappropriate resources to prepare a proposal, just for the sake of submitting a proposal. Submitting a poor-quality proposal can leave the customer with a negative impression, which can hurt the contractor's chances of winning future contracts from that customer.

8. *Project resources.* Are appropriate resources available to perform the project if the contractor is selected as the winner? Contractors

REINFORCE YOUR LEARNING

2. *What are some factors that a contractor should consider when deciding whether to respond to an RFP?*

need to be sure that the appropriate individuals within their organization will be available to work on the project. If, after being awarded the contract, the contractor discovers that the team must be made up of individuals other than those originally planned for the project, the chances of successfully completing the project may diminish. The result could be a dissatisfied customer who will not ask the contractor to respond to future RFPs. If a contractor is not sure that it has the resources to perform the project, it needs a plan for securing the resources needed to successfully perform the project (such as hiring new people or having consultants or subcontractors perform some work elements).

Contractors need to be realistic about their ability to prepare proposals and about the probability of winning the contract. The proposal selection process is competitive—the customer will select one winner from among competing proposals. For a contractor, success is winning the contract, not merely submitting a proposal. Submitting a lot of nonwinning proposals in response to RFPs can hurt a contractor's reputation. So, although it is often the right thing to do, sometimes the hardest thing for a contractor to do is to decide to *no-bid* an RFP.

Figure 3.2 is an example of a Bid/No-Bid Checklist, which a contractor might use in deciding whether or not to submit a proposal in response to a request for proposal. Such a checklist might be used by the decision makers in the contractor's organization to reach a consensus. The checklist in Figure 3.2 illustrates the consensus of key individuals from a training consulting firm. It summarizes their deliberations over whether or not to bid on an RFP from Ace Manufacturing, Inc. to conduct a substantial supervisory training program for employees at seven plant locations nationwide. Do you think they should submit a proposal to Ace?

DEVELOPING A WINNING PROPOSAL

It is important to remember that *the proposal process is a competitive process.* A customer uses a request for proposals to solicit competing proposals from contractors. Each contractor, therefore, must keep in mind that its proposal will be competing with other contractors' proposals to be selected by the customer as the winner. Submitting a proposal that meets the customer's statement of work and requirements in the RFP is not sufficient to be selected as the winning contractor. Many or all of the proposals will likely meet the requirements. The customer will select the one that it expects will provide the best value.

A proposal is a selling document; it is not a technical report. In the proposal the contractor must convince the customer that the contractor

- understands what the customer is looking for
- can carry out the proposed project
- will provide the greatest value to the customer
- is the best contractor to solve the problem

FIGURE 3.2   Bid/No-Bid Checklist

Bid/No-Bid Checklist		
Project Title: Supervisory Training Program		
Customer: ACE Manufacturing, Inc.		**Due Date:** 5/31

Score each factor as High, Medium, or Low

Factor	Score	Comments
1. Competition	H	Local university has been providing most of the training to ACE in the past
2. Risk	L	Requirements in RFP are well defined
3. Consistent with our mission	H	Training is our business
4. Opportunity to extend our responsibilities	H	Some tasks require videoconferencing, which we haven't done before
5. Reputation with customer	L	Have not done any training for ACE before
6. Availability of funds	H	ACE has funds budgeted to implement the training
7. Resources available to prepare quality proposal	M	Lynn will have to reschedule her vacation. Will probably need to work over Memorial Day weekend to finish proposal
8. Resources available to perform project	M	Will have to hire subcontractors for several specific training topics

Our advantages, strengths, or distinct capabilities:

• Good track record in supervisory training—we have many repeat customers
• More flexible than local university in meeting ACE's need for on-site training during 2nd and 3rd shift operations

Our weaknesses:

• Most of our customers have been in the service sector, such as hospitals. ACE is a manufacturer
• President of ACE is a graduate of local university and a large contributor to it

- will capitalize on its successful experience with previous related projects
- will do the work professionally
- will achieve the intended results
- will complete the project within budget and on schedule
- will satisfy the customer

In the proposal the contractor must highlight the unique factors that differentiate it from competing contractors. The contractor proposal must emphasize the benefits to the customer if the customer selects the contractor to perform the project.

Proposals should be written in a simple, concise manner; they should not be wordy or redundant. They should use terminology with which the customer is familiar and avoid abbreviations, acronyms, jargon, and other words that the customer may not know or understand. Simple illustrations and graphics should be used when possible. Overly complex illustrations should be avoided; several simple graphics will likely be easier for the customer to understand than one complicated graphic. When a point is made or an approach or concept proposed, it should be supported with logic, rationale, or data. Proposals must be specific in addressing the customer's requirements as laid out in the RFP. Proposals written in generalities will cause the customer to question whether the contractor really understands what needs to be done and how to do it. For example, suppose one of the requirements in a customer's RFP is that a specialized piece of machinery be designed to produce twenty parts per minute. A contractor proposal stating that "the machine to be designed will in fact produce twenty parts per minute" is more convincing than one stating that "the machinery will be designed to produce the maximum number of parts per minute." The customer will be doubtful about the latter statement, since "maximum" could be something less than twenty parts per minute.

REINFORCE YOUR LEARNING

3. The proposal process is a _____ process. A proposal is a _____ document.

Finally, proposals must be realistic, in terms of the proposed scope, cost, and schedule, in the eyes of the customer. Proposals that promise too much or are overly optimistic may seem unbelievable and again raise doubt about whether the contractor understands what needs to be done and how to do it.

PROPOSAL PREPARATION

The preparation of a proposal can be a straightforward task performed by one person, or it can be a resource-intensive effort requiring a team of organizations and individuals with various expertise and skills. In the simple case of designing and printing an annual report, an experienced commercial printer (the contractor), after meeting with the customer regarding the requirements, may be able to prepare a proposal within a short period of time without involving other individuals. However, in the case where a government agency has issued an RFP for a multimillion-dollar project to design and construct a new regional rapid transit system, each interested contractor may have to assemble a team of many individuals and subcontractors to help develop the proposal. In such situations the contractor may designate a *proposal manager* who coordinates the efforts of the proposal team to ensure that a consistent, comprehensive proposal is prepared by the due date stated in the RFP.

Developing a comprehensive proposal for a large project should be treated as a project itself; thus, the proposal manager needs to meet with the proposal team to develop a schedule for completing the proposal by the customer's due date. The schedule should include the dates by which various individuals will have drafts of their assigned portions of the proposal, dates for conducting reviews with appropriate people on the proposal team, and the date on which the proposal will be finalized. The proposal schedule must allow time for review and approval by management within the contractor's organization. Time must also be provided for preparing any graphic illustrations, typing, copying, and delivery of the proposal to the customer, who may be hundreds of miles away from the contractor.

Proposals in response to RFPs for very large technical projects can be multivolume documents that include engineering drawings and hundreds of pages of text. And, yes, such proposals are often due within thirty calendar days of the RFP's issuance! Contractors who bid on such large projects usually do pre-RFP marketing, and so they may have a draft proposal prepared before the customer even issues a formal RFP. During the thirty-day response period, the contractor can first revise the proposal to incorporate any unanticipated requirements and then use any remaining time to "package" a first-class professional proposal.

Customers do not pay contractors to prepare proposals. Contractors absorb such costs as normal marketing costs of doing business, in anticipation of winning contracts and making profits on them.

As stated previously, a proposal is a selling document, not a technical report. It may consist of several pages or several volumes, containing hundreds of pages, illustrations, and tabulations. A proposal should contain sufficient detail to convince the customer that the contractor will provide the best value to the customer. Too much detail in a proposal may overwhelm the customer and needlessly increase the proposal preparation costs for the contractor.

PROPOSAL CONTENTS

REINFORCE YOUR LEARNING

4. A proposal should address three topics or contain three sections. What are they?

Proposals are often organized into three sections: technical, management, and cost. For large proposals, these could be three separate volumes. The amount of detail the contractor includes will depend on the complexity of the project and the contents of the RFP. Some RFPs state that contractor proposals that exceed a certain number of pages won't be accepted by the customer. After all, customers are anxious to do an expeditious evaluation of all proposals submitted, and they may not have the time to review a large number of voluminous proposals.

Technical Section

The objective of the technical section of the contractor proposal is to *convince the customer that the contractor understands the need or problem and can provide the least risky and most beneficial solution.* The technical section should contain the following elements:

1. *Understanding of the problem.* The contractor should state its understanding of the customer's problem or need in its own words. The contractor should not merely restate the problem statement that appears in the customer's RFP. This first part of the technical section must show the customer that the contractor thoroughly understands the problem to be solved or the need to be addressed and establish the basis for the solution proposed later in the technical section. The contractor may want to describe, in narrative or graphic form, the customer's current condition. For example, if the problem is a high reject rate from a manufacturing process, the contractor may want to incorporate a flowchart of the customer's current manufacturing process that indicates where the rejects are occurring and what other problems they may be causing, such as production bottlenecks. Customers will feel more confident working with a contractor who they believe really understands their problem.

2. *Proposed approach or solution.* Some problems lend themselves to a specific proposed solution—for example, an RFP to reconfigure a large office to accommodate 10 percent more people. Other problems, however, do not. A problem may require that an analysis and development task be conducted as part of the proposed project before a specific solution can be described in detail. In such cases, the contractor proposal must describe the approach or methodology that would be used in developing the solution. For example, if an RFP is for a specialized non–contact inspection system to measure certain characteristics of a complexly shaped product made of an advanced material, it would be unrealistic for the customer to expect the contractors to design such a system as part of the proposal itself; rather, such engineering design and development would be done as part of the proposed project. However, in the proposal, the contractor must convince the customer that the approach proposed for designing, developing, and building such a system is logical and realistic and would lead to the contractor's supplying a system that would successfully meet the customer's requirements.

   This part of the technical section might contain the following:

   a. A description of how the contractor would collect, analyze, and evaluate data and information about the problem.

   b. Methods that would be used by the contractor to evaluate alternative solutions or further develop the proposed solution to the problem. This portion could include a discussion of various experiments, tests, or physical or computer models the contractor would use or has used on similar projects.

   c. The rationale for the proposed approach or solution. This rationale could be based on experiments previously conducted by the contractor, the contractor's experience in solving similar problems, or a unique patented technology the contractor would use to solve the problem.

d. Confirmation that the proposed solution or approach would meet each of the physical, operational, and performance requirements stated in the customer's RFP. For example, if the RFP for the design and construction of a day care center states that certain furnishings must be at a specific height to accommodate children under forty-eight inches tall, the proposal must state that the contractor will meet that requirement. Not addressing each of the customer's requirements will raise doubt in the customer's mind about the proposed solution and could hurt a contractor's chances of winning the contract, especially if competing contractors' proposals state that they will meet the requirements.

If the contractor cannot meet a specific customer requirement, that fact should be stated in the contractor proposal. A variation from specified requirements is known as an **exception.** For each exception taken to a customer requirement, the contractor should explain why the requirement will not or cannot be met and propose an alternative. Although contractors should avoid taking exceptions to customer requirements, there may be circumstances where an exception is appropriate. For example, if the customer requires an electric heating system for an office building, the contractor may take exception and show in the proposal that the initial and operating costs for a natural gas heating system would be less expensive for the customer. However, the customer may have very good reasons beyond cost for requiring an electric heating system and may reject proposals that take exception to that requirement.

3. *Benefits to the customer.* The contractor should state how the proposed solution or approach would benefit the customer. Benefits could be quantitative and/or qualitative and could include cost savings; reduced processing time; reduced inventory; better customer service; less scrap, rejects, or errors; improved safety conditions; more timely information; and reduced maintenance. This portion of the proposal *should help convince the customer of the value of the proposed approach* compared with proposals from competing contractors.

REINFORCE YOUR LEARNING

5. *What is the objective of the technical section of a proposal?*

Management Section

The objective of the management section of the contractor proposal is to *convince the customer that the contractor can do the proposed work (the project) and achieve the intended results.* The management section should contain the following elements:

1. *Description of work tasks.* The contractor should define the major tasks that will be performed in carrying out the project and provide a brief description of what each major task includes. The contractor should not merely restate the statement of work that may be

included in the customer's RFP. The proposal need not include a lengthy list of detailed activities; such an activity list would be developed during the initial planning effort of the project phase, after the contract is awarded.

2. *Deliverables*. The contractor should include a list of all deliverables (tangible products or items) that will be provided during the project, such as reports, drawings, manuals, and equipment.

3. *Project schedule*. The contractor should provide a schedule for performing the major tasks required to complete the project. The schedule must show that the contractor can complete the project within the time frame stated in the RFP. The task schedule can be given in any one of several formats: a list of tasks with their estimated start and completion dates; a bar chart, often called a *Gantt chart* (covered in Chapter 9), with the estimated duration of each task represented by a bar along a horizontal timeline; or a network diagram in which the tasks are portrayed graphically so as to show the sequence and interdependencies among the tasks.

   In addition to the major tasks, the schedule might include dates for other key events such as important review meetings, customer approval activities, and completion of deliverable items such as progress reports, drawings, manuals, or equipment.

4. *Project organization*. The contractor should describe how the work and resources will be organized to perform the project. For large projects involving many people and subcontractors, it may be appropriate to include an organization chart (covered in Chapter 7), which gives the major project functions along with the name of the specific individual who will be assigned responsibility for each function. Resumes of the key people who will be assigned to the project should be included to convince the customer that their significant related experience will be brought to bear to ensure the project's success. In addition to or in place of an organization chart, the contractor may include a responsibility matrix (covered in Chapter 9) that lists the major project tasks and the name of the person, organization, or subcontractor responsible for the achievement of each task.

5. *Related experience*. To help convince the customer that the contractor can do the project, the contractor should provide a list of similar projects it has completed. The contractor should briefly describe each past project and explain how the experience from that project will be helpful in successfully performing the proposed project. The contract dollar value of each project should also be provided to give the customer a sense of the contractor's ability to manage projects the size of the proposed one. The probability of a contractor's winning a contract for a several-hundred-thousand-dollar project is not very high if all its previous related experience is on $20,000 projects. For each previous similar project, the contractor might want to include the name, title, and phone number of an individual the current customer could contact to check on the contractor's performance. Reference letters from satisfied customers might also be included. This type of

information will be particularly helpful if the contractor has a strong performance record.

REINFORCE YOUR LEARNING

6. *What is the objective of the management section of a proposal?*

6. *Equipment and facilities.* Some projects require the contractor to use or have access to unique equipment such as computers, software, manufacturing equipment, or testing facilities. In these cases, the contractor may want to provide a list of the equipment and special facilities it has, in order to convince the customer that it has the necessary resources.

Cost Section

The objective of the cost section of the contractor proposal is to *convince the customer that the contractor's price for the proposed project is realistic and reasonable.* In some cases, the customer may want only the bottom-line total cost of the project. Some customers also want to see the costs for optional items. For example, a couple who is asking several contractors for proposals for building a house may be looking for the total cost plus costs for options such as landscaping, a deck, a finished basement, a built-in swimming pool, and a fence around the backyard. Government agency RFPs usually require contractors to provide a detailed breakdown of the various costs.

REINFORCE YOUR LEARNING

7. *What is the objective of the cost section of a proposal?*

The cost section usually consists of tabulations of the contractor's estimated costs for such elements as the following:

1. *Labor.* This portion gives the estimated costs for the various classifications of people who are expected to work on the project. It might include the estimated hours and hourly rate for each person or classification, such as senior engineer, designer, machinist, or programmer. The estimated hours must be realistic. If they are too high and have too much "fat" in them, the total estimated costs may be higher than what the customer is willing to pay. On the other hand, if the estimated hours are too low, the contractor may lose money on the project. The hourly rate is usually based on the annual salary for each person or the average annual salary for each classification plus an additional percentage to cover employee fringe benefits (health insurance, retirement, and so forth). These salaries are then divided by the number of normal work hours in a year (for example, 40 hours a week times 52 weeks totals 2080 hours) to determine the hourly labor rate for each person or classification.

2. *Materials.* This portion gives the cost of materials the contractor needs to purchase for the project. For example, the cost of materials for a remodeling project might include lumber, new windows, electrical and plumbing supplies, and carpeting.

3. *Subcontractors and consultants.* When contractors do not have the expertise or resources to do certain project tasks, they may hire subcontractors or consultants to perform those tasks. For example, a project to make over a church basement into a day care center might require that the contractor hire a subcontractor to remove any asbestos and a consultant to provide advice on state

REINFORCE YOUR LEARNING

8. What elements might each of the three sections of a proposal contain?

regulations and codes for day care facilities. The contractor usually asks the subcontractors and consultants to submit a proposal of work scope and cost for their tasks. The contractor then includes these costs in the overall cost for the project.

4. *Equipment and facilities rental.* Sometimes the contractor will have to rent special equipment, tools, or facilities solely for the project.

5. *Travel.* If travel (other than local travel) is required during the project, the costs for travel (such as air fare), lodging (hotel rooms), and meals need to be included. The contractor must first estimate the number and length of trips. For example, if the customer is a government agency in Washington, D.C., and the contractor is in California, the costs associated with travel to Washington for review meetings with the customer need to be included.

6. *Documentation.* Some customers want the contractor to show separately the costs associated with the project documentation deliverables. This would be the cost of printing manuals, drawings, or reports or the cost of producing videotapes.

7. *Overhead.* Contractors will add a percentage to costs in items 1 through 6 to cover their normal **overhead**—the **indirect costs** of doing business, such as insurance, depreciation, accounting, general management, marketing, and human resources. Of course, in informal projects such as organization of a town celebration by volunteers, such overhead costs are not applicable.

8. *Escalation.* For large projects that are expected to take several years to complete, the contractor needs to include the costs of escalation in wage rates and materials costs over the length of the project. For example, for a three-year project, the contractor will want to anticipate a 4-percent wage increase in each of the last two years of the project. If the same project requires that the contractor purchase most of the materials during the third year, the current materials cost estimates may need to be increased by a certain percentage to cover the expected cost of the materials at the time they will be purchased.

9. *Contingency.* **Contingency,** or **management reserve,** is an amount the contractor may want to include to cover the unexpected—items that have been overlooked or tasks that have to be redone because they did not work the first time.

10. *Fee or profit.* Items 1 through 9 are costs. The contractor must now add an amount for its fee or profit. The total cost plus the profit is the contractor's price for the proposed project.

PRICING CONSIDERATIONS

When contractors prepare a proposal, they are generally competing with other contractors to win a contract. Therefore, they need to be careful not to overprice the proposed project, or else the customer may select a lower-priced contractor. However, contractors must be equally careful not to underprice the proposed project; otherwise, they may lose money rather than making a profit or may have to request additional funds from the customer, which could be embarrassing and hurt the contractor's reputation.

REINFORCE YOUR LEARNING

9. What are some items a contractor needs to consider when determining a price for a proposed project?

The contractor must consider the following items when determining the price for the proposed project:

1. *Reliability of the cost estimates.* Does the contractor have confidence that the total cost for the proposed project is complete and accurate? The contractor should take the time to think through the project and estimate costs at a high level of detail, rather than making a ballpark estimate. Ideally the costs should be based on a recent similar project or, in the case of materials cost estimates, on current price lists, catalogs, or quotations. It may be advisable to ask experienced individuals or specialists to help estimate the labor effort. In general, the more detailed the cost estimates, the better.

2. *Risk.* If the proposed project involves an endeavor that has not been undertaken before, such as a research and development project to come up with a drug to control a disease, it may be necessary to include a large amount of contingency, or management reserve, funds.

3. *Value of the project to the contractor.* There may be situations in which the contractor is willing to live with a tight or low price. For example, if the contractor doesn't have many other projects, it may need to lay off workers unless new contracts are obtained. In such a case, the contractor may include only a very small fee to increase the chances of winning the contract and avoid having to lay off people. Another example of a project that may be particularly valuable to the contractor is a project that provides an opportunity to extend capabilities or expand into new types of projects. A building contractor who has been doing only remodeling projects may want to get into building complete homes and may be willing to make a low profit in order to gain entry into the market and establish a reputation.

4. *Customer's budget.* A contractor who knows how much money the customer has budgeted for a project should not submit a price that exceeds what the customer has available. This is where good pre-RFP marketing is important. By helping a potential customer identify a need or submitting unsolicited proposals with cost estimates, a contractor can help the customer determine a budget for the project. Then, if the customer issues a competitive RFP (and doesn't disclose the amount budgeted for the project), the contractor with the customer budget "intelligence" information may be in a better position to submit a proposal with an acceptable price than are contractors who have not done similar homework.

5. *Competition.* If many contractors are expected to submit proposals in response to a customer RFP or if some competing contractors are hungry for work, it may be necessary to submit a price that includes only a small profit to increase the chances of winning the contract.

PROPOSAL SUBMISSION AND FOLLOW-UP

The customer's RFP will usually provide instructions regarding the due date by which proposals must be submitted and the name and address of the person to whom the proposals should be submitted. Some customers want the contractor to provide several copies of the proposal because the proposal will be distributed to various individuals within the organization for review and evaluation. From the customer's point of view, it is easier and less costly to have the contractor make the necessary copies. This is especially true for large projects where proposals may be several hundred pages long and may include large drawings or color graphics. Government agencies are very strict about having proposals submitted on time; those submitted late will not be accepted—and the contractor's efforts will have been wasted. Rather than trust the mail, some contractors hand deliver proposals to ensure that they arrive on time. Other contractors have been known to send two sets of proposals by different express mail services to ensure that at least one set arrives at its destination on time. Such precautions are usually taken for multimillion-dollar projects or when thousands of hours have been spent in pre-RFP marketing and proposal preparation.

Contractors must continue to be proactive even after the proposal is submitted. The contractor should call the customer to confirm that the proposal was received. After several days, the contractor should contact the customer again and ask whether the customer has any questions or needs clarification of anything in the proposal. Such follow-up needs to be done in a professional manner in order to make a favorable impression on the customer. If the contractor appears aggressive rather than responsive, the customer may view the contractor as an intrusive element trying to influence the proposal evaluation process. A contractor must always consider whether and how aggressively other competing contractors are following up with the customer after proposals have been submitted.

Industrial and, especially, government customers usually do not respond to attempted follow-up communications from contractors so that no contractor gains an unfair advantage in influencing the proposal evaluation process. Such customers will initiate any needed communications. The contact will generally be in the form of a written list of specific questions that need to be answered or points that need to be clarified about a particular contractor's proposal. A written response from the contractor is required by a certain date.

CUSTOMER EVALUATION OF PROPOSALS

Customers evaluate contractors' proposals in many different ways. Some customers first look at the prices of the various proposals and select, for example, only the three lowest-priced proposals for further evaluation. Other customers initially screen out those proposals with prices above their budget or those whose technical section doesn't meet all the requirements stated in the RFP. Other customers, especially on large projects, create a proposal review team that uses a scorecard to determine whether each proposal meets all requirements in the RFP and to rate the proposal against predefined evaluation criteria.

Figure 3.3 illustrates a proposal evaluation scorecard. This scorecard was used by AJACKS Information Services Company to review

FIGURE 3.3   Proposal Evaluation Scorecard

AJACKS Information Services Company
Proposal Evaluation

Project Title: _Technical Information Needs of Manufacturers_

Contractor: _Galaxy Market Research Inc._

Score all criteria on a scale from 1 (low) to 10 (high)

Evaluation Criteria	Weight A	Score B	Points AxB	Comments
1. Approach	30	4	120	Shallow description of methodology
2. Experience	30	3	90	Little experience with manufacturing firms
3. Price	30	9	270	Lowest price bid Supported by details
4. Schedule	10	5	50	Schedule is overly optimistic
Total	100		530	

Advantages of this proposal:

- This is the lowest price proposal received. It appears the salaries of Galaxy's staff are low compared to those of other proposers.

Concerns about this proposal:

- Galaxy may not fully comprehend the requirements.
- Low salaries in its budget may reflect low levels of experience of the staff Galaxy plans to use.
- Optimistic schedule (3 months) to complete project may indicate Galaxy doesn't fully comprehend the work scope.

contractor proposals submitted in response to the request for proposal in Chapter 2 (Figure 2.2). It is an evaluation of a proposal from Galaxy Market Research, Inc., one of five contractors that submitted proposals to AJACKS. Each person on the customer's proposal evaluation team completes a scorecard for each of the contractor proposals. These scorecards are then used by the proposal evaluation team to reach a consensus as to which contractor, if any, to select as the winner. The scorecards are not the sole mechanism for evaluating proposals and selecting the winner. They are usually used as input to the decision-making process.

Sometimes the technical and management proposals are evaluated first, without consideration of cost. Those proposals with the highest points on the technical/management review are then evaluated for their costs. The customer weighs the technical/management merit against the costs to determine which proposal offers the best value.

Some of the criteria that might be used by customers in evaluating contractor proposals include the following:

- Compliance with the customer's statement of work and requirements in the request for proposal
- Contractor's understanding of the customer's problem or need
- Soundness and practicality of the contractor's proposed approach to solving the problem
- Contractor's experience and success with similar projects
- The experience of key individuals who will be assigned to work on the project
- Management capability, including the contractor's ability to plan and control the project to ensure that the work scope is completed within budget and on schedule
- Realism of the contractor's schedule. Is it realistic considering the resources the contractor plans to assign to the project? Does it meet the customer's schedule as stated in the RFP? How detailed is the schedule?
- Price. Customers may evaluate not only the contractor's total price for the project but also the detailed costs in the cost section of the proposal. Customers are concerned about the reasonableness, realism, and completeness of the contractor's costs. Did the contractor use sound cost-estimating methodology? Are the labor hours, classifications, and rates appropriate for the type of project? Were any items left out? The customer wants to be sure that a contractor isn't "low-balling" the price to win the contract, expecting to come back to the customer for additional funds if the project overruns its proposed cost. It is unethical and may be illegal for contractors to intentionally low-ball their price.

In some instances, especially when a large number of proposals are received, the proposal evaluation process will produce a short list of proposals the customer considers to be acceptable and of good value. The customer may then ask each of these contractors to give an oral presentation of its proposal. This provides a final opportunity for each contractor to convince the customer that its proposal will provide the best value. The customer may also ask each of these contractors to submit a **best and final offer (BAFO)**. This gives the contractor one last chance to reduce its price and possibly win the contract. However, the customer usually requires the contractor to provide a written rationale for any cost reductions to make sure that they are reasonable. The contractor, for instance, might review the people to be assigned to the project and determine that for some tasks individuals with lower labor cost rates could be used, or the contractor might decide that some travel could be eliminated or trips combined to reduce costs.

Once the customer has selected the winning contractor, the contractor is informed that it is the winner, subject to successful negotiation of a contract.

TYPES OF CONTRACTS

Just because the contractor has been selected as the winner doesn't mean the contractor can start doing the work. Before the project can proceed, a contract must be signed between the customer and the contractor—the final step in this second phase of the life cycle.

A **contract** is a vehicle for establishing good customer-contractor communications and arriving at a mutual understanding and clear expectations to ensure project success. It is an agreement between the contractor, who agrees to provide a product or service (deliverables), and the customer, who agrees to pay the contractor a certain amount in return. The contract must clearly spell out the deliverables the contractor is expected to provide. For example, a contract will state that the project result will meet certain specifications or that certain documentation will be provided. The contract must also state the terms by which the customer will make payments to the contractor. There are basically two types of contracts: fixed price and cost reimbursement.

Fixed-Price Contracts

In a **fixed-price contract,** the customer and the contractor agree on a price for the proposed work. The price remains fixed unless the customer and contractor agree on changes. This type of contract provides low risk for the customer, since the customer will not pay more than the fixed price, regardless of how much the project actually costs the contractor. However, a fixed-price contract is high risk for the contractor, because if the cost of completing the project is more than originally planned, the contractor will make a lower profit than anticipated or even lose money.

A contractor bidding on a fixed-price project must develop accurate and complete cost estimates and include sufficient contingency costs. However, the contractor needs to be careful not to overprice the proposed project, or else a competing contractor with a lower price may be selected.

Fixed-price contracts are most appropriate for projects that are well defined and entail little risk. Examples include the construction of a standard model house and the design and production of a brochure for which the customer has provided detailed specifications regarding format, content, photos, color, number of pages, and number of copies.

Cost-Reimbursement Contracts

In a **cost-reimbursement contract,** the customer agrees to pay the contractor for all actual costs (labor, materials, and so forth), regardless of amount, plus some agreed-upon profit. This type of contract provides high risk for the customer, since contractor costs can overrun the proposed price—as when a car repair service provides an estimate for repairing a transmission but presents a final bill that is higher than the original estimate. In cost-reimbursement contracts, the customer usually requires that, throughout the project, the contractor regularly compare actual expenditures with the proposed budget and reforecast cost-at-completion, comparing it with the original proposed price. This allows the customer to take action if it looks as if the project will overrun the original proposed budget costs. This type of contract is low risk for the contractor, because all costs will be reimbursed by the customer. The contractor cannot lose money on this type of contract. However, if the contractor's costs do overrun the proposed budget, the contractor's reputation will be hurt, in turn hurting the contractor's chances of winning contracts in the future.

Cost-reimbursement contracts are most appropriate for projects that involve risk. Examples include the development of a new robotics device to assist during surgery or the environmental clean-up of a contaminated site.

REINFORCE YOUR LEARNING

10. *Write the word* low *or* high *in each box, depending on the degree of risk for the customer and contractor associated with each type of contract.*

	Customer	Contractor
Fixed price	low	high
Cost reimbursement	high	low

CONTRACT PROVISIONS

The following are some miscellaneous provisions that may be included in project contracts:

1. *Misrepresentation of costs.* States that it is illegal for the contractor to overstate the hours or costs expended on the project.
2. *Notice of cost overruns or schedule delays.* Outlines the circumstances under which the contractor must notify the customer immediately of any actual or anticipated cost overruns or schedule delays, submitting in writing both the reason and a plan for corrective action to get the costs back within budget or the schedule back on track.
3. *Approval of subcontractor.* Indicates when the contractor needs to obtain advance approval from the customer before hiring a subcontractor to perform a project task.
4. *Customer-furnished equipment or information.* Lists the items (such as parts for conducting tests) that the customer will provide to the contractor throughout the project and the dates by which the

customer will make these items available. This provision protects the contractor from incurring schedule slippage caused by delays in the customer's furnishing information, parts, or other items.

5. *Patents*. Covers ownership of patents that may result from conducting the project.

6. *Disclosure of proprietary information*. Prohibits one party from disclosing to anyone else or using for any purpose other than work on the project confidential information, technologies, or processes utilized by the other party during the project.

7. *International considerations*. Specifies accommodations that must be made for customers from other countries. Contracts for projects that are done for a foreign customer or are conducted in part in a foreign country may require the contractor to make certain accommodations, such as

   - observing certain holidays or work rules
   - spending a certain percentage of the contract costs for labor or materials within the customer's country
   - providing project documentation, such as manuals and reports, in the customer's language

8. *Termination*. States the conditions under which the customer can terminate the contract, such as nonperformance by the contractor.

9. *Terms of payment*. Addresses the basis on which the customer will make payments to the contractor. Some types of payments are

   - monthly payments, based on actual costs incurred by the contractor
   - equal monthly or quarterly payments, based on the expected overall duration of the project schedule
   - percentages of the total contract amount, paid when the contractor completes predefined milestones
   - single payment at completion of the project

   In some cases, such as when the contractor needs to purchase a significant amount of materials and supplies during the early stages of the project, the customer provides an initial down payment at the start of the contract.

10. *Bonus/penalty payments*. Some contracts have a bonus provision, whereby the customer will pay the contractor a bonus if the project is completed ahead of schedule or exceeds other customer performance requirements. On the other hand, some contracts include a penalty provision, whereby the customer can reduce the final payment to the contractor if the project is not completed on schedule or if performance requirements are not met. Some of these penalties can be substantial, such as 1 percent of the total contract price for each week the project extends beyond the required project completion date, up to a maximum of 10 percent. A ten-week schedule overrun could wipe out the contractor's profit and cause a loss.

11. *Changes*. Covers the procedure for proposing, approving, and implementing changes to the project scope or schedule. Changes can be initiated by the customer or proposed by the contractor.

Some changes may necessitate a change in price (increase or decrease); others may not. All changes must be documented and approved by the customer before they are incorporated into the project. Customers usually want the contractor to provide a price estimate, along with an indication of the schedule impact, for a proposed change before they will allow the contractor to implement the change. If a contractor makes changes without the customer's approval or with only oral approval from someone in the customer's organization who may not be authorized to give it, the contractor runs the risk of being unable to collect payment for the changes.

SUMMARY

The development of proposed solutions by interested contractors or by the customer's internal project team is the second phase of the project life cycle. This phase starts when the RFP becomes available at the conclusion of the needs identification phase and ends when an agreement is reached with the person, organization, or contractor selected to implement the proposed solution.

Contractors should develop relationships with potential customers long before the customers prepare requests for proposal. Contractors should maintain frequent contacts with past customers and current customers and initiate contacts with potential new customers. During these contacts, contractors should help customers identify areas in which the customers might benefit from the implementation of projects that address needs, problems, or opportunities. These pre-RFP/proposal efforts are crucial to establishing the foundation for eventually winning a contract from the customer.

Because the development and preparation of a proposal takes time and money, contractors interested in submitting a proposal in response to an RFP must be realistic about the probability of being selected as the winning contractor. Evaluating whether or not to go forward with the preparation of a proposal is sometimes referred to as the bid/no-bid decision. Some factors that a contractor might consider in making a bid/no-bid decision are the competition, the risk, its business mission, the ability to extend its capabilities, its reputation with the customer, the availability of customer funds, and the availability of resources for the proposal and the project.

It is important to remember that the proposal process is a competitive process and that the proposal is a selling document that should be written in a simple, concise manner. In the proposal the contractor must highlight the unique factors that differentiate it from competing contractors. The contractor proposal must also emphasize the benefits to the customer if the customer selects the contractor to perform the project. The customer will select the contractor that it expects will provide the best value.

Proposals are often organized into three sections: technical, management, and cost. The objective of the technical section of the contractor proposal is to convince the customer that the contractor understands the need or problem and can provide the least risky and most beneficial solution. The technical section should show an understanding of the problem, a proposed approach or solution, and the benefits to the customer. The objective of the management section of the contractor proposal is to convince the customer that the contractor can do the proposed work and achieve the intended results. The management section should contain a description of work tasks, a list of deliverables, a project schedule, a description of the organization of the project, a list detailing related experience, and a list of any special equipment and facilities the contractor has. The objective of the cost section of the contractor proposal is to convince the customer that the contractor's price for the proposed project is realistic and reasonable. The cost section usually consists of tabulations of the contractor's estimated costs for such elements as labor, materials, subcontractors and consultants, equipment and facilities rental, travel, documentation, overhead, escalation, contingency, and a fee or profit.

When contractors prepare proposals, they are generally competing with other contractors to win a contract. Therefore, they must consider the reliability of the cost estimates, the risk, the value of the project to the contractor, the customer's budget, and the competition when determining the price for the proposed project.

Customers evaluate contractors' proposals in many different ways. Sometimes the technical and management proposals are evaluated first, without consideration of cost. Those proposals with the highest points on the technical/management review are then evaluated for their costs. The customer weighs the technical/management merit against the costs to determine which proposal offers the best value. Some of the criteria that might be used by customers in evaluating contractor proposals include compliance with the customer's statement of work, the contractor's understanding of the customer's problem or need, the soundness and practicality of the contractor's proposed solution to the project, the contractor's experience and success with similar projects, the experience of key individuals who will be assigned to work on the project, the contractor's ability to plan and control the project, the realism of the contractor's schedule, and the price.

Once the customer has selected the winning contractor, the contractor is informed that it is the winner, subject to successful negotiation of a contract. A contract is an agreement between the contractor, who agrees to provide a product or service (deliverables), and the customer, who agrees to pay the contractor a certain amount in return.

There are basically two types of contracts: fixed price and cost reimbursement. In a fixed-price contract, the customer and the contractor agree on a price for the proposed work. The price remains fixed unless the customer and contractor agree on changes. This type of contract provides low risk for the customer and high risk for the contractor. In a cost-reimbursement contract, the customer agrees to pay the contractor for all actual costs (labor, materials, and so forth), regardless of amount, plus some agreed-upon profit. This type of contract provides high risk for the customer, since contractor costs can overrun the proposed price, and low risk for the contractor.

A contract may include miscellaneous provisions covering misrepresentation of costs, notice of cost overruns or schedule delays, approvals for any subcontractors, customer-furnished equipment or information, patent ownership, disclosure of proprietary information, international considerations, termination, terms of payment, bonuses or penalties, and procedures for making changes.

QUESTIONS

1. Describe what is meant by pre-RFP/proposal marketing. Why should contractors do it?
2. Discuss why contractors must make bid/no-bid decisions and the factors involved in making these decisions.
3. Give an example of when a contractor should bid and when a contractor should not bid.
4. Define *proposal,* and describe the purpose of a proposal.
5. List the three major sections of a proposal and the purpose and elements of each.
6. What factors must be considered when a contractor develops the proposal price? Why is this not an easy task?
7. Should a contractor try to contact a customer after a proposal has been submitted? Why or why not?
8. How do customers evaluate proposals? What factors might they consider?
9. Should the lowest-priced proposal always be selected as the winner? Why or why not? Give examples.
10. Describe two different types of contracts, when each should be used, and the risks associated with each.
11. Give examples of some miscellaneous provisions that might be found in a contract.
12. Develop a complete proposal in response to the RFP you created for question 10 at the end of Chapter 2.

WORLD WIDE WEB EXERCISES

If you have difficulty accessing any of the Web addresses listed here, you can find these exercises (with up-to-date addresses) on the home page of Dr. James P. Clements, co-author of this book, at

www.towson.edu/~clements

1. Information about the *International Journal of Project Management,* an excellent journal on project management, can be obtained from its publisher's Web site at

**www.elsevier.nl/inca/publications/
store/3/0/4/3/5/30435.pub.shtml**

Visit the publisher's home page (or conduct an Internet search using the publisher's name and the title of the journal). Explore what this journal is all about, the topics it covers, and its intended audience.

2. Print out the list of articles from the most recent edition of the *International Journal of Project Management*. Are there any articles on developing proposals? If so, what aspects do they discuss?

3. Do any of these articles relate to other topics covered thus far in this book? If so, which ones?

4. Sign up on-line for a free sample copy.

CASE STUDY

Maggie Pressman, Paul Goldberg, and Steve Youngblood are equal partners in their own consulting business, which specializes in designing and installing computer-based information systems for physicians. These systems usually include patient records, prescriptions, billings, and medical insurance processing. In some cases, the physician customers have a manual system and want to computerize it; in other situations, they have an existing computer system that needs to be upgraded and enhanced.

In most cases, the consulting firm purchases the necessary hardware as well as some packaged software. They add some of their own customized software to meet the specific requirements of the physician, and they install the complete, integrated system. They also provide training for the employees in the physician's office. The cost of most of these projects ranges from $10,000 to $40,000, depending on the amount of hardware needed. Most physicians are willing to spend such amounts rather than hire an additional office person to keep up with the ever-increasing paperwork.

Dr. Houser, one of the physicians for whom Paul had done a project in the past, left her private practice to join a large regional medical practice. This organization has six offices throughout the region, with an average of eight physicians in each office. Two of the offices also include a pharmacy. The organization employs a total of two hundred people. Dr. Houser contacted Paul and asked if his consulting firm would be interested in submitting a proposal to upgrade the information system for this entire regional medical practice. The project will include integrating the six offices and two pharmacies into one system; the physicians will eventually hire an information systems person to oversee the operation of the system. Presently each office has its own system.

Dr. Houser tells Paul that some of the other physicians have patients who work for large consulting firms they think could do the job. She says that a team of representatives from the six offices and two pharmacies, with the help of the organization's purchasing manager, has prepared a request for proposal. The proposals are due in two weeks. The RFP was issued two weeks ago to the larger consulting firms, which are already working on their proposals. The purchasing manager was not familiar with Paul's consulting firm, and that is why he didn't receive a copy of the RFP.

She tells Paul that she's sorry she can't talk to him more about this, but she hasn't been involved like some of the other physicians, who discussed ideas with their patients who work at the larger consulting firms *before* the RFP was issued. Dr. Houser says that she will have the purchasing manager send Paul the RFP if he is interested and will be able to submit a proposal within two weeks.

"Sure," Paul says, "I'll drive over this afternoon and pick it up!" He asks if she knows how much money the medical practice has allocated for the project, but she doesn't.

Paul picks up the RFP and makes copies for Maggie and Steve. Paul is enthusiastic about the opportunity when he meets with them. "If we do this project, it will propel us into a whole new business arena," Paul tells them. "This is the big break we've been waiting for!" he shouts.

Maggie moans, "This couldn't have come at a worse time. I'm working on three projects for other physicians, and they're all hounding me to finish up. In fact, one of them is not very satisfied. He said that if I don't finish his project in two weeks, he doesn't want it and won't recommend us to other physicians. I'm working sixteen hours a day to keep up. I'm just overcommitted. I agree with you, Paul, it is a great opportunity, but I'm afraid I won't be able to spend any time helping with the proposal."

Steve wonders out loud, "Preparing the proposal is one thing, but can we do the project? I think we have the expertise among the three of us to do such a project, but this is a really big project, and we have other customers, too."

Paul replies, "We can hire more people. I have a few friends who would probably want some part-time work. We can do it! If we don't go after projects like this, we'll always be a small firm, each of us working twelve-hour days for peanuts. And these small jobs for individual offices aren't going to last forever. Someday they'll all be computerized, and we'll be out of business. What do we have to lose by submitting a proposal? We can't win if we don't submit one!"

Case Questions

1. Why didn't this team receive the RFP at the same time the larger consulting firms did?
2. Why is this team being considered as a candidate to submit a proposal?
3. What should Maggie, Paul, and Steve do? In explaining your answer, address the concerns of each of the three team members.

Group Activity

Break the course participants into teams of three or four to discuss the case and decide whether the consulting firm should submit a proposal. Each team must provide reasons for its decision. Have each team choose a spokesperson to present its decision and reasons for that decision to the entire class.

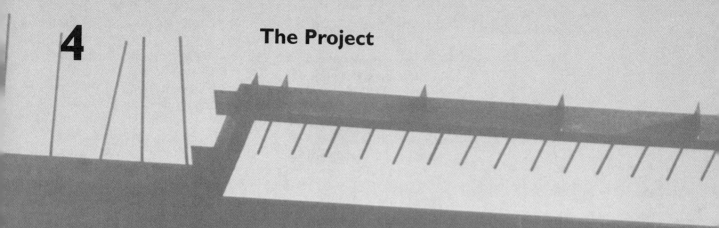

4

The Project

Project Management Makes Housing Affordable

To the everyday observer, Deer Meadow, a family-centered apartment community in Bloomfield, Connecticut, appears to be an upscale condominium complex. In reality, it is an affordable housing project that demonstrates how effective project management can help society.

Enterprise Builders, Inc., a merit shop general contractor and construction management firm headed by Paul Berg and located in Simsbury, Connecticut, was selected to manage the project. The scope of the project involved construction of a low-density housing development consisting of apartment buildings on a 13.5-acre rural site. It would contain forty-eight two- and three-bedroom garden-style apartments ranging in size from 1,000 to 1,300 square feet. The plans called for children's play areas, ample parking, and attractive landscaping.

The project team from Enterprise Builders established clear lines of communication and defined objectives, such as (1) to construct the project within the budget of $3.75 million, (2) to stay on or ahead of schedule, (3) to perform as a team in the best interests of the project, (4) to anticipate the needs of the project and identify potential problems before they occurred, and (5) to end with a satisfied client. In addition, they consistently applied project management techniques and ideas.

Thanks to the dedication of the project team and the use of project management techniques, this attractive family-oriented apartment community was completed in less than eight months, a month ahead of schedule, and $300,000 under budget. Also, as a result of their success at Deer Meadow, another affordable housing project in Connecticut was awarded to Enterprise Builders and its project team. This second project was valued at $8.75 million and set on a fifty-acre site. However, possibly the greatest satisfaction for the project team was helping to make affordable housing available to families who would not otherwise have the opportunity to live in such pleasant surroundings. "I live in a palace!" stated a tenant who had just moved into one of the new apartments.

Source: P. Berg, "Making Affordable Housing Attainable Through Modern Project Management," PM Network, August 1994.

Critical Success Factors

A study was conducted to test the importance of certain factors that were believed to be critical to project success. Although the researchers specifically studied information systems projects, they pointed out that the factors presented were general enough to apply to almost any type of project. Seventy-eight survey questionnaires were obtained from fifty different firms. The results showed that the top ten major factors were

1. Clearly defined goals and project mission
2. Top management support
3. A competent project manager
4. A competent project team
5. Sufficient resources
6. Client/customer involvement and consultation
7. Good communications
8. Responsiveness to clients
9. Proper monitoring and feedback
10. Appropriate technology

Source: J. Jiang, G. Klein, and J. Balloun, "Ranking of System Implementation Success Factors," Project Management Journal, December 1996.

Performing, or doing, the project—implementing the proposed solution—is the third phase of the project life cycle shown in Figure 4.1. This phase starts after a contract or agreement is drawn up between the customer and the contractor or project team, and it ends when the project objective is accomplished and the customer is satisfied that the work has been completed in a quality manner, within budget, and on time. The fourth and final phase of the project life cycle involves terminating the project. This chapter discusses these last two phases of the project life cycle. You will become familiar with

FIGURE 4.1   Project Life Cycle

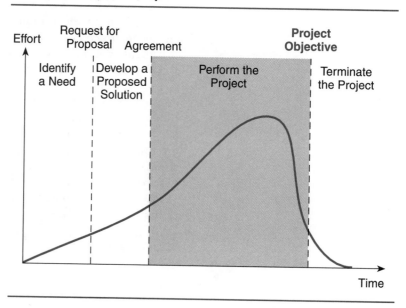

- the elements involved in establishing a project plan
- the steps in the project control process
- actions that should be taken when a project is terminated

PLANNING THE PROJECT

REINFORCE YOUR LEARNING

1. What are the two parts of the project phase of the life cycle?

The third phase of the project life cycle has two parts—doing the detailed planning for the project and then implementing that plan to accomplish the project objective. Before jumping in and starting the project itself, the contractor or project team must take sufficient time to properly plan the project. It is necessary to lay out a roadmap, or game plan, that shows how the project tasks will be accomplished within budget and on schedule. Trying to perform a project without a plan is like attempting to assemble a child's bicycle without first reading the instructions. Individuals who think planning is unnecessary or a waste of time invariably need to find time later on to re-do things. It is important to *plan the work, then work the plan*. Otherwise, chaos and frustration will result, and the risk of project failure will be higher.

The planning part of the project phase involves taking the plan, schedule, and budget in the proposal to much greater detail. The time and expense required to do such detailed planning is not usually warranted during the proposal (second) phase of the life cycle. Detailed planning involves the same steps as the front-end planning discussed in Chapter 1:

1. *Clearly define the project objective.* The definition must be agreed upon by the customer and the individual or organization who will perform the project.

2. *Divide and subdivide the project scope into major "pieces," or **work packages**.* Although major projects may seem overwhelming when viewed as a whole, one way to conquer even the most monumental endeavor is to break it down. A **work breakdown structure** is a hierarchical tree of work elements or items accomplished or produced by the project team during the project. The work breakdown structure usually identifies the organization or individual responsible for each work package. (Work breakdown structures will be discussed further in Chapter 9.)

3. *Define the specific activities that need to be performed for each work package in order to accomplish the project objective.*

4. *Graphically portray the activities in the form of a **network diagram**.* This diagram shows the necessary sequence and interdependencies of activities to achieve the project objective. (Network diagrams will be discussed further in Chapter 9.)

5. *Make a **time estimate** for how long it will take to complete each activity.* It is also necessary to determine the types of resources and how many of each resource are needed for each activity to be completed within the estimated duration.

6. *Make a **cost estimate** for each activity.* The cost is based on the types and quantities of resources required for each activity.

7. *Calculate a project schedule and budget to determine whether the project can be accomplished within the required time, with the allotted funds, and with the available resources.* If not, adjustments must be made to the project scope, activity time estimates, or resource assignments until an achievable, realistic **baseline plan** (a roadmap for accomplishing the project scope on time and within budget) can be established.

Planning determines what needs to be done, who will do it, how long it will take, and how much it will cost. The result of this effort is a baseline plan. Taking the time to develop a well-thought-out plan is critical to the successful accomplishment of any project. Many projects have overrun their budgets, missed their completion dates, or only partially satisfied their technical specifications because there was no viable baseline plan before the project was started.

It is important that the people who will be involved in performing the project also participate in planning the work. They are usually the most knowledgeable about what detailed activities need to be done. Also, by participating in the planning of the work, these individuals become committed to accomplishing it according to the plan. Participation builds commitment.

PERFORMING THE PROJECT

Once the baseline plan has been developed, project work can proceed. The project team, led by the project manager, will implement the plan and perform the activities, or work elements, in accordance with the plan. The pace of project activity will increase as more and various resources become involved in performing the project tasks.

For a project to put on a town festival, the major work elements might include the following:

1. Preparing promotions—newspaper advertisements, posters, tickets, and so forth.
2. Selecting volunteers.
3. Organizing games, including constructing booths and acquiring prizes.
4. Contracting for amusement rides and obtaining the necessary permits.
5. Identifying performers to entertain and constructing the grandstand stage.
6. Arranging for food, including making the food and building concession stands.
7. Organizing all the support services, such as parking, clean-up, security, and restroom facilities.

For the more technical project of designing, building, and installing a specialized automated high-speed packaging machine in the customer's factory, major work elements might include the following:

1. Developing both preliminary and detailed designs, including preparation of specifications, drawings, flowcharts, and a list of materials.
2. Preparing plans for testing of the component, subsystems, and system by the contractor, both prior to shipping the equipment to the customer's plant and also after it has been installed at the customer's plant, to ensure that the equipment meets the customer's requirements. The customer may want to review and approve the test plans before the start of testing.
3. Conducting design review meetings, both internally and with the customer. Based on these design review meetings, the customer may initiate or approve changes to the original proposal. These changes could have an impact on the scope, schedule, and price. The customer may need to amend the contract, and the contractor may have to do some replanning of the project to incorporate any changes.
4. Ordering materials and parts.
5. Fabricating components and parts.
6. Writing and testing software.
7. Assembling and testing hardware, including testing components, assembling components into subassemblies, testing subassemblies, assembling subassemblies into the system, and testing the entire hardware system.
8. Integrating hardware and software and testing the system. Customer representatives may want to witness and document the test results to ensure that they meet the contract specifications.
9. Preparing installation requirements, such as floor plans and utility requirements (electrical, plumbing, and so forth), and identifying what items the customer will be responsible for during installation.
10. Preparing training materials (manuals, videotapes, computer simulations) to train the customer to operate and maintain the new equipment.

11. Shipping the equipment to the customer's factory and installing it.
12. Conducting training for the customer.
13. Conducting final acceptance tests to show that the equipment meets all of the customer's specified requirements.

CONTROLLING THE PROJECT

While the project work is being performed, it is necessary to monitor progress to ensure that everything is going according to plan. This involves measuring actual progress and comparing it to planned progress. To measure actual progress, it is important to keep track of which activities have actually been started and/or completed, when they were started and/or completed, and how much money has been spent or committed. If, at any time during the project, comparison of actual progress to planned progress reveals that the project is behind schedule, overrunning the budget, or not meeting the technical specifications, corrective action must be taken to get the project back on track. (Corrective action is discussed further in Part 3.)

Before a decision is made to implement corrective action, it may be necessary to evaluate several alternative actions to make sure the corrective action will bring the project back within the scope, time, and budget constraints of the objective. Be aware, for instance, that adding resources to make up time and get back on schedule may result in overrunning the planned budget. If a project gets too far out of control, it may be difficult to achieve the project objective without sacrificing the scope, budget, schedule, or quality.

The key to effective **project control** is measuring actual progress and comparing it to planned progress on a timely and regular basis and taking corrective action immediately, if necessary. Hoping that a problem will go away without corrective intervention is naive. The earlier a problem is identified and corrected, the better. Based on actual progress, it is possible to forecast a schedule and budget for completion of the project. If these parameters are beyond the limits of the project objective, corrective actions need to be implemented at once.

The **project control process** involves regularly gathering data on project performance, comparing actual performance to planned performance, and taking corrective actions if actual performance is behind planned performance. This process must occur regularly throughout the project.

Figure 4.2 illustrates the steps in the project control process. It starts with establishing a baseline plan that shows how the project scope (tasks) will be accomplished on time (schedule) and within budget (resources, costs). Once this baseline plan is agreed upon by the customer and the contractor or project team, the project can start.

A regular **reporting period** should be established for comparing actual progress with planned progress. Reporting may be daily, weekly, bi-weekly, or monthly, depending on the complexity or overall duration of the project. If a project is expected to have an overall duration of a month, the reporting period might be as short

FIGURE 4.2 Project Control Process

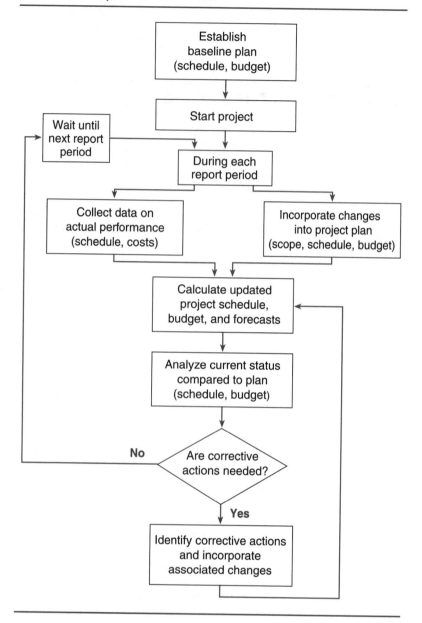

as a day. On the other hand, if a project is expected to run five years, the reporting period might be a month.

During each reporting period two kinds of data or information need to be collected:

1. *Data on actual performance.* This includes
   - the actual time that activities were started and/or finished
   - the actual costs expended and committed
2. *Information on any changes to the project scope, schedule, and budget.* These changes could be initiated by the customer or the project

REINFORCE YOUR LEARNING

3. *What are the two kinds of data or information that need to be collected during each reporting period?*

team, or they could be the result of an unanticipated occurrence such as a natural disaster, a labor strike, or the resignation of a key project team member.

It should be noted that once changes are incorporated into the plan and agreed on by the customer, a new baseline plan has to be established. The scope, schedule, and budget of the new baseline plan may be different from those of the original baseline plan.

It is crucial that the data and information discussed above be collected in a timely manner and used to calculate an updated project schedule and budget. For example, if project reporting is done monthly, data and information should be obtained as late as possible in that monthly period so that when an updated schedule and budget are calculated, they are based on the latest possible information. In other words, a project manager should not gather data at the beginning of the month and then wait until the end of the month to use it to calculate an updated schedule and budget, because the data will be outdated and may cause incorrect decisions to be made about the project status and corrective actions.

Once an updated schedule and budget have been calculated, they need to be compared to the baseline schedule and budget and analyzed for variances to determine whether the project is ahead of or behind schedule and under or over budget. If the project status is okay, no corrective actions are needed; the status will be analyzed again for the next reporting period.

If it is determined that corrective actions are necessary, however, decisions must be made regarding how to revise the schedule or the budget. These decisions often involve a trade-off of time, cost, and scope. For example, reducing the duration of an activity may require either increasing costs to pay for more resources or reducing the scope of the task (and possibly not meeting the customer's technical requirements). Similarly, reducing project costs may require using materials of a lower quality than originally planned. Once a decision is made on which corrective actions to take, they must be incorporated into the schedule and budget. It is necessary to calculate a revised schedule and budget to determine whether the planned corrective measures result in an acceptable schedule and budget. If not, further revisions will be needed.

The project control process continues throughout the project phase of the life cycle. In general, the shorter the reporting period, the better the chances of identifying problems early and taking effective corrective actions. As mentioned earlier, if a project gets too far out of control, it may be difficult to achieve the project objective without sacrificing the scope, budget, schedule, or quality. There may be situations in which it is wise to increase the frequency of reporting until the project is back on track. For example, if a five-year project with monthly reporting is endangered by a slipping schedule or an increasing budget overrun, it may be prudent to reduce the reporting period to one week in order to monitor the project and the impact of corrective actions more closely.

The project control process is an important and necessary part of performing the project. Just establishing a sound baseline plan is not sufficient, since even the best laid plans don't always work out. *Project management is a proactive approach to controlling a project,* to ensure that the project objective is achieved even when things don't go according to plan.

This third phase of the life cycle ends when the customer is satisfied that the requirements have been met and the project objective has been accomplished.

TERMINATING THE PROJECT

The fourth and final phase of the project life cycle is terminating the project. It starts after the project work has been completed, as shown in Figure 4.3, and includes various actions to properly close out the project.

The purpose of properly terminating a project is to learn from the experience gained on the project in order to improve performance on future projects. Therefore, the activities associated with terminating the project should be identified and included in the project's baseline plan—they should not be done merely as spontaneous afterthoughts. These activities might include organizing and filing project documents, receiving and making final payments, and conducting post-project evaluation meetings within both the contractor's and the customer's organization.

The termination phase starts when performance of the project is completed and the result is accepted by the customer. In some situations, this might be a somewhat formal event in which an automated system satisfies a set of criteria or passes tests that were stated in the contract. Other projects, such as a weekend of homecoming activities at a university, are completed merely with the passage of time.

FIGURE 4.3   Project Life Cycle

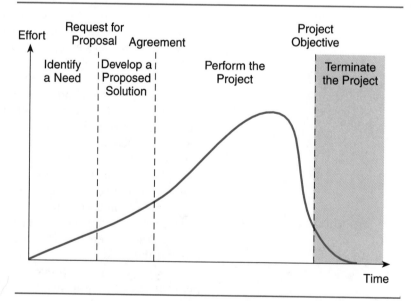

When a contractor completes a project for a customer, the contractor must verify that all the agreed-on deliverables were, in fact, provided. Such deliverables might include training or procedures manuals, drawings, flowcharts, equipment, software, brochures, reports, and data. During project termination, the contractor or organization that performed the project should ensure that copies of appropriate project-related documentation are properly organized and filed so that they can be readily retrieved for use in the future, if necessary. In the future, the contractor may want to use some actual cost and schedule information from this completed project to help develop the schedule and cost estimates for a proposed project. Or, if the project involved, say, staging an arts festival, the project team should organize all its documentation—including suggestions for improving aspects of the festival—for use by the project team that will do the festival the following year.

REINFORCE YOUR LEARNING
5. *What is the purpose of properly terminating a project?*

Another activity that must be performed during the termination phase is assuring that all payments have been collected from the customer. Many contracts include a progress payment clause, which states that the customer will make the final payment at the completion of the project. In some cases, the final payment is a high percentage of the total project price—for example, 25 percent. Similarly, it should be verified that all payments have been made to any subcontractors or consultants and for any purchased materials or items. Once all payments have been received and made, the project "books," or accounting records, can be closed, and a financial analysis of the project can be made, in which actual costs are compared to the project budget.

During the project termination phase, the project manager should prepare a written performance evaluation of each member of the project team and mention how each has expanded her or his knowledge as a result of the project assignment, as well as what areas she or he needs to develop further. If a project team member does not report directly to the project manager within the company's organizational structure, the project manager should provide a copy of the performance evaluation to the person's immediate supervisor.

Finally, no successful project should end without some type of celebration. This could range from an informal pizza party after work to a more formal event, with speakers from the customer's organization and awards or certificates of recognition for project participants.

Another important activity during the termination phase is holding post-project evaluation meetings. These meetings should be conducted internally, within the organization that performed the project, as well as with the customer. The purpose of such meetings is to evaluate performance of the project, to determine whether the anticipated benefits from the project were actually achieved, and to identify what could be done to improve performance on future projects.

Internal Post-Project Evaluation

Internally, there should be two types of meetings: individual meetings with team members and a group meeting with the project team. They should be held as soon as possible after the completion of the

FIGURE 4.4   Post-Project Evaluation Team Meeting Agenda

> ## POST-PROJECT EVALUATION
> ### Team Meeting
>
> ### AGENDA
>
> 1. Technical performance
>   Work scope
>   Quality
>   Managing changes
> 2. Cost performance
> 3. Schedule performance
> 4. Project planning and control
> 5. Customer relationships
> 6. Team relationships
> 7. Communications
> 8. Problem identification and resolution
> 9. Recommendations for future projects

project, and they should be announced in advance so that people can be prepared.

The project manager should have an individual meeting with each of the team members. These meetings allow team members to give their personal impressions of performance of the project and what could be done better on future projects. Such individual meetings allow people to speak openly, without the constraints of a group meeting. For example, they can mention any problems in working relationships with other team members. Of course, the project manager must assure team members that any such disclosures will be kept confidential. Once the individual meetings with team members are complete, the project manager can identify common issues brought up in those meetings. With this information, the project manager can then develop an agenda for a group meeting with the entire project team.

At the group meeting with the project team, the project manager should discuss what happened during performance of the project and identify specific recommendations for improvement. A sample agenda for such a post–project evaluation team meeting is shown in Figure 4.4.

Following are some topics that might be discussed under each of the agenda items:

1. *Technical performance.* How did the final scope of the work compare to the scope of the work at the start of the project? Were there many changes to the work scope? Were the changes handled properly in

terms of approvals and documentation? What impact did the changes have on project costs and schedule? Was the work scope totally completed? Were the project work and deliverables completed in a quality manner, and did they meet the expectations of the customer?

2. *Cost performance.* How did the final project costs compare with the original project budget and with the last project budget, which included any relevant changes in project scope? If there was a fixed-price contract, was it profitable, or did the project organization lose money? If there was a cost-reimbursement contract, was the project completed within the customer's budget? Were there any particular work packages that overran or underran their budgets by more than 10 percent? If so, why? What were the causes of any cost overruns? Were the cost estimates realistic?

3. *Schedule performance.* How did the actual project schedule compare with the original schedule? If the project was late, what were the causes? How was performance on the schedule associated with each work package? Were the activity duration estimates realistic?

4. *Project planning and control.* Was the project planned in sufficient detail? Were the plans updated in a timely manner to incorporate changes? Was actual performance compared with planned performance on a regular basis? Were data on actual performance accurate and collected in a timely manner? Was the planning and control system used on a regular basis by the project team? Was it used for decision making?

5. *Customer relationships.* Was every effort made to make the customer a participant in the success of the project? Was the customer asked on a regular basis about the level of satisfaction with the progress of the project? Were there regularly scheduled face-to-face meetings with the customer? Was the customer informed of potential problems in a timely manner and asked to participate in the problem-solving process?

6. *Team relationships.* Was there a feeling of "team" and a commitment to the success of the project? Were there any conditions that impeded teamwork?

7. *Communications.* Was the team kept informed of the project status and potential problems in a timely manner? Was the project environment conducive to open, honest, and timely communications? Were project meetings productive? Were written communications within the team and with the customer sufficient, insufficient, or overburdening?

8. *Problem identification and resolution.* Were mechanisms in place for team members to identify potential problems early? Was problem solving done in a thorough, rational manner?

9. *Recommendations.* Based on the team's discussion and evaluation of the above items, what specific recommendations can be made to help improve performance on future projects?

REINFORCE YOUR LEARNING

6. *What are the two types of internal post-project evaluation meetings the project manager should have?*

After the evaluation meeting, the project manager should issue a brief written report to management with a summary of project performance and the recommendations.

Customer Feedback

Just as important as the internal meeting is a post-project evaluation meeting with the customer. The purposes of this meeting should be to determine whether the project provided the customer with the anticipated benefits, to assess the level of customer satisfaction, and to obtain any feedback that would be helpful in future business relationships with this or other customers. Meeting participants should include the project manager, other key project team members, and key representatives of the customer's organization who were involved with the project. The project manager should take care to schedule the meeting for a time when the customer is in a position to really say whether the project met expectations and achieved the anticipated benefits. In the case of a project to develop an eight-page color brochure for a customer, a meeting can be held shortly after the final printed brochure is given to the customer, because the customer will know immediately whether the brochure met expectations. However, in the case of a project that supplied a customer with a specialized automated assembly machine expected to reduce the product defect rate from 10 percent to 2 percent, it may be several months after the machine is installed before the customer can verify whether the defect rate was reduced. This time may be needed for the operators to learn how to properly operate the equipment or for the company to verify a reduction in returned merchandise.

Ideally, the contractor should sit down with the customer and ask open-ended questions. This provides an opportunity for customers not only to express their level of satisfaction but also to provide detailed comments about the parts of the project with which they were satisfied or dissatisfied. These comments will not come as a surprise if the project manager has been continually monitoring the level of customer satisfaction throughout the project. If the customer is satisfied with the project, the contractor or organization that performed the project is presented with several opportunities. First, the contractor should ask the customer about any other projects the contractor could do—perhaps without going through a competitive RFP process. If the customer is satisfied with the brochure, for instance, the contractor should ask if any other brochures, annual reports, or marketing materials are needed. Likewise, if the customer is satisfied with the automated assembly machine, the contractor should ask whether other parts of the manufacturing process need to be studied for additional productivity improvements. Second, the contractor should ask permission to use the customer as a reference with potential customers. The contractor may even want to feature the customer in a brochure, maybe with a picture and a quote stating how satisfied the customer was with the contractor's performance. Another publicity angle is writing up a news story about the project in collaboration with the customer and issuing it as a press release to the appropriate newspapers and other media.

Another way to get feedback from the customer regarding satisfaction with the results of the project is through a post-project customer evaluation survey, as shown in Figure 4.5. The project manager gives this survey form to the customer and, possibly, other project stakeholders

REINFORCE YOUR LEARNING

7. *List three reasons to have a post-project evaluation meeting with the customer.*

FIGURE 4.5   Post-Project Customer Evaluation Survey

Post-Project Customer Evaluation Survey

Please complete this brief survey to help us evaluate and improve our project management performance. If more space is needed for responses, please attach additional pages.

Project Title: _____

	Degree of Satisfaction
	Low High
1. Completeness of Work Scope	1 2 3 4 5 6 7 8 9 10
Comments _____	
2. Quality of Work	1 2 3 4 5 6 7 8 9 10
Comments _____	
3. Schedule Performance	1 2 3 4 5 6 7 8 9 10
Comments _____	
4. Budget Performance	1 2 3 4 5 6 7 8 9 10
Comments _____	
5. Communications	1 2 3 4 5 6 7 8 9 10
Comments _____	
6. Customer Relations	1 2 3 4 5 6 7 8 9 10
Comments _____	
7. Overall Performance	1 2 3 4 5 6 7 8 9 10
Comments _____	

What **benefits** did you _____ actually realize or _____ anticipate as a result of this project?

A. Quantitative Benefits

B. Qualitative Benefits

Suggestions on how we can improve our performance on future projects:

Name: _____ Date: _____

to complete and return. For large projects, several individuals in the customer's organization may contribute to formulating the responses.

When there are multiple customers or end users of the results of a project, it may be difficult to get feedback from them. For example, after a volunteer group organizes a week-long town festival, how does it get feedback from the people who attended about their level of satisfaction and their suggestions for improving next year's event? Or consider a project in which a new software product was developed. The immediate customer is the company's product manager, but the true customers are the people who eventually purchase the software. The product manager may be satisfied with the resultant product, but how does the project team determine whether the end users are satisfied? In both of these cases—the town festival and the new software product—the project team may use some type of survey or focus group to obtain feedback from the end users.

Early Project Termination

There may be circumstances that require a project to be terminated before it is completed. For example, suppose a company is working on a research and development project with an advanced material that has certain properties at extremely low temperatures. After some development work and testing, it is determined that further development of the material could cost much more and take far longer than originally thought. If the company decides that the probability is low that further expenditures on the project will yield a successful outcome, the project will be stopped, even though the company has several million dollars invested in it. Another circumstance that can cause a project to be terminated early is a change in a company's financial situation—for example, if a company's sales are going down or if the company is acquired by another company.

Projects also can be terminated by the customer because of dissatisfaction. For example, if the buyers of a house are not satisfied with the quality of the contractor's work or are frustrated with schedule delays, they may terminate the agreement with the contractor and hire another contractor to finish the project. Similarly, if the government is funding the design and production of new military aircraft and project costs begin to significantly overrun the budget, the government may terminate the contract.

REINFORCE YOUR LEARNING

8. *For a contractor, what are two potential consequences of having a project terminated early by a dissatisfied customer?*

Having a project terminated early by a dissatisfied customer can really hurt a contractor's business. The contractor may incur a financial loss due to early termination and may have to lay off some of the employees who were working on the project. More importantly, the contractor's reputation may be tarnished. There will likely be no future business from the dissatisfied customer, and a tarnished reputation could make it difficult for the contractor to obtain business from other customers. One way to avoid early termination of a project due to customer dissatisfaction is to monitor the level of customer satisfaction continually throughout the project and take corrective action at the first hint of any dissatisfaction.

SUMMARY

Performing, or doing, the project—implementing the proposed solution—is the third phase of the project life cycle. This phase starts after a contract or agreement is drawn up between the customer and the contractor or project team, and it ends when the project objective is accomplished and the customer is satisfied that the work has been completed in a quality manner, within budget, and on time.

This third phase has two parts: doing the detailed planning for the project and then implementing that plan to accomplish the project objective. It is necessary to develop a plan that shows how the project tasks will be accomplished within budget and on schedule. Planning determines what needs to be done, who will do it, how long it will take, and how much it will cost. The result of the planning effort is a baseline plan for performing the project. It is important that the people who will be involved in performing the project also participate in planning the work. Participation builds commitment. Once a plan has been established, the project team, led by the project manager, implements the plan.

While the project work is being performed by the project team, it is necessary to monitor progress to ensure that everything is going according to plan. The project control process involves regularly gathering data on project performance, comparing actual performance to planned performance, and taking corrective actions if actual performance is behind planned performance. Project management is a proactive approach to controlling a project, to ensure that the project objective is achieved even when things don't go according to plan.

The fourth and final phase of the project life cycle is terminating the project. It starts after the project work has been completed. The purpose of this phase is to learn from the experience gained on the project in order to improve performance on future projects. Post-project evaluation activities include both individual meetings with team members and a group meeting with the project team. It is also important to meet with the customer to assess the level of customer satisfaction and determine whether the project provided the customer with the anticipated benefits. Some projects are terminated before their completion for various reasons. Projects may be terminated by the customer because of dissatisfaction. This can result in a financial loss and tarnish the reputation of the contractor or organization performing the project. One way to avoid early termination due to customer dissatisfaction is to monitor the level of customer satisfaction continually throughout the project and take corrective action at the first hint of any dissatisfaction.

QUESTIONS

1. Which phase of the life cycle involves performing the project? When can this phase be started?

2. Describe why planning is so important, and list the steps involved in detailed planning.
3. Think about a project on which you are currently working or have recently worked on. Describe the planning that you did before you started.
4. Describe what might be involved in actually performing a project. List the activities that must be performed for a project on which you are currently working.
5. Why is it important to control a project after it has started? How is this done?
6. What can be done if the actual progress on a project doesn't match the expected progress?
7. Describe the project control process. Discuss how it can be applied to a project on which you are currently working or one you have recently worked on.
8. Why should a project have a well-defined reporting period?
9. During each reporting period, what kinds of data need to be collected?
10. Discuss what needs to be done as part of terminating a project. Why are these activities important?
11. Discuss the internal post-project evaluation process and the two types of meetings involved.
12. What are some ways you can obtain feedback from a customer after a project has been completed? How would you use this information?
13. Why are some projects terminated before they are completed? When would it be wise to do so?

WORLD WIDE WEB EXERCISES

If you have difficulty accessing any of the Web addresses listed here, you can find these exercises (with up-to-date addresses) on the home page of Dr. James P. Clements, co-author of this book, at

www.towson.edu/~clements

1. Check out the Web site for ProjectNet at

www.projectnet.co.uk

2. Explore some of the links, including "What Is Project Management?" "Project Manager Today," "Case Studies," and "Associations." Report what you find.
3. *Project Manager Today* is a printed magazine that provides a monthly update on news about project management. Check out the electronic version, which gives a selection of news and features from each issue. It can be reached either from ProjectNet's home page or directly at

www.projectnet.co.uk/pm/pmt/pmt.htm

Print out at least one recent issue of this electronic magazine.

4. ProjectNet provides excellent project management case studies on line. These case studies can be reached either from ProjectNet's home page or directly at

www.projectnet.co.uk/pm/pmcase.htm

Print out and read at least one of these case studies. Summarize in one page what it's all about and answer all of the questions at the end of the case study.

5. Check out the project management association news, which can be reached either from ProjectNet's home page or directly at

www.projectnet.co.uk/pm/pmassoc.htm

Find at least three project management associations outside of the United States.

CASE STUDY

Delta, Inc. manufactures electronic testing equipment. Its products are known for their quality, and they command a premium price in the marketplace because of their reputation.

Hannah Elkton is vice president of marketing, Jim Anderson is sales manager, and Cathy Perez is product development manager. Jim and Cathy both work for Hannah. Cathy came to the company two years ago from a competing firm when she was bypassed for a promotion. At Delta, she initiated a project to develop a lower-cost testing device that would compete with products in the lower end of the market, such as those manufactured by her previous employer. After nearly twelve months of development work, the product met Cathy's expectations. Manufacturing of the new product started soon afterward, and it hit the marketplace about three months ago.

Jim, a Delta employee for twenty-five years, felt slighted when Cathy initiated the development project without seeking his input. He believes that he has a knowledge of the marketplace and knows what will or will not sell.

One day Jim schedules a meeting with Hannah and Cathy. He opens the meeting by announcing, "I wanted to get together to tell you that we are having a big problem. My sales representatives say that we have some very dissatisfied customers who purchased Cathy's new cheap testing device."

"What specifically is the problem?" asks Cathy.

"I don't exactly know for sure, but my sales reps tell me they aren't interested in peddling them if they aren't working right," responds Jim.

"How can you come to a meeting like this and make accusations without having the facts? What kind of problems and how many?" demands Cathy. "Maybe your sales reps don't want to sell this product because you're giving them a lower commission on it."

Jim quickly answers, "Maybe if you had tried to find out what our customers need and want, rather than what you thought they wanted, the product would be more successful. As far as I'm concerned, you've wasted a lot of money developing this piece of junk. Money that has cut company profits and reduced bonuses this year for me and my sales reps."

Hannah breaks in, "We must get some factual data on what precisely the problems are and how to correct the situation. We can't let a problem like this tarnish our reputation and hurt the sales of our other products."

Cathy and Jim respond simultaneously, "Let me do it."

Case Questions
1. Why is there a problem at Delta, Inc.?
2. What should Hannah do? How should she proceed?
3. How could the problem have been avoided?
4. What lessons can be learned for future projects?

Group Activity
Form teams of three students each. With each team member assuming the role of one of the people in the case study, have each group debate the causes of and solutions to this problem.

Then have each group address the four individual questions listed above, either by writing a brief report or by giving a brief presentation of their answers to the class.

People: The Key to Project Success

The chapters in this section focus on the importance of the people involved in a project. It is the people, not the procedures and techniques, that are critical to accomplishing the project objective. Procedures and techniques are merely tools to help people do their jobs.

The project manager provides leadership to the project team to accomplish the project objective—leadership in planning, organizing, and controlling the work effort. The ultimate responsibility of the project manager is to make sure that the customer is satisfied that the work scope is completed in a quality manner, within budget, and on time. The project manager must possess the skills to inspire the project team and win the confidence of the customer.

The project team is a group of individuals working interdependently to achieve the project objective. Teamwork is cooperative effort by members of the project team to achieve this common goal. The effectiveness of the project team can make the difference between project success and project failure. Although plans and project management techniques are necessary, it's the people—the project manager and the project team—that are the key to project success.

To ensure the success of projects, various structures are used to organize people to work on them. Regardless of how the project team is organized, though, communication between the project team and the customer, within the project team, and between the project team and its upper management is critical to success.

5

The Project Manager

The Rise of the Project Manager

With the elimination of large numbers of middle managers, there is a new breed of worker on the rise—the project manager. Just consider some of these quotes from a recent article in *Fortune* magazine:

"Project management is going to be huge in the next decade," says William Dauphiman, a partner at Price Waterhouse. "The project manager is the linchpin in the organizations we're creating."

"While automation and worker empowerment have replaced day-to-day management in many organizations, there still needs to be some oversight, and that is where the project manager comes in—everything has become projects, and that is the way we do business," says Fannie Mae's CIO.

"The project manager is ultimately responsible for what is done, and bringing a job in on time and on budget has always been the key," states David Milligan, the director of project operations for ASEA Brown Boveri's combustion engineering systems.

"Project management is the wave of the future," states an in-house newsletter from General Motors' technology and training group.

Source: T. Stewart, "The Corporate Jungle Spawns a New Species: The Project Manager," *Fortune,* July 10, 1995.

A Dozen Rules for the Project Manager

According to Jeffrey Pinto and Om Kharbanda, projects and project management are the wave of the future. However, organizations of today simply do not have enough project managers who possess the problem-solving, communication, team-building, and leadership skills needed to succeed. Most project managers, unfortunately, are never properly trained and fall into their responsibilities by happenstance.

To study this situation, Pinto and Kharbanda conducted numerous interviews with senior project managers in which they asked a simple question: "What information were you never given as a novice project manager that, in retrospect, could have made your job easier?" The answers form what they call the Vital Dozen Rules for Project Managers:

1. Understand the problems, opportunities, and expectations of a project manager.
2. Recognize that project teams will have conflicts, but this is a natural part of group development.
3. Understand who the stakeholders are and their agendas.
4. Realize that organizations are very political and use politics to your advantage.
5. Realize that project management is "leader intensive" but that you must be flexible.
6. Understand that project success is defined by four components: budget, schedule, performance criteria, and customer satisfaction.
7. Realize that you must build a cohesive team by being a motivator, coach, cheerleader, peacemaker, and conflict resolver.
8. Notice that your team will develop attitudes based on the emotions you exhibit—both positive and negative.
9. Always ask "what-if" questions and avoid becoming comfortable with the status of the project.
10. Don't get bogged down in minutiae and lose sight of the purpose of the project.
11. Manage your time efficiently.
12. Above all, plan, plan, plan.

Source: J. Pinto and O. Kharbanda, "Lessons for an Accidental Profession," *Business Horizons,* March–April 1995.

I t is the people—not the procedures and techniques (covered in later chapters)—that are critical to accomplishing the project objective. Procedures and techniques are merely tools to help people do their jobs. For example, an artist needs to have paint, canvas, and brushes in order to paint a portrait, but it is the skills and knowledge of the artist that allow a portrait to be created with these tools. So, too, in project management: The skills and knowledge of the people are vital for producing the result. This chapter focuses on one very important person—the project manager. You will become familiar with

- the responsibilities of the project manager
- the skills needed to successfully manage projects and techniques for developing those skills
- approaches to effective delegation
- ways the project manager can manage and control changes to the project

RESPONSIBILITIES OF THE PROJECT MANAGER

It is the responsibility of the project manager to make sure that the customer is satisfied that the work scope is completed in a quality manner, within budget, and on time. The project manager has primary responsibility for providing leadership in planning, organizing, and controlling the work effort to accomplish the project objective. In other words, *the project manager provides the leadership to the project team to accomplish the project objective.* If the project team were an athletic team, the project manager would be the coach; if it were an orchestra, the project manager would be the conductor. The project manager coordinates the activities of the various team members to ensure that they perform the right tasks at the proper time, as a cohesive group.

Planning

First, the project manager clearly defines the project objective and reaches agreement with the customer on this objective. The manager then communicates this objective to the project team in such a manner as to create a vision of what will constitute successful accomplishment of the objective. The project manager spearheads development of a plan to achieve the project objective. By involving the project team in developing this plan, the project manager ensures a more comprehensive plan than he or she could develop alone. Furthermore, such participation gains the commitment of the team to achieve the plan. The project manager reviews the plan with the customer to gain endorsement and then sets up a project management information system—either manual or computerized—for comparing actual progress to planned progress. It's important that this system be explained to the project team so that the team can use it properly to manage the project.

REINFORCE YOUR LEARNING

1. What two benefits does the project manager realize by involving the team in developing the plan?

Organizing

Organizing involves securing the appropriate resources to perform the work. First, the project manager must decide which tasks should be done inhouse and which tasks should be done by subcontractors or consultants. For tasks that will be carried out inhouse, the project manager gains a commitment from the specific people who will work on the project. For tasks that will be performed by subcontractors, the project manager clearly defines the work scope and deliverables and negotiates a contract with each subcontractor. The project manager also assigns responsibility and delegates authority to specific individuals or subcontractors for the various tasks, with the understanding that they will be accountable for the accomplishment of their tasks within the assigned budget and schedule. For large projects involving a large number of individuals, the project manager may designate leaders for specific groups of tasks. Finally, and most important, the task of organizing involves creating an environment in which the individuals are highly motivated to work together as a project team.

REINFORCE YOUR LEARNING

2. The project manager secures the _____ to perform the work and then assigns _____ and delegates _____ to specific individuals for the various tasks.

Controlling

To control the project, the project manager implements a project management information system designed to track actual progress and compare it with planned progress. Such a system helps the manager distinguish between busy-ness and accomplishments. Project team members monitor the progress of their assigned tasks and regularly provide data on progress, schedule, and costs. These data are supplemented by regular project review meetings. If actual progress falls behind planned progress or unexpected events occur, the project manager takes immediate action. He or she obtains input and advice from team members regarding appropriate corrective action and how to replan those parts of the project. It's important that problems, or even potential problems, be identified early and action taken. The project manager cannot take a "let's wait and see how things work out" approach—things never work out on their own. He or she must intervene and be proactive, resolving problems before they become worse.

The project manager plays the leadership role in planning, organizing, and controlling the project but does not try to do it alone. She or he involves the project team in these functions to gain their commitment to successful completion of the project.

REINFORCE YOUR LEARNING

3. The project manager implements a project management information system to serve what two functions?

SKILLS OF THE PROJECT MANAGER

The project manager is a key ingredient in the success of a project. In addition to providing leadership in planning, organizing, and controlling the project, the manager should possess a set of skills that will both inspire the project team to succeed and win the confidence of the customer. Effective project managers have strong leadership ability, the ability to develop people, excellent communication skills, good interpersonal skills, the ability to handle stress, problem-solving skills, and time management skills.

REINFORCE YOUR LEARNING

4. The project manager has primary responsibility for providing leadership for what three management functions?

Leadership Ability

It is said that leadership is getting things done through others; the project manager achieves results through the project team. Project leadership involves inspiring the people assigned to the project to work as a team to successfully implement the plan and achieve the project objective. The project manager needs to create for the team a vision of the result and benefits of the project—for example, the project manager may describe a new layout for a plant that will be the result of a project and articulate the benefits of this project, such as the elimination of bottlenecks, increased throughput, and reduced inventory. When project team members can envision the result, they will be more motivated to work as a team to successfully complete the project.

REINFORCE YOUR LEARNING

5. *Project leadership involves _____ the people assigned to the project to work as a team to successfully implement the _____ and achieve the _____ _____.*

Effective project management requires a participative and consultative leadership style, in which the project manager provides guidance and coaching to the project team. This style is preferred over a hierarchical, autocratic, and directive management approach. Leadership requires that the project manager provide direction, not directions. The project manager establishes the parameters and guidelines for what needs to be done, and the project team members determine how to get it done. The effective manager does not tell people how to do their jobs.

Project leadership requires involvement and empowerment of the project team. Individuals want to have ownership and control of their own work. They want to show that they can accomplish goals and meet challenges. The project manager should involve individuals in decisions affecting them and should empower them to make decisions within their assigned areas of responsibility. Creating a project culture that empowers the project team means not only assigning responsibility for tasks to team members but also delegating the authority to make decisions regarding the accomplishment of those tasks. Team members will embrace the responsibility for planning their work, deciding how to accomplish their tasks, controlling the progress of their work, and solving problems that may impede progress. They will accept accountability for performing their work scope within budget and on schedule.

In empowering individuals to make decisions affecting their work, the project manager should establish clear guidelines and, if appropriate, any limits. For example, team members may be authorized to implement their own remedy for solving a problem as long as the decision doesn't result in overrunning the budget or schedule; otherwise, consultation with a team leader or the project manager may be required. Likewise, when a decision by an individual or group of individuals within the team could have a negative impact on the work, budget, or schedule of other team members, consultation with the project manager would be required. For example, suppose one team member wants to hold up ordering certain materials until she confirms particular test results, but doing so will cause the work of other team members to fall behind schedule. In this instance, the project manager might want to involve all appropriate team members in a problem-solving meeting.

REINFORCE YOUR LEARNING

6. *Project leadership requires _____ and _____ of the project team.*

The capable project manager understands what motivates team members and creates a supportive environment in which individuals work as part of a high-performing team and are energized to excel.

REINFORCE YOUR LEARNING

7. *The capable project manager understands what _____ team members and creates a _____ environment in which individuals work as part of a high-performing team.*

A project manager can create such an environment by encouraging participation and involvement by all members of the project team. Techniques include facilitating project meetings so as to draw all individuals into the discussions, soliciting an individual's ideas when meeting separately with that person, and having various team members participate in presentations to the customer or the company's upper management. The project manager shows that he or she values the contributions of each team member when he or she seeks their advice and suggestions. And by example, the project manager encourages team members to seek advice from one another. In addition to allowing each member to tap the knowledge and expertise of other team members, this approach creates a sense of support and mutual respect within the team for the unique expertise each person brings to the team.

The project manager must be careful not to create situations that cause individuals to become discouraged. When expectations are unclear, discouragement is likely to result. Consider the following example: On Monday, the project manager tells Gayle to get a specific task done as soon as possible. Then, on Friday, he asks her whether the task is done yet. When Gayle says she won't have it done until next Friday, he looks annoyed and says, "I really needed it done by today!" If he had a specific deadline, he should have communicated it to Gayle at the start.

Another way of discouraging a project team is to subject members to unnecessary procedures, such as the weekly preparation of written status reports that basically duplicate what is verbalized at the weekly project meetings. Unproductive team meetings can also decrease motivation.

The underutilization of individuals creates another problematic situation. Assigning people to work that is well below their level of competence and not challenging will decrease their motivation. Even more detrimental is "over-managing" people by telling them how to do their work. Such an approach will cause individuals to think that the project manager doesn't trust them; it will create a feeling of "If you're going to tell me how to do my job, why don't you just do it yourself!" So, effective project managers not only do things that establish a supportive environment but also are careful not to do things that can have the opposite effect.

The project manager can foster motivation through recognition of the project team as a whole and of individual members. This is done throughout the project, not just at the end of the project. People want to feel that they are making a contribution to the project and need to be recognized. Recognition can take many forms—it need not be monetary. It can come in the form of verbal encouragement, praise, a sign of appreciation, or rewards. Such positive reinforcement helps stimulate desired behavior; behavior that is recognized or rewarded gets repeated. A project team might be recognized for completing a major task under budget and ahead of schedule or for identifying an innovative way to accelerate the project schedule. Such recognition will encourage the team to try to repeat such feats in the future.

One way the project manager provides recognition is by exhibiting a genuine interest in the work of each person on the project team. This can be accomplished by focusing full and undivided attention on individuals when they are explaining their work and then asking them questions about the work. A brief concluding comment such as "thank you," "good job," or "sounds great" will show the person that her or his contributions are recognized and appreciated. Other forms of recognition include a congratulatory or "thanks for the nice job" memo; some publicity, such as an article or photograph in the company newsletter; a presentation of a certificate or plaque; or assigning the person a more responsible position on the project team.

Recognition should be carried out as soon as possible after the action that is being recognized. If too much time elapses between the good deed and the recognition, there will be little impact on future performance, and the individual may feel that the project manager is not interested in the contribution that was made. When possible, recognition activities should involve other people in addition to the person being recognized. Individuals appreciate being acknowledged in front of their peers. The project manager might, for example, make a positive comment about the team or specific individuals during a project meeting or in front of the customer or the company's upper management. The project manager should try to make the recognition event fun—perhaps by presenting the person with some type of novelty award or taking the person to lunch. The effective project manager never monopolizes the spotlight or tries to take credit for the work of others.

The project manager sets the tone for the project team by establishing an environment of trust, high expectations, and enjoyment. To foster an atmosphere of trust, the project manager lives up to his or her word and follows through on his or her commitments. By doing so, the project manager sets an example, demonstrating that follow-through is expected of everyone on the project team. If the project manager fails to follow up on any suggestions, questions, or concerns that are brought up, he or she will lose credibility. In cases where things can't or don't work out as intended or expected, the project manager needs to provide an explanation so that his or her credibility is not lost.

Capable project managers have high expectations of themselves and of each person on the project team. They believe that people tend to live up to what is expected of them. If the project manager shows confidence in the team members and has high expectations for their performance, team members will usually rise to the occasion and deliver. Project managers tend to be optimistic that, at times, even apparently insurmountable obstacles to accomplishing the project can be overcome. If the project manager doesn't balance her or his high expectations and optimism with reality, however, the project team can become frustrated. Examples of unrealistic expectations include committing to an overly ambitious schedule for completing a complicated task and expecting a newly developed sophisticated software product to work right the first time without any glitches. A project manager who is perceived as foolhardy or reckless will not win the confidence of the project team or the customer.

REINFORCE YOUR LEARNING

8. *People want to feel that they are making a _____ to the project and need to be _____.*

REINFORCE YOUR LEARNING

9. *A project manager sets the tone for the project team by establishing an environment of _____, high _____, and _____.*

Projects should be fun. Project managers should enjoy their work and encourage the same positive attitude on the part of the project team members. Most people working on projects look for affiliation and socialization; they don't want to work in isolation. The project team needs to go through socialization before it can function effectively as a high-performing team. The project manager can facilitate this socialization process by creating a sense of camaraderie among team members. One technique is to initiate periodic social gatherings—lunches, picnics, or pizza parties—for the project team. Another technique is to try to situate all the project team members in one office location, if feasible. Having an open office environment, rather than having everyone behind a closed door, will further foster socialization by making it easier for people to interact. Finally, the project manager should look for opportunities to celebrate successes, especially early in the project. As early milestones are achieved, the project manager might bring donuts to a team meeting or order boxed lunches for everyone at the conclusion of a staff meeting. Such activities create a forum for socialization, informal chatter, and team building, and they make the job enjoyable. Who said work shouldn't be fun!

REINFORCE YOUR LEARNING

10. *People working on projects look for _____ and _____; they don't want to work in _____.*

Leadership requires that the project manager be highly motivated and set a positive example for the project team—in other words, practice what she or he preaches. If a project manager expects people to stay late to finish up work to keep the project on schedule, she has to be there too; she can't leave early. Everything the project manager does and says sets an example for the team in terms of expected behavior. A project manager must maintain a positive attitude—no negative comments, no whining, no bad-mouthing or blaming, and no derogatory remarks—and make it clear that such behavior is not acceptable while working on the team. Effective project managers have a "can do" attitude—a desire to achieve and overcome obstacles. They thrive on challenges and getting things done. They focus on ways to get the job done rather than on reasons why it can't be done. A good project manager is not deterred by barriers or excuses. She or he has self-confidence and exhibits confidence in the project team members.

It is said . . .

REINFORCE YOUR LEARNING

11. *Leadership requires that the project manager be highly _____ and set a _____ _____ for the project team.*

> There are those who make things happen
> those who let things happen, and
> those who wonder what happened.

The project manager leads by making things happen!

Ability to Develop People

The effective project manager has a commitment to the training and development of people working on the project. He or she uses the project as an opportunity to add value to each person's experience base so that all members of the project team are more knowledgeable and competent at the end of the project than when they started it. The project manager should establish an environment where people can learn from the tasks they perform and the situations they experience or observe, and he or she must communicate to the team the importance of continuous self-development activities. One way of encouraging such activities is to talk about the importance of self-development at project team meetings. Another way is to meet with project team members individually at the start of their project assignments and encourage them to take advantage of their assignments to expand their knowledge and skills. A good project manager believes that all individuals are valuable to the organization and that they can make greater contributions through continuous learning. He or she stresses the value of self-improvement by encouraging individuals to take the initiative—for example, to ask for new or challenging assignments or to participate in seminars. A project presents many opportunities for people to expand their technical knowledge as well as further develop skills in communication, problem solving, leadership, negotiating, and time management.

A capable project manager provides opportunities for learning and development by encouraging individuals to assume the initiative, take risks, and make decisions. Rather than create a fear of failure, the manager acknowledges that mistakes are part of the learning and growth experience. The project manager can try to provide "stretch" assignments that require individual team members to extend their knowledge and accomplish more than they may think they can. For instance, a design task that involves the use of optics technology for sensors may be assigned to an engineer who has only limited familiarity with optics technology. This will require the engineer to learn more about optics, making her more valuable to the organization on future projects.

Another thing the project manager can do is identify situations in which less experienced people can learn from more experienced people. For example, a person who has been compiling test data may be assigned to work with an analyst so that he can learn how to analyze and interpret the data. In such situations, the project manager should tell the experienced people that part of their job on the project is to mentor, coach, and teach the less experienced people.

A final way in which the project manager can develop people is by having them attend formal training sessions. For example, if an individual on the project team has no experience in making stand-up presentations or has poor presentation skills, the project manager might have him attend a seminar on how to make effective presentations. The individual might then be given opportunities to apply what he has learned by making presentations at team meetings. The project manager might even provide coaching to help him improve to the point where he can make an effective presentation to the customer.

During discussions with individual team members, the project manager should ask, "What have you learned from working on the project?" Each response will help the manager determine what further development activities or learning opportunities are needed. Asking such questions also sends the message that the project manager values and expects continuous self-improvement.

REINFORCE YOUR LEARNING

12. A good project manager believes that all individuals are _____ to the organization and that they can make greater contributions through _____ _____ .

REINFORCE YOUR LEARNING

13. Rather than create a fear of _____ , the project manager acknowledges that mistakes are part of the _____ and _____ experience.

REINFORCE YOUR LEARNING

14. A good project manager values and expects continuous _____ .

Communication Skills

REINFORCE YOUR LEARNING

15. *List five reasons it is important for the project manager to have frequent communication.*

Project managers must be good communicators. They need to communicate *regularly* with the project team, as well as with any subcontractors, the customer, and their own company's upper management. Effective and frequent communication is crucial for keeping the project moving, identifying potential problems, soliciting suggestions to improve project performance, keeping abreast of customer satisfaction, and avoiding surprises. A high level of communication is especially important early in the project to build a good working relationship with the project team and to establish clear expectations with the customer.

Effective project managers communicate and share information in a variety of ways. They have meetings with the project team, the customer, and the company's upper management, as well as informal conversations with these individuals. They also provide written reports to the customer and upper management. All these tasks require that the project manager have good oral and written communication skills. It is said that one learns more by listening than by talking. Therefore, good project managers spend more time listening than talking. They don't dominate a conversation. They listen to the expectations and needs expressed by the customer and the ideas and concerns expressed by the project team. To initiate dialogue on important issues, they start discussions and conversations; to stimulate dialogue, they ask questions and solicit comments and ideas. For example, when a project manager introduces a topic at a team meeting, she might ask for others' reactions or ideas, rather than just giving her views on the topic and then moving to the next agenda item. Every project manager should get out of her or his office on a regular basis and drop in on individual team members—for instance, to follow up on a comment or idea that the person expressed at a team meeting but that was not pursued at the meeting.

REINFORCE YOUR LEARNING

16. *A high level of communication is especially important early in the project to help build a good _____ _____ with the project team and to establish clear _____ with the customer.*

REINFORCE YOUR LEARNING

17. *What are three ways in which a project manager communicates?*

The project manager establishes ongoing communication with the customer to keep the customer informed and to determine whether there are any changes in expectations. The project manager needs to keep abreast of the degree of customer satisfaction throughout the project by regularly talking with the customer—for example, maybe scheduling a phone discussion with the customer every Friday afternoon.

Communication by project managers needs to be timely, honest, and unambiguous. Effective communication establishes credibility and builds trust. It also prevents rumors from starting. Suppose a team member is temporarily assigned to another project where her expertise is needed to help solve a critical problem. When the project team discovers that one of the members is no longer working on the project, rumors may start that she was let go for overrunning her budget or that she quit because she was unhappy. The project manager needs to call a team meeting to inform the members that she was temporarily reassigned and will return to the project in a couple of weeks.

REINFORCE YOUR LEARNING

18. *Good project managers spend more time _____ than _____.*

REINFORCE YOUR LEARNING

19. *Give three reasons the project manager should establish ongoing communication with the customer.*

It's important for the project manager to provide timely feedback to the team and customer. Both the good news and the bad news should be shared promptly. For the project team to be effective, members need to have up-to-date information—especially customer feedback that may necessitate changes to the project work scope, budget, or schedule.

The project manager should create an atmosphere that fosters timely and open communication without any fear of reprisal, and he or she must accept differing viewpoints. For example, an individual who is having difficulty completing a task should feel that he can bring the problem to the attention of the project manager without being admonished.

Project communication is discussed further in Chapter 8.

Interpersonal Skills

Good interpersonal skills are essential for a project manager. Such skills depend on good oral and written communication skills, as discussed in the previous section. The project manager needs to establish clear expectations of members of the project team so that everyone knows the importance of his or her role in achieving the project objective. The project manager can do so by involving the team in developing a project plan that shows which people are assigned to which tasks and how those tasks fit together. Much like the coach of an athletic team, the project manager should emphasize that everyone's contribution is valuable to successfully executing the plan.

It's important that the project manager develop a relationship with each person on the project team. This may sound like a time-consuming activity, but it isn't necessarily so. It requires making the time to have an informal conversation with each person on the project team and with each key individual in the customer's organization. These conversations, initiated by the project manager, can take place during work or outside the office. They can occur over lunch, while traveling with the person on a business trip, or while sitting next to the individual at a Little League game. Such situations provide an opportunity for the project manager to get to know the various people on the project team—what motivates them, how they think things are going, what concerns they have, and how they feel about things. For example, suppose Carlos mentions that he enjoys doing demonstrations but would like to further develop his formal presentation skills. With such knowledge, the project manager can ask Carlos to provide a demonstration at the next customer review meeting of the graphics software he has developed. Or, the project manager might ask Carlos to give a presentation at the next internal project review meeting, which Carlos may find a less stressful forum for practicing his presentation skills. Carlos's self-improvement goal might not have been uncovered in any situation other than an informal conversation initiated by the project manager.

The project manager should try to learn about the personal interests of each individual without being intrusive. One technique is for the project manager to mention his or her own hobbies or family and see whether the team member picks up on the topic. The project manager should look for areas of common interest with each indi-

REINFORCE YOUR LEARNING

20. *Why does communication by project managers need to be timely, honest, and unambiguous?*

REINFORCE YOUR LEARNING

21. *The project manager should have an informal _____ with each person on the project team and with each key individual in the _____ organization.*

vidual, such as tennis, cooking, college sports, children, or home-town.

In informal conversations, the project manager should use open-ended questions and do a lot of listening. It's amazing how much information you can get in response to a simple question like "How are things going?" Show genuine interest in what an individual says, however; if you seem disinterested, the person will not pursue the conversation. Thus, it is important to provide feedback and encouraging comments, such as "That's interesting" or "Tell me more about that."

Good interpersonal skills enable a project manager to empathize with individuals when special circumstances arise—whether a team member is discouraged because of technical problems in developing software or is distracted by the stress of a spouse's recuperation from an automobile accident. Of course, the project manager must be genuine in offering encouragement and support.

When he or she encounters a member of the project team, whether in the hallway or at the supermarket, the project manager should capitalize on the opportunity. Rather than make do with a mere "Hi" or "Good afternoon," she or he should stop and try to engage the team member in a conversation, even if brief. It can be on any topic, from "Are you ready for our meeting with the customer next week?" to "Did your daughter's soccer team win yesterday?" An effective project manager develops and maintains these interpersonal relationships throughout the duration of the project.

A project manager needs good interpersonal skills to try to influence the thinking and actions of others. Throughout the project, the project manager will have to persuade and negotiate with the customer, the project team, and the company's upper management. For example, the manager of a construction project might need to try to persuade the customer to forgo a change in the project scope that would require an increase in costs. Or the manager of a project to present a talent show for the benefit of a local charity might have to use her interpersonal skills to persuade a local celebrity to work on the project. These situations cannot be handled in a heavy-handed manner; good interpersonal skills are required to bring about the desired outcome.

A project manager also needs good interpersonal skills to deal with disagreement or divisiveness among team members. Such situations can require delicate handling on the project manager's part in order to mediate a resolution in which no one loses face and the project work is not affected. The subject of conflict resolution is discussed further in Chapter 6.

Ability to Handle Stress

Project managers need to be able to handle the stress that can arise from work situations. Stress is likely to be high when a project is in jeopardy of not meeting its objective because of a cost overrun, a schedule delay, or technical problems with the equipment or system; when changes in scope are requested by the customer; or when conflict arises within the project team regarding the most appropriate

REINFORCE YOUR LEARNING

22. The project manager should use _____ questions and do a lot of _____ .

solution to a problem. Project activity can get both tense and intense at times. The project manager cannot panic; she or he has to remain unruffled. The effective project manager is able to cope with constantly changing conditions. Even with the best laid plans, projects are subject to unforeseen events that can cause immediate turmoil. The project manager needs to remain composed and make sure that panic and frustration do not beset the project team, the customer, or the company's upper management.

In certain situations, the project manager needs to act as a buffer between the project team and either the customer or upper management. If the customer or upper management is not satisfied with the progress of the project, the project manager has to take the blame and make sure that the project team doesn't become discouraged. She or he needs to communicate any discontent to the project team in a manner that will inspire the team to meet the challenge. Similarly, there may be times when the project team has complaints about the customer's requirements or unwillingness to make changes. Here, too, the project manager needs to act as the buffer, absorbing the complaints and redirecting them into challenges for the project team to overcome.

The project manager needs to have a good sense of humor. Used appropriately, humor can help a project manager handle the stress and break the tension. Since the project manager sets an example for the project team and demonstrates what is acceptable and unacceptable behavior on the project, any humor must be in good taste. A manager should not tell inappropriate jokes or have improper items hanging on the office wall, and he or she must make it known to the project team right from the beginning that such behavior is unacceptable and will not be tolerated.

REINFORCE YOUR LEARNING

23. *The project manager needs to have a good sense of* _____ *and needs to stay* _____ *fit.*

The project manager can improve her or his ability to handle stress by keeping physically fit through regular exercise and good nutrition. The project manager also can organize stress relief activities for the project team, such as a softball game, golf outing, or hiking trip.

Problem-Solving Skills

A project manager needs to be a good problem solver. Although it's easier to identify problems than to solve them, good problem solving starts with the early identification of a problem or potential problem. Early identification of a problem will allow more time to develop a well thought-out solution. In addition, if a problem is identified early, it may be less costly to solve and may have less impact on other parts of the project. Good problem identification requires a timely and accurate data-driven information system; open and timely communication among the project team, the subcontractors, and the customer; and some "gut feelings" based on experience.

The project manager should encourage project team members to identify problems early and solve them on their own. The project team needs to be self-directed in solving problems and not require instigation from the project manager.

When a problem is potentially critical and likely to jeopardize accomplishment of the project objective, team members need to communicate this information to the project manager early so that he or she can lead the problem-solving effort. Once such a problem has been identified, the project manager may need to seek additional data and ask clarifying questions to really understand the problem and its magnitude. Team members should be asked whether they have any suggestions for how the problem might be solved. Working with the appropriate members of the project team, the project manager should then use analytical skills to evaluate the information and develop the optimal solution. It's important that the project manager possess the ability to see the "big picture" and how potential solutions might affect other parts of the project, including relationships with the customer or upper management. After the optimal solution has been developed, the project manager delegates implementation of the solution to the appropriate individuals on the project team.

Problem solving is discussed further in Chapter 6.

Time Management Skills

Good project managers manage their time well. Projects require a lot of energy because they involve many concurrent activities and unexpected events. To make optimal use of the time available, project managers have to have self-discipline, be able to prioritize, and show a willingness to delegate.

Time management is discussed thoroughly in Chapter 6.

DEVELOPING THE SKILLS NEEDED TO BE A PROJECT MANAGER

People are not born with the skills needed to be effective project managers; rather, they develop those skills. There are various ways to develop the skills necessary to be an effective project manager.

1. *Gain experience.* Work on as many projects as you can. Each project presents a learning opportunity. It's helpful if the projects aren't all the same. For example, if you're a civil engineer with a large architectural firm and you just worked on a project to design a high school, you might then look for an opportunity to be assigned to another type of project such as designing a museum or a church. Also, look for different assignments on each project. On one project you might develop software, while on another project you might ask to be a group leader or to have an opportunity to interact more with the customer. The purpose of varying projects and assignments is to expose yourself to as many project managers, customers, and other experienced project people as possible. Each experience presents an opportunity to learn from other people.

   You can ask someone to be your *mentor* while you work on a project. This should be someone who you think has the skills that you're trying to develop. You should also observe how the other project participants employ their skills. See what they do—right and wrong. For example, suppose you want to develop your presentation skills. When people make presentations on the project, observe what they do right—such as showing enthusiasm or engaging the audience—and what they do wrong—such as blocking the visual aids so that not everyone can see them or telling an inappropriate joke at the start of the presentation. Making a mental note of such things will help you when you have to make a presentation. It is less painful to learn from others' mistakes than from your own.

2. *Seek out feedback from others.* If you want to improve your problem-solving skills, for example, ask a mentor whether she has observed anything you could do better in problem-solving situations. If she tells you that you have a tendency to jump to conclusions prematurely, you can work on taking more time to find out all the facts or listen to others' viewpoints.

3. *Conduct a self-evaluation, and learn from your mistakes.* If you completed a project task but overran the budget or were behind schedule, for example, ask yourself what happened, what you could have done differently, and what you will do differently the next time. Maybe you need to work on time management—focusing on the most important activities first.

4. *Interview project managers who have skills that you want to develop in yourself.* If you want to develop leadership skills, for example, seek out project managers who you think are effective leaders. Ask them how they developed their skills and what suggestions they have. Offer to buy them lunch, if that's the only time you can meet them. It may be a worthwhile investment.

5. *Participate in training programs.* There are plenty of seminars, workshops, video and audio tapes, and self-study materials on all of the skills discussed in the previous section. There are even courses and seminars on the topic of project management. When participating in seminars, look for opportunities to learn from three sources: the instructor, the materials, and the other participants.

6. *Join organizations.* For example, membership in the Project Management Institute will provide opportunities for you to participate in meetings and conferences with other people involved in project management. Joining Toastmasters will give you a chance to develop effective presentation skills. See Appendix B for a list of project management organizations.

REINFORCE YOUR LEARNING

26. a. Identify one skill you want to develop.

b. Identify three things you can do to develop that skill.

c. Select one of the three things listed above and pick a date by which you will have done it.

7. *Read.* Subscribe to journals, or look up articles related to the skills you want to develop. There are plenty of articles on improving your skills. Ask other people if they know of any good books or articles on a specific topic; their endorsement may save you time searching for good materials.

8. *Volunteer.* The workplace is not the only place where you can develop skills. Opportunities may not be available at work to develop certain skills. Consider getting involved with a volunteer organization, in which you not only can contribute to the community or a specific cause but also can try your hand at developing leadership skills.

Learning and development are lifetime activities—there's no finish line. Your employer can support and encourage you and provide the resources (time and money). The organization has to budget funds for training and staff development activities. You, however, have the primary responsibility for developing your skills. You have to take the initiative and have the desire. *You* have to make it happen.

DELEGATION

REINFORCE YOUR LEARNING

27. *Delegation involves* _____ *the project team to achieve the* _____ _____ *and each team member to accomplish the* _____ _____ *for his or her area of responsibility.*

Delegation involves empowering the project team to achieve the project objective and empowering each team member to accomplish the expected results for his or her area of responsibility. It's the act of allowing individuals to successfully carry out assigned tasks. Delegation implies more than just assigning tasks to specific members of the project team. It includes giving team members the responsibility to accomplish job objectives and the authority to make decisions and take actions to achieve the expected results, as well as accountability for accomplishing those results.

Members of the project team are given specific results to achieve in terms of the work scope, tangible results or products to be delivered, the available budget, and the allowable time frame or schedule for their assigned areas of responsibility. They plan their own methods for accomplishing the desired results, and they exercise control over the resources they need to do the work.

Delegation is a must for an effective project manager. It is part of the project manager's responsibility for organizing the project. Delegation is *not* "passing the buck." The project manager is still ultimately responsible for achieving the project results. The project manager who understands and practices delegation ensures effective performance by the project team and creates the conditions necessary for cooperation and teamwork.

Effective delegation requires effective communication skills. The project team members need to realize that the job of implementing the project has been delegated to them. The project manager has the responsibility for providing a clear understanding of what is expected in terms of specific results. It's not sufficient for the project manager to say "Rashid, you work on the mechanical design" or "Rosemary, you handle the publicity." Rather, she or he needs to define what specifically constitutes each task and the desired result of the task. This includes its work scope, tangible results or products to be delivered, expected quality, budget, and schedule. These elements should be defined and agreed upon by the project manager and project team members before any work begins. However, the project manager *should not tell the individuals how to do the task.* That should be left up to the individuals so that they can be creative. If people are told how to do tasks, they will not be as committed to achieving the desired result and will feel that the project manager lacks confidence in their capabilities.

REINFORCE YOUR LEARNING

28. *Project managers should not tell individuals* _____ *to do the assigned tasks.*

If team members are to successfully accomplish their tasks, they need to be given the resources necessary and the authority to exercise control over those resources. Resources can include people, money, and facilities. Team members should be able to call on other team members' expertise when needed, purchase needed materials, and have access to needed facilities. Team members should be given the authority to make decisions regarding the use of resources as long as they stay within the constraints of the budget and schedule.

Delegation involves selecting the project team members who are best qualified to perform each task and then empowering them to do it. Since the project manager makes such selections or assignments based on each person's capabilities, potential, and workload, she or he needs to know the capabilities, capacity, and limitations of each member of the project team. The project manager can't delegate to a particular individual a set of tasks that requires more person-days than the individual has available. For example, one person, working alone, can't be expected to paint six rooms in a week when it is estimated that it takes two days to paint each room. Similarly, the project manager can't expect individuals to perform tasks for which they do not have the appropriate expertise. For example, an individual without the appropriate knowledge of chemistry or analysis techniques cannot be expected to perform a chemical analysis. Delegation does, however, provide an opportunity to give challenging, or "stretch," assignments to individuals in order to develop and extend their expertise and skills. Therefore, when the project manager is delegating, he or she considers not only the person's current capabilities, but also the person's potential. Stretch assignments energize people to take on the challenge and show that they can meet the project manager's expectations.

When a project manager empowers team members to make decisions associated with performing their work, he or she gives them freedom to take action to accomplish the work and freedom from interference. Yet, the project manager should realize that in performing the work and making decisions, people may make errors and failure may occur. If the project manager is critical of mistakes, he or she will train people to seek him or her out to review and approve every little thing they do. Such fear of failure will paralyze the project team. Effective delegation requires that the project manager have confidence in each member of the project team.

When the project team is carrying out its tasks, the project manager should let team members do their jobs; however, he or she should be available to coach and advise individuals when needed. An effective project manager is careful not to disempower individuals by giving them directives, by telling them how to do things, or by making decisions for them. Rather, he or she shows confidence in their capabilities and encourages them.

Delegation requires that individuals be accountable for achieving the expected results of their tasks. To support team members in controlling their work efforts, the project manager needs to establish a project management information and control system. This system should keep the project manager and the team informed and support decision making. The system may include a computerized information reporting system and the requirement that regular meetings be held with the project team or individual team members to check on progress. Such a system should focus on measuring and evaluating progress toward the expected result of each task, not merely on monitoring busy-ness. The project manager is interested in knowing whether the work scope for each task is progressing according to plan and whether it will be completed within the available budget and on the required schedule. He or she cannot accept a report that "the team worked until 10:00 p.m. all week" as an indication that the work is on track. The project manager makes it known that delegation requires team members to be accountable for achieving the expected results, not just to keep busy. Empowered individuals accept this accountability. When monitoring progress, the project manager should offer encouragement to team members. He or she should show genuine interest in their work and offer recognition and appreciation of their progress.

Following are some common barriers to effective delegation and what can be done to overcome them.

- The project manager has a personal interest in the task or thinks she can do it better or faster herself. In this case, she must force herself to let go and have confidence in other individuals. She needs to understand that other people may not do things exactly the way she would.
- The project manager lacks confidence in the capability of others to do the work. In this case, he should be sure that he knows the capabilities, potential, and limitations of each member of the project team so that he can select the most appropriate person for each task.
- The project manager is afraid that he will lose control of the work and not know what is going on. In this case, he should set up a system for regularly monitoring and evaluating progress toward the expected results.
- Team members fear criticism for mistakes or lack self-confidence. In this case, the project manager has to show confidence in each individual, offer regular encouragement, and understand that mistakes are opportunities for learning rather than occasions for criticism.

Figure 5.1 shows various degrees of delegation. The sixth degree supports full empowerment of the project team. In most cases, the project manager should delegate to this degree. However, there may be some situations that require delegating to a lesser degree. For example, a lesser degree of delegation might be advisable if there was a critical problem in meeting the project objective, such as a potentially significant cost overrun or continuing test failures of a prototype. Similarly, a lesser degree of delegation might be appropriate if the person performing the work was in a stretch assignment.

Figure 5.2 is a checklist for rating your effectiveness at delegation. It can be used by the project manager as a self-assessment instrument, or the project manager may choose to have the project team complete the checklist in order to get feedback on his or her effectiveness at delegation. In either case, the project manager should then focus on improving in areas that were rated low.

REINFORCE YOUR LEARNING

31. *Delegation requires that individuals be _____ for achieving the expected results.*

FIGURE 5.1   Degrees of Delegation

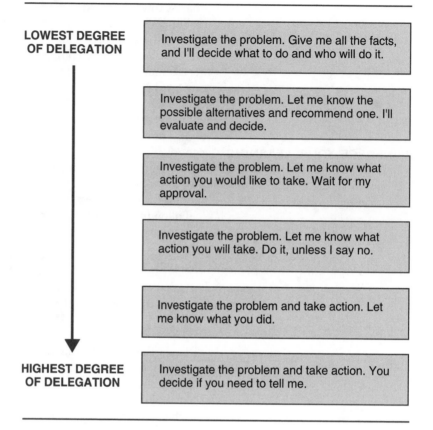

LOWEST DEGREE OF DELEGATION

Investigate the problem. Give me all the facts, and I'll decide what to do and who will do it.

Investigate the problem. Let me know the possible alternatives and recommend one. I'll evaluate and decide.

Investigate the problem. Let me know what action you would like to take. Wait for my approval.

Investigate the problem. Let me know what action you will take. Do it, unless I say no.

Investigate the problem and take action. Let me know what you did.

HIGHEST DEGREE OF DELEGATION

Investigate the problem and take action. You decide if you need to tell me.

MANAGING CHANGE

The one thing that you can be sure will happen during a project is change. Despite the best laid plans, changes will still occur. Changes may be

- initiated by the customer,
- initiated by the project team,
- caused by unanticipated occurrences during the performance of the project, or
- required by the users of the project results.

An important aspect of the project manager's job is to manage and control changes in order to minimize any negative impact on the successful accomplishment of the project objective. Some changes are trivial, but others may significantly affect the project work scope, budget, or schedule. Deciding to change the color of a room before it is painted is a trivial change. Deciding that you want a two-story house after the contractor has already put up the framing for a single-story house is a major change, which would certainly increase the cost and probably delay the completion date.

FIGURE 5.2   Delegation Checklist

How Effective Are You at Delegating?					
	Not at All		Somewhat		Very Much
1. Does your team have a clear understanding of the results expected?	1	2	3	4	5
2. Does your team have all the resources needed to accomplish what was delegated?	1	2	3	4	5
3. Do you focus on the results you expect from team members, rather than on the details of how they do their work?	1	2	3	4	5
4. Do you have a system to follow up and monitor progress?	1	2	3	4	5
5. Do team members understand how and when they are to let you know how they are progressing and when to seek your advice?	1	2	3	4	5
6. Does your team understand how progress will be measured and evaluated?	1	2	3	4	5
7. Can your team speak freely to you about problems, without fear of criticism?	1	2	3	4	5
8. Do team members feel they have the freedom to perform their work without your over-managing them?	1	2	3	4	5
9. Do team members feel they can perform their work without fear of making a mistake?	1	2	3	4	5
10. Do you encourage team members to make decisions within the level of authority you delegated to them?	1	2	3	4	5
11. Do you provide coaching as needed?	1	2	3	4	5
12. Do you encourage and are you supportive of your team's suggestions?	1	2	3	4	5

The impact a change has on accomplishing the project objective may be affected by when during the project the change is identified. Generally, **the later in the project that changes are identified, the greater their effect on accomplishing the project objective.** The aspects most likely to be affected are the project budget and the completion date. This is particularly true when work that has already been completed needs to be "undone" in order to accommodate the required change. For example, it would be very expensive to change the plumbing or wiring in a new office building after the walls and ceilings were completed because some of the walls and ceilings would need to be torn out first. Then new walls and ceilings would have to be installed. However, if such a change were made much earlier in the project—for instance, while the building was still

REINFORCE YOUR LEARNING

33. The project manager's job is to _____ and _____ changes in order to _____ any negative impact on the successful accomplishment of the project objective.

being designed—accommodation would be easier and less costly. The drawings could be changed so that the plumbing and wiring could be installed correctly the first time.

At the start of the project, procedures need to be established regarding how changes will be documented and authorized. These procedures must cover communication between the project manager and the customer and between the project manager and the project team. If changes are agreed upon orally rather than in writing and there is no indication of the impact the changes will have on the work scope, cost, or schedule, project costs can be greater than expected and schedules can run later than expected. Let's say, for example, that Mrs. Smith calls her contractor and tells him to add a fireplace to the house he is building for her. Based on her oral authorization, the contractor installs the fireplace and chimney. Then, when he informs Mrs. Smith of the additional costs, she is shocked.

"You should have told me before you went ahead and did the work," she says.

"But you told me to go ahead and do it. It sounded like your mind was made up," he says.

"Well, I'm not going to pay this much; it's outrageous!" Mrs. Smith responds. And the hassle continues.

Whenever a customer requests changes, the project manager should have the appropriate project team members estimate the effects on the project cost and schedule. The project manager should then present these estimates to the customer and request the customer's approval before proceeding. If the customer agrees to the changes, the project schedule and budget should be revised to incorporate the additional tasks and costs. Sometimes customers try to squeeze in changes for free by making them sound trivial or by circumventing the project manager and dealing with one of the individuals on the project team. The project manager needs to be sure that team members won't casually agree to changes that may require additional person-hours. Otherwise, if the customer does not agree to pay for the changes, the contractor will have to absorb the costs for the additional person-hours and risk overrunning costs for a particular task or the entire project.

REINFORCE YOUR LEARNING

34. At the start of the project, the project manager needs to establish _____ regarding how changes will be _____ and _____.

Sometimes changes are initiated by the project manager or project team. For example, suppose a member of the project team came up with a new design approach that used a different type of computer system than the customer originally wanted but would substantially reduce the project cost. In this case, the project manager would present a proposal for the change to the customer and get the customer's approval before making the change. The customer would probably give approval if the change reduced costs without any degradation to system performance. On the other hand, if the project manager asked the customer to extend the project completion date or to provide additional funding because the project team had run into difficulties that had caused schedule slippage or cost overruns, the customer might not agree. The contractor might have to absorb the cost overrun or spend additional money to temporarily add more resources to get the project back on schedule.

The project manager needs to make it clear to the project team that team members should not make any changes to their work that will increase costs beyond budgeted amounts, delay the schedule, or produce results that do not meet the customer's expectations. For example, on a technical project a software engineer may think that he will please the customer by making slight enhancements to the software beyond what is required. However, he will not please the project manager if he overruns the budget for the software development task because of all the time he spends making a bunch of "slight enhancements" that are nice but aren't necessary!

Some changes become necessary as a result of unanticipated occurrences, such as an early snowstorm that slows down the construction of a building, failure of a new product to pass tests, or the untimely death or resignation of a key member of the project team. These occurrences will have an impact on the project schedule and/or cost and will require that the project plan be modified. In some cases, unanticipated events can cause the project to be terminated. For example, if early test results in a research project to develop an advanced ceramic material are not promising, the company may decide to terminate the project rather than spend more money with diminishing chances of success.

Perhaps the most difficult type of change to manage is that required of the users of the project results. In some situations, the project manager is responsible not only for managing the project to develop a new or improved system but also for implementing the resultant system among its users, who will have to change the way they perform their work. For example, in a project to design, develop, and implement a new computerized ordering, billing, and collection system to replace the current manual systems, the project manager might be responsible not only for managing the project to design and develop the new system, but also for getting the users to accept the change from the old manual system to the new computerized system.

There are some things a project manager can do to facilitate implementation of such a change. Open communication and a climate of trust are prerequisites for introducing change, reducing resistance to change, and gaining commitment to the change. It is important to gain the users' support for and commitment to the new system, not merely their agreement that they need a better system. The project manager needs to share information about the change with the users. Such communication has to be carried out promptly, fully, honestly, and regularly. This means that the project manager must initiate discussions with the users before the new system is even designed, not wait until it is ready to be implemented. Discussing the system early will help squelch the rumor mill. The project manager needs to tell the users why the change is being made and how it will affect and benefit them. They need to believe that the change will benefit them; otherwise, they will resent it rather than support it.

Discussions or meetings provide a good opportunity for people to express their concerns, fears, and anxieties. Anxiety and fear of the unknown can induce stress in people and build up resistance to change. During meetings to discuss the impending change, the project manager should not get into debates or be defensive. He or she should empathize with people's concerns and fears, not discount or trivialize them. If possible, the project manager should have users participate up front in the decision to change from, say, manual methods to a computerized system. Then he or she needs to involve them in planning and designing the system; after all, they are the people who will be using it. The users also need to be involved in planning how to implement the new system—how to make the changeover from the manual system to the computerized one. The project manager can provide support and rewards to help ensure successful implementation of the new system. A reward to the users might be that they receive computer skills training that will make them more knowledgeable and valuable. Finally, the project manager needs to be patient; only when the new system becomes fully utilized will the expected benefits be achieved.

Changes are going to occur on projects. The project manager has to manage and control the changes so that the project doesn't get out of control.

SUMMARY

It is the responsibility of the project manager to make sure that the customer is satisfied that the work scope is completed in a quality manner, within budget, and on time. The project manager has primary responsibility for providing leadership in planning, organizing, and controlling the work effort to accomplish the project objective. In terms of planning, the project manager has to clearly define the project objective and reach agreement with the customer on this objective. In terms of organizing, the project manager must secure the appropriate resources to perform the work. In terms of controlling, the project manager needs to track actual progress and compare it with planned progress.

The project manager is a key ingredient in the success of a project and needs to possess a set of skills that will help the project team succeed. The project manager should be a good leader who inspires the people assigned to the project to work as a team to successfully implement the plan and achieve the project objective; be committed to the training and development of the people working on the project; be an effective communicator who interacts regularly with the project team, as well as with any subcontractors, the customer, and her or his own company's upper management; and have good interpersonal skills. It is important that the project manager develop a relationship with each person on the project team and effectively use his or her interpersonal skills to try to influence the thinking and actions of others. An effective project manager can handle stress and has a good sense of humor. In addition, he or she is a good problem solver. Although it's easier to identify problems than to solve them, good problem solving starts with the early identification of a problem or potential problem. Good project managers also manage their time well.

These essential skills can be developed through experience, by seeking out feedback from others, by conducting a self-evaluation and learning from your own mistakes, by interviewing effective project managers, by participating in training programs, by joining organizations, through reading, and through involvement with volunteer organizations in which these skills can be tested.

Project managers need to be good delegators. Delegation involves empowering the project team to achieve the project objective and empowering each team member to accomplish the expected results for her or his area of responsibility. It's the act of allowing individuals to successfully carry out assigned tasks.

One other important component of the project manager's job is managing and controlling changes in order to minimize any negative impact on the successful accomplishment of the project objective. In order to do this successfully, the project manager should, at the beginning of the project, establish procedures regarding how changes will be documented and authorized.

QUESTIONS

1. Describe what the project manager should do in order to perform the planning function. Give some specific examples.
2. Describe what the project manager should do in order to perform the organizing function. Give some specific examples.
3. Describe what the project manager should do in order to perform the controlling function. Give some specific examples.
4. What are some essential skills for an effective project manager? How can these skills be developed?
5. Describe why a project manager needs good oral and written communication skills.
6. What is meant by the term *interpersonal skills?* Give some examples of interpersonal skills, and describe why they are important.
7. What are some things a project manager can do to help create an environment in which a project team will feel motivated?
8. What is meant by the term *delegation?* Why is delegation essential for project management? Give some examples.
9. What are some barriers to effective delegation?
10. Why is it important to manage change during a project? How is change initiated? Give some specific examples.
11. Describe some ways a project manager can make a project more fun and team members more committed.
12. Think of a project that you have worked on. Describe what made the project manager for that project effective or ineffective. How could the project manager have done a better job?

WORLD WIDE WEB EXERCISES

If you have difficulty accessing any of the Web addresses listed here, you can find these exercises (with up-to-date addresses) on the home page of Dr. James P. Clements, co-author of this book, at

www.towson.edu/~clements

1. Jerry Madden, Associate Director of the Flight Projects Directorate at NASA's Goddard Space Flight Center, has compiled an excellent Web site, which lists 100 rules for NASA project managers. The rules cover a wide range of areas, including communication, decision making, ethics, and failures. The Web address is

pscinfo.pscni.nasa.gov/online/msfc/
project_mgmt/100_Rules.html

   Print out the list of rules, and comment on at least ten of them.

2. The Department of Defense (DOD) has been promoting effective project management for a long time. Check out their Web site for the Software Program Managers Network at

www.spmn.com

3. What is the DOD Web site all about? Check out at least three of the links. Describe what you found.

4. Revisit the home page of the Project Management Institute (first visited in Chapter 2) at

www.pmi.org

   Either check out their career link from their home page or go directly to

www.pmi.org/jobs/job_list.htm

5. Reach the code of ethics for project managers from the Project Management Institute's home page or go directly to it at

www.pmi.org/mem_info/pmpcode.htm

   Print out and summarize the code.

6. From the Project Management Institute's home page, check out the link for Awards. Describe the Project of the Year Award, the PMI Fellow Award, and the Person of the Year Award, and any other awards that are listed.

CASE STUDY

Codeword is a medium-size firm that designs and manufactures electronic systems for military aircraft. It competes with other firms to win contracts to provide such systems. Its primary customer is the government. When Codeword receives a contract, it creates a project to complete the work. Most projects range from $10 million to $50 million in cost and from one to three years in duration. Codeword can have six to twelve projects going on at any one time, in various stages of completion—some just starting and others finishing.

Codeword has a handful of project managers who report to the general manager; other people report to their functional manager. For example, the electronic engineers all report to the manager of electrical engineering, who reports to the general manager. The functional manager assigns particular individuals to work on various projects. Some people work full time on a project, while others split their time among two or three projects. Although individuals are assigned to work for a project manager on a specific project, administratively they still report to their functional manager.

Jack Kowalski has been with the company for about eight years, since graduating from college with a B.S. in electronic engineering. He has worked his way up to senior electronics engineer and reports to the manager of electrical engineering. He has worked on many projects and is well respected within the company. Jack has been asking for an opportunity to be a project manager. When Codeword is awarded a $15 million contract to design and manufacture an advanced electronics system for a new aircraft, the general manager promotes Jack to project manager and asks him to run this project.

Jack works with the functional managers to get the best people available assigned to the project. Most of the people are buddies, who have worked with Jack on previous projects. However, with Jack's position as senior electronics engineer vacant, the manager of electrical engineering has no one with the appropriate level of expertise to assign to Jack's project. So the manager hires a new person, Alfreda Bryson. Lured away from a competitor, she has a Ph.D. in electronic engineering and twenty years' experience. She was able to command a high salary—more than Jack is making. She is assigned to Jack's project full time as the senior electronics engineer.

Jack takes a special interest in Alfreda's work and asks to meet with her to discuss her design approaches. Yet most of these meetings turn into monologues, with Jack suggesting how Alfreda should do the design and paying little attention to what she says.

Finally, Alfreda asks Jack why he is spending so much more time reviewing her work than that of the other engineers on the project. He responds, "I don't have to check theirs. I know how they work. I worked with them on other projects. You're the new kid on the block, and I want to be sure you understand the way we do things here, which may be different than at your previous employer."

On another occasion, Alfreda shows Jack what she thinks is a creative design approach that will result in a lower-cost system. Jack tells her, "I don't even have a Ph.D. and I can see that that won't work. Don't be so esoteric; just stick to basic sound engineering."

During a business trip with Dennis Freeman, another engineer assigned to the project who has known Jack for six years, Alfreda says that she is frustrated with the way Jack treats her. "Jack is acting more like the electronics engineer for the project than the project manager," she tells Dennis. "Besides, I have forgotten more about designing electronics than Jack ever knew! He really isn't up to date on electronic design methodologies." She also tells Dennis that she's planning to discuss the matter with the manager of electrical engineering and that she'd never have taken the job with Codeword if she'd known it was going to be like this.

Case Questions

1. Do you think Jack is ready to serve as a project manager? Why or why not?

2. How could Jack have prepared for his new role?
3. What is the major problem with the way Jack interacts with Alfreda?
4. Why do you think Alfreda hasn't had an open discussion with Jack about the way he's treating her?
5. If Alfreda approaches Jack directly, how do you think he will respond?
6. How do you think the manager of electrical engineering will respond to this situation? What should he do?

Group Activity

Course participants should split into groups of four or five students to discuss the following questions:

- What should be done to remedy the situation?
- What could have been done to prevent the situation?

Each group must then choose a spokesperson to present its conclusions to the entire class.

6

The Project Team

Team Building and Project Management: How Are We Doing?

Donald Tippett and James Peters stress that building a cohesive, motivated project team is a key to the ultimate accomplishment of project goals, and therefore team building is an essential project management skill. To study how well project managers are doing with respect to team building, they distributed nearly 100 survey forms to various organizations. Overall, the results showed that companies are doing a poor job of team building. For example, many team members reported that often they don't know enough about each other's jobs to appreciate the contributions others are making; few project managers are taking the time to brief team members regarding specific responsibilities and performance standards; project managers are not helping team members grow and advance professionally; project managers aren't effectively communicating feedback on job performance; and team members don't believe management understands the distinction between rewarding people for individual accomplishments and rewarding people for accomplishments as members of a team.

Tippett and Peters recommend that project managers (1) show respect and consideration for all employees as valued members of the team, (2) make sure each individual understands his or her job responsibility and the performance standards,

(3) establish good communication with employees as individuals and as a team, (4) establish clear individual and group goals, (5) properly reward teamwork and team-building efforts, and (6) demonstrate loyalty to the team.

Source: D. Tippett and J. Peters, "Team Building and Project Management: How Are We Doing?" *Project Management Journal,* December 1995.

Building Commitment in Project Teams

According to Gerard Rossy and Russell Archibald, one of the greatest challenges or sources of difficulty for the project manager relates to commitment. She or he must first get the necessary commitments to the project objectives and then ensure that they are fulfilled. Rossy and Archibald found that two general types of behaviors are needed to build commitment. The first is supporting behaviors, which lead to and build overall commitment. The second is innovating behaviors, which create opportunities and the desire to exceed initial performance expectations and goals through improvements.

Four key supporting behaviors are (1) identifying those activities and goals that deserve the highest priority and allocating time and resources accordingly, (2) being a visible role model for other members of the team, (3) rewarding contribution and fulfillment of commitments, and (4) managing actions or comments that communicate a negative attitude or feeling. Four key innovating behaviors are (1) searching for improvements in design, performance, costs, and schedules; (2) challenging the expectations of team members so they don't limit their own performance as a result of their *a priori* expectations; (3) creating an open and flexible environment; and (4) encouraging and supporting responsible risk taking.

Source: G. Rossy and R. Archibald, "Building Commitment in Project Teams," *Project Management Journal,* June 1992.

REINFORCE YOUR LEARNING

1. *A team is a group of individuals working _____ to achieve a common _____ .*

A *team* is a group of individuals working interdependently to achieve a common goal. *Teamwork* is cooperative effort by members of a team to achieve that common goal. The effectiveness—or lack thereof—of the project team can make the difference between project success and project failure. Although plans and project management techniques are necessary, it is the people—the project manager and the project team—that are the key to project success; project success requires an effective project team. This chapter covers the development and maintenance of an effective project team. You will become familiar with

- the development and growth of teams
- characteristics of effective project teams and barriers to effectiveness

REINFORCE YOUR LEARNING

2. *Teamwork is a _____ effort by members of a team to achieve a _____ goal.*

- team building
- sources of conflict during the project and approaches to handling conflict
- problem solving
- effective time management

PROJECT TEAM DEVELOPMENT AND EFFECTIVENESS

A personal relationship between two people takes time to develop. Initially, you may be curious about each other, but apprehensive about letting your guard down and opening yourself up to the other person. As you get to know each other a little more, you may begin to notice differences in your attitudes and values, and disagreements may arise. You may be anxious about whether the relationship will or should continue. As you work through your differences, you may get to know each other better and become friends. Finally, you may develop a close relationship that helps you to be open with each other, accept each other's differences, and enjoy participating together in activities that are of mutual interest.

Likewise, teams evolve through various stages of development. In many projects, people who have never worked together are assigned to the same project team. This group of individuals must develop into an effective team to successfully achieve the project objective.

Stages of Team Development and Growth

B.W. Tuckman has defined four stages of team development: forming, storming, norming, and performing (see Figure 6.1).

FORMING

Forming is the initial stage of the team development process. It involves the transition from individual to team member. Similar to the early "courting" phase of a relationship, it is when individuals on the team begin to get acquainted. During this stage, team members generally have positive expectations and are eager to get started on the work to be accomplished. The group begins to establish an identity and attempts to define and plan the tasks that need to be done. In this phase, however, little actual work is accomplished because of the high level of anxiety that individuals have about the work itself and about their relationships with each other. Team members are unsure of their own roles and the roles of the other members of the project team. In the forming stage, the team needs direction. Members depend on the project manager to provide direction and structure.

REINFORCE YOUR LEARNING

3. *During the forming stage, _____ actual work is accomplished because of the _____ level of anxiety that individuals have.*

Feelings characteristic of this stage include excitement, anticipation, suspicion, anxiety, and hesitancy. Individuals do a lot of questioning in the forming stage: What is our purpose? Who are the other team members? What are they like? Individuals are anxious about whether they will fit in with the other members and be accepted. They may be hesitant to participate because they are unsure how

FIGURE 6.1   Stages of Team Development

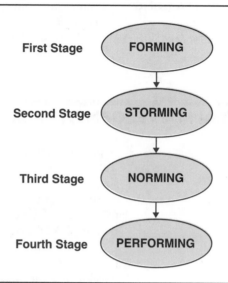

other members will react. Members wonder whether their input will be valued and whether their role in the project aligns with their personal and professional interests.

During the forming stage, the project manager needs to provide direction and structure. In giving orientation to the project team, the project manager must clearly communicate the project objective and create a vision of the successful result of the project and the benefits it will provide. Project constraints regarding the work scope, quality levels, budget, and schedule must be stated. The project manager also needs to discuss the make-up of the project team: the reasons team members were selected, their complementary skills and expertise, and each person's role in helping to accomplish the project objective. Establishing structure is another task the project manager must perform in this phase. This includes defining initial processes and procedures for team operation and addressing such items as communication channels, approvals, and paperwork. These processes and procedures may be improved by the team as it develops through its later stages. To relieve some of the anxiety, the project manager should discuss his or her management style and expectations regarding the work and behavior of the people on the project team. It's also important to get the team working on some initial tasks. Here is where the project manager gets the team to participate in developing the project plans.

STORMING

The second stage of team development is known as *storming*. Like the teenage years, it's usually tough on everyone, but you have to go through it. You can't get around it or avoid it.

The project objective is clearer in this stage. Members start to apply their skills to work on their assigned tasks, and work begins to

REINFORCE YOUR LEARNING

6. During the storming stage, _____ emerges and _____ increases.

REINFORCE YOUR LEARNING

7. During the storming stage, team members wonder how much _____ and _____ they have.

REINFORCE YOUR LEARNING

8. During the storming stage, the project manager needs to provide _____ and foster _____ _____ .

progress slowly. Reality sets in, though, and it may not match individuals' initial expectations. For example, tasks may be more extensive or difficult than anticipated, or cost or schedule constraints may be tighter than expected. As team members begin to perform their tasks, they feel increasing dissatisfaction with dependence on the direction or authority of the project manager. For example, they may have negative reactions to the project manager and to the operating processes and procedures that were established in the forming stage. Team members now begin to test the limits and flexibility of the project manager and the ground rules. During the storming stage, conflict emerges and tension increases. There is a need for agreement on methods for handling and resolving conflict. Motivation and morale are low in this stage. Members may resist team formation—they want to express their individuality as opposed to team allegiance.

The storming stage is characterized by feelings of frustration, anger, and hostility. As individuals begin to perform their tasks, they have more questions about their roles and responsibilities with respect to other team members. As they begin to follow operating procedures, they question the viability and necessity of such procedures. Members wonder how much control and authority they have.

In the storming stage, the project manager still needs to be directive, but less directive than in the forming stage. She or he needs to provide clarification and better definition of individual responsibilities and of interfacing activities among team members. It is necessary to begin involving the team in problem-solving activities and to start sharing decision making so as to empower the team. The project manager should acknowledge and tolerate any dissatisfaction expressed by team members—not become defensive or take it personally. This is the time for the project manager to provide an understanding and supportive environment. It's important to give members an opportunity to express their concerns. The project manager has to provide guidance and foster conflict resolution—not try to suppress any dissatisfaction, in the hope that it will go away by itself. If dissatisfaction is not addressed, it will build up and could result in dysfunctional behavior later, putting the successful completion of the project at risk.

NORMING

After struggling through the storming stage, the project team moves into the *norming* stage of development. Relationships among team members and between the team and the project manager have become settled. Interpersonal conflicts have been resolved for the most part. In general, the level of conflict is lower than it was in the storming stage. Dissatisfaction, too, is reduced, as individuals' expectations align with the reality of the situation—the work to be done, the resources available, the constraints, and the other individuals involved. The project team has accepted its operating environment. Project procedures are improved and streamlined. Control and decision making are transferred from the project manager to the project team. Cohesion begins to develop. There is a sense of team. Individuals feel accepted as part of the team, and they accept others as part of the team. There is an appreciation of each member's contribution to achieving the project objective.

Trust begins to develop in this stage, as team members start to confide in one another. There is a greater sharing of information, ideas, and feelings; cooperation increases. Team members give and ask for feedback and feel that they can freely and constructively express their emotions and criticisms. A feeling of camaraderie emerges as the team goes through a socialization process. Personal friendships may develop that reach beyond the work environment.

During the norming stage, the project manager minimizes directiveness and takes on a more supportive role. Work performance accelerates and productivity increases. The project manager should recognize the project team for the progress being made.

PERFORMING

The fourth and final stage of team development and growth is the *performing* stage. In this stage, the team is highly committed and eager to achieve the project objective. The level of work performance is high during this stage. The team feels a sense of unity and pride in its accomplishments. Confidence is high. Communication is open, frank, and timely. During this stage, members work individually or in temporary sub-teams, as needed. There is a great degree of interdependency—members frequently collaborate and willingly help each other with work beyond their own assigned tasks. The team feels fully empowered. As problems are identified, appropriate team members form sub-teams to solve the problems and decide how the solution should be implemented. There is a feeling of satisfaction as progress is made and recognized. Individual members realize that they are experiencing professional growth as a result of working on the project.

During the performing stage, the project manager fully delegates responsibility and authority, thereby empowering the project team. He or she focuses on helping the team execute the project plan and giving recognition to team members for their progress and accomplishments. At this stage, the project manager concentrates on project performance with respect to the budget, schedule, scope, and plan. The project manager's role is to facilitate and support the development and implementation of corrective actions if actual progress falls behind planned progress. It is also at this stage that the project manager acts as a mentor, supporting the professional growth and development of the people working on the project.

Figure 6.2 graphically illustrates the levels of work performance and sense of team during the four stages of team development and growth. The amount of time and effort it takes a team to move through each of the stages depends on several factors, including the number of people on the team, whether or not team members have worked together before, the complexity of the project, and the teamwork skills of the members.

FIGURE 6.2   Level of Functioning at Various Stages of Team Development

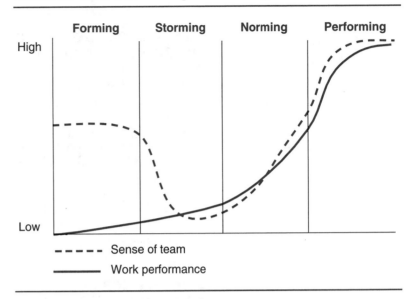

The Effective Project Team

Putting a group of people together to work on a project does not create a team. A project team is more than a group of individuals assigned to work on one project. A project team is a group of interdependent individuals working cooperatively to achieve the project objective. Helping these individuals develop and grow into a cohesive, effective team takes effort on the part of the project manager and each member of the project team. As was noted at the beginning of the chapter, the effectiveness—or lack thereof—of the project team can make the difference between project success and project failure. Although plans and project management techniques are necessary, it is the people— the project manager and project team—that are the key to project success; project success requires an effective project team.

Characteristics associated with effective project teams include

- a clear understanding of the project objective
- clear expectations of each person's role and responsibilities
- a results orientation
- a high degree of cooperation and collaboration
- a high level of trust

A CLEAR UNDERSTANDING OF THE PROJECT OBJECTIVE

The scope, level of quality, budget, and schedule must be well defined for a project team to be effective. If the project objective is to be achieved, each team member must have the same vision of the project result and the benefits it will provide.

CLEAR EXPECTATIONS OF EACH PERSON'S ROLE AND RESPONSIBILITIES

Members of an effective team know how their work must fit together, because they participated in developing the project plans. Team members appreciate each other's expertise, skills, and contributions to achieving the project objective. Each person accepts responsibility for carrying out her or his part of the project.

A RESULTS ORIENTATION

Each person on an effective project team has a strong commitment to achieving the project objective. By setting a good example, the project manager sets the tone for the energy level. Team members are enthusiastic and willing to spend the time and energy necessary to succeed. For example, individuals are willing to work extra hours or weekends or skip lunches when necessary in order to keep the project on track.

A HIGH DEGREE OF COOPERATION AND COLLABORATION

Open, frank, and timely communication is the norm on an effective project team. Members readily share information, ideas, and feelings. They are not shy about asking other members for help. Team members act as resources for each other, beyond just doing their assigned tasks. They want to see other members succeed in their tasks and are willing to help and support them if they are stuck or faltering. They give and accept feedback and constructive criticism. Because of this cooperation, the team is creative in problem solving and timely in decision making.

A HIGH LEVEL OF TRUST

Members of an effective team understand interdependency and accept that everyone on the team is important to project success. Each member can count on the other members to do what they say they will do—and do it at the expected level of quality. Team members care for and about one another. Because differences are accepted, members feel free to be themselves. Differences of opinion are encouraged, freely expressed, and respected. Individuals are able to raise issues that may result in disagreement or conflict without concern about retribution. Effective project teams resolve conflict through constructive and timely feedback and positive confrontation of the issues. Conflict is not suppressed; rather, it is seen as normal and as an opportunity for growth and learning.

Figure 6.3 is a checklist for rating the effectiveness of a project team. It is recommended that team members complete this assessment instrument periodically during the project. After the scores of all team members have been summarized, the team, including the project manager, should discuss how to improve in any areas that were rated low.

REINFORCE YOUR LEARNING

15. *An effective project team has a clear understanding of the _____ and clear expectations of each person's _____ and _____.*

REINFORCE YOUR LEARNING

16. *Effective project teams have a _____ orientation; each person has a strong commitment to achieving the _____ _____. There is a high degree of _____ and _____.*

REINFORCE YOUR LEARNING

17. *Effective project teams have a high level of _____. They are able to resolve conflict through constructive and timely _____ and positive _____ of the issues.*

FIGURE 6.3   Team Effectiveness Checklist

How Effective Is Your Project Team?					
	Not at All		Somewhat		Very Much
1. Does your team have a clear understanding of its goal?	1	2	3	4	5
2. Are the project scope, level of quality, budget, and schedule well defined?	1	2	3	4	5
3. Does everyone have clear expectations of his or her own role and responsibilities?	1	2	3	4	5
4. Does everyone have clear expectations of other members' roles and responsibilities?	1	2	3	4	5
5. Does everyone know the expertise and skills that each person brings to the team?	1	2	3	4	5
6. Is your team results oriented?	1	2	3	4	5
7. Does everyone have a strong commitment to achieving the project objective?	1	2	3	4	5
8. Does your team have a high level of enthusiasm and energy?	1	2	3	4	5
9. Does your team have a high degree of cooperation and collaboration?	1	2	3	4	5
10. Are open, frank, and timely communications the norm?	1	2	3	4	5
11. Do members readily share information, ideas, and feelings?	1	2	3	4	5
12. Do members feel free to ask other members for help?	1	2	3	4	5
13. Do members willingly help one another?	1	2	3	4	5
14. Do team members give feedback and constructive criticism?	1	2	3	4	5
15. Do team members accept feedback and constructive criticism?	1	2	3	4	5
16. Is there a high level of trust among the project team members?	1	2	3	4	5
17. Do members follow through on what they say they will do?	1	2	3	4	5
18. Is there an openness to differing viewpoints?	1	2	3	4	5
19. Do team members accept one another and their differences?	1	2	3	4	5
20. Does your team constructively resolve conflicts?	1	2	3	4	5

Barriers to Team Effectiveness

Although every project team has the potential to be highly effective, there are often barriers that impede a team's achievement of the level of effectiveness of which it is capable. Following are barriers that can hinder project team effectiveness and some suggestions for overcoming them.

UNCLEAR GOALS

The project manager needs to articulate the project objective, as well as the project scope, level of quality, budget, and schedule. He or she needs to create a vision of the project result and the benefits it will provide. This information needs to be communicated at the very first project meeting. At this meeting, the project manager needs to ask team members if they understand this information and answer any questions they may have. The information should then be provided in written form, along with any clarification given during the initial project meeting, to each individual on the project team. Periodically, the project manager needs to discuss the project objective at project status review meetings. At these meetings, he or she should always ask whether anyone has any questions about what must be accomplished. Telling the team what the project objective is only once, at the beginning of the project, is not sufficient. The project manager must say it, write it, distribute it, and repeat it frequently.

UNCLEAR DEFINITION OF ROLES AND RESPONSIBILITIES

Individuals may feel that their roles and responsibilities are ambiguous or that there is overlap in the responsibilities of some individuals. At the beginning of the project, the project manager should meet individually with each member of the project team, to tell the member why she or he was selected for the project, describe her or his expected role and responsibilities, and explain how they relate to the other team members' roles and responsibilities. Project team members need to feel free to ask the project manager to clarify any areas of ambiguity or overlap whenever they become apparent. As the project team develops the project plan, each member's tasks should be identified using a tool such as a work breakdown structure, a responsibility matrix, a Gantt chart, or a network diagram (all of these are discussed in Part 3 of the text). Copies of these documents should be given to everyone so that each team member can see not only her or his own assigned tasks but also other member's tasks and how they all fit together.

LACK OF PROJECT STRUCTURE

Individuals may feel that everyone is working in a different direction or that there are no established procedures for team operation. This, too, is a reason for the project manager to have the team participate in developing the project plan.

REINFORCE YOUR LEARNING

18. *The project manager needs to articulate the project _____ frequently. At periodic meetings, he or she should always ask whether anyone has any _____ about what must be accomplished.*

REINFORCE YOUR LEARNING

19. *The project manager should meet individually with each team member, to tell the member why he or she was _____ for the project and describe her or his expected _____ and _____ .*

A tool such as a network diagram (discussed in Part 3) shows how everyone's work fits together to accomplish the project objective. At the beginning of the project, the project manager should establish preliminary operating procedures that address such issues as communication channels, approvals, and documentation requirements. Each procedure, as well as the rationale for establishing it, needs to be explained to the team at a project meeting. The procedures should also be provided in written form to all team members. If some team members do not follow the procedures or circumvent them, the project manager needs to reinforce the importance of everyone's consistently following established procedures. However, the project manager needs to be open to suggestions for eliminating or streamlining procedures when they no longer contribute to the effective and efficient performance of the project.

REINFORCE YOUR LEARNING

20. *The project manager needs to establish preliminary operating _____ at the beginning of the project, but be open to suggestions for _____ or _____ them when they no longer _____ to the effective and efficient performance of the project.*

LACK OF COMMITMENT

Team members may not appear to be committed to their project work or the project objective. To counter such indifference, the project manager needs to explain to each individual the importance of his or her role on the team and how he or she can contribute to the success of the project. The project manager also needs to ask team members what their personal and professional interests are and look for ways that the project assignment might help satisfy these interests. She or he should try to determine what motivates each individual and then create a project environment where these motivators are available. The project manager also needs to recognize the accomplishments of each person and support and encourage his or her progress.

REINFORCE YOUR LEARNING

21. *The project manager should try to determine what _____ each individual and then create a project _____ where these motivators are available.*

POOR COMMUNICATION

Poor communication occurs when team members lack knowledge about what is happening on the project and individuals don't share information. It's important for the project manager to have regular project status review meetings with a published agenda. Various project team members should be asked to give a briefing on the status of their work. Participation and questions should be encouraged. All project documents—such as plans, budgets, schedules, and reports—should be kept up to date and distributed in a timely manner to the entire project team. The project manager should encourage team members to get together to share information, collaborate, and solve problems as needed, rather than wait for official project meetings. Also, physically locating all members of the project team in the same office area can enhance project communications.

REINFORCE YOUR LEARNING

22. *It's important for the project manager to have regular project _____ _____ meetings with a published agenda. _____ and questions should be encouraged during such meetings.*

POOR LEADERSHIP

To keep the project team from feeling that the project manager is not providing effective leadership for the team, the project manager has to be willing to periodically solicit feedback from the project team by asking questions like "How am I doing?" or "How can I improve my leadership?" However, she or he must first establish a project environment in which individuals feel free to provide feedback without fear of retribution. The project manager should state at an early project meeting that feedback will be requested periodically and that others' suggestions for improving her or his leadership skills are welcome. For example, a project manager might say that she is interested in improving her leadership skills so as to enhance her own contribution to the success of the project. Of course, she then must be willing to follow up on appropriate suggestions, whether they involve additional training, changing her behavior, or modifying project procedures.

TURNOVER OF PROJECT TEAM MEMBERS

When team composition changes often—that is, when new people are continually being assigned to a project and others leaving—the flow of individuals may be too dynamic for the team to jell. A project team made up of a small number of individuals with long-term assignments will be more efficient than a project team composed of a large number of individuals with short-term assignments. The project manager should select for the project team people who are sufficiently versatile in expertise and skills that they can contribute to many areas of the project and thus be assigned to a project for a long period of time. Although the project manager should not try to run the project with a multitude of individuals with narrow expertise who will be assigned to the project for only short intervals, in some cases it may be appropriate for individuals with specific expertise to be assigned to the project for only one task or for a limited period of time.

DYSFUNCTIONAL BEHAVIOR

Sometimes an individual exhibits behavior that is disruptive to the development of an effective team—hostility, excessive clowning around, or the making of disparaging personal remarks, for example. The project manager needs to meet with this individual, point out the disruptive behavior, and explain that it is unacceptable because of the impact it's having on the rest of the project team. The individual might be offered coaching, a training seminar, or counseling, if appropriate. The project manager must make it clear, however, that if the dysfunctional behavior continues, the person will be released from the project team. Of course, the project manager needs to be prepared to follow through, if necessary.

Being an Effective Team Member

Being a member of a project team should be an enriching and satisfying growth experience for each individual. However, growth will not just happen by itself. It requires a sense of responsibility, hard work, open mindedness, and a desire to further develop yourself. Although the project manager is ultimately responsible for the success of a project, each member of the project team shares in that responsibility. Each member of the project team needs to help create and foster a positive and effective project environment.

REINFORCE YOUR LEARNING

23. *A project manager should periodically solicit others' suggestions for improving her or his _____ skills.*

REINFORCE YOUR LEARNING

24. *A project team made up of a _____ number of individuals with _____-term assignments will be more efficient than a project team composed of a _____ number of individuals with _____-term assignments.*

REINFORCE YOUR LEARNING

25. *What are some barriers to team effectiveness?*

Effective team members plan, control, and feel accountable for their individual work efforts. They have high expectations of themselves and strive to accomplish their assignments under budget and ahead of schedule. They manage their time well. They make things happen, they don't just let them happen. Effective team members don't simply work on a task until they are told to stop—they're self-directed and follow through on assignments and action items. They take pride in doing quality work instead of expecting other team members to finish, clean up, or re-do any of their shabby or incomplete work. Each team member can count on all the other team members to perform their respective tasks in a quality and timely manner so as not to delay or impede the work of other team members.

Effective team members participate and communicate. They don't sit back and wait to be asked; they speak up and participate in meetings. They take the initiative, communicating with other team members and the project manager in a clear, timely, and unambiguous manner. They provide constructive feedback to each other. In particular, effective team members feel responsible for identifying problems—or potential problems—as early as possible, without pointing the finger or blaming other individuals, the customer, or the project manager for causing the problems. Effective team members are not only problem identifiers but also problem solvers. When a problem has been identified, they suggest alternative solutions and are ready and willing to collaborate with other team members to solve the problem, even if it is outside of their assigned area of responsibility. Effective team members do not have a "that's not my problem" or "that's not my job" attitude; rather, they are willing to pitch in to help the team achieve the project objective.

Effective team members help to create a positive, constructive project environment in which there is no room for divisiveness. They're sensitive to the diverse composition of the project team and show respect for all members of the team. They respect others' viewpoints. They don't let pride, stubbornness, or arrogance get in the way of collaboration, cooperation, and compromise. Effective team members put the success of the project above personal gain.

It has been said that there is no I in TEAM—there are no individual winners or losers. When a project is successful, everybody wins!

Team Building

Legendary baseball manager Casey Stengel once said, "It's easy to get the players. Gettin' 'em to play together, that's the hard part." Team building—developing a group of individuals to accomplish the project objective—is an ongoing process. It is the responsibility of both the project manager and the project team. Team building helps to create an atmosphere of openness and trust. Members feel a sense of unity and a strong commitment to accomplishing the project objective. Chapter 5 discussed various things that the project manager can do in order to foster and support team building. Here we will discuss a few things that the project team can do to help the team-building process.

REINFORCE YOUR LEARNING

26. *Effective team members plan, control, and feel _____ for their individual work efforts. They have high _____ of themselves.*

REINFORCE YOUR LEARNING

27. *Effective team members _____ and _____. They are not only problem identifiers, but also _____ _____.*

REINFORCE YOUR LEARNING

28. *Think about projects in which you have been involved. What are some characteristics of individual team members that made them effective contributors?*

REINFORCE YOUR LEARNING

29. *Team building is the responsibility of both the _____ _____ and the _____ _____.*

Socializing among team members supports team building. The better team members get to know one another, the more team building is enhanced. To ensure that individual members communicate with one another frequently, situations need to be created that foster socializing among team members. Team members can initiate some of these situations.

The team can request that team members be physically located in one office area for the duration of the project. When team members are located near one another, there is a greater chance that they will go to each other's offices or work areas to talk. Also, they will pass each other more frequently in common areas such as hallways and have a chance to stop and talk. Discussions should not always be work related. It's important that team members get to know one another on a personal basis, without being intrusive. A certain number of personal friendships will develop during the project. Having the entire project team located in one area prevents that "us versus them" feeling that can arise when parts of the team are located in different parts of a building or plant. Such a situation can result in a project team that is really a set of several subgroups rather than a true team.

REINFORCE YOUR LEARNING

30. _____ among team members supports _____ _____.

Individual members need to _____ with one another frequently.

The project team can initiate social events to celebrate project events, such as reaching a critical milestone—a system's passing a test or a successful design review meeting with the customer—or events can be scheduled periodically just for stress relief. An after-work pizza party, a team luncheon, an informal lunch in the conference room, a weekend family picnic, and a trip to see a sports event or theater production are examples of events the team can organize to foster socializing and team building. It's important that such activities include everyone on the team. Though some individuals may not be able to participate, everyone should at least be invited and encouraged to participate. Team members should use these events to get to know as many other team members (and their families, if they participate) as possible. A good rule of thumb is to always try to sit next to someone you don't know too well and strike up a conversation—ask questions, listen to what the other person says, look for areas of common interest. It is important for individuals to avoid forming cliques composed of several people who always hang together at every event. Engaging in social events not only helps to develop a sense of camaraderie but also makes it easier for team members to engage in open and frank communication while working on the project.

In addition to organizing social activities, the team can periodically call team meetings, as opposed to project meetings. The purpose of team meetings is to discuss openly such questions as the following: How are we working as a team? What barriers are impeding teamwork (such as procedures, resources, priorities, or communications)? What can we do to overcome these barriers? What can we do to improve teamwork? If the project manager participates in team meetings, he or she should be treated as an equal—team members should not look to the manager for the answers, and he or she should not pull rank and override the consensus of the team. It's a team meeting, not a project meeting. Only team-related issues, not project items, should be discussed.

Team members should foster team building in whatever ways they can. They should not expect the project manager alone to be responsible for team building.

CONFLICT ON PROJECTS

You might think that conflict is bad and should be avoided. However, conflict on projects is inevitable. Differences of opinion are natural and must be expected. It would be a mistake to try to suppress conflict, as conflict can be beneficial. It provides an opportunity to gain new information, consider alternatives, develop better solutions to problems, enhance team building, and learn. As part of the team-building process, the project manager and project team need to openly acknowledge that conflict is bound to occur during the performance of the project and reach a consensus on how it should be handled. Such a discussion needs to take place at the beginning of the project, not when the first situation occurs or after there has been an emotional outburst.

The following sections discuss the sources of conflict on a project and approaches to handling these conflicts.

Sources of Conflict

During a project, conflict can emerge from a variety of situations. It can involve members of the project team, the project manager, and even the customer. Here are seven sources of potential conflict on projects.

WORK SCOPE

Conflict can arise from differences of opinion on how the work should be done, how much work should be done, or at what level of quality the work should be done. Take the following cases:

- In a project to develop an order tracking system, one team member thinks that bar coding technology should be used, whereas another individual thinks that keypad data entry stations should be used. This is a conflict over the technical approach to the job.
- In a town festival project, one team member thinks that mailing an advertisement about the festival to each household in the town is sufficient, whereas another thinks that the mailing should be sent to all residents in the county and advertisements should be placed in newspapers. This is a conflict over how much work should be included.
- As part of a project to build a home, a contractor has put one coat of paint on each room in the house. Upon inspection, however, the customer is not satisfied that one coat is sufficient and demands that the contractor put on a second coat at no additional cost. This is a conflict over the level of quality of the work.

RESOURCE ASSIGNMENTS

Conflict can arise over the particular individuals assigned to work on certain tasks or over the quantity of resources assigned to certain tasks. In the project to develop an order tracking system, the person assigned the task of developing the application software might want to be assigned to work on the database because it would give her an opportunity to expand her knowledge and skills. In the town festival project, the team members charged with painting the booths might think that they need more volunteers assigned to help them in order to finish the work in time.

SCHEDULE

Conflict can result from differences of opinion about the sequence in which the work should be done or about how long the work should take. When, during the planning stage at the beginning of the project, a team member estimates that her tasks will take six weeks to complete, the project manager may respond, "That's too long. We'll never get the project done on time. You have to do it in four weeks."

COST

Conflict often arises over how much the work should cost. For example, suppose a market research company provided a customer with an estimated cost for conducting a nationwide survey and then, when the project was about 75 percent complete, told the customer that the project would probably cost 20 percent more than originally estimated. Or suppose more people were assigned to a late project to bring it back on schedule, but now expenditures are way above budget. Who should pay for the cost overruns?

PRIORITIES

Conflict is likely to result when people are assigned to work on several different projects concurrently or when various people need to use a limited resource at the same time. For example, suppose an individual has been assigned to work part of her time on a project team within her company to streamline some of the company's procedures. However, she has a sudden increase in her regular workload, and her failure to spend the anticipated amount of time on her project assignments is holding up the project. Which has priority—her project assignment or her regular work? Or suppose a company has one powerful computer capable of doing complicated scientific data analysis. Several project teams need access to the computer during the same time period in order to maintain their respective schedules. The team that can't use the computer will behind schedule. Which project team has priority?

ORGANIZATIONAL ISSUES

A variety of organizational issues can cause conflict, particularly during the storming stage of team development (discussed earlier in the chapter). There may be disagreement over the need for certain procedures established by the project manager with respect to paperwork or approvals. Conflict can result from poor or ambiguous project communication, from a lack of information sharing, or from failure to make timely decisions. For example, conflict is likely to arise if the project manager insists that all communications flow through him or her. Another case may be that there are not enough project status review meetings. When one is held, information is unveiled that would have been helpful to others if it had been known several weeks earlier. As a result, some team members may have to re-do some of their work. Finally, there could be conflict between some or all of the project team members and the project manager because of his or her leadership style.

PERSONAL DIFFERENCES

Conflict can emerge among members of the project team because of prejudices or differences in individuals' values and attitudes. In the case of a project that is behind schedule, if one team member is working evening hours to try to get the work back on schedule, she may resent the fact that another member always leaves at the normal time in order to have dinner with his wife before she leaves for her evening job.

There may be times during the project when there are no conflicts. On the other hand, there will be times when there are many conflicts from various sources that need to be handled. Conflict is inevitable on projects, but it can be beneficial if handled properly.

REINFORCE YOUR LEARNING

31. What are common sources of conflict on projects?

Handling Conflict

Conflict is not just for the project manager to handle and resolve; conflict between team members should be handled by the individuals involved. Handled properly, conflict can be beneficial. It causes problems to surface and be addressed. It stimulates discussion and requires individuals to clarify their views. Conflict can force individuals to search for new approaches; it can foster creativity and enhance the problem-solving process. If it is handled properly, conflict helps team building. However, if it is not handled properly, conflict can have a negative impact on the project team. It can destroy communication—people stop talking and sharing information. It can diminish team members' willingness to listen to and respect others' viewpoints. It can break down team unity and reduce the level of trust and openness.

Researchers Blake and Mouton and Kilmann and Thomas have identified five approaches that people use to handle conflict.

REINFORCE YOUR LEARNING

32. Handled properly, conflict can be _____.

AVOIDING OR WITHDRAWING

In the avoiding or withdrawing approach, individuals in conflict retreat from the situation in order to avoid an actual or potential disagreement. For example, if one person disagrees with a second person, the second individual may simply remain silent. This approach can cause the conflict to fester and then escalate at a later time.

COMPETING OR FORCING

In the competing or forcing approach, conflict is viewed as a win–lose situation. The value placed on winning the conflict is higher than the value placed on the relationship between the individuals, and the individual who is in a position to do so handles the conflict by exerting power over the other individual. For example, in a conflict between the project manager and a member of the project team regarding which technical approach to use for designing a system, the project manager may simply pull rank and say, "Do it my way." This approach to handling conflict can result in resentment and deterioration of the work climate.

ACCOMMODATING OR SMOOTHING

The accommodating or smoothing approach emphasizes the search for areas of agreement within the conflict and minimizes the value of addressing differences. Topics that may cause hurt feelings are not discussed. In this approach, the value placed on the relationship between the individuals is greater than the value placed on resolution of the issue. Although this approach may make a conflict situation livable, it does not resolve the issue.

COMPROMISING

In the compromising approach, team members search for an intermediate position. They focus on splitting the difference. They search for a solution that will bring some degree of satisfaction to each individual. The solution, however, may not be the optimal one. Take the case where members of the project team are establishing duration estimates for various project tasks. One member says, "I think it'll take fifteen days." Another says, "No way; it shouldn't take that long. Maybe five or six days." So they quickly split the difference and agree on ten days, which may not be the best estimate.

COLLABORATING, CONFRONTING, OR PROBLEM SOLVING

In the collaborating, confronting, or problem-solving approach, team members confront the issue directly. They look for a win–win outcome. They place high value on both the outcome and the relationship between the individuals. Each person must approach the conflict with a constructive attitude and a willingness to work in good faith with the others to resolve the issue. There is an open exchange of information about the conflict as each sees it. Differences are explored and worked through to reach the best overall solution. Each individual is willing to abandon or redefine his or her position as new information is exchanged, in order to arrive at the optimal solution. For this approach to work, it is necessary to have a healthy project environment (see the earlier discussion of effective project teams) in which relationships are open and nonhostile and people don't fear retribution if they're honest with each other.

REINFORCE YOUR LEARNING

33. What are five approaches to handling conflict?

Differences can escalate into emotional arguments. When individuals try to resolve a conflict, they cannot let themselves be drawn into an emotional state. They need to be able to manage, but not suppress, their emotions. They need to take the time to understand the other person's point of view. The following section provides a helpful approach to collaborative problem solving.

Unnecessary conflict can be avoided or minimized through early involvement of the project team in planning; clear articulation of each member's role and responsibilities; open, frank, and timely communication; clear operating procedures; and sincere team-building efforts by the project manager and project team.

PROBLEM SOLVING

It is unusual for a team to complete a project without encountering some problems. Normally, various kinds of problems arise along the way, some more serious than others. For example, the project can fall a few weeks behind schedule, jeopardizing completion by the customer's required date. Or the project may be in budget trouble—maybe 50 percent of the money has been spent, but only 40 percent of the work has been accomplished. Some problems are of a technical nature—a new optical sensor system is not providing the required data accuracy, or a new piece of high-speed assembly equipment continues to jam up and ruin expensive components. How effectively the project team solves problems may make the difference between project success and project failure. Therefore, a disciplined, creative, and effective approach to problem solving is needed. Here is a nine-step approach to problem solving, followed by a discussion of brainstorming—a technique helpful in several steps of the problem-solving approach.

A Nine-Step Approach to Problem Solving

The nine-step problem-solving approach is as follows:

1. *Develop a problem statement.* It's important to start with a written statement of the problem, which gives definition and boundaries to the problem. The problem statement provides a vehicle for reaching agreement among the members of the problem-solving team about the exact nature of the problem they are trying to solve. The problem statement should include a quantitative measure of the extent of the problem.
   - An example of a poor problem statement is "We are behind schedule." An example of a better problem statement is "We are two weeks behind schedule. It looks as if we will miss our customer's due date, which is four weeks from now, by two weeks unless we do something. If we don't make the customer's due date, she will be entitled to a 10 percent price reduction according to the contract."
   - Another example of a poor problem statement is "The sensor system doesn't work." A better statement is "The sensor system is giving erroneous data when it measures the rounded corners of parts."

   The more specific or quantitative the problem statement, the better, because any measures can be used as criteria later on to evaluate whether the problem has indeed been solved.

2. *Identify potential causes of the problem*. There can be many reasons why a problem has occurred or is occurring. This is especially true of technical problems. Take a project involving the development of a multiple-user computer system, in which the problem is that data are not being passed from the central computer to all the user work stations. The cause could be a hardware or software problem, or it could be a problem with the central computer or with some of the work stations. A technique often used to identify potential causes of a problem is *brainstorming*. This technique will be discussed later in this chaper.

3. *Gather data and verify the most likely causes*. In the early stages of the problem-solving process, the team is often reacting to symptoms rather than dealing with what might be causing the problem. This is particularly likely to happen when the problem is described in terms of symptoms. Suppose a person goes to a doctor and says he has been getting headaches. The doctor realizes that there could be many causes, such as stress, a tumor, a change in diet, or a problem in the environment. So the doctor will attempt to gather additional data about some of the most likely causes—by asking questions and possibly having the patient undergo some tests. The doctor will then use this information to narrow down the list of possible causes of the problem. It's important for the team to get beyond the symptoms and gather the facts before moving on to the next step: identifying possible solutions. Otherwise, much time may be wasted developing solutions to symptoms rather than to the cause of the problem. Gathering data, whether it be through asking questions, interviewing people, running tests, reading reports, or analyzing data, takes time. However, it must be done to focus the team's work in the rest of the problem-solving process.

4. *Identify possible solutions*. This is the fun and creative step in the problem-solving process. It's also a critical step in the process. Team members need to be careful not to jump to the first solution suggested or even the most obvious solution. They will be disappointed later on when that first or obvious solution doesn't work and it's back to the drawing board. For example, when a project is two weeks behind schedule, the obvious solution may be to just ask the customer if it's okay for the project to be delivered two weeks late. However, that solution could backfire. If the project manager approaches the customer and asks if it's okay for the project to be delivered late, the customer may react negatively, threaten not to do business with his company ever again, and call his boss to complain about the project's being late. The brainstorming technique, discussed later, is very useful in this step to help identify several possible solutions.

5. *Evaluate the alternative solutions*. Once various potential solutions have been identified in step 4, it is necessary to evaluate them. There may be many good, yet different, solutions to the problem. Each viable solution should be evaluated. The question then becomes, "Evaluated against what?" Criteria have to be established. So in this step, the problem-solving team has to first estab-

lish the criteria against which alternative solutions will be evaluated. Once the criteria have been established, the team may want to use an evaluation scorecard similar to the one in Figure 3.3 in Chapter 3. Each criterion can be weighted differently, depending on how important it is. For example, the cost of implementing the solution may be weighted more heavily than the estimated time it will take to implement. Like step 3, this step may take some time if you need to gather data in order to intelligently evaluate the alternative solutions. For example, it may take time to pull together information on the costs of parts or materials needed for some of the solutions, especially if you need to get price estimates from other vendors or suppliers. Each person on the problem-solving team should complete an evaluation scorecard for each of the possible solutions. These scorecards will be used in the next step.

6. *Determine the best solution.* In this step, the evaluation scorecards completed in step 5 by each member of the problem-solving team are used to help determine the best solution. They become a basis for discussion among the team members. The scorecards are not used as the sole mechanism for determining the best solution; they are used as input to the decision-making process. Here is where it becomes important to have a well-rounded team in terms of relevant expertise. The decision as to which is the best solution is based on the knowledge and expertise of the members of the problem-solving team, in conjunction with the evaluation scorecards.

7. *Revise the project plan.* Once the best solution has been selected, it's necessary to prepare a plan for implementing that solution. Specific tasks need to be identified, along with their estimated costs and durations. The persons and resources needed for each task must also be identified. The project team members who will be responsible for implementing the solution should develop this planning information. It must then be incorporated into the overall project plan to determine what impact the solution will have, if any, on other parts of the project. Of specific interest is whether the selected solution will cause other problems. For example, the best solution to the technical problem with the sensor system may be to order a new part from a vendor, but if it takes two months for the vendor to make and ship the part, this solution may cause the whole project to fall behind schedule and jeopardize meeting the required project completion date. If this risk wasn't taken into account in step 5, the problem-solving team may have to re-visit the solution to determine whether it is still the best solution.

8. *Implement the solution.* Once a plan has been developed for implementing the best solution, the appropriate team members should go ahead and perform their respective tasks.

9. *Determine whether the problem has been solved.* Once the solution has been implemented, it's important to determine whether the problem has indeed been solved. Here is where the team goes back to the problem statement in step 1 and compares the results of implementing the solution to the measure of the problem

defined in the problem statement. The team has to ask itself, "Did the selected solution accomplish what we hoped it would? Is the problem solved?" The solution may have only partially solved the problem, or perhaps it didn't solve the problem at all. For example, maybe after the new part ordered for the sensor system was installed, the system still gave erroneous data. If the problem has not been solved, the problem-solving team needs to go back to steps 2 and 3 to see what else could be causing the problem.

Depending on the magnitude and complexity of the problem, the above nine-step problem-solving process can take a few hours or several months. The problem-solving team should include those individuals most familiar with the problem as well as individuals with specific expertise that may be required. Sometimes the individual with the necessary expertise may be an outsider to the project team, such as a consultant who can provide a fresh perspective.

REINFORCE YOUR LEARNING

34. What are the nine steps involved in problem solving?

Brainstorming

Brainstorming is a technique used in problem solving in which all members of a group contribute spontaneous ideas. Before team members select a solution to a problem, they should make sure that they have explored as broad a range of options and ideas as possible. Brainstorming is a way to generate a lot of ideas and have fun doing it. Brainstorming generates excitement, creativity, better solutions, and greater commitment. It is particularly useful in two of the steps in the nine-step approach to problem solving: step 2, identify potential causes of the problem, and step 4, identify possible solutions.

In brainstorming, the *quantity* of ideas generated is more important than the *quality* of the ideas. The objective is for the group to produce as many ideas as possible. Members should be encouraged to come up with novel and unorthodox ideas.

The team sits around a table, with a facilitator at a flip chart or chalk board to record ideas. To start the process, one member states an idea. For example, during a brainstorming session for a project that is two weeks behind schedule, the first member might say, "Work overtime." It would then be the next member's turn to state an idea, such as "Bring in some temporary help." And so forth. The process continues around the table, with each person stating only one idea at a time. Anyone who can't think of an idea when it's his or her turn can simply say "Pass." Some people will come up with ideas that *build* on ideas previously mentioned by others. *Building* involves combining several ideas into one idea or improving on another's idea. As the ideas are given, the facilitator writes them on the flip chart or chalk board. This round-robin process continues until no one can come up with any more ideas or the time limit is up.

Two important rules must be followed for brainstorming to work: *no discussion* and *no judgmental comments*. As soon as a participant has stated his or her idea, it's the next person's turn. Individuals should simply state an idea—not discuss, justify, or try to sell it. Other participants are not allowed to make any comments at all, supportive or judgmental, and no one may ask questions of the person who stated the idea. Obviously such "killer" comments as "That will never work," "That's a stupid idea," or "The boss won't go for that" are not allowed, but participants also must be cautioned not to use body language—raised eyebrows, a cough, a smirk, or a sigh—to send judgmental messages.

Brainstorming can be an effective and fun way of helping a problem-solving team come up with the best possible solution.

TIME MANAGEMENT

People involved in projects are usually very busy working on their assigned tasks, communicating, preparing documents, attending meetings, and traveling. Therefore, good time management is essential for a high-performance project team. Following are some suggestions to help you effectively manage your time:

1. *At the end of each week, identify several (two to five) goals that you want to accomplish the following week.* List the goals in priority order, with the most important (not the most urgent) first. Take into consideration the time you will have available; look at your schedule for the week to see whether you have meetings or other commitments. Don't attempt to create a multiple-page, exhaustive list of all the things you would like to do. Keep this list of goals within sight so you will look at it frequently.
2. *At the end of each day, make a to-do list for the next day.* The items on the daily to-do list must support the achievement of the goals you set for the week. List items in priority order, again with the most important (not necessarily the easiest or the most urgent) first. Before you prepare the to-do list, look at your schedule for the day to see how much time you have available to devote to accomplishing the items on your list. You may have meetings or appointments that will reduce the amount of time available. You should also allow some flextime in your day's schedule to accommodate unexpected things that may come up. Don't make an exhaustive list of everything you'd like to accomplish when there's no time to get it all done—that just causes frustration.

    List only what you can realistically accomplish. Don't get in the habit of feeling that whatever isn't accomplished can just be rolled over to the next day. You will find more items rolled over than accomplished!

    It's important to write out the to-do list, not just keep it in your head. Writing it out builds commitment to doing it.
3. *Read the daily to-do list first thing in the morning, and keep it in sight all day.* Set everything else aside, and start working on the first item. Focus and self-discipline are extremely important. Don't divert your attention to less important items that may be less chal-

lenging, such as reading your mail or filing. As you complete an item, cross it off the list; this will provide a sense of accomplishment. Then start right in on the next item. Again, don't let yourself get sidetracked into working on less important items in between completing the items on your list.

4. *Control interruptions.* Don't let phone calls, email messages, or walk-in visitors divert you from working on the items on your to-do list. You may want to set aside a block of time each day to return and make phone calls and email rather than letting them interrupt your work throughout the day. There may be times when you want to close your door so that people will know not to interrupt you. When you are working on a particular item on your to-do list, clear away other paperwork to eliminate the temptation to reach over and start working on something else.

5. *Learn to say no.* Don't let yourself get drawn into activities that will consume your time but not contribute to accomplishing your goals. You might have to turn down invitations to participate in meetings or trips, serve on committees, or review documents. You may have to cut short hallway conversations. Learn to say no, or you'll overcommit yourself and end up a very busy person without accomplishing your goals.

REINFORCE YOUR LEARNING
36. What are some things you can do to manage your time effectively?

6. *Make effective use of waiting time.* For example, always carry reading material with you in case you get stuck in an airport, a traffic jam, or a dentist's office.

7. *Try to handle most paperwork only once.* Go through your incoming mail or email at the end of the day so that it won't divert you from working on your day's to-do list. There may be something in your mail that will lead you to add an item to the to-do list you prepare for the next day. When going through your mail, take action on each document while you are holding or reading it:
   - If it's junk mail, throw it out or delete it without reading it.
   - If you can throw it out or delete it after you read it, do so; file it only if you can't get it somewhere else if you need it.
   - If a response is required, either hand-write a response on the document and return it to the originator or type a brief email reply.
   - If the document will require an extended period of time to read, either incorporate time to read it on one of your future to-do lists (if the item could make an important contribution to your weekly goals) or put it in your briefcase so that you can read it when you're stuck waiting somewhere (see item 6 above).

8. *Reward yourself at the end of the week if you accomplished all your goals.* Make sure you're honest with yourself. Reward yourself for accomplishing all your goals, not for working hard and being busy but not accomplishing your goals. In your mind, the reward must be an incentive and payoff tied directly to accomplishing your goals. If you don't accomplish your weekly goals, you should not reward yourself. Otherwise, the reward will be meaningless and will not constitute an incentive to accomplish the goals.

SUMMARY

A team is a group of individuals working interdependently to achieve a common goal. Teamwork is the cooperative effort by members of a team to achieve that common goal. The effectiveness—or lack thereof—of the project team can make the difference between project success and project failure.

Project teams evolve through various stages of development. Forming, the initial stage of the team development process, involves the transition from individual to team member. In this stage, individuals on the team begin to get acquainted. During the storming stage, conflict emerges and tension increases. Motivation and morale are low in this stage. Members may even resist team formation. However, after struggling through the storming stage, the team moves into the norming stage of development. Relationships among team members and between the team and the project manager have become settled, and interpersonal conflicts have been resolved for the most part. The fourth and final stage of team development and growth is the performing stage. In this stage, the team is highly committed and eager to achieve the project objective. The members feel a sense of unity.

Characteristics often associated with effective project teams include a clear understanding of the project objective, clear expectations of each person's role and responsibilities, a results orientation, a high degree of cooperation and collaboration, and a high level of trust. Barriers to team effectiveness include unclear goals, unclear definition of roles and responsibilities, lack of project structure, lack of commitment, poor communication, poor leadership, turnover of project team members, and dysfunctional behavior.

Team building—developing a group of individuals to accomplish the project objective—is an ongoing process. It is the responsibility of both the project manager and the project team. Socializing among team members supports team building. To facilitate socializing, team members can request that they be physically located in one office area for the duration of the project and they can participate in social events.

Conflict on projects is inevitable. During a project, conflict can emerge from a variety of situations. It can involve members of the project team, the project manager, and even the customer. Sources of potential conflict on projects include differences of opinion on how the work should be done, how much work should be done, at what level of quality the work should be done, who should be assigned to work on which tasks, the sequence in which the work should be done, how long the work should take, and how much the work should cost. Conflict can also arise because of prejudices or differences in individuals' values and attitudes.

Conflict is not just for the project manager to handle and resolve; conflict among team members should be handled by the individuals involved. Handled properly, conflict can be beneficial because it causes problems to surface and be addressed.

It is unusual for a team to complete a project without encountering some problems along the way. A good nine-step problem-solving approach is to develop a problem statement, identify potential causes of the problem, gather data and verify the most likely causes, identify possible solutions, evaluate the alternative solutions, determine the best solution, revise the project plan, implement the solution, and determine whether the problem has been solved. Brainstorming is a technique used in problem solving in which all members of a group contribute spontaneous ideas. In brainstorming, the quantity of ideas generated is more important than the quality of the ideas.

Good time management is essential for a high-performance project team. To effectively manage their time, team members should identify weekly goals, make a to-do list for each day, focus on accomplishing the daily to-do list, control interruptions, learn to say no to activities that don't move them closer to their goals, make effective use of waiting time, handle paperwork only once, and reward themselves for accomplishing their goals.

QUESTIONS

1. Discuss the stages of team development. Address the process, problems, and level of productivity of each.
2. What are some characteristics associated with effective project teams? Can the same be said for an effective couple, orchestra, or professional sports team? Why or why not?
3. What are some common barriers to team effectiveness? Think of a team project that you have worked on. Discuss any barriers to success.
4. Why is it said that there is no *I* in TEAM? Do you agree or disagree? Why?
5. When working on a class project, how can you be an effective team member?
6. Describe three activities that facilitate the process of team building. Must the project manager initiate all of these?
7. Discuss some types of conflict that might arise during a project. Describe two situations in which you have experienced these types of conflict.
8. Describe the methods for handling conflict on a project. How was the conflict handled in the two situations you described in your answer to question 7?
9. The manager at a local bank noticed that after a new information system was installed at the bank, some of the customer transactions were not getting posted. The manager knew that this problem could lead to serious financial difficulties as well as unhappy customers. Describe how she could apply the nine-step problem-solving process described in the chapter to solve the problem.
10. With a friend, conduct a brainstorming session to name as many as you can of the parts of the body spelled with only three letters.
11. How can people more effectively manage their time? Which of these suggestions do you currently practice?

12. For the next week, attempt to manage your time better. Heed all the advice given in the book. At the end of the week, write a summary of your experience.

WORLD WIDE WEB EXERCISES

If you have difficulty accessing any of the Web addresses listed here, you can find these exercises (with up-to-date addresses) on the home page of Dr. James P. Clements, co-author of this book, at

www.towson.edu/~clements

1. Check out the Web site for the Project Manager's Palette at

www.4pm.com/frmain.html

2. Visit their discussion forum called PMChat.
3. Download (for free) or read on line chapters from some of their books.
4. Read at least one issue of PMtalk, the free newsletter they produce twice a month. You can link to it from their home page or go directly to

www.4pm.com/discussion.html

You might want to sign up to receive it.
5. View and describe their excellent on-line slide show about establishing measures of project success. You can link to it from their home page or go directly to

www.4pm.com/demo/classroom.htm

6. Read and print out their presentation on effective ways to criticize a project team member's performance. You can link to it from their home page or go directly to

www.4pm.com/articles/critic.html

7. Read their "Ongoing Saga of the Project from Hell." You can reach it from their home page or go directly to

www.4pm.com/articles/hell.html

Provide a one-page summary, with comments, of this project.
8. Explore some of the other links from Project Manager's Palette.

CASE STUDY

RD Processing, Inc. is a firm that provides data processing services to other local businesses. It has been in business twenty years now and has ninety employees. Sixty employees are located in the Big Tower building, in an office park on the outskirts of a major city. Forty of these people work on the fifth floor, where the company has been renting space for the past twelve years; the other twenty are on the ninth floor, where the firm was able to rent additional space as it grew. The people from these two areas see one another in the building cafeteria, but don't really know one another well. Six months ago RD Processing acquired DataHelps, a similar firm, when that firm's owner decided to retire. DataHelps has been in business ten years, has thirty employees, and is located on the other side of the city in the Green Valley professional building.

Big Tower II, a new office building, was recently completed next to the original Big Tower building. Maria Alomar, owner of RD Processing, has an option to rent an entire floor in Big Tower II. This would be enough space to consolidate all ninety employees in one space and still leave some room for growth.

Maria has established a project team of three people, one from each of the current spaces, to come up with a proposed layout for the new building space. Christina Lin, who works on the fifth floor, is a supervisor and has been with the firm eighteen years. Jessica Tarasco, who works on the ninth floor, is the firm's computer specialist and has been with the company five years. Sharon Nesbitt, a data processing clerk located in the Green Valley professional building, has worked for DataHelps since it started ten years ago.

The project team is having its first meeting in the company's conference room on the fifth floor of the Big Tower building. Sharon arrives late. It's only her second visit to the Big Tower building, and traffic was heavier than she expected. Christina speaks first. "I pretty much know the work flow and the bottlenecks and have a pretty good idea of how we should lay out the new office space we'll be moving into."

"Are we all really going to move into the new space?" asks Sharon.

"Yes," responds Christina abruptly.

Jessica speaks up. "One of my neighbors told me that his company went through a similar consolidation, and they surveyed all the employees to get their input. Maybe we should do something like that."

"We don't need to waste time doing that," states Christina. "I've been here long enough to know what needs to be done."

"I guess you're right," says Jessica.

Christina continues, "Now let's get to work. I suggest . . . "

Sharon interrupts. "Consolidation? Did I hear you say consolidation? Does that mean that we're going to be downsizing? Is *that* what this is all about? I heard rumors about layoffs when RD Processing acquired DataHelps."

"That's ridiculous!" retorts Christina.

"Layoffs? Really?" queries Jessica. "They'll never lay me off, not with my computer skills. They need me too much. Besides, I could get another job in a minute."

"We're getting off the topic," interjects Christina. "Can we get to work, or we'll be here all day."

"Wait a minute," interrupts Sharon again. "We've got some bigger issues here than some dumb office layout! I'm telling you, none of the people in the Green Valley building want to move to the new building. We like it where we are. We can walk to the shopping mall at lunch, and employees have their kids in the day care center right down the street. And we're going to have to drive an extra thirty minutes to and from work every day. The people might not be able to get to the day care center before it closes at 6 o'clock. I think we have a lot of other problems to solve before we worry about an office layout. Aren't there any alternatives?"

"I'm open," says Jessica.

Christina sighs, looks down, and says matter of factly, "You're making this more complicated than it needs to be. Now, can we please get to the office layout? Isn't that what we're supposed to be doing?"

Case Questions

1. Why is Maria considering moving to a new office building?
2. What are some of the advantages and disadvantages of the move?
3. Are Christina, Jessica, and Sharon functioning effectively as a team? Why or why not?
4. What should Christina, Jessica, and Sharon have done differently?
5. Give some suggestions for how this team can function more effectively.

Group Activity

Have an open discussion among the course participants regarding the following questions:

- How should the team proceed?
- What could have been done to prevent this situation?
- How could each of the team members have handled the situation better?

7

Types of Project Organizations

In Search of Structural Excellence

Differences in organizational goals, resources, and environments make it difficult to identify the single ideal structure for all organizations. In fact, organizations may not even have a common ideal structure. Dissimilarities in their strategy, size, technology, environment, industry type, stage of development, and current organizational trend may call for different structures.

The three most common structures are discussed in detail in this chapter. The article cited below discusses the structure followed by Procter and Gamble.

Source: A. Martinsons, "In Search of Structural Excellence," *Leadership & Organization Development Journal,* March 1994.

Matrix Management

According to Richard E. Anderson, the matrix approach to corporate organization is making a strong comeback in the 1990s. In the 1970s, matrix management was in vogue. Dow Corning's matrix organization was championed by its chairman, William C. Gogin, in a classic *Harvard Business Review* article in 1974. Companies such as GE, Xerox, Texas Instruments, TRW, Digital Equipment Corporation, and Citibank employed the structure. After a few years of success, however, the matrix organization faded from view, and numerous critics of this structure began to emerge.

Now it appears as though the structure, with a few modifications, is becoming popular again. Recent studies show that team members often favor the matrix management approach over more traditional approaches; they report that it leads to more successful relationships and projects. In addition, Anderson stresses that matrix organizational structures can aid decentralization, employee empowerment, and customer service initiatives and help deliver results more effectively.

Source: R. Anderson, "Matrix Redux," *Business Horizons,* November/December 1994; W. C. Gogin, "How the Multidimensional Structure Works at Dow Corning," *Harvard Business Review,* January/February 1974.

Although there are various ways in which people can be organized to work on projects, the most common types of organization structures are functional, project, and matrix. The examples here relate to industrial companies; however, the concepts are applicable to other sectors such as service businesses and not-for-profit organizations (for example, educational institutions and hospitals). You will become familiar with

- the characteristics of the three types of organization structures
- the advantages and disadvantages of each

FUNCTIONAL-TYPE ORGANIZATION

REINFORCE YOUR LEARNING

1. *The functional organization emphasizes the importance of the contribution of each functional component's* _____ *to the company's products.*

Figure 7.1 represents a **functional organization structure** for an industrial business that sells standard electronics products. Functional organization structures are typically used in businesses that primarily sell and produce standard products and seldom conduct external projects. For example, a company that manufactures and sells video recorders and players may have a functional organization structure. In the functional organization structure, groups consist of individuals who perform the same function, such as engineering or manufacturing, or have the same expertise or skills, such as electronics engineering or testing. Each functional group, or component, concentrates on performing its own activities in support of the company's business mission. The focus is on the technical excellence and cost competitiveness of the company's products, as well as the importance of the contribution of each functional component's expertise to the company's products.

A company with a functional structure may periodically undertake projects, but these are typically in-house projects rather than projects for external customers. Projects in a functional-type organization might involve developing new products, designing a company information system, redesigning the office floor plan, or updating the company policy and procedures manual. For such projects, a *multifunctional*

FIGURE 7.1   Functional Organization Structure

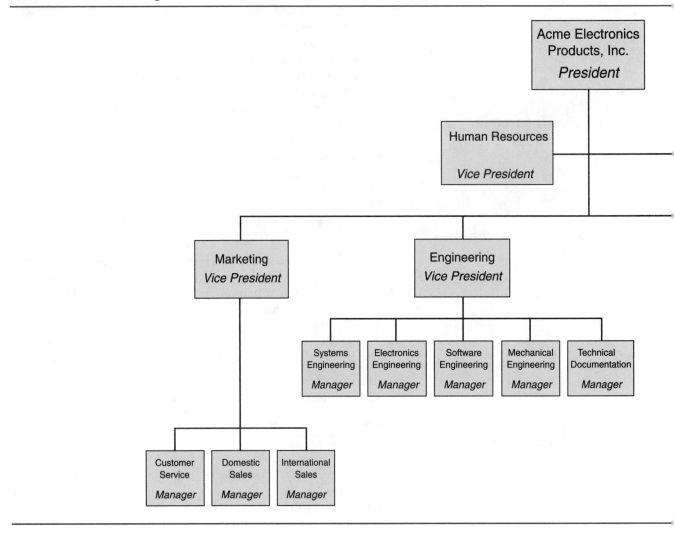

project team or *task force* is formed, with members selected by company management from the appropriate subfunctions in marketing, engineering, manufacturing, and procurement. Team members may be assigned to the project either full-time or part-time, for a part of the project or for the entire project duration. In most cases, however, individuals continue to perform their regular functional jobs while they serve part-time on the project task force. One of the team members—or possibly one of the functional vice presidents—is designated as the project leader or manager.

In a functional-type organization, the project manager does not have complete authority over the project team, since administratively the members still work for their respective functional managers. And because they view their contribution to the project in terms of their technical expertise, their allegiance remains to their functional managers. If there is conflict among the team members, it usually works

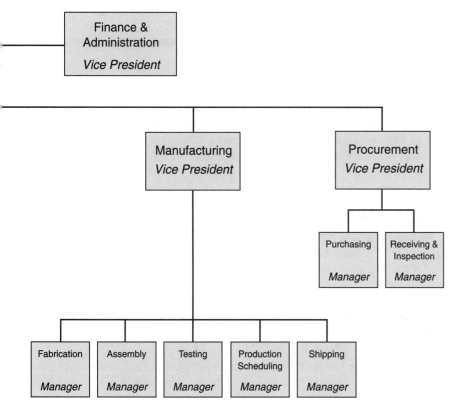

its way through the organization hierarchy to be resolved, slowing down the project effort. On the other hand, if the company president does give the project manager the authority to make decisions when there is disagreement among team members, decisions might reflect the interests of the project manager's own functional component rather than the best interests of the overall project. For example, take the situation in which there is disagreement about the design of a new product and the project manager, who is from the engineering function, makes a decision that reduces the engineering design cost of the product but increases the manufacturing cost. In reporting project progress to the company president, the project manager then makes some biased comments regarding the viewpoints of team members from other functional components, such as, "If manufacturing were more willing to consider other production methods, they could make the product for a lower cost. Engineering has already reduced its design costs." Such a situation could require the company president to get drawn into handling the conflict.

The functional organization structure can be appropriate for internal company projects. However, since projects are not a part of the normal routine, it's necessary to establish a clear understanding of the role and responsibilities of each person assigned to the project task force. If the project manager does not have full authority for project decisions, then she or he must rely on leadership and persuasion skills to build consensus, handle conflict, and unify the task force members to accomplish the project objective. The project manager also needs to take the time to regularly update the other functional managers in the company on the status of the project and thank them for the support of their people assigned to the task force.

There may be situations in which a task force is assigned to work on a project that is strictly within a particular functional component. For example, the manager of technical documentation may form a task force of editors and documentation specialists to develop common standards for all technical documents. In such a case, the particular functional manager has full authority over the project, and conflict can be handled more quickly than when it arises within a multifunctional project team.

Companies with functional organization structures seldom perform projects involving external customers, as such organizations do not have project managers designated to manage customer-funded projects. Rather, functional-type organizations concentrate on producing their products and selling them to various customers.

REINFORCE YOUR LEARNING

3. *A company with a functional structure may periodically form project task forces to work on _____ projects, but will seldom perform projects involving _____ customers.*

PROJECT-TYPE ORGANIZATION

Figure 7.2 illustrates a **project organization structure** for a business that sells rapid transit projects to cities and counties. An average customer order will be for a multimillion-dollar project that will require several years for engineering, manufacturing, and installation. This company is in the projects business; it does not produce standard products. It's working on multiple projects at any one time, at various stages of completion. As projects wind down and are completed, the company hopes to get contracts for new projects. People are hired to work on a specific project; they may be reassigned from a project just completed if they have the appropriate expertise. Each project team is dedicated to only one project. When their project is completed, unless team members are assigned to another project they might be laid off.

In the project-type organization, each project is operated like a mini-company. All the resources needed to accomplish each project are assigned full-time to work on that project. A full-time project manager has complete project and administrative authority over the project team. (In the functional-type organization, the project manager may have project authority, but the functional managers retain administrative and technical authority over his or her people who are assigned to the team.) The project-type organization is well positioned

FIGURE 7.2   Project Organization Structure

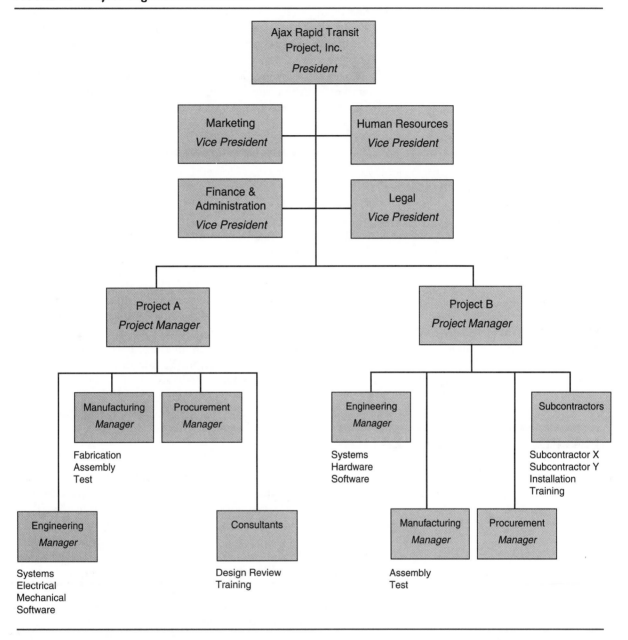

REINFORCE YOUR LEARNING

4. In a project-type organization, all resources are assigned _____-time to work on a particular project. The project manager has complete _____ and _____ authority over the project team.

to be highly responsive to the project objective and customer needs because each project team is strictly dedicated to only one project.

A project-type organization can be cost-inefficient both for individual projects and for the company. Each project must pay the salaries of its dedicated project team, even during parts of the project when they are not busy. For example, if a delay in one part of the project leaves some resources with no work to do for several weeks, project funds must cover these costs. If the amount of unapplied time becomes excessive, the project can become unprofitable and drain the profits from other projects. From a company-wide viewpoint, a project-type organization can be cost-inefficient because of the duplication of resources or tasks on several concurrent projects. Because resources are not shared, they may not be diverted to a similar concurrent project even when they are not busy on or being used for the project to which they are dedicated. Also, there is little opportunity for members of different project teams to share knowledge or technical expertise, since each project team tends to be isolated and focused strictly on its own project. However, there may be some company-wide support functions that serve all the projects. Figure 7.2 shows, for example, that the human resources function serves all projects, since it wouldn't make sense for each project to hire its own human resources staff. And, by having a common human resources functional component, the company is likely to have consistent human resources policies and employee benefits.

In a project-type organization, detailed and accurate planning and an effective control system are required to assure optimum utilization of the project resources in successfully completing the project within budget.

Project organization structures are found primarily in companies that are involved in very large projects. Such projects can be of high (multimillion) dollar value and long (several years) duration. Project organization structures are prevalent in the construction and aerospace industries. They are also used in the nonbusiness environment, such as for a volunteer-managed fund-raising campaign, town centennial celebration, class reunion, or variety show.

REINFORCE YOUR LEARNING

5. *A project-type organization can be cost-_____.*

REINFORCE YOUR LEARNING

6. *Project organization structures are found primarily in companies that are involved in very _____ projects.*

MATRIX-TYPE ORGANIZATION

Figure 7.3 shows a **matrix organization structure** for a business that sells custom computer-based automation systems. Each customer order is for a unique system. Some systems sell for as little as $50,000 and take four to six months to design and produce, whereas others cost several million dollars and take up to three years to complete. Like Ajax Rapid Transit Project, Inc. in Figure 7.2, Specialized Computer Systems, Inc. is in the projects business; however, its business involves a greater number of smaller-sized projects. It's working on multiple projects at any one time, and these projects vary in size and complexity. Projects are continually being completed and started.

The matrix-type organization is kind of a hybrid—a mix of both the functional and project organization structures. It provides the project and customer focus of the project structure, but it retains the functional expertise of the functional structure. The project and functional components of the matrix structure each have their responsibilities in contributing jointly to the success of each project and the company. The project manager is responsible for the project results, while the functional managers are responsible for providing the resources needed to achieve the results.

The matrix-type organization provides for effective utilization of company resources. The functional components (systems engineer-

REINFORCE YOUR LEARNING

7. *The matrix organization structure provides the project and customer focus of the _____ structure, but it retains the functional expertise of the _____ structure.*

ing, testing, and so forth), home of the technical staff, provide a pool of expertise to support ongoing projects.

Project managers come under the projects component of the organization. When the company receives an order for a new system, the vice president of projects assigns a project manager to the project. A small project may be assigned to a project manager who is already managing several other small projects. A large project may be assigned a full-time project manager.

The project manager then meets with the appropriate functional managers to negotiate the assignment of various individuals from the functional components to work on the project. These individuals are assigned to the project for the length of time they are needed. Some individuals may be assigned to the project full-time, while others may be assigned only part-time. Some people may be assigned to a project for its entire duration; others may work on only one part of the project or even off and on throughout the project, depending on when their expertise is needed and how many of their hours the project budget can support. In a matrix-type organization, it's not unusual for an individual from a functional component to be assigned part-time to several concurrent projects. Figure 7.3 shows, for example, that Jack, Cathy, Rose, Chris, and Katie are all working part-time on two projects. Some projects do not require certain types of expertise. For example, projects A and C do not require any mechanical engineering activity, and project A does not include any training. Thus, sharing of individuals' time among several projects results in effective utilization of resources and minimizes overall costs for each project and for the entire company.

As projects or particular assignments are completed, available individuals are assigned to new projects. The objective is to maximize the number of functional person-hours applied to work on projects (within the constraints of individual project budgets) and minimize the unapplied time (since the salary costs for unapplied time have to be absorbed by the company, reducing overall company profitability). Of course, unapplied time must be provided for vacations, holidays, illness, training activities, and work on proposals for new projects.

It is important to note that if the total amount of unapplied time of the functional staff is high, the company may be unprofitable even though each project is completed within its budgeted hours. This will happen if the company is not working on enough projects to utilize the people in some of the functional components. The company always needs to have new projects coming in as other projects are completed, in order to maintain a high applied-time rate for the functional staff. If the amount of unapplied time is excessive, individuals may have to be laid off. The company needs to be continually on the lookout for opportunities to develop projects for new or past customers or to develop proposals in response to Requests for Proposal, as discussed in Chapter 3.

The matrix-type organization provides opportunities for people in the functional components to pursue career development through assignment to various types of projects. As they broaden their experience, individuals become more valuable for future assignments and

FIGURE 7.3   Matrix Organization Structure

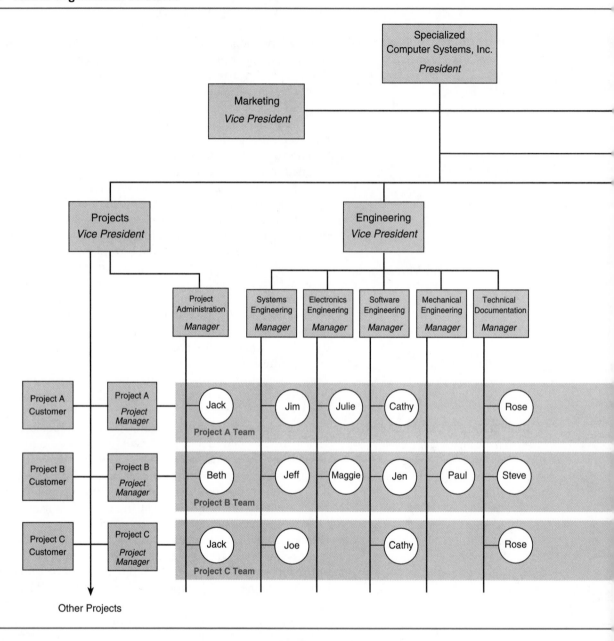

enhance their eligibility for higher-level positions within the company. As each individual in a particular functional component develops a broad base of experience, the functional manager gains greater flexibility to assign individuals to different kinds of projects.

All of the individuals assigned to a given project constitute the project team, under the leadership of a project manager who integrates and unifies their efforts. Individuals assigned to several small projects will be members of several different project teams. Each member of a project team has a dual reporting relationship; in a sense, each mem-

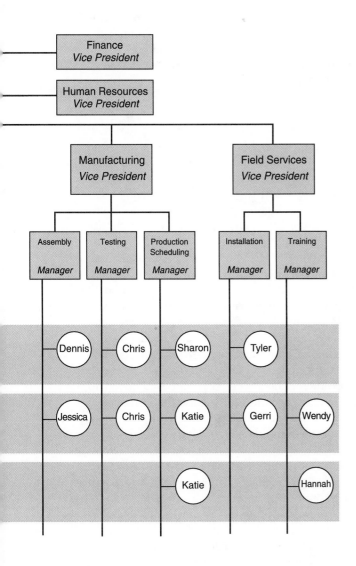

ber has two managers—a (temporary) project manager and a (permanent) functional manager. For a person assigned to several concurrent projects, changing work priorities can cause conflict and anxiety.

It's critical to specify to whom the team member reports and for what responsibilities or tasks. Therefore, it's important that the project management responsibilities and the functional management responsibilities be delineated in a matrix-type organization.

In the matrix organization structure, the *project manager* is the intermediary between the company and the customer. The project

REINFORCE YOUR LEARNING

11. *In a matrix organization, the project manager defines _____ has to be done, by _____, and for how much _____ to meet the project _____ and satisfy the customer.*

manager defines what has to be done (work scope), by when (schedule), and for how much money (budget) to meet the project objective and satisfy the customer. She or he is responsible for leading the development of the project plan, establishing the project schedule and budget, and allocating specific tasks and budgets to the various functional components of the company organization. Throughout the project, the project manager is responsible both for controlling the performance of the work within the project schedule and budget and for reporting project performance to the customer and to the company's upper management. A project administrator may be assigned to each project to support the project manager and project team in planning, controlling, and reporting.

REINFORCE YOUR LEARNING

12. *In a matrix organization, each functional manager is responsible for _____ the work will be accomplished and _____ will do each task.*

Each functional manager in a matrix organization structure is responsible for how the assigned work tasks will be accomplished and who (which specific people) will do each task. The functional manager of each organization component provides technical guidance and leadership to the individuals assigned to projects. He or she is also responsible for ensuring that all tasks assigned to that functional component are completed in accordance with the project's technical requirements, within the assigned budget, and on schedule.

In a multiple-project environment, each functional manager can have many individuals assigned to parts of many concurrent projects, particularly if projects are too small to require full-time people or if projects need certain expertise for only brief periods. The functional manager must continually monitor the assignments of the individuals within her or his functional component and make any needed reallocations in response to changing conditions on various projects, such as schedule delays or customer changes. For example, if a project is delayed because the customer is taking longer than anticipated to review and approve engineering drawings or because the shipment of a piece of equipment from a vendor is taking longer than estimated, individuals assigned to the project should be temporarily reassigned to other projects, if possible. In a situation in which a project is behind schedule and in jeopardy of not being completed by the customer's required due date, the functional manager might temporarily assign people from projects that are not in jeopardy.

REINFORCE YOUR LEARNING

13. *The matrix organization structure allows for fast response upon problem identification because it has both a _____ and a _____ path for the flow of _____.*

The matrix-type organization provides a checks–and–balances environment. The fact that potential problems can be identified through both its project and its functional structure reduces the likelihood that problems will be suppressed beyond the point where they can be corrected without jeopardizing the success of the project. The matrix organization structure allows for fast response upon problem identification because it has both a horizontal (project) and a vertical (functional) path for the flow of information.

REINFORCE YOUR LEARNING

14. *List three common types of structures that can be used to organize people to work on projects.*

The vice president of projects, to whom the project managers report, plays an important role in the matrix structure (see Figure 7.3). This individual can resolve priority conflicts between two or more projects within the organization. For example, if two projects are competing to use a particular resource (a technical specialist, maybe, or a piece of test equipment) the vice president of projects can decide the priority in terms of least overall risk to the company and customer relationships (especially if the company has other current or proposed projects for a given customer). Through the project administration function, the vice president of projects can establish consistent procedures for managing projects, such as procedures for planning and budgeting, data gathering, using information systems, and project reporting.

ADVANTAGES AND DISADVANTAGES

The previous sections discussed the characteristics of the functional-, project-, and matrix-type organizations. Table 7.1 lists some of the more significant advantages and disadvantages that are particular to each of the three organization structures.

Functional Organization Structure

By bringing specialists from the same discipline together in the same organizational unit, a functional-type organization reduces duplication and overlap of activities. It provides the benefits associated with specialization: an environment in which individuals can share and keep up with the knowledge and skills of their particular discipline. For example, all individuals in a computer engineering unit can share software and discuss approaches to developing computer systems.

Functional-type organizations can be insular, though, with each functional component concerned about only its own performance. Teamwork with other functions is not emphasized, and there is little cross-fertilization of ideas among functions. Project focus is not emphasized either, and decisions may be parochial rather than in the best interests of the overall project. The hierarchical structure causes communication, problem resolution, and decision making to be slow. Take the case in which there is a problem with product failures. Engineering thinks it's because manufacturing is not producing the product properly. Manufacturing claims it's because engineering didn't design it properly or because there were errors in the engineering drawings provided to manufacturing. Such a problem could work its way up and down through the chain of command, and its resolution may rest with the company president. The functional-type organization lacks customer focus. There is a stronger allegiance to the function than to the project or the customer.

REINFORCE YOUR LEARNING

15. What are some advantages and disadvantages of the functional organization structure?

Project Organization Structure

In a project-type organization, all the individuals on the project team work for the project manager. Therefore, she or he has full control over the resources, including authority over how the work gets done and by whom. There is no conflict with other projects over priorities or resources, since all the resources for a project are totally dedicated to that project. The project organization is highly responsive to the customer. For example, if the customer makes changes to the project work scope, the project manager has the authority to immediately reassign resources to accommodate the changes.

TABLE 7.1   Advantages and Disadvantages of Organization Structures

	Advantages	Disadvantages
Functional Structure	• No duplication of activities • Functional excellence	• Insularity • Slow response time • Lack of customer focus
Project Structure	• Control over resources • Responsiveness to customers	• Cost-inefficiency • Low level of knowledge transfer among projects
Matrix Structure	• Efficient utilization of resources • Functional expertise available to all projects • Increased learning and knowledge transfer • Improved communication • Customer focus	• Dual reporting relationships • Need for balance of power

REINFORCE YOUR LEARNING
16. *What are some advantages and disadvantages of the project organization structure?*

The project organization structure can be cost-inefficient because of underutilization of resources. With individuals assigned full-time to the project, there may be times when things are slow and team members are not working at a high level of productivity. When things are slow, individuals have a tendency to stretch out their work to fill up the time available. If there's nothing else to work on, a one-week task can stretch out to two or three weeks, causing project costs to increase. Also, if some people do not have any tasks to do for temporary periods, their unapplied time is still a cost to the company and erodes the company's profitability. Another factor increasing cost-inefficiency is the potential for duplication of activities on several concurrent projects. For example, if project teams ordered their materials and supplies jointly instead of independently, they could probably get better prices from vendors.

In the project organization structure, there is a low level of knowledge transfer among projects. Individuals are dedicated to working on one project. They do not have a functional "home" to be a source of shared functional expertise and knowledge. Also, at the end of a project, people may be laid off if there is not a new project to which they can be assigned. In such cases, what they learned on the project is lost to the company. In a project-type organization, team members experience high anxiety about reassignment as their project nears completion, especially since they don't have a functional home to which they can return.

Matrix Organization Structure

The matrix organization structure tries to capitalize on the advantages of both the functional and project structures while overcoming their disadvantages. The matrix structure allows efficient utilization of resources by having individuals from various functions assigned to work part-time, if necessary, on specific projects or by having them assigned for only a limited duration to certain projects. Furthermore, it's not unusual for individuals in a specific function to be working on two or more projects concurrently. Because they have a functional home, individuals can be moved among projects as necessary in order to accommodate any project changes. For example, if one project is delayed, the functional manager can deploy some of its team members to other projects rather than have their unapplied time increase costs to the company.

The matrix structure provides a core of functional expertise that is available to all projects, and thus this expertise is better utilized. Individuals in a functional component have a common discipline and can collaborate with and learn from one another. This functional component provides a home for individuals at the end of a project while they are waiting to be assigned to other projects. Their knowledge stays with the company, ready to be used on future projects. As people work on more and various projects, they experience greater learning and growth, and their knowledge and skills are transferred from project to project.

The matrix structure also facilitates improved communication, allowing for more timely problem identification and conflict resolution. Project team members have two channels through which to send up a warning about a potential problem—they can inform the project manager and the functional manager. These dual communication paths increase the chances that problems will be identified rather than suppressed.

Finally, the matrix organization is customer focused. The project manager is the designated focal point for communication with the customer, and the functional units are set up to support projects.

REINFORCE YOUR LEARNING

17. What are some advantages and disadvantages of the matrix organization structure?

Members of a project team in a matrix organization structure have a dual reporting relationship: Temporarily they report to a project manager, while administratively they still report to their functional manager. If an individual is assigned to work on several projects, she or he can have several managers. This can cause anxiety and conflict over work priorities. These individuals have a permanent allegiance to their functional home, which is strained by their required allegiance to the project team. A company that uses a matrix organization structure must establish operating guidelines to assure a proper balance of power between project managers and functional managers. Conflicts will arise between project managers and functional managers regarding priorities, the assignment of specific individuals to projects, technical approaches to the work, and changes to projects. If there is an imbalance of power, such conflicts may not be resolved in a manner that will be in the best interests of either the customer or the company.

SUMMARY

The three most common structures used to organize people to work on projects are functional, project, and matrix. These structures are applicable to a large majority of businesses and not-for-profit organizations.

The functional organization structure is typically used in businesses that primarily sell and produce standard products and seldom conduct external projects. The focus is on the technical excellence and cost competitiveness of the company's products, as well as the importance of each functional component's contribution of expertise to the company's products. For projects, a multifunctional project team or task force is formed, with members selected from the appropriate subfunctions. In this structure, the project manager does not have complete authority over the project team, since administratively the members still work for their respective functional managers. If there is conflict among the team members, it usually works its way through the organization hierarchy to be resolved. A company with a functional organization structure may periodically form project task forces to work on internal projects, but will seldom perform projects involving external customers.

The project organization structure is used by companies that are working on multiple projects at any one time and do not produce standard products. People are hired to work on a specific project, and each project team is dedicated to only one project. When the project is completed, team members may be assigned to another project if they have the appropriate expertise. A full-time project manager has complete project and administrative authority over the project team. A project-type organization is well positioned to be highly responsive to the project objective and customer needs because each project team is strictly dedicated to only one project. From a company-wide viewpoint, a project-type organization can be cost-inefficient because of the duplication of resources or tasks on several concurrent projects. Also, there is little opportunity for members of different project teams to share knowledge or technical expertise. Project organization structures are found primarily in companies that are involved in very large projects with high dollar values and long durations.

The matrix-type organization is kind of a hybrid—a mix of both the functional and project organization structures. It's appropriate for companies that are working on multiple projects at any one time and projects that vary in size and complexity. It provides the project and customer focus of the project structure, but it retains the functional expertise of the functional structure. The project and functional components of the matrix structure each have their responsibilities in contributing jointly to the success of each project and the company. In addition, the matrix-type organization provides for effective utilization of company resources. The sharing of individuals' time among several projects results in effective utilization of resources and minimizes overall costs for each project and for the entire company. All of the individuals assigned to a given project constitute the project team, under the leadership of a project manager who integrates and unifies their efforts.

In the matrix structure, the project manager is the intermediary between the company and the customer. The project manager defines what has to be done, by when, and for how much money to meet the project objective and satisfy the customer. The project manager is responsible for leading the development of the project plan, establishing the project schedule and budget, and allocating specific tasks and budgets to various functional components of the company organization. Each functional manager is responsible for how the assigned work tasks will be accomplished and who will do each task.

The advantages of a functional organization structure are no duplication of activities and functional excellence. Disadvantages include insularity, slow response time, and lack of customer focus. The project organization structure has control over resources and responsiveness to customers as advantages. Cost-inefficiency and low level of knowledge transfer among projects are its disadvantages. The advantages of a matrix organization structure include efficient utilization of resources, functional expertise available to all projects, increased learning and knowledge transfer, improved communication, and customer focus. Its disadvantages are the dual reporting relationships and the need for a balance of power.

QUESTIONS

1. Describe what a functional-type organization is. Make sure you discuss the advantages and disadvantages of this structure.
2. Describe what a project-type organization is. Make sure you discuss the advantages and disadvantages of this structure.
3. Describe what a matrix-type organization is. Make sure you discuss the advantages and disadvantages of this structure.
4. Which type of organization structure is often used by companies that produce standard products? Why?
5. Discuss some of the problems that might be encountered when a functional-type organization develops new products.
6. Why is a project-type organization considered to be like a mini-company?
7. Why is a project-type organization sometimes considered to be expensive?
8. Which organization structure is considered to be a hybrid? How so?
9. What makes a matrix organization structure so effective?
10. How does a matrix-type organization provide for career development?
11. What are the responsibilities of the project manager in a matrix-type organization?
12. What are the responsibilities of the functional manager in a matrix-type organization?
13. What are the responsibilities of the vice president of projects in a matrix-type organization?

WORLD WIDE WEB EXERCISES

If you have difficulty accessing any of the Web addresses listed here, you can find these exercises (with up-to-date addresses) on the home page of Dr. James P. Clements, co-author of this book, at

www.towson.edu/~clements

1. There is a popular project management association in the United Kingdom called the Association for Project Management (APM), which publishes a magazine called *Project*. Visit their Web site at

www.asterisk.co.uk/project/Pmgen.html

2. Obtain information about the Association for Project Management—its aims and objectives, structure, branches, and so forth— from their home page.
3. View some selected features from *Project*. You can link to it from the APM's home page or go directly to

www.asterisk.co.uk/project/Pmproj.html

4. Do any of these articles relate to project organizations? If so, describe how.
5. Use some of the links provided to visit other project management sites. Describe what you find.

CASE STUDY

Multi Projects, Inc. is a well-established consulting firm with 400 employees. It has many projects going on at the same time for various clients. It has a good reputation, and nearly 30 percent of its business is from previous clients. It targets growing companies for future business and has been successful in this area, too. Because of the growth, things have been quite hectic, with employees trying to keep up with the work, keep old clients satisfied, and bend over backward to accommodate new clients. Multi Projects has been hiring new employees—in fact, it has grown from 300 to 400 employees over the past two years.

Multi Projects has a matrix organization structure. As new projects come in, a project manager is assigned. One project manager may be assigned to several projects at one time, depending on the sizes of the projects. Projects range in value from $20,000 to $1,000,000 and can be from one month to two years in duration. Most projects are about six months in duration and worth about $60,000 to $80,000. The firm performs a range of consulting services, including market research, manufacturing system design, and executive recruiting. Its clients are medium to large corporations and include banks, manufacturers, and government agencies.

Multi Projects just got a call from Growin Corporation, which wants to go forward with a project that Multi Projects proposed nearly six months ago. Partners at Multi Projects are surprised by the good news. They had thought the project was dead. They're also very interested in carrying out a first project for Growin Corporation because it's a rapidly growing company. Multi Projects sees an opportunity to do several projects with Growin Corporation in the future.

Jeff Armstrong has been assigned as project manager for the Growin Corporation project. He has been with Multi Projects for about a year and has been anxious to get a challenging project to manage. He worked on the proposal for the Growin project.

Tyler Bonilla is a senior systems engineer. He has been with Multi Projects eight years. He has an excellent reputation, and previous clients with whom he has worked usually request that he be assigned to their projects. He enjoys his work even though he's extremely busy. He is currently working full-time on a project for Goodold Company, a previous client. Goodold said that one of the reasons it does business with Multi Projects, rather than with another consulting firm, is the great work Tyler does on their projects.

Jennifer Fernandez is the manager of systems engineering. She has been with Multi Projects about fifteen years. Tyler reports to Jennifer, but because of his heavy workload and associated travel he doesn't get to see Jennifer very often, other than at her monthly staff meetings.

Julie Capriolo is the project manager for the Goodold Company project. She has been with Multi Projects about two years. Tyler is assigned to her project full-time. The project has a tight schedule, and everyone is putting in extra hours. Julie feels a lot of pressure, but she has a good project team—she relies heavily on Tyler. She had heard from a friend who used to work with Jeff that Jeff is very ambitious and will do whatever it takes to make himself look good. This hadn't been of concern to Julie because she and Jeff have separate projects and don't run into each other very often.

The day Jeff is assigned to be project manager on the Growin Corporation project, he runs into Tyler in the hallway. "We got the Growin project," he tells Tyler.

"Great," responds Tyler.

Jeff continues, "You know, one of the big reasons they gave the project to us rather than another consulting firm is because we promised you'd be the lead systems engineer on the project, Tyler. They were impressed with you when we met with them to present our proposal. When do you think you can start work on the project?"

"Unfortunately, I can't. I'm tied up on the Goodold project, and things are really hectic. I'll be on that project for another four months," says Tyler.

"No way!" exclaims Jeff. "This Growin project is too important to me—I mean, to us. I'll take care of it."

"You'd better talk to Jennifer," Tyler tells him.

Jeff stops by Jennifer's office. She's busy, but he interrupts her. "I gotta have Tyler Bonilla on my Growin project. He wants to work on it, but he said I should talk to you."

"That's impossible," says Jennifer. "He's assigned to Julie Capriolo's Goodold project for the next four months."

"Julie? Who's she? Never mind. I'll find her and work it out. You probably have somebody else you can assign to her project," replies Jeff as he quickly bolts out of her office in search of Julie.

"That's my decision, not yours or Julie's!" shouts Jennifer. But by that time Jeff is gone and doesn't hear what she says.

Julie is meeting with her project team in the conference room. Jeff knocks on the door and opens it. "Is there a Julie in here?" he asks.

"I'm Julie," she responds.

"I need to talk to you ASAP. It's important. Oh, by the way, sorry for interrupting." Looking toward Tyler, who's in the meeting, Jeff says, "Hey, Tyler, catch you later, buddy, after I talk with Julie." Jeff then shuts the door and goes back to his office. Julie is noticeably disturbed at the interruption.

After her meeting, Julie calls Jeff. "This is Julie. What did you want to talk to me about that was so urgent?"

"About reassigning Tyler to my project. He's interested, and I've already talked to Jennifer about it," answers Jeff.

"That's impossible," declares Julie. "He's critical to the Goodold project."

"Sorry," says Jeff, "but if the Growin project is successful, we'll get more business from them than we ever got from the Goodold company."

"It's already after 6 o'clock and I have to be out of town for a week, but I'll discuss this with Jennifer as soon as I get back," snaps Julie.

"Yeah, sure, whatever," responds Jeff.

The next day Jeff calls a meeting with Jennifer and Tyler. He starts by telling them, "I called this meeting to figure how soon Tyler can begin working on the Growin project and how you [looking toward Jennifer] can get somebody to take his place on what's-her-name's project."

"I think Julie should be here for this discussion," says Jennifer.

"She couldn't make it. Apparently she's out of town for a week, and we need to get going on the Growin project." Jeff tells her. "We need to prepare for a meeting with them next week. Besides, Tyler is the one we're talking about, and he'd rather work on the Growin project. Right, Tyler?"

"Ah, well, now that you've asked, I am getting tired of working on the Goodold projects," replies Tyler. I'm not learning anything new. I mean, it's okay, but I'd like a change."

Jennifer is astonished. "You never mentioned that to me, Tyler."

Jeff breaks in, "Well, I guess it's settled. Jennifer, you assign somebody else to the Goodold project who'll feel a little more challenged and tell Julie when she gets back. In the meantime, me and my buddy Tyler have got a lot of work to do to look good for our meeting with the Growin people next week."

Case Questions

1. Why is Jeff so anxious to get started on the Growin project?
2. Why is Tyler in such high demand?

3. What is wrong with Jeff's approach to handling this situation?
4. What should Jennifer do to resolve this situation?
5. What advantages of the matrix-type organization are apparent from this story?
6. What disadvantages of the matrix-type organization are apparent from this story?

Group Activity

Have an open discussion among course participants regarding the following questions:

- What should Jennifer do next?
- What should Tyler do?
- What could have been done to prevent this situation?
- How could each of the four individuals have handled the situation better?

8

Project Communication and Documentation

How You Say It Does Make a Difference

Discussions with numerous successful people have confirmed that communication skills are crucial for success. Oral communication, written communication, and listening skills often make the difference between the very successful person and the person who is not as successful.

According to Joseph O'Brian, project managers with difficulties in written and oral communication need only master a few essentials in order to eliminate their problems. In writing memos and letters, they should eliminate unnecessary remarks, avoid jargon, and use only simple, plain, good English. Moreover, managers should refrain from making jokes and obscure references and from using official communications to blow off steam. As for oral communication, such as presentations and speeches, project managers should prepare in advance, mentally punctuate while speaking, and make eye contact.

Effective communication skills actually begin with active listening, according to Helga Drummond. Active listening not only ensures accurate acquisition of information but also leads to personal development. Listening effectively, therefore, requires the mental organization of information received, as well as the continuous evaluation and interpretation of its contents. Oral and visual acknowledgments let the other person know that you're listening effectively.

Sources: J. O'Brian, "How You Say It Does Make a Difference," *Supervisory Management,* April 1994; H. Drummond, "Talking and Listening," *International Journal of Bank Marketing,* October 1993.

The Role of Communication in Global Business

As the United States competes more and more on a global basis, the importance of effective communication continues to increase. Richard Ramsey points out that U.S. businesses can continue to compete effectively with their counterparts from other countries only if the quantitative bias in U.S. firms and business schools is eliminated. Studies show that U.S. companies and educational institutions have consistently emphasized mathematically oriented, quantitative approaches to project management, such as linear programming and decision trees. These techniques have value, but emphasizing such approaches can lead managers to overlook the importance of communication and quality teams. To rectify the situation, universities and business schools must train students in the importance of effective oral and written communication, nonverbal skills, and intercultural communication.

These same skills are no less essential for the project manager. Without effective communication, projects are often doomed to failure.

Source: R. Ramsey, "The Role of Communication in Global Business," *Bulletin of the Association for Business Communication,* March 1994.

This chapter discusses an element vital to the effective performance of a project—communication. Communication takes place between the project team and the customer, among the project team members, and between the project team and its upper management. Communication may involve two people or a group of people. It can be oral or written. It can be face to face or involve some medium, such as phone, voice mail, electronic mail, letters, memos, video conferencing, or groupware. It can be formal, such as a report or a presentation at a meeting, or informal, such as a hallway conversation or an email message. This chapter covers many communication formats. You will become familiar with

- suggestions for enhancing personal communications, such as face-to-face discussions, phone conversations, letters, and memos
- effective listening
- various types of project meetings and suggestions for effective meetings
- formal project presentations and suggestions for effective presentations
- project reports and suggestions for preparing useful reports
- project documentation and keeping track of changes

PERSONAL COMMUNICATION

Effective and frequent personal communication is crucial to keep the project moving, identify potential problems, solicit suggestions for improving project performance, keep abreast of whether the customer is satisfied, and avoid surprises. Personal communication can occur through words or nonverbal behavior, such as body language. It can be face to face or use some medium, including telephone, voice mail, electronic mail, letters, memos, video conferencing, or groupware. Personal communication can be oral or written.

Oral Communication

Personal oral communication can be face to face or via telephone. It can be by means of voice mail or video conferencing. Information can be communicated in a more accurate and timely manner through oral communication. Such communication provides a forum for discussion, clarification, understanding, and immediate feedback. Face-to-face communication also provides an opportunity to observe the body language that accompanies the communication. Even phone conversations allow the listener to hear the tone, inflection, and emotion of the voice. Body language and tone are important elements that enrich oral communication. Face-to-face situations provide an even greater opportunity for enriched communication than phone conversations do.

REINFORCE YOUR LEARNING

1. Identify two types of personal oral communication.

Body language can be used not only by the person talking, but also by the listener, as a way of providing feedback to the person talking. Positive body language can include direct eye contact, a smile, hand gestures, leaning forward, and nodding acknowledgment or agreement. Negative body language can be a frown, crossed arms, slouching, fidgeting, gazing or looking away, doodling, or yawning. In personal communications *people need to be sensitive to body language reflective of the cultural diversity of the participants,* whether they're other team members or the customer. When communicating with individuals from other cultures or countries, you need to be aware of their customs regarding greetings, gestures, gift giving, and protocol. For example, hand gestures, proximity to the person with whom you are communicating, and touching have different meanings in different cultures.

REINFORCE YOUR LEARNING

2. Body language can be used not only by the person talking, but also by the _____, as a way of providing _____ to the person talking.

When communicating orally, a person must be careful not to use remarks, words, or phrases that can be construed to be sexist, racist, prejudicial, or offensive. Comments do not have to be made directly to a particular person to be offensive. Remarks made in a group setting can be distasteful to some individuals in the group. They may find certain statements hurtful to themselves or to an acquaintance. Comments about ethnic customs, surnames, dialects, religious practices, physical characteristics or appearance, or mannerisms can be offensive, even if the offense is unintentional or the comment is said in jest.

REINFORCE YOUR LEARNING

3. In personal communication, people need to be sensitive to body language reflective of the _____ _____ of the participants.

A high degree of face-to-face communication is especially important early in a project to foster team building, develop good working relationships, and establish mutual expectations. Locating the project team in a common area facilitates communication. It's much easier to walk over to someone's office to ask something than to call the person on the phone and maybe wait several days for your call to be returned. However, voice mail allows individuals to communicate orally in a timely manner when face-to-face communication is not possible. It is not always feasible to locate the project team in a common area, especially if the team includes members or subcontractors from different geographic locations. In such cases, video conferencing can be helpful, if available.

Project team members need to be proactive in initiating timely communication with other team members and the project manager to get and give information, rather than waiting until an upcoming project team meeting that could be several weeks away. The project manager, in particular, should get out of the office on a regular basis and drop in on individual team members. She or he should take the initiative to visit the customer or the firm's upper management for face-to-face communication, rather than waiting to be summoned to a meeting. If a visit to the customer requires distant travel, the manager should initiate regular phone discussions between visits.

Oral communication should be straightforward and unambiguous. Sometimes attempting to be overly tactful, especially in communicating a problem or concern, can mislead and result in unclear expectations. You should check for understanding of what you wanted to communicate by asking for feedback. If you're not sure whether a point you made was understood by the other person, ask the other person to state his or her understanding of what you said. Similarly, if you aren't clear on a point the other person was trying to communicate, paraphrase what you think the other person said to ensure mutual understanding.

Finally, the timing of oral communication is important. For example, you shouldn't barge into a colleague's office and interrupt him if he is in the middle of doing something important. Rather, in such a situation, ask him when would be a good time to get together. You should indicate about how long you need to talk with him and what you want to discuss. He will then know whether to expect a ten-minute discussion on a trivial subject or a one-hour discussion on a critical subject. Similarly, when making a phone call to another person, you should state at the start what topics you want to discuss and how long it might take, then ask if now is a good time or if you should call back at a more convenient time.

Written Communication

Personal written communication is generally carried out through internal memos to the project team and external letters to the customer or others outside the firm, such as subcontractors. Memos and letters can be transmitted in hardcopy or through electronic mail (email) or groupware.

Memos and letters are ways to communicate efficiently with a group of people when it's impractical to have a meeting or when the

REINFORCE YOUR LEARNING

4. *Project team members need to be _____ in initiating timely communication to _____ and _____ information.*

REINFORCE YOUR LEARNING

5. *Identify two methods you can use to generate feedback during oral communication.*

information needs to be disseminated in a timely manner. Written communication should be used only when necessary and not just to generate paperwork. Project participants are usually very busy and do not have time to read trivial memos containing information that could have been communicated orally at the next project meeting.

A memo or letter may be appropriate as a follow-up to a face-to-face conversation or a phone call, so as to confirm decisions or actions rather than relying on a person's memory. When a memo is used to confirm oral communication, other people who were not involved in the oral communication but who may need to know the information can be given copies. Also, such written communication can be important if a member of the project team leaves the project—the replacement person will have a record of communications regarding previous actions and decisions.

Written communication should be used mostly to inform, confirm, and request—for example, to remind the project team that the customer will be visiting on a certain date or to ask team members to provide written input for a quarterly project progress report to the client.

Memos and letters should be clear and concise and should not include lengthy dissertations or voluminous extraneous attachments. Project participants are busy with their assigned work tasks and will perceive being flooded with paperwork or email as more of a hindrance than a help.

REINFORCE YOUR LEARNING

6. *What are two forms of personal written communication?*

EFFECTIVE LISTENING

"I know that you believe that you understand what you thought you heard me say. But what you don't realize is that what you thought you heard is not what I meant."

REINFORCE YOUR LEARNING

7. *Failure to _____ can cause a _____ in communication between people.*

The heart of communication is not words, but understanding. Not only to be understood, but also to understand. Half of making communication effective is listening. Failure to listen can cause a breakdown in communication.

Here are some common barriers to effective listening:

- *Pretending to listen.* You listen and think faster than the average person talks. This may lead to drifting, boredom, or thinking about what you want to say in response.
- *Distractions.* If you try to do something else, such as answer the phone or read, while someone is talking to you, you won't be able to focus on the person talking. It's also easy to get distracted by people walking by or what's happening outside the window.
- *Bias and closed-mindedness.* Hearing what supports your views and turning off the things with which you disagree is known as selective listening. Bias in listening can also be attributed to feelings about the speaker's dress, looks, tone of voice, or mannerisms.
- *Impatience.* If you are anxious for the person talking to get to the point or waiting for a chance to interrupt and speak, you may tune out what the speaker is saying.

- *Jumping to conclusions.* If you begin to draw conclusions about what is being said before the person talking has finished, you may not hear the whole story or all the facts.

Listening is more than just letting the other person talk. It must be an active, not a passive, process. Active listening increases understanding and reduces conflict. Here are some suggestions for improving listening skills:

- *Focus on the person talking.* Looking at the person who is speaking helps you concentrate, and you can see the speaker's body language.
- *Engage in active listening.* Provide verbal and nonverbal feedback to the person talking. This can include body language, such as nodding in acknowledgment of something the person said, smiling, or simply leaning forward attentively. It can be a verbal comment that doesn't require a response from the speaker, such as, "That's interesting," "I see," or "Uh huh." It can be paraphrasing what the speaker said, as in "What you're saying is . . . " or "What you mean is . . . ." Such paraphrasing will give the speaker an opportunity to clear up any misunderstandings.
- *Ask questions.* When you need clarification or more information about something the person said, ask a probing question such as "Could you tell me more about that?"
- *Don't interrupt.* When a person is talking, listen to the whole thought or wait for an appropriate pause before breaking in with a question or comment. Don't interrupt and change the subject before the person talking has completed the message.

Good listening skills are important if project team members are to be effective in communicating with one another and with the customer.

MEETINGS

A meeting can be a vehicle for fostering team building and reinforcing team members' expectations, roles, and commitment to the project objective. This section covers various types of meetings that may take place during a project and provides suggestions for ensuring that meetings are effective.

Types of Project Meetings

The three most common types of project meetings are

- Status review meetings
- Problem-solving meetings
- Technical design review meetings

It's not unusual for a contract between a customer and a project contractor to outline requirements for periodic status review meetings and specific technical review meetings.

STATUS REVIEW MEETINGS

A project status review meeting is usually led or called by the project manager; it generally involves all or some of the project team, plus the customer and/or the project team's upper management. The primary purposes of such a meeting are to inform, to identify problems, and to identify action items. Project status meetings should be held on a regularly scheduled basis so that problems and potential problems can be identified early and surprises that could jeopardize accomplishing the project objective can be prevented. For example, project status review meetings might be held weekly with the project team and less frequently with the customer—perhaps monthly or quarterly, depending on the overall duration of the project and the contractual requirements.

A sample agenda for a project status review meeting is shown in Figure 8.1. Here are some of the subjects that might be discussed under each of the agenda items:

REINFORCE YOUR LEARNING

10. *What are the primary purposes of a status review meeting?*

- *Accomplishments since last meeting.* Key project milestones that were reached should be identified, and actions on items from previous meetings should be reviewed.
- *Cost, schedule, and work scope—status.* Performance should be compared to the baseline plan. It's important that status be based on up-to-date information regarding completed tasks and actual expenditures.
- *Cost, schedule, and work scope—trends.* Any positive or negative trends in project performance should be identified. Even if a project is ahead of schedule, the fact that the schedule has been slipping over the past several weeks might indicate that corrective action should be initiated now, before the project falls behind schedule.
- *Cost, schedule, and work scope—forecasts.* Based on current status, trends, and the project tasks yet to be completed, the forecasted project completion date and forecasted cost at completion should be reviewed and compared to the project objective and the baseline plan.
- *Cost, schedule, and work scope—variances.* Any differences should be identified between actual progress and planned progress with respect to cost and schedule for project work packages and tasks. These variances can be positive—for example, being ahead of schedule—or they can be negative—such as overrunning the budget given the amount of work that has been accomplished. Negative variances will help pinpoint both current problems and potential problems. Particular attention should be given to those parts of the project that have had negative variances which are continuing to get worse.
- *Corrective actions.* In some instances, corrective actions to address problems and potential problems might take place right at the status review meeting—for example, receiving customer or management approval to proceed with the purchase of certain materials or authorization of overtime to get the project back on schedule. In other cases, separate problem-solving meetings may be

FIGURE 8.1   **Project Status Review Meeting Agenda**

PROJECT STATUS REVIEW
Team Meeting

AGENDA

8:00 AM	Accomplishments since last meeting	
	• Hardware	Steve
	• Software	Katie
	• Documentation	Wendy
8:30	Cost, schedule, and work scope	Jack
	• Status	
	• Trends	
	• Forecasts	
	• Variances	
8:45	Corrective actions, if necessary	As appropriate
9:15	Opportunities for improvement	All
9:30	Open discussion	All
9:50	Action item assignments	Jack
10:00	Adjourn	

required so that appropriate members of the project team can develop corrective actions.

- *Opportunities for improvement.* These should also be identified, along with problem areas and associated corrective actions. For example, a member of the project team might point out that the technical specifications could be met by using an alternative material or piece of equipment, which is substantially less expensive than the one the team originally planned to use. Or a team member might suggest that substantial time could be saved by replicating and slightly modifying existing computer software rather than developing completely new software.
- *Action item assignment.* Specific action items should be identified and assigned to specific team members. For each action item, the person responsible and the estimated completion date should be noted. The completion date should be estimated by the person responsible for the action item. When people verbalize their commitment to a date at a meeting in front of other people, they will usually strive to meet that date.

It should be noted that listening to the information provided at a status review meeting is one way, but not the only way, for a project manager to get a true understanding of the project status. He or she needs to validate what was said at the status review meeting through personal communication with individual members of the project team. The project manager should also ask to see any tangible products, or deliverables, such as drawings, prototypes, or reports. This will both validate that the item is really complete (and not just almost or essentially complete) and show that the project manager is genuinely interested in the individual's work and acknowledges its importance to the successful achievement of the project objective.

PROBLEM-SOLVING MEETINGS

When a problem or potential problem is identified by an individual project team member, that person should promptly call a problem-solving meeting with other appropriate individuals, not wait for a future status review meeting. Identifying and resolving problems as early as possible is critical to project success.

The project manager and the project team need to establish guidelines at the beginning of the project regarding who should initiate problem-solving meetings and when, as well as the level of authorization required to implement corrective actions.

Problem-solving meetings should follow a good problem-solving approach, such as the following:

1. Develop a problem statement.
2. Identify potential causes of the problem.
3. Gather data and verify the most likely causes.
4. Identify possible solutions.
5. Evaluate the alternative solutions.
6. Determine the best solution.
7. Revise the project plan.
8. Implement the solution.
9. Determine whether the problem has been solved.

This nine-step problem-solving approach was discussed in greater detail in Chapter 6.

REINFORCE YOUR LEARNING

11. *True or false: When members of the project team identify problems or potential problems, they should wait until the next scheduled status review meeting to bring them up for discussion.*

TECHNICAL DESIGN REVIEW MEETINGS

Projects that involve a design phase, such as an information system project, may require one or more technical design review meetings to ensure that the customer agrees with or approves of the design approach developed by the project contractor.

Take the example of a company that hires a consultant to design, develop, and implement an information system to track customer orders from order entry through receipt of payment. The company may require that the consultant review the system design with appropriate company representatives before the next phase of the project—detailed development of the system and purchase of hardware and software—is approved. At a later stage in the project, the company may want certain employees to review and approve the computer interface and output formats developed by the consultant to ensure that they meet the needs and expectations of the people who will be using the system.

In many technical projects there are two design review meetings:

1. *A preliminary design review meeting* when the contractor has completed the initial conceptual specifications, drawings, or flowcharts. The purpose of this preliminary design review meeting is to get the customer's agreement that the design approach meets the technical requirements and to gain approval from the customer before the contractor orders materials that have a long delivery time (so as not to delay the project schedule).

2. *A final design review meeting* when the contractor has completed the detailed specifications, drawings, screen and report formats, and such. The purpose of this final design review meeting is to gain approval from the customer before the contractor starts building, assembling, and producing the project deliverables.

REINFORCE YOUR LEARNING

12. *On technical projects there are often two design review meetings: a _____ design review meeting and a _____ design review meeting.*

Effective Meetings

Before, during, and after a meeting, the person calling or conducting the meeting can take various steps to ensure that the meeting is effective.

BEFORE THE MEETING

- *Determine whether a meeting is really necessary* or whether another mechanism, such as a conference call, is more appropriate.
- *Determine the purpose of the meeting.* For instance, is it to share information, plan, collect input or ideas, make a decision, persuade or sell, solve a problem, or evaluate status?
- *Determine who needs to participate in the meeting,* given its purpose. The number of participants should be the minimum number needed to achieve the purpose of the meeting. Project team members are usually busy on their work tasks and do not want to participate in meetings to which they have nothing to contribute or from which they have nothing to gain. Individuals who are invited to attend the meeting should know why they are being asked to participate.
- *Distribute an agenda well in advance of the meeting* to those invited. The agenda should include:

  Purpose of the meeting

  Topics to be covered. (Items should be listed from most important to least important. If time runs out, the most important items will have been covered.)

  Time allocated for each topic and who will cover the topic, make the presentation, or lead the discussion.

  Figure 8.2 is a sample agenda for a project review meeting with a customer. Accompanying the agenda should be any documents or data the participants need to review *prior* to the meeting. Sufficient time should be given between distribution of the announcement and the date of the meeting to allow participants to prepare for the meeting adequately. Some participants may need to collect and analyze data or prepare presentation or handout materials.

FIGURE 8.2   Customer Project Review Meeting Agenda

PROJECT REVIEW
Meeting with Customer

AGENDA

8:00 AM	Opening comments	Jeff
8:15	Technical review	
	• System design	Joe
	• Training	Cathy
	• Installation plans	Jim
10:00	Break	
10:15	Project status	Jeff
	• Schedule	
	• Cost	
11:00	Proposed changes	Joe
11:45	Decisions and action items	Jeff
12:00	Open discussion (box lunches)	
1:00	Adjourn	

REINFORCE YOUR LEARNING

13. *To ensure that a meeting is effective, what are some steps that the person calling or conducting the meeting should take before the meeting?*

• *Prepare visual aids or handouts.* Graphics, charts, tables, diagrams, pictures, and physical models are effective visual aids. Often these materials focus the discussion and prevent a lot of rambling and misunderstanding. A picture is worth a thousand words!

• *Make meeting room arrangements.* The room should be large enough that people aren't cramped and uncomfortable. Seats should be arranged so that all participants can see each other; this will foster participation. The appropriate visual aids and accessories (projector, screen, videotape player, flip charts, chalkboard) should be in the room and be tested before the meeting starts. Refreshments should be ordered if the meeting is going to be long. For example, box lunches may be served in order to allow meeting discussions to continue over a working lunch.

In some cases, a conference room may be designated the "project room," where all project meetings are held or where project team members can meet for problem-solving discussions. Sometimes such project rooms have project plans, schedules, status charts, and system diagrams posted on the walls for easy reference by all project team members.

DURING THE MEETING

- *Start the meeting on time.* If the meeting leader waits for a few late-comers, people will get in the habit of showing up late, because they know the meeting won't start on time anyway. If the meeting starts on time, people will get in the habit of arriving on time rather than suffer the embarrassment of entering a meeting already in progress.

- *Designate a note-taker.* Someone should be assigned (preferably before the meeting) to take notes. The notes should be concise, and they should cover decisions and action items, assignments, and estimated completion dates. Detailed meeting minutes can be a burden both to take and to read later and therefore should be avoided.

- *Review the purpose of the meeting and the agenda.* Be concise, and don't give a lengthy discourse.

- *Facilitate—don't dominate—the meeting.* The project manager should not lead all the discussions, but rather should get other participants to lead the discussions on their assigned topics. A good facilitator will

  Keep the meeting moving and within the scheduled time frame.

  Encourage participation, especially from individuals who appear hesitant to participate.

  Limit discussion by participants who have a tendency to talk too much, repeat themselves, or stray from the topic at hand.

  Control interruptions and side conversations.

  Clarify points that are made.

  Summarize discussions and make transitions to the next topics on the agenda.

  It's helpful to discuss meeting guidelines at a project team meeting at the beginning of the project so that everyone understands what behavior is expected during project meetings. An example of a code of conduct for team meetings is shown in Figure 8.3.

- *Summarize the meeting results* at the end of the meeting, and make sure all participants have a clear understanding of all decisions and action items. The meeting leader should verbalize these items to help avoid any misunderstandings.

- *Do not overrun the scheduled meeting time.* Participants may have other commitments or subsequent meetings. If all agenda items are not covered, it's better to schedule another meeting for the people involved with those items. These should be the lower-priority items anyway, since the agenda topics should have been arranged in order of most to least important.

- *Evaluate the meeting process.* Occasionally, at the end of a meeting, the participants should openly discuss what took place and determine whether any changes should be made to improve the effectiveness of future meetings.

  Figure 8.4 is a checklist for rating the effectiveness of a meeting. The project team members might complete this assessment instrument periodically during the project. After the scores of all

FIGURE 8.3   Team Meeting Code of Conduct

TEAM MEETING

NEW PIG CORPORATION

TEAM QUALITY MANAGEMENT

CODE OF CONDUCT

- Stick to the topic at hand.
- Arrive on time and end on time.
- One person talks at a time.
- Everyone has the responsibility to participate. Be prepared.
- Be frank, honest, and sincere.
- Limit sarcastic and cynical remarks to zero.
- The overall tone of the meetings will be positive.
- Eliminate negativity.
- Make criticism constructive.
- Pay attention. Seek first to understand, then to be understood.
- No gossip.
- Ideas belong to the group, not to the individual.
- The team speaks wih one voice after the decision is made. Leave united.
- Reinforce positive behavior.
- Keep your cool. If you lose it, you are wrong—no one else.

REINFORCE YOUR LEARNING
14. *True or false: It's always a good idea to wait for everyone to arrive before starting a meeting, even if it's beyond the scheduled start time.*

team members have been summarized, the team, including the project manager, should discuss how to improve in the areas that were rated low.

AFTER THE MEETING

Publish the meeting results within 24 hours after the meeting. The summary document should be concise and kept to one page if possible. It should confirm decisions that were made and list the action

FIGURE 8.4   Meeting Effectiveness Checklist

How Effective Are Your Meetings?

	Not at All		Somewhat		Very Much
1. Is the agenda sent in time to allow presentation?	1	2	3	4	5
2. Is the agenda properly sequenced?	1	2	3	4	5
3. Is sufficient time allocated for each item?	1	2	3	4	5
4. Is the room set up appropriately?	1	2	3	4	5
5. Do appropriate participants attend?	1	2	3	4	5
6. Do meetings start on time?	1	2	3	4	5
7. Do attendees know why they were invited?	1	2	3	4	5
8. Are meeting objectives understood?	1	2	3	4	5
9. Are objectives for each agenda item clear?	1	2	3	4	5
10. Are meetings kept on track and not allowed to digress?	1	2	3	4	5
11. Is there balanced participation of all attendees?	1	2	3	4	5
12. Do attendees listen to each other?	1	2	3	4	5
13. Does the leader maintain control?	1	2	3	4	5
14. Do meetings have a positive, productive tone?	1	2	3	4	5
15. Do meetings finish on time?	1	2	3	4	5
16. Are decisions and action items documented and the documents distributed?	1	2	3	4	5
17. Are meetings a valuable use of time?	1	2	3	4	5

items, including who is responsible, the estimated completion date, and expected deliverables. It may also list who attended and who was absent. The meeting results should be distributed to all individuals who were invited, whether or not they actually attended the meeting. The meeting notes should not include a detailed narrative of the meeting discussions. Figure 8.5 is a sample action item list from a meeting.

Effective meetings, like successful projects, require good planning and good performance.

PRESENTATIONS

Often the project manager or members of the project team are called on to give a formal presentation. The audience may be representatives of the customer's organization, the project organization's upper

FIGURE 8.5   Action Item List

ACTION ITEMS from March 1 Project Status Review Meeting		
Action	**Who**	**By When**
1. Revise system requirements document	Tyler	March 10
2. Schedule review meeting with customer	Jim	March 11
3. Change purchase order for computers from 15 to 20	Maggie	March 19

4. Evaluate feasibility of bar coding
   and optical character recognition
   for data entry
	Hannah	March 19

management, the project team itself, or the public, such as at a conference. The audience may be one person (the customer) or several hundred attendees at a national conference. The presentation may last ten minutes or an hour or more. The subject could be an overview of the project; the current status of the project; a serious problem that is jeopardizing successful achievement of the project objective, such as a forecasted schedule delay or cost overrun; or an attempt to persuade the customer to expand or redirect the project work scope.

In such situations, you, the speaker, are in the spotlight. Following are some suggestions that may help you prepare and deliver your presentation.

PREPARING FOR THE PRESENTATION

- *Determine the purpose of the presentation.* Is it to inform or to persuade? What do you want to accomplish? For example, do you want the audience to understand the project, or do you want the customer to agree to suggested changes in the project work scope?
- *Know the audience.* What is their level of knowledge or familiarity with the subject? What is their rank—are they senior managers and key decision makers, or are they your peers?
- *Make an outline of the presentation.* Only after you have made an outline should you write out the presentation. Read it over and over and over, but don't try to memorize it.
- *Use simple language that the audience will understand.* Don't use jargon or acronyms that the audience may not understand. Don't use sophisticated or technical vocabulary that the audience may not understand. Don't try to impress the audience with your word power! Don't make remarks that can be construed to be sexist, racist, prejudicial, offensive, sarcastic, or profane.

- *Prepare notes or a final outline that you will use or refer to during your presentation.* Yes, it is all right to use notes.
- *Practice, practice, practice—more than you think you should.* You may want to do a trial run in front of your peers. Ask for their feedback; solicit suggestions on how you might improve the presentation.
- *Prepare visual aids and test them.* Make sure the visual aids are readable from the most distant seat in the room where the presentation will be given. If it will be given in a large auditorium, make sure the visual aids are very large. Visual aids such as graphs, diagrams, and tables should be simple and not too busy—there shouldn't be a lot of text and diagrams shouldn't be too detailed. There should be one idea per chart or slide. Multicolor graphics are more appealing than plain black and white, but choose colors carefully—you can overwhelm your audience with too many colors or color combinations that are difficult to read.
- *Make copies of handout materials.* If audience members don't have to take a lot of notes, they will be able to give their full attention to the presentation.
- *Request the audiovisual equipment well in advance.* Whether it's an overhead projector, slide projector, microphone, lectern, pointer, or video projector, you don't want to find at the last minute that it's not available.
- *Go into the meeting room when it's empty or not in use and get a feel for the surroundings.* Stand in the place where the presentation will be made (in the front of the room, at the lectern, or on the stage). Test the projector and microphone.

DELIVERING THE PRESENTATION

- *Expect a bit of nervousness; all speakers experience it.* Just remember that you know more about what you are talking about than most of the audience members do.
- *Know the first two or three sentences of your presentation.* The opening lines are crucial; have them down pat. They must be delivered in a confident and relaxed manner. This is where credibility is established with the audience. You can't afford to fumble over the opening lines or say something that may alienate the audience.
- *Use the 3-T approach in your presentation:*

  First, tell them what you are going to tell them (your outline).
  Then, tell them (the body of your presentation).
  Finally, tell them what you told them (your summary).

- *Talk to the audience, not at it.* Maintain as much eye contact with the audience as possible, and refer to your notes as little as possible (you'll be glad you practiced plenty of times beforehand).
- *Speak clearly and confidently.* Don't speak too quickly or too slowly. Speak in short, understandable sentences—not long, complex, rambling sentences. Pause appropriately after a key point or before moving on to a new item. Use appropriate inflection in your voice to help make a point. Do not present your speech in a monotone.

REINFORCE YOUR LEARNING

*16. What are some important
things to keep in mind when
delivering a presentation?*

- *Use appropriate animation to help make a point.* Use hand movements, facial expressions, and body language. Don't stand frozen to one spot; move around, if appropriate. In a large auditorium, it's better to have a portable microphone than to be locked to a lectern with a fixed microphone. If you do walk around, whether in a small meeting room or an auditorium, always face the audience when you speak; never speak with your back to the audience. For example, do not face the projector screen and read your visual aid to the audience. Elaborate on the single idea illustrated by each visual aid and give examples, if appropriate.
- *Do not stand in front of your visual aids.* Don't stand in a position where you block any of the audience's view of the projector screen, flip chart, or whatever.
- *Build interest in your presentation* by developing your "story" with logic and rationale. Gradually increase the tempo of your presentation.
- *Keep to the key points in your outline.* Don't digress or wander off the topic or your outline. You will waste time and confuse the audience.
- *When making key points, explain to the audience why they are important.*
- *Sum up your points on a particular item before moving on to the next item on your outline.*
- *Know your closing lines.* The closing is as important as the opening. Tie the closing to the purpose of the presentation. Finish with conviction and confidence.
- *Allow time for interaction with the audience, if appropriate.* Ask if there are any questions. You should state at the beginning of your presentation whether there will be time for questions at the end of the presentation or whether the audience can interrupt with questions during the presentation. The latter option can be risky if you have a fixed time slot or an agenda to complete. However, if it's a presentation to a customer conducted in a small meeting room, responding to questions on the fly may be more appropriate than expecting the customer to hold all questions until the end of the presentation. In fact, part of your presentation strategy may be to draw the customer into a discussion to expose his or her opinions.
- *When responding to questions, be sincere, candid, and confident.* If you don't know the answer or can't divulge the answer, say so; that's a legitimate answer. Don't be defensive in responding.

REPORTS

Written reports are just as important as oral reports in communicating information about a project. The required types, content, format, frequency, and distribution of reports that the project organization must prepare may be specified by the customer in the contract.

Some reports may be distributed to a large audience. It's important to know who will be receiving copies of reports. The audience could be very diverse and could include people who are very knowledgeable about the project, as well as individuals who know only what they read in the periodic reports they receive. Recipients of the reports may have different levels of technical sophistication, and some may not understand certain technical language or jargon.

It is important to keep in mind that *reports must be written to address what is of interest to the readers, not what is of interest to the person writing the report.*

The following sections discuss two common types of project reports and suggestions for ensuring that reports are useful.

Types of Project Reports

The two most common types of project reports are

- Progress reports
- Final report

PROGRESS REPORTS

It is important to keep in mind that a progress report is not an activity report. *Do not confuse activity or busy-ness with progress and accomplishment.* The customer, in particular, is interested in project accomplishments—what progress has been made toward achieving the project objective—rather than what activities the project team was busy on.

Reports on project progress can be prepared by project team members for the project manager or their functional manager (in a matrix organization), by the project manager for the customer, or by the project manager for the project company's upper management.

Progress reports usually cover a specified period, called the **reporting period.** This period could be a week, a month, a quarter, or whatever best fits the project. Most progress reports cover only what happened during the reporting period rather than cumulative progress since the beginning of the project.

A sample outline for a project progress report is shown in Figure 8.6. Items that might be included in a project progress report include the following:

- *Accomplishments since prior report.* This section should identify key project milestones that were reached. It could also include a report on achievement (or lack of achievement) of specific goals set for the reporting period.
- *Current status of project performance.* Data on cost, schedule, and work scope are compared to the baseline plan.
- *Progress toward resolution of previously identified problems.* If no progress has been made on items brought up in previous progress reports, an explanation should be provided.
- *Problems or potential problems since prior report.* Problems can include (1) technical problems such as prototypes that do not work or test results that are not what they were expected to be; (2) schedule problems such as delays encountered because some tasks took

FIGURE 8.6   Project Progress Report Outline

PROJECT PROGRESS REPORT
for the period July 1 to September 30

TABLE OF CONTENTS

1. Accomplishments since prior report
2. Current status of project performance
   - 2.1 Cost
   - 2.2 Schedule
   - 2.3 Work scope
3. Progress toward resolution of previously identified problems
4. Problems or potential problems since prior report
5. Planned corrective actions
6. Milestones expected to be reached during next report period

---

longer than expected, materials were delivered late or bad weather caused construction delays; and (3) cost problems such as cost overruns because materials cost more than originally estimated or more person-hours were expended on tasks than had been planned.

- *Planned corrective actions*. This section should specify the corrective actions to be taken during the next reporting period to resolve each of the identified problems. It should include a statement explaining whether the project objective will be jeopardized, with respect to scope, quality, cost, or schedule, by any of these corrective actions.
- *Milestones expected to be reached during next reporting period*. These goals should be in accordance with the latest agreed-upon project plan.

None of the information in the progress report should be a surprise to the readers. For example, any identified problems should already have been discussed orally prior to the preparation of the written progress report.

FINAL REPORT

The project final report is usually a summary of the project. It is not an accumulation of the progress reports, nor is it a blow-by-blow story of what happened throughout the project. The final report might include the following:

- *Customer's original need*
- *Original project objective*
- *Customer's original requirements*
- *Actual versus anticipated benefits* to the customer as a result of the project

- *Degree to which the original project objective was met.* If it was not met, an explanation should be included.
- *Brief description of the project*
- *Future considerations.* This section could include actions the customer might want to consider in the future to enhance or expand the project results. For example, if the project was constructing an office building, future considerations might be to add a parking deck, a fitness center, or a day care center adjacent to the building. If the project was organizing an arts festival, future considerations might be to change the time of year or to take action to improve the pedestrian traffic flow.
- *A list of all deliverables* (equipment, materials, software, documents such as drawings and reports, and so on) provided to the customer
- *Test data* from the final-acceptance testing of a system or piece of equipment, on the basis of which the customer accepted the project results

REINFORCE YOUR LEARNING

19. *True or false: A project final report is an accumulation of the progress reports prepared during the project.*

Preparing Useful Reports

Taking into consideration the following guidelines when you are preparing project reports will help ensure their usefulness and value to the recipients:

- *Make your reports concise.* Don't try to impress the recipients with volume. The volume of a report does not equate to project progress or accomplishment. If reports are kept brief, there is a better chance that they will be read. Furthermore, report preparation can be a time-consuming activity; the project manager should therefore try to minimize the time needed by the project team to develop input to the project reports.
- *Write as you would speak.* Use short, understandable sentences rather than compound, complex, paragraph-length sentences. Long paragraphs will tempt the reader to skip down the page and miss important points. Use simple language that the various recipients will understand. Don't use jargon or acronyms that some readers may not understand. Read the report aloud for content and style. Is it easily readable and understandable, or does it sound stilted and confusing?
- *Put the most important points first*—in the report and in each paragraph. Some readers have a tendency to read the first sentence and then skim over the rest of the paragraph.
- *Use graphics where possible*—such as charts, diagrams, tables, or pictures. Remember, a picture is worth a thousand words. Don't make the graphics too busy. Have one concept or point per graphic. It's better to have several clean graphics than a single cluttered one.
- *Pay as much attention to the format of the report as to the content.* The report should be open, inviting, and organized in a manner that is understandable to the readers. It should not be cluttered or in a small-sized type font that is difficult to read. It should not contain unclear copies of materials or graphics or forms that have been reduced to an illegible size.

REINFORCE YOUR LEARNING

20. *What are some important guidelines to keep in mind when preparing a report?*

Written reports, like oral communication, leave an impression—positive or negative—with the audience. Care and thought should be given to preparing reports, and report preparation should be looked upon as an opportunity to make a positive impression, rather than as a burdensome, time-consuming activity. It may be worthwhile to ask periodically for feedback from the recipients of the reports regarding the usefulness of the reports in meeting their needs and interests and to solicit any suggestions they might have for enhancing the reports.

PROJECT DOCUMENTATION AND CONTROLLING CHANGES

In addition to project reports, many other documents may be created by either the contractor's project team or the customer during the project. Some examples are a map of tent locations at a campground for a scout camping trip, assembly instructions for booths for a town festival, drawings for a house addition, and a printout of a computer program for controlling the movements of a robot. Project documents can be text, drawings, forms, lists, manuals, photographs, videotapes, or software. They can be on large paper (for example, an engineering drawing or blueprints) or on a computer disk or CD-ROM (for example, a document or software).

Revisions to project documents can result from changes initiated by the customer or by the project team. Some changes are trivial; others are major, affecting the project work scope, cost, and schedule. An example of a minor change is updating the drawings and assembly instructions for festival booths because a benefactor donated canopies for all the booths. An example of a major change is a change in the location, size, and type of some of the windows, requested by the customer upon seeing the house being built. In this case, it's important that the contractor stop work on those particular windows and inform the customer of any additional costs or schedule delays that might be caused by the requested changes. These changes should be documented in writing for the customer, and the customer should approve the changes before work proceeds and any new materials are ordered.

REINFORCE YOUR LEARNING

21. Revisions to project documents can result from changes initiated by the _____ or by the _____ _____.

Throughout a project, various project documents will be revised to incorporate changes. It is important for the project team to know which is the latest version of a document, so that they can perform their work correctly based on the most current information and documentation. For example, the buyer wouldn't want the builder to use outdated drawings if the architect had just made revisions that changed the locations of interior walls.

It's good practice to put on each page of each type of document (1) the date of the latest revision, (2) a sequential revision number, and (3) the initials of the person who made the changes. For example, a notation in the lower right corner of a floor plan for an office arrangement may indicate

Rev. 4, 06/20/97, ES

This means that the latest version of the floor plan is Revision number 4, which was made on June 20, 1997, by Elisabeth Smith (ES).

Just as important as keeping up to date with revision numbers and dates on documents is timely distribution of updated documents to appropriate people on the project. When changes are made to documents, the updated documents should immediately be given to any project team members whose work will be affected by the changes. Also, when revised documents are distributed, they should be accompanied by a cover memo explaining the changes that were made to the previous document. This will be helpful to people receiving the document—they won't need to go back and compare the new document to the old one and try to find the changes. If only a few changes are made to a document, distribution of the particular pages that were changed may be all that is required. When changes are extensive, though, it may make sense to distribute the entire revised document rather than all the revised pages.

Early in the project, agreement should be reached between the contractor and the customer, as well as between the project manager and the project team, regarding the way changes will be documented and authorized. If changes are consented to orally rather than in writing and there is no indication given of the impact the changes will have on the work scope, cost, or schedule, there are bound to be problems down the road.

Project team members should be careful about casually agreeing to changes without knowing whether they will necessitate additional person-hours. If the customer does not agree to pay for extra person-hours, the contractor must absorb the costs and risk overrunning costs for a particular task or the project. See Chapter 5 for a further discussion of managing change.

REINFORCE YOUR LEARNING

22. *Early in the project, agreement should be reached regarding the way changes will be _____ and _____ .*

SUMMARY

Project communication takes various forms, including personal communication, meetings, presentations, reports, and project documentation. Communication can be face to face or use some medium, including telephones, voice mail, electronic mail, video conferencing, or groupware. It can be formal or informal. Personal communication can be either oral or written. Oral communication can be face to face or via telephone. Information can be communicated in a more accurate and timely manner through oral communication. Such communication provides a forum for discussion, clarification, understanding, and immediate feedback. Body language and tone are important elements in oral communication. Body language and customs reflective of cultural diversity must be considered in communications. Oral communication should be straightforward, unambiguous, free of technical jargon, and not offensive. Asking for or providing feedback enhances understanding.

Personal written communication is generally carried out through internal memos or external letters. Such means can be used to effectively communicate with a large group of people, but should not be used for trivial matters. Written communications should be clear and concise and should be used mostly to inform, confirm, and request.

Listening is an important part of making communication effective. Failure to listen can cause a breakdown in communication. Common barriers to effective listening include pretending to listen, distractions, bias and closed-mindedness, impatience, and jumping to conclusions. Listening skills can be improved by focusing on the person talking, engaging in active listening, asking questions, and not interrupting.

Project meetings are another forum for project communication. The three most common types of project meetings are status review, problem-solving, and technical design review meetings. The purposes of a status review meeting are to inform, identify problems, and identify action items. Items often covered at such a meeting include accomplishments since the last meeting; cost, schedule, and work scope—status, trends, forecasts, and variances; corrective actions; opportunities for improvement; and action item assignment. Problem-solving meetings are called when problems or potential problems arise. They should be used to develop a problem statement, identify potential causes, gather data, identify and evaluate possible solutions, determine the best solution, revise the plan, implement the solution, and evaluate it. Technical design review meetings are for projects that include a design phase. They often include a preliminary design review meeting, in which the customer reviews the initial conceptual design, and a final design review meeting, in which the customer reviews completed, detailed design documents. These meetings are a mechanism for gaining customer approval before proceeding with the remainder of the project effort.

Before any meeting, the purpose of the meeting and the people who need to participate should be determined, an agenda should be prepared and distributed, materials should be prepared, and room arrangements should be made. The actual meeting should start on time; notes should be taken and the agenda should be reviewed. The meeting leader should facilitate, not dominate, the meeting. After the meeting, decision and action items should be published and distributed.

Project managers and team members are often called on to give formal presentations. In preparing for the presentation, it's important to determine the purpose of the presentation, find out about the target audience, make an outline, develop notes and visual aids, make copies of handout materials, and practice. You should start by telling the audience what you are going to tell them, then tell it to them, then summarize the presentation by telling them what you told them. The presentation should be clear, simple, and interesting and should conclude within the allotted time.

Written reports are often required during a project. The two most common types of project reports are progress reports and final reports. Progress reports often cover accomplishments since the prior report, the current project status, any potential problems that have been identified and corrective actions that are planned, and goals that should be accomplished during the next reporting period. Final reports provide a summary of the project and often include items such as the customer's original need, the original project objective and requirements, benefits resulting from the project, a description of the project, and a list of deliverables produced. All reports should be clear and concise and written as you would speak. They should be written to address what is of interest to the readers, not the writer.

Throughout a project, many types of documents may be created, such as manuals or drawings. They may need to be revised as a result of changes made by the customer or the project team. Early in the project, agreement should be reached regarding how changes will be documented and authorized.

QUESTIONS

1. Discuss why oral communication is important to project success, and describe several ways of enhancing such communication.
2. Discuss why written communication in the form of memos and external letters is important to project success, and describe several ways of enhancing such communication.
3. Why are listening skills important in effective communications? How can you improve your listening skills?
4. For the next few days, observe the body language of the people with whom you communicate. Describe some of the positive and negative things they do.
5. Discuss why it's important to be sensitive to the diverse composition of a project team, especially with regard to communication.
6. What is the purpose of status review meetings? When should they be conducted? What should be covered at such meetings?
7. Why are problem-solving meetings conducted? Who should call such meetings? Describe the approach that should be followed.
8. What is the purpose of technical design review meetings? What are the two different types of technical design reviews? Who participates? What should be covered in each type of meeting?
9. What should be done before a meeting to properly prepare for the meeting?
10. What should be done during a meeting to ensure that the meeting will be effective?
11. What should happen after a meeting, and how soon should it happen?
12. If you were asked to advise someone on how to prepare for and deliver an important presentation, what would you say? For each step listed, state why it is important.
13. Why are progress reports an integral part of project communications? What should they include?
14. Describe the primary purpose of a final report and items that you might include in it.
15. Why is it important to control the changes made to project documents? How can you achieve effective control?

WORLD WIDE WEB EXERCISES

If you have difficulty accessing any of the Web addresses listed here, you can find these exercises (with up-to-date addresses) on the home page of Dr. James P. Clements, co-author of this book, at

www.towson.edu/~clements

1. Check out the Web site for the WWW Project Management Forum at

www.pmforum.org

2. What is this site all about?
3. Information about numerous resources can be obtained from this site, including a list of project management journals, magazines, and books. Explore some of these links.
4. Describe the mission statement of this organization.
5. Describe what you find in the link for Content and Resources.
6. Describe what you find in the link for Global PM Forum.
7. Describe what you find in the Journal link.

CASE STUDY

Cathy Buford is the design leader on a project team for a large, complex technical project for a very demanding customer. Joe Jackson is an engineer assigned to her design team.

It's about 9:30 a.m. when Joe walks into Cathy's office. Her head is down and she's hard at work.

"Hey Cathy," says Joe, "going to the Little League game tonight? Ya know, I volunteered to coach this year."

"Oh. Hi, Joe. I'm really busy," Cathy tells him.

Joe then proceeds to sit down in Cathy's office. "I hear your kid is a pretty good ball player."

Cathy shuffles some papers and tries to focus on her work. "Huh? I guess so. I am so swamped."

"Yeah, me too," Joe says. "I had to take a break to get away from it for a while."

"Since you're here," Cathy says, "I've been thinking that maybe you should evaluate using bar coding or optical character recognition technology for data entry. It might . . ."

Joe interrupts, "Look at those dark clouds forming outside. I hope the game isn't rained out tonight."

Cathy continues, "Some of the advantages of these technologies are . . . ." She goes on for a few minutes. "So what do you think?"

"Huh? No, they won't work," is Joe's response. "Trust me. Besides the customer is a low-tech kind of guy, and it would increase the project costs."

"But if we can show the customer that it could save him money and reduce input errors," Cathy persists, "he probably would pay the extra needed to implement the technologies."

"Save him money!" Joe exclaims. "How? By laying off people? We already have too much downsizing in this country. And the government and politicians aren't doing anything about it. It doesn't matter who you vote for. They're all the same."

"By the way, I still need your input to the progress report," Cathy reminds him. "I need to mail it to the customer tomorrow. As you know, I'll need about eight to ten pages. We need a thick report to show the customer how busy we've been."

"What? Nobody told me," says Joe.

"I sent the design team an email a couple of weeks ago saying I needed everyone's input by last Friday. You could probably use the material you've prepared for the project status review meeting tomorrow afternoon," Cathy responds.

"I have to make a presentation at the meeting tomorrow? That's news to me," Joe tells her.

"It was on the agenda distributed last week," says Cathy.

"I don't have time to keep up with all the stuff in my in basket," Joe snorts. "Well, I'll just have to wing it. I'll use some of the transparencies from my pitch six months ago. Nobody will know the difference. Those meetings are a waste of time anyway. Nobody cares about them. Everybody thinks they are just a waste of two hours each week."

"Anyway, can you email me your input for the progress report by the end of the day?" asks Cathy.

"I have to leave early for the game."

"What game?"

"Aren't you listening to anything I say? The Little League game."

"Maybe you should start working on it now," Cathy suggests.

"I just have to talk to Jim first about the game tonight." says Joe. "Then I'll write up a couple of paragraphs. Can't you just take notes at the meeting tomorrow when I give my pitch? That should give you what you need for the report."

"It can't wait until then. The report has to be in the mail tomorrow, and I'll be working on it late into the night."

"So, you won't be at the game?"

"Just send me your input through email."

"I'm not being paid to be a typist," Joe declares. "I can write it much faster. You can get somebody to type it. You'll probably want to edit it anyway. The last report to the customer looked completely different from the input I provided. It looked like you completely rewrote it."

Cathy looks back down at her desk and attempts to continue her work.

Case Questions

1. What are some of the communication problems?
2. What should Cathy do?
3. What do you think Joe will do?
4. How could Cathy and Joe have handled this situation better?

5. What could have been done to prevent the communication problem between Cathy and Joe?

Group Activity

Two participants in the class act out this scenario. Immediately afterward, have a class discussion that addresses the five questions above.

Part 3

Project Planning and Control

The chapters in Part 3 address techniques for planning and controlling a project in order to successfully achieve the project objective. Planning determines *what* needs to be done, *who* will do it, *how long* it will take, and *how much* it will cost. Taking the time to develop a well-thought-out plan is critical to the successful accomplishment of the project objective. Developing a detailed plan includes (1) defining the specific activities needed to perform the project and assigning responsibility for each, (2) determining the sequence in which those activities must be accomplished, (3) estimating the time and resources that will be needed for each activity, and (4) preparing a project schedule and budget. Many projects have overrun their budgets, missed their completion dates, or only partially met their technical specifications because no viable plan was created before the project was started. To avoid this, you must *plan the work, then work the plan.*

Once a plan has been established, it must be implemented. This means performing the work according to the plan and controlling the work so that the project scope is accomplished within budget and on schedule. Once the project starts, it's necessary to monitor progress to ensure that everything is going according to the plan. This involves measuring actual progress and comparing it to planned progress. If, at any time, the project is not proceeding according to plan, corrective action must be taken and replanning must be done. The key to effective project control is comparing actual progress with the plan on a timely and regular basis and taking any needed corrective action immediately.

9 Planning

A Philosophy of Planning

Planning is an essential part of project management. Without an effective plan, the chance of failure is greatly increased for any project. In essence, the plan is a roadmap that shows you how to get from where you currently are to where you want to be. Without it, you probably won't end up where you want to be. Unfortunately, that is the way many projects are managed—without an effective roadmap. To help overcome this problem, Andrew Smith, director of quality for the Delta Catalytic Corporation in Calgary, Alberta, compiled what he calls "thirty nuggets of wisdom" that can help improve the entire process of planning. The following are among these nuggets.

1. The essence of planning is to stop and think before you actually start a project, in order to consider how it can best be done.
2. Focus on the work, not on whether it will make you look good or bad.
3. When faced with a problem, always ask how the company handled it before, in order to gain some insights.
4. Avoid the tendency to be overly optimistic, especially at the initial phase of the project—if you think the project will actually take an additional month, say so.
5. Validate the project plan with those involved in the project—if there is disagreement, then set it straight before you proceed.

6. Become an expert at calling project meetings, especially for planning purposes.
7. Don't rely solely on a chart to communicate your project plan—include a brief narrative.
8. Always look ahead, and do this with your project team.
9. Don't set the plan until the required data are available and are accurate.
10. Be effective in the distribution, timeliness, comprehensiveness, conciseness, format, and consistency of your plans.

For additional nuggets of wisdom read the material in this chapter, and when you get a chance, read Andrew Smith's article in *PM Network*.

Source: A. Smith, "A Personal Philosophy of Planning," *PM Network,* June 1995.

Better Project Plans

Wilson Mar, who works with a consortium of project management experts who pioneered the use of tools and techniques to analyze, design, and communicate project plans, describes many useful things to consider when building project plans. He states that although a project plan is sometimes expected to be a crystal ball that predicts exactly when certain events will happen, it's better to view the project plan as a framework for coordinating work, communicating ideas, and analyzing the impact of change.

One of the suggestions he makes for improving project plans is to intimately involve the team in the planning process by having workers estimate the duration of their own work, because they know it best. Also, he suggests using the different personalities on the team. For example, have detail-minded people check that the plan is complete and help with proofreading, have anxious people make a list of potential difficulties, and have confident people resolve roadblocks and come up with contingency actions. Another suggestion is to accept that plans must sometimes be revised and that they should not be "set in concrete," since that doesn't reflect the real world. Mar stresses the fact that honesty and openness should be built into plans, and he recommends that descriptions of what needs to be accomplished be based on the value that is added, as in "generate a list of ideas," "identify management concerns," and "incorporate feedback."

In conclusion, Mar states that project plans should be structured more as a checklist of accomplishments than as an accumulation of expenses. An understanding of the topics presented in this chapter will prepare you to develop a high-quality project plan.

Source: W. Mar, "New Paradigms for Project Plans," *PM Network,* June 1993.

This chapter describes techniques used to plan the work elements and activities that need to be carried out in order to accomplish a project. You will become familiar with

- clearly defining the project objective
- developing a work breakdown structure
- developing a network diagram
- utilizing a project management methodology called the systems development life cycle for information systems development projects

Planning is the systematic arrangement of tasks to accomplish an objective. The plan lays out what needs to be accomplished and how it is to be accomplished. The plan becomes a benchmark against which actual progress can be compared; then, if deviations occur, corrective action can be taken.

It is important that the people who will be involved in performing the work are also involved in planning the work. They are usually the most knowledgeable about what detailed activities need to be done and how long each should take. By participating in the planning of the work, individuals will become committed to accomplishing it according to the plan and within the schedule and budget. *Participation builds commitment.* In large, multi-year projects that involve hundreds or even thousands of people, it's not possible to involve everyone in the initial planning. As the project progresses, however, it may be possible to involve many of these individuals in developing more detailed plans.

PROJECT OBJECTIVE

The first step in the planning process is to define the project objective—the expected result or end product. The objective must be clearly defined and agreed upon by the customer and the organization or contractor that will perform the project. The objective must be clear, attainable, specific, and measurable. Achievement of the project objective must be easily recognizable by both the customer and the contractor. The objective is the target—the tangible end product that the project team must deliver.

For a project, the objective is usually defined in terms of scope, schedule, and cost—it requires completing the work within budget by a certain time. For example, the objective of a project might be to "introduce to the market in ten months and within a budget of $2,000,000 a new electronic household cooking product, which meets certain predefined performance specifications." Another example is to "produce a four-color, sixteen-page, back-to-school merchandise catalog and mail it by July 31 to all targeted potential customers in the county, within a budget of $40,000."

A project objective such as "complete the house" is too ambiguous, since the customer and the contractor may have different views of what is meant by "complete." A better objective is to "complete the house by May 31 in accordance with the floor plans and specifi-

REINFORCE YOUR LEARNING

1. *For a project, the objective is usually defined in terms of* _____, _____, *and* _____.

cations dated October 15 and within a budget of $150,000." The specifications and floor plans provide the details as to the scope of the work that the contractor agreed to perform. Therefore, no arguments should arise about whether the landscaping and carpeting were to be included or about the size of the entrance door, the color of paint in the bedrooms, or the style of lighting fixtures—all of these should have been spelled out in the specifications.

Ideally, the project objective should be clear and concise at the beginning of the project. However, sometimes the project objective needs to be modified as the project proceeds. The project manager and the client must agree on all changes to the initial project objective. Any such changes might affect the work scope, completion date, and final cost.

WORK BREAKDOWN STRUCTURE (WBS)

Once the project objective has been defined, the next step is to determine what work elements, or activities, need to be performed to accomplish it. This requires developing a list of all the activities. There are two approaches to preparing such a list. One approach is to have the project team "brainstorm" the list of activities. This approach is suitable for small projects; however, for larger, more complex projects, it's difficult to develop a comprehensive list of activities without forgetting some items. For such projects, creating a **work breakdown structure (WBS)** is a better approach.

The WBS breaks a project down into manageable pieces, or items, to help ensure that all of the work elements needed to complete the project work scope are identified. It's a hierarchical tree of end items that will be accomplished or produced by the project team during the project. The accomplishment or production of all of these items constitutes completion of the project work scope.

An example of a WBS for a town festival is shown in Figure 9.1. The graphic structure subdivides the project into smaller pieces called **work items.** Not all branches of the WBS have to be broken down to the same level. The lowest-level item of any one branch is called a **work package.** Most work packages in Figure 9.1 are at the second level, but four work items are further divided into a more detailed third level; one work item (List of Volunteers) is not broken down beyond the first level. The WBS usually indicates the organization or individual responsible for each work item.

The criteria for deciding how much detail or how many levels to put in the WBS are (1) the level at which a single individual or organization can be assigned responsibility and accountability for accomplishing the work package and (2) the level at which you want to control the budget and monitor and collect cost data during the project. There is not a single correct WBS for any project. For example, two different project teams might develop somewhat different WBSs for the same project.

FIGURE 9.1   Work Breakdown Structure for Festival Project

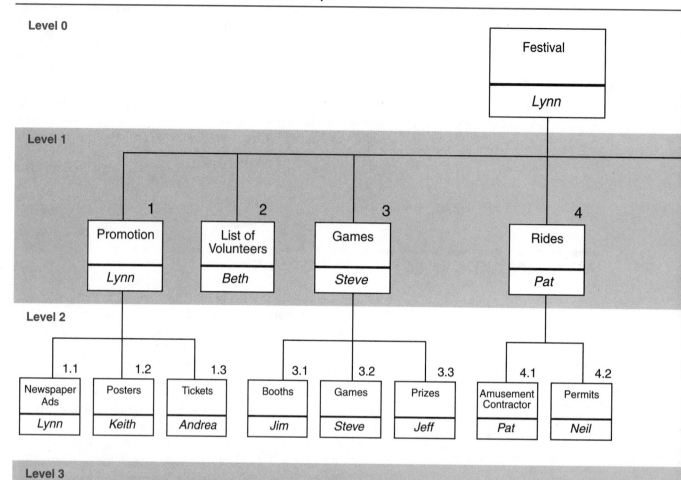

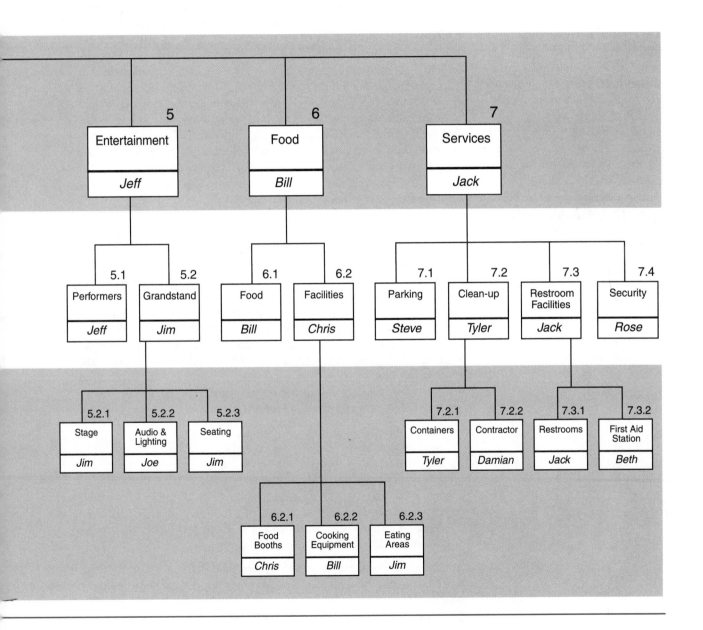

RESPONSIBILITY MATRIX

The **responsibility matrix** is a method used to display, in tabular format, the individuals responsible for accomplishing the work items in the WBS. It's a useful tool because it emphasizes who is responsible for each work item and shows each individual's role in supporting the overall project. Figure 9.2 shows the responsibility matrix associated with the WBS in Figure 9.1 for the festival project.

Some responsibility matrices use an X to show who is responsible for each work item; others use a P to designate primary responsibility and an S to indicate support responsibility for a specific work item. For example, Figure 9.2 indicates that Jim has primary responsibility for the game booths, with Chris and Joe supporting this effort. It is a good idea to show only one individual as the lead, or primary, person responsible for each work item. Designating two individuals as co-chairpersons increases the risk that certain work will "fall through the cracks" because each person assumes that the other person is going to do it.

REINFORCE YOUR LEARNING

5. *A responsibility matrix shows which individual is responsible for accomplishing each*
   _____ _____ *in the work breakdown structure.*

DEFINING ACTIVITIES

As noted earlier, a list of specific, detailed activities necessary to accomplish the overall project can be generated through team brainstorming, especially for small projects. However, for projects in which a work breakdown structure is used, individual activities can be defined by the person or team responsible for each work package. An **activity** is a defined piece of work that consumes time. It does not necessarily require the expenditure of effort by people—for example, waiting for concrete to harden can take several days but does not require any human effort.

For work package 3.1 in Figure 9.1, game booths, the following eight detailed activities may be identified:

Design booths
Specify materials
Buy materials
Construct booths
Paint booths
Dismantle booths
Move booths to festival site and reassemble
Dismantle booths and move to storage

When all the detailed activities have been defined for each of the work packages, the next step is to graphically portray them in a **network diagram** that shows the appropriate sequence and interrelationships to accomplish the overall project work scope.

DEVELOPING THE NETWORK PLAN

Network planning is a technique that is helpful in planning, scheduling, and controlling projects that consist of many interrelated activities.

FIGURE 9.2   Responsibility Matrix for Festival Project

WBS Item	Work Item	Andrea	Beth	Bill	Chris	Damian	Jack	Jeff	Jim	Joe	Keith	Lynn	Neil	Pat	Rose	Steve	Tyler
	Festival		S	S			S	S				P		S		S	
1	**Promotion**	S									S	P					
1.1	Newspaper Ads											P					
1.2	Posters										P						
1.3	Tickets	P	S									S					
2	**List of Volunteers**		P						S						S		
3	**Games**							S	S							P	
3.1	Booths				S				P	S							
3.2	Games														S	P	
3.3	Prizes							P							S		
4	**Rides**												S	P			
4.1	Amusement Contractor													P			
4.2	Permits												P	S			
5	**Entertainment**							P	S	S							
5.1	Performers				S			P									
5.2	Grandstand								P	S							
5.2.1	Stage								P	S							
5.2.2	Audio & Lighting									P							
5.2.3	Seating				S				P								
6	**Food**			P	S												
6.1	Food			P											S		
6.2	Facilities			S	P				S								
6.2.1	Food Booths			P					S	S							
6.2.2	Cooking Equipment			P													
6.2.3	Eating Areas								P						S		
7	**Services**						P								S	S	S
7.1	Parking														P		
7.2	Clean-up					S											P
7.2.1	Containers																P
7.2.2	Contractor					P											
7.3	Restroom Facilities		S				P										
7.3.1	Restrooms						P										
7.3.2	First Aid Stations		P														
7.4	Security					S				S					P		

KEY: **P** = Primary responsibility; S = Support responsibility.

Two network planning techniques, **program evaluation and review technique (PERT)** and the **critical path method (CPM),** were developed in the 1950s. Since that time, other forms of network planning, such as the **precedence diagramming method (PDM)** and the **graphical evaluation and review technique (GERT),** have been developed. All of these fall under the general category of network planning techniques, because they all make use of a network diagram to show the sequential flow and interrelationships of activities.

In the past, there were distinguishable methodological differences between PERT and CPM. Today, however, when most people refer to a CPM diagram or PERT chart, they mean a generic network diagram. See Figures 9.8 and 9.9 (discussed later in this chapter) for examples of network diagrams for a project to conduct a consumer market study; Figure 9.14 is an example for a project to develop a sales reporting system.

Network planning techniques are often compared with a somewhat more familiar tool known as a **Gantt chart,** sometimes called a **bar chart.** This is an older planning and scheduling tool, developed in the early 1900s; however, it remains very popular today, mainly because of its simplicity.

The Gantt chart combines the two functions of planning and scheduling. Figure 9.3 shows a Gantt chart for a consumer market study. Activities are listed down the left-hand side, and a time scale is shown along the bottom. The estimated duration for each activity is indicated by a line or bar spanning the period during which the activity is expected to be accomplished. Columns that indicate who is responsible for each task can be added to the chart.

With Gantt charts, the scheduling of activities occurs simultaneously with their planning. The person drawing the activity lines or bars must be aware of the interrelationships of the activities—that is, which activities must be finished before others can start and which activities can be performed concurrently. One of the major drawbacks to the traditional Gantt chart is that it does not graphically display the interrelationships of activities. Therefore, it's not obvious which other activities will be affected if one activity is delayed. However, most project management software packages can produce Gantt charts that display the interdependencies among tasks by using connecting arrows.

Because planning and scheduling are done simultaneously in a traditional Gantt chart, it is cumbersome to make changes to the plan manually. This is especially true if an activity at the beginning of the project is delayed and thus many of the remaining lines or bars have to be redrawn. Network techniques, on the other hand, separate the planning and scheduling functions. A network diagram is the result, or output, of the planning function and is not drawn to a time scale. From this diagram a schedule is developed (this topic will be covered in detail in the next chapter). Separating the two functions makes it much easier to revise a plan and calculate an updated schedule.

FIGURE 9.3   Gantt Chart for Consumer Market Study Project

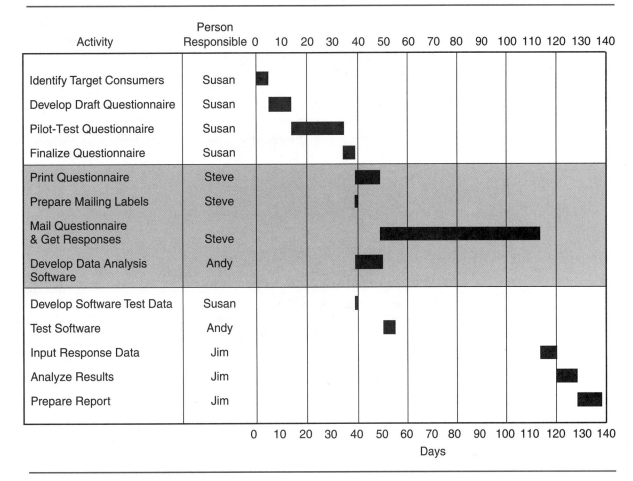

Network Principles

There are a few basic principles that must be understood and followed in preparing a network diagram. There are also different formats that can be used in drawing the diagram. One format is **activity in the box (AIB),** also known as activity on the node (AON), and another format is **activity on the arrow (AOA).**

REINFORCE YOUR LEARNING

6. Identify two formats for drawing a network diagram.

ACTIVITY IN THE BOX (AIB)

In the AIB format, each activity is represented by a box in the network diagram, and the description of the activity is written within the box, as shown below.

```
┌─────────────┐
│    Get      │
│ Volunteers  │
├───┬─────────┤
│ 7 │         │
└───┴─────────┘
```

Activities consume time, and their description usually starts with a verb. Each activity is represented by one and only one box. In addition, each box is assigned a *unique* activity number. In the above example, the activity "Get Volunteers" has been given activity number 7.

Activities have a **precedential relationship**—that is, they are linked in a precedential order to show which activities must be finished before others can start. Arrows linking the activity boxes show the direction of precedence. *An activity cannot start until all of the preceding activities that are linked into it by arrows have been finished.*

Certain activities have to be done in a serial order. For example, as shown below, only after "Wash Car" is finished can "Dry Car" start.

Some activities may be done concurrently. For example, as shown below, "Get Volunteers" and "Buy Materials" can be done concurrently; when they are *both* finished, "Construct Booth" can start. Similarly, when "Paint Booth" is finished, *both* "Dismantle Booth" and "Clean Up" can start and be worked on concurrently.

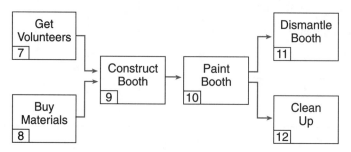

ACTIVITY ON THE ARROW (AOA)

In the AOA format, an activity is represented by an arrow in the network diagram, and the activity description is written above the arrow, as shown below.

Collect Data →

Each activity is represented by one and only one arrow. The tail of the arrow designates the start of the activity, and the head of the arrow represents the completion of the activity. The length and slope of the arrow are in no way indicative of the activity's duration or importance (unlike the situation in the Gantt chart, in which the length of the line or bar indicates the duration of the activity).

In the AOA format, activities are linked by circles called **events.** An event represents the finish of activities entering into it and the start of activities going out of it. In the AOA format, each event—not each activity—is assigned a unique number. For example, the activities shown below, "Wash Car" and "Dry Car," have a serial relationship and are linked together by event 2. Event 2 represents the completion of "Wash Car" and the start of "Dry Car."

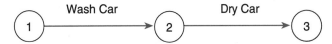

The event at the beginning (tail of the arrow) of the activity is known as the activity's **predecessor event,** and the event at the end (head of the arrow) of the activity is known as the activity's **successor event.** For the activity "Wash Car," the predecessor event is 1 and the successor event is 2; for the activity "Dry Car," the predecessor event is 2 and the successor event is 3.

All activities going into an event (circle) must be finished before any activities leading from that event can start. For example, as shown below, the activities "Get Volunteers" and "Buy Materials" can be done concurrently, but only when they are *both* finished can the activity "Construct Booth" start. Similarly, when "Paint Booth" is finished, *both* "Dismantle Booth" and "Clean Up" can start and be worked on concurrently.

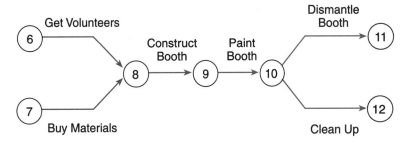

DUMMY ACTIVITIES

In the activity-on-the-arrow format, there is a special type of activity known as a **dummy activity,** which consumes zero time and is represented by a dashed arrow in the network diagram. Dummy activities, which are used only with the activity-on-the-arrow format, are needed for two reasons: to help in the unique identification of activities and to show certain precedential relationships that otherwise could not be shown.

In drawing an activity-on-the-arrow network diagram, there are two basic rules with regard to the unique identification of activities:

1. Each event (circle) in the network diagram must have a unique event number—that is, no two events in the network diagram can have the same event number.
2. Each activity must have a unique combination of predecessor and successor event numbers.

Activities A and B below both have the predecessor–successor event number combination 1–2. This is not allowed in an AOA network diagram, because if someone referred to activity 1–2, you would not know whether activity A or activity B was being discussed.

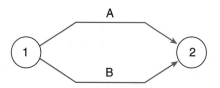

If computer software is used to calculate a project schedule based on an activity-on-the-arrow network diagram, it will probably require that each activity be identified by a unique predecessor–successor event number combination.

The insertion of a dummy activity, as shown below, allows activities A and B to have unique predecessor–successor event number combinations. In (a), activity A is referred to as 1–3 and activity B as 1–2. Similarly, in (b), activity A is referred to as 1–2 and activity B as 1–3. Both approaches are acceptable ways of dealing with this situation.

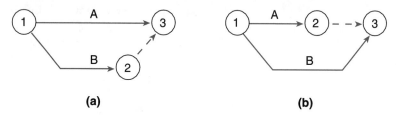

Let's consider an example of a case in which a dummy activity must be used to show precedential relationships that otherwise could not be shown. The situation is as follows:

• Activities A and B can be done concurrently.
• When activity A is finished, activity C can start.
• When both activity A and activity B are finished, activity D can start.

To portray this logic a dummy activity must be used, as shown below.

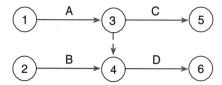

The dummy activity 3–4 in a sense extends activity A to show that, in addition to being necessary in order to start activity C, its finish is also needed (along with the finish of activity B) in order to start activity D.

The format shown below is incorrect because it indicates that activities A and B must both be finished in order for activities C and D to start, when, in fact, only activity A (not A and B) must be finished in order for activity C to start.

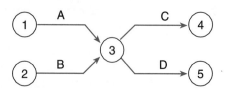

REINFORCE YOUR LEARNING

9. Dummy activities are used only when the _____ format is used for drawing a network diagram. Dummy activities are shown using a _____ _____ .

An advantage of the activity-in-the-box format is that the logic can be shown without the use of dummy activities. For example, below is the AIB format for the relationship shown above; no dummy activity is needed.

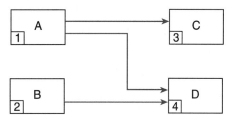

LOOPS

Shown below in AIB and AOA formats is an illogical relationship among activities known as a *loop*. In preparing a network diagram, drawing activities in a loop is not allowed because it portrays a path of activities that perpetually repeats itself.

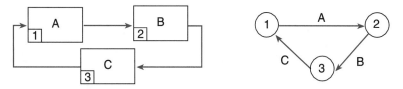

LADDERING

Some projects have a set of activities that are repeated several times. For example, consider a project involving the painting of three rooms. Painting each room requires (1) preparing the room to be painted, (2) painting the ceiling and walls, and (3) painting the trim. Assume that three experts will be available—one to do the preparation, one to paint the ceilings and walls, and one to do the trim.

It may seem logical to draw a network diagram for the project as shown in Figure 9.4 or 9.5. However, Figure 9.4 indicates that all the activities must be done in serial order, which means that at any one

FIGURE 9.4 Activities Performed Serially

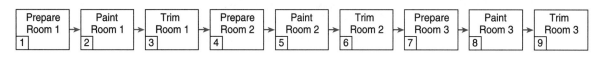

(a) Activity-in-the-Box Format

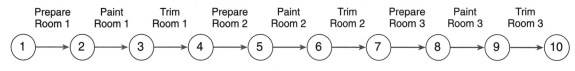

(b) Activity-on-the-Arrow Format

FIGURE 9.5   Activities Performed Concurrently

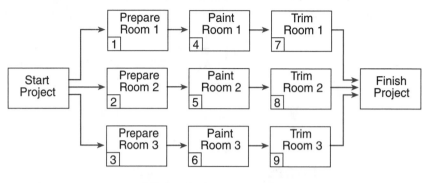

(a) Activity-in-the-Box Format

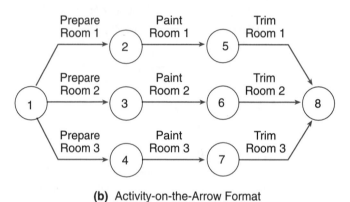

(b) Activity-on-the-Arrow Format

time only one person is working while two other people are waiting. Figure 9.5, on the other hand, indicates that all three rooms can be done concurrently, which is not possible because only one expert is available for each type of activity.

Figure 9.6 shows a technique known as **laddering,** which can be used to diagram this project. It indicates that each expert, after finishing one room, can start working on the next room. This approach will allow the project to be completed in the shortest possible time while making the best use of available resources (the experts).

Preparing the Network Diagram

Given a list of activities and a knowledge of network principles, you can prepare a network diagram. First, select the format to be used—activity in the box or activity on the arrow. Next, start drawing the activities in their logical precedential order, as the project should progress from its beginning to its completion. When deciding on the sequence in which the activities should be drawn to show their log-

FIGURE 9.6   Laddering

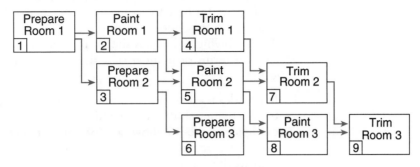

(a) Activity-in-the-Box Format

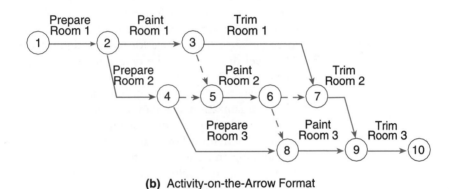

(b) Activity-on-the-Arrow Format

ical precedential relationship to one another, you should ask the following three questions regarding each individual activity:

1. Which activities must be finished *immediately* before this activity can be started?
2. Which activities can be done concurrently with this activity?
3. Which activities cannot be started until this activity is finished?

By answering these questions for each activity, you should be able to draw a network diagram that portrays the interrelationships and sequence of activities needed to accomplish the project work scope.

The entire network diagram should flow from left to right, although some arrows may flow from right to left to prevent the overall diagram from becoming too long. Unlike the Gantt chart, the network diagram is *not* drawn to a time scale. It is easier to visualize the entire project if the network diagram can be drawn to fit on a large sheet of paper. If the network is very large, however, it may require multiple pages. In such cases, it may be necessary to create a reference system or set of symbols to show the linkages between activities on different pages.

When initially drawing the network diagram for a project, don't be too concerned about drawing it neatly. It's better to sketch out a rough draft of the diagram and make sure the logical relationships among the activities are correct. Then, go back later and draw a neater diagram (or have the computer generate the diagram if you are using project management software).

The following guidelines should be considered in deciding how detailed (in terms of number of activities) a network diagram for a project should be:

1. If a work breakdown structure has been prepared for the project, then activities should be identified for each work package. For example, Figure 9.7 shows a WBS for a project involving a consumer market study and the activities that have been identified for each work package.

2. It may be preferable to draw a summary-level network first and then expand it to a more detailed network. A *summary network* is one that contains a small number of higher-level activities rather than a large number of detailed activities. In some cases, a summary network may suffice for use throughout a project.

3. The level of detail may be determined by certain obvious interface or transfer points:
   - If there is a change in responsibility—that is, a different person or organization takes over responsibility for continuing the work—it should define the end of one activity and the start of other activities. For example, if one person is responsible for building an item and another person is responsible for packaging it, these should be two separate activities.
   - If there is a tangible, deliverable output or product as a result of an activity, it should define the end of one activity and the start of other activities. Some examples of outputs include a report, a drawing, the shipment of a piece of equipment, and the design of computer software. In the case of a brochure, the production of a draft brochure should be defined as the end of one activity; another activity, perhaps "Approve Draft Brochure," would follow.

4. Activities should not be longer in estimated duration than the time intervals at which actual project progress will be reviewed and compared to planned progress. For example, if the project is a three-year endeavor and the project team plans to review project progress monthly, then the network should contain no activities with estimated durations greater than 30 days. If there are activities with longer estimated durations, they should be broken up into more detailed activities with durations of 30 days or less.

Whatever the level of detail used in the initial network diagram, some activities may be broken down further as the project progresses. It's always easier to identify activities that need to be done in the near term (during the next several weeks or months) than to identify activities that are a year in the future. It is not unusual to add more detail to a network diagram as the project moves forward.

In some cases, an organization may do similar projects for different customers, and certain portions of these projects may include the same types of activities in the same logical precedential relationships.

FIGURE 9.7   Work Breakdown Structure for Consumer Market Study Project

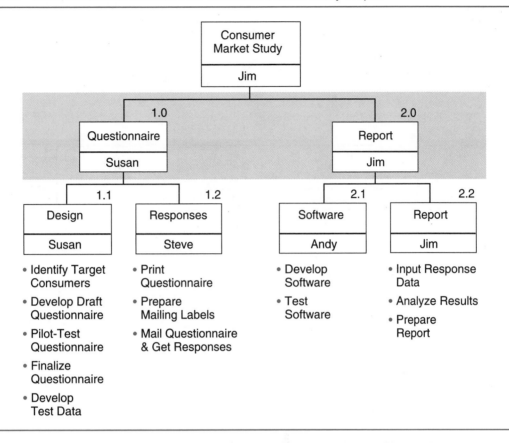

If so, it may be worthwhile to develop standard *subnetworks* for these portions of the projects. Having standard subnetworks can save effort and time when a network diagram is developed for an overall project. Standard subnetworks should be developed for those portions of projects for which the logical relationships among the activities have been well established through historical practice. These subnetworks may, of course, be modified as necessary for a particular project.

Finally, when the entire network diagram has been drawn, it's necessary to assign a unique activity number either to each activity (box), if you are using the activity-in-the-box format, or to each event (circle), if you are using the activity-on-the-arrow format.

Figures 9.8 and 9.9 show complete network diagrams for the consumer market study project in the AIB and AOA formats, respectively. Notice the addition of the person responsible on these diagrams.

The choice between the activity-in-the-box format and the activity-on-the-arrow format is a matter of personal preference. Both formats use a network based on precedential relationships. The network is a roadmap that displays how all the activities fit together to accomplish the project work scope. It also is a communication tool for the project team because it shows who is responsible for each activity and how that person's work ties into the overall project.

FIGURE 9.8 Network Diagram for Consumer Market Study Project (Activity-in-the-Box Format)

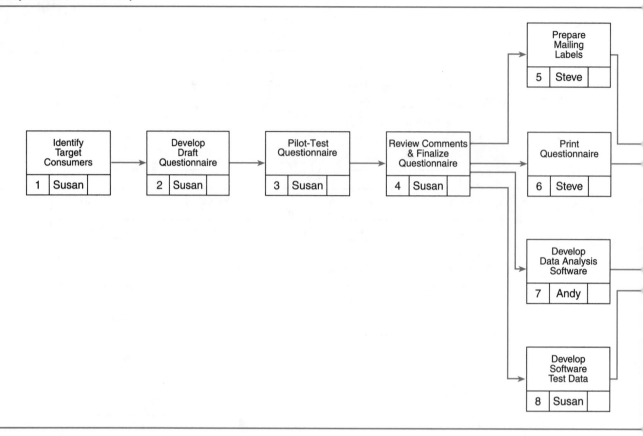

PLANNING FOR INFORMATION SYSTEMS DEVELOPMENT

Because of the rapidly increasing number of information technology-related projects that are being undertaken, it seems appropriate to include a section in each of the next few chapters on project management practices in information systems development. An **information system (IS)** is a computer-based system that accepts data as input, processes the data, and produces useful information for users. Information systems include computerized order entry systems, automatic teller machines, and billing, payroll, and inventory systems. The development of an IS is a challenging process that requires extensive planning and control to ensure that the system meets user requirements and is finished on time and within budget.

A project management planning tool, or methodology, called the **systems development life cycle (SDLC)** is often used to help plan, execute, and control IS development projects. The SDLC consists of a set of phases or steps that need to be completed over the

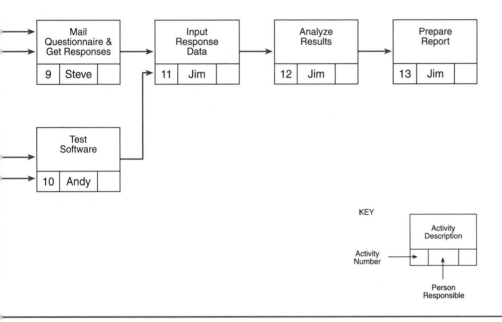

course of a development project. Many people view the SDLC as a classic problem-solving approach. It consists of the following steps:

1. *Problem definition.* Data are gathered and analyzed, and problems and opportunities are clearly defined. Technical, economic, operational, and other feasibility factors are defined and studied to determine, at least initially, whether the IS can be successfully developed and used.
2. *System analysis.* The development team defines the scope of the system to be developed, interviews potential users, studies the existing system (which might be manual), and defines user requirements.
3. *System design.* Several alternative conceptual designs are produced that describe input, processing, output, hardware, software, and the database at a high level. Each of these alternatives is then evaluated, and the best one is selected for further design and development.
4. *System development.* The actual system is brought into existence. Hardware is purchased, and software is either purchased,

**FIGURE 9.9   Network Diagram for Consumer Market Study Project
(Activity-on-the-Arrow Format)**

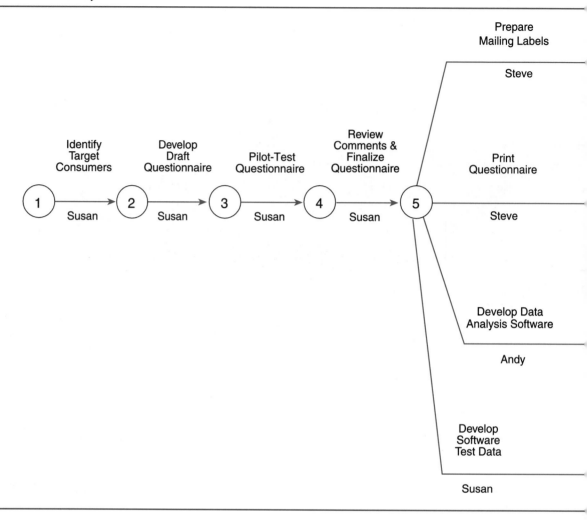

REINFORCE YOUR LEARNING
11. *Refer to Figure 9.9.*
   a. In order to start "Test Software," which activities must have been completed immediately beforehand?

   b. True or false: Once "Print Questionnaire" is finished, "Mail Questionnaire & Get Responses" can start immediately.

customized, or developed. Databases, input screens, system reports, telecommunication networks, security controls, and other features are also developed.

5. *System testing.* After individual modules within the system have been developed, testing can begin. Testing involves looking for logical errors, database errors, errors of omission, security errors, and other problems that might prevent the system from being successful. After the individual modules are tested and problems are corrected, the entire system is also tested. Once the users and the developers are convinced that the system is error-free, the system can be implemented.

6. *System implementation.* The existing system is replaced with the new, improved system, and users are trained. Several methodologies exist for converting from the existing system to the new system with minimal interruption to the users.

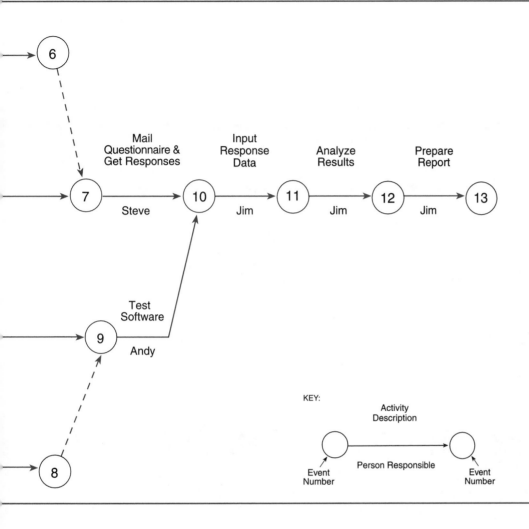

The SDLC concludes with implementation of the system. The system life cycle itself continues with a formal review of the development process after the system is up and running, and then continues with maintenance, modifications, and enhancements to the system.

An IS Example: ABC Office Designs

A corporation called ABC Office Designs has a large of number of sales representatives who sell office furniture to major corporations. Each sales representative is assigned to a specific state, and each state is part of one of four regions in the country. To enable management to monitor the number and amount of sales for each representative, for each state, and for each region, ABC has decided to build an IS. In addition, the IS needs to be able to track prices, inventory, and the competition.

FIGURE 9.10   Work Breakdown Structure for Sales Reporting System Project

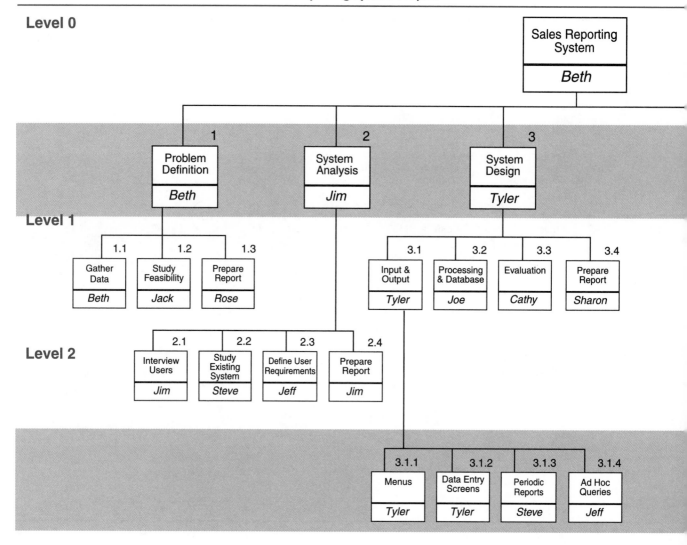

The IS Department within the corporation has assigned Beth Smith to be the project manager of the Sales Reporting System development project. With the help of her staff, Beth identified all of the major tasks that need to be accomplished and developed the work breakdown structure shown in Figure 9.10. Notice that the WBS follows the SDLC. At level one, the major tasks are problem definition, analysis, design, development, testing, and implementation. Each of these tasks is further broken down into level-two tasks, and a few are broken down further into level-three tasks.

After the project team developed the WBS, the responsibility matrix shown in Figure 9.11 was developed. Notice that this table reflects all of the activities shown in the WBS. In addition, it shows who has primary responsibility and secondary responsibility for each task.

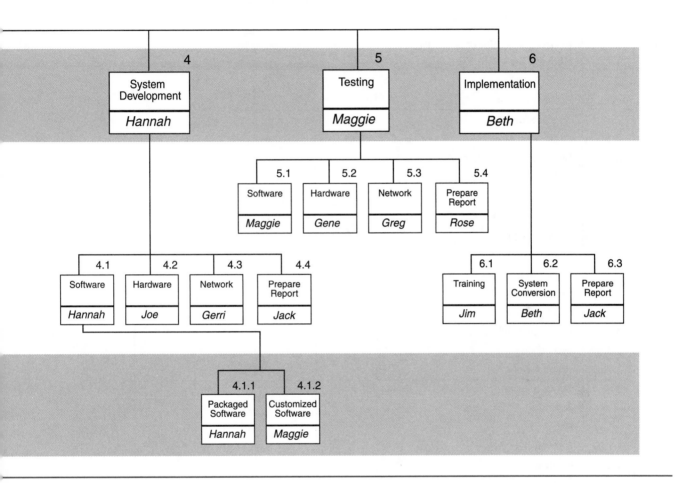

After each task was assigned team members, the project manager put together a Gantt chart of the major tasks to be accomplished. The Gantt chart is shown in Figure 9.12. Notice that the Gantt chart provides a clear visual representation of the activities to be performed and the time frame in which each will be done. The project manager has allocated 5 weeks for problem definition, 10 weeks for system analysis, 10 weeks for system design, 15 weeks for system development, 8 weeks for system testing, and 5 weeks for system implementation. The project, as shown, needs to be completed within 50 weeks.

After completing the Gantt chart, the project manager felt that it was important to develop a network diagram to show the interdependencies that exist between tasks. Before Beth did this, however, she and the project team created a list of all tasks to be done, with the immediate predecessor for each task listed to the right of the task, as

FIGURE 9.11   Responsibility Matrix for Sales Reporting System Project

WBS Item	Work Item	Beth	Jim	Jack	Rose	Steve	Jeff	Tyler	Cathy	Sharon	Hannah	Joe	Gerri	Maggie	Gene	Greg
	Sales Reporting System	P	S					S			S			S		
1	**Problem Definition**	P		S	S											
1.1	Gather Data	P	S										S			
1.2	Study Feasibility			P		S	S		S	S						
1.3	Prepare Report	S			P											
2	**System Analysis**		P			S	S									
2.1	Interview Users		P		S						S			S		
2.2	Study Existing System					P										
2.3	Define User Requirements						P									
2.4	Prepare Report		P													
3	**System Design**							P	S	S	S					
3.1	Input & Output					S	S	P								
3.1.1	Menus		S					P								
3.1.2	Data Entry		S					P								
3.1.3	Periodic Reports					P	S						S			
3.1.4	Ad Hoc Questions					S	P						S			
3.2	Processing Database											P			S	S
3.3	Evaluation	S	S	S					S							
3.4	Prepare Report									P	S					
4	**System Development**			S							P	S	S			
4.1	Software										P	S	S	S		
4.1.1	Packaging										P	S	S	S		
4.1.2	Customize Software											S	S	P		
4.2	Hardware							S				P				
4.3	Network												P			
4.4	Prepare Report			P												
5	**Testing**				S									P	S	S
5.1	Software					S	S							P		
5.2	Hardware											S	S		P	
5.3	Network									S	S					P
5.4	Prepare Report				P									S	S	S
6	**Implementation**	P	S	S												
6.1	Training		P								S		S			
6.2	System Conversion	P									S		S			
6.3	Prepare Report	S	S	P												

KEY: **P** = Primary responsibility; S = Support responsibility.

FIGURE 9.12   Gantt Chart for Sales Reporting System Project

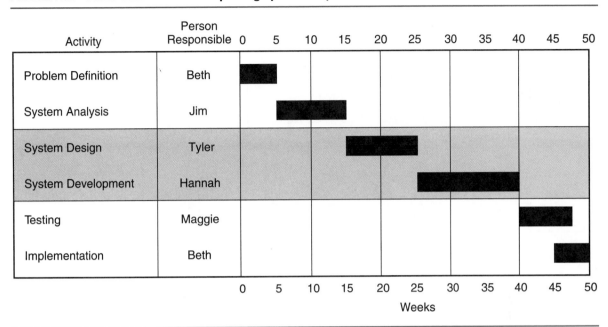

FIGURE 9.13   List of Activities and Immediate Predecessors

SALES REPORTING SYSTEM PROJECT

Activity	Immediate Predecessors
1. Gather Data	—
2. Study Feasibility	—
3. Prepare Problem Definition Report	1, 2
4. Interview Users	3
5. Study Existing System	3
6. Define User Requirements	4
7. Prepare System Analysis Report	5, 6
8. Input & Output	7
9. Processing & Database	7
10. Evaluation	8, 9
11. Prepare System Design Report	10
12. Software Development	11
13. Hardware Development	11
14. Network Development	11
15. Prepare System Development Report	12, 13, 14
16. Software Testing	15
17. Hardware Testing	15
18. Network Testing	15
19. Prepare Testing Report	16, 17, 18
20. Training	19
21. System Conversion	19
22. Prepare Implementation Report	20, 21

FIGURE 9.14   Network Diagram for Sales Reporting System Project (Activity-in-the-Box Format)

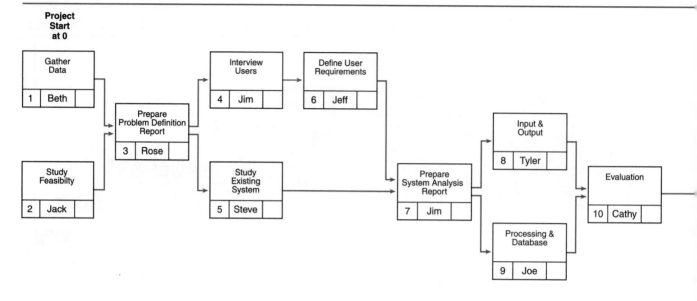

shown in Figure 9.13. Notice that before "Prepare Problem Definition Report" can start, both "Gather Data" and "Study Feasibility" must be finished. Similarly, before "Prepare System Analysis Report" can start, both "Study Existing System" and "Determine User Requirements" must be completed.

With this list Beth then prepared the network diagram using the activity-in-the-box format as shown in Figure 9.14.

PROJECT MANAGEMENT SOFTWARE

A wide variety of affordable project management software packages are available for purchase. These packages allow the project manager and the project team to plan and control projects in a completely interactive mode. See Appendix A at the end of the book for a thorough discussion of project management software, including a list of vendors.

Common features of project management software allow the user to

- create lists of tasks with their estimated durations
- establish interdependencies among tasks

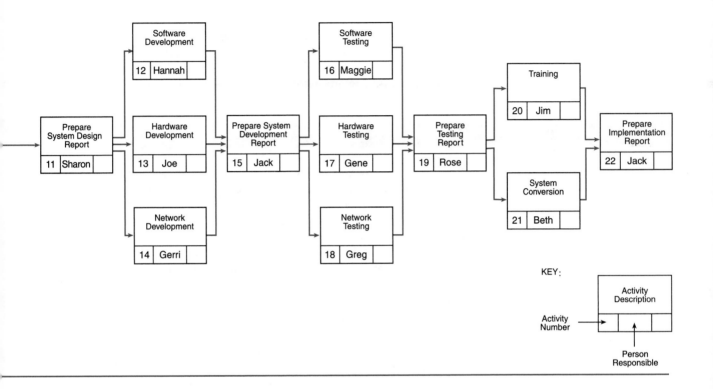

- work with a variety of time scales, including hours, days, weeks, months, and years
- handle certain constraints—for example, a task cannot start before a certain date, a task must be started by a certain date, labor unions allow no more than two people to work on the weekends
- track team members, including their pay rates, hours worked thus far on a project, and upcoming vacation dates
- incorporate company holidays, weekends, and team member vacation days into calendaring systems
- handle shifts of workers (day, evening, night)
- monitor and forecast budgets
- look for conflicts—for example, overallocated resources and time conflicts
- generate a wide variety of reports
- interface with other software packages such as spreadsheets and databases
- sort information in a variety of ways—for example, by project, by team member, or by work package
- handle multiple projects
- work on-line and respond quickly to changes in schedule, budget, or personnel

- compare actual costs with budgeted costs
- display data in a variety of ways, including both Gantt charts and network diagrams

Note: As mentioned earlier, most project management software has the ability to provide Gantt charts that display the interdependencies among tasks by connecting tasks and their predecessors by lines with arrowheads. The network diagrams most commonly displayed with project management software use the activity-in-the-box format. The user can move back and forth between the Gantt charts and the network diagrams with a click of the mouse.

SUMMARY

Planning is the systematic arrangement of tasks to accomplish an objective. The plan lays out what needs to be accomplished and how it is to be accomplished. The plan becomes a benchmark against which actual progress can be compared; then, if deviations occur, corrective action can be taken.

The first step in the planning process is to define the project objective—the expected result or end product. The project objective is usually defined in terms of scope, schedule, and cost. The objective must be clearly defined and agreed upon by the customer and the organization or contractor that will perform the project.

Once the project objective has been defined, the next step is to determine what work elements, or activities, need to be performed to accomplish it. This requires developing a list of all the activities.

The work breakdown structure (WBS) breaks a project down into manageable pieces, or items, to help ensure that all of the work elements needed to complete the project work scope are identified. It's a hierarchical tree of end items that will be accomplished or produced by the project team during the project. It usually indicates the organization or individual responsible for each work item.

A responsibility matrix is often developed to display, in tabular format, the individuals responsible for accomplishing the work items in the WBS. It's a useful tool because it emphasizes who is responsible for each work item and shows each individual's role in supporting the overall project.

Finally, network planning is a technique that is helpful in planning, scheduling, and controlling projects that consist of many interrelated activities. In addition, it is also useful for communicating information about projects. There are several different network plan formats that can be used; the two most popular are activity in the box (AIB) and activity on the arrow (AOA).

In the activity-in-the-box format, each activity is represented by a box in the network diagram, and the description of the activity is written within the box. In the activity-on-the-arrow format, each activity is represented by an arrow in the network diagram, and the activity description is written above the arrow.

After a list of activities has been created, a network diagram can be prepared. When deciding on the sequence in which the activities should be drawn to show their logical precedential relationship to one another, you must determine (1) which activities must be finished immediately before each activity can be started, (2) which activities can be done concurrently, and (3) which activities cannot be started until prior activities are finished.

Project planning is a critical activity in developing an information system (IS). A project management planning tool, or methodology, called the systems development life cycle (SDLC) is often used to help plan, execute, and control IS development projects. The SDLC consists of a set of phases or steps: problem definition, system analysis, system design, system development, system testing, and system implementation. All of these need to be completed over the course of a development project.

Numerous project management software packages are available to help project managers plan, track, and control projects in a completely interactive way.

QUESTIONS

1. What is meant by *planning a project?* What does this encompass?
2. Should the people who will actually perform the work be involved in planning the work? If so, why?
3. What is meant by the term *project objective?* What might happen if a project objective is not clearly written? Give three examples of clearly written project objectives.
4. What is a work breakdown structure? In describing a WBS, discuss the terms *end product, work item,* and *work package.*
5. What is a *responsibility matrix?* Discuss how it is related to a work breakdown structure.
6. What is an activity? Does it always require human effort? Refer to Figure 9.1. Provide a detailed list of activities needed to accomplish work package 3.3. Do the same for work package 4.2.
7. Draw a Gantt chart for a project on which you are currently working or have recently worked. What are some of the major advantages and disadvantages of Gantt charts?
8. Describe the differences between the activity-in-the-box format and the activity-on-the-arrow format.
9. What is meant by the terms *predecessor event* and *successor event?*
10. Refer to Figure 9.9. What activities must be accomplished before "Input Response Data" can start? What activities can start after "Review Comments & Finalize Questionnaire" has finished? List two activities that can be done concurrently.
11. What is a dummy activity? In which networking format is it used? Why? When?
12. Consider a project with the following requirements: Activities A and B can be done concurrently. Activities C and D can start immediately after activity A is finished. Activities E and F can

start only after activities A and B are finished. Draw the network diagram for this project using the activity-on-the-arrow format.

13. Are loops allowed in a network diagram? Why or why not?

14. When would you use laddering in a network diagram? Give an example, different from the one provided in the chapter, and draw the corresponding network diagram in both the activity-in-the-box and the activity-on-the-arrow formats.

15. Discuss the steps you should follow when drawing a network diagram. When deciding on the sequence in which the activities should be drawn to show their logical precedential relationship, what three questions should you ask regarding *each* activity?

16. What are information systems? Give some examples of information systems. Why is planning such a critical activity in the development of an IS?

17. What is the systems development life cycle? What phases does it include? Describe each phase.

18. Why would you recommend project management software to someone involved in project management? What features and benefits does it provide?

19. Draw a network diagram representing the following logic: As the project starts, activities A and B can be performed concurrently. When A is finished, activities C and D can start. When B is finished, activities E and F can start. When activities D and E are finished, activity G can start. The project is complete when activities C, F, and G are finished. Use both the activity-in-the-box and the activity-on-the-arrow formats.

20. Draw a network diagram representing the following information: The project starts with three activities, A, B, and C, which can be done concurrently. When A is finished, D can start; when B is finished, F can start; when B and D are finished, E can start. The project is complete when activities C, E, and F are finished. Use both the activity-in-the-box and the activity-on-the-arrow formats.

21. Draw a network diagram that represents the following IS development task list. Use both the activity-in-the-box and the activity-on-the-arrow formats.

Activity	Immediate Predecessor
1. Problem Definition	—
2. Study Current System	1
3. Define User Requirements	1
4. Logical System Design	3
5. Physical System Design	2
6. System Development	4, 5
7. System Testing	6
8. Convert Database	4, 5
9. System Conversion	7, 8

22. Find as many errors as you can in the following network diagram:

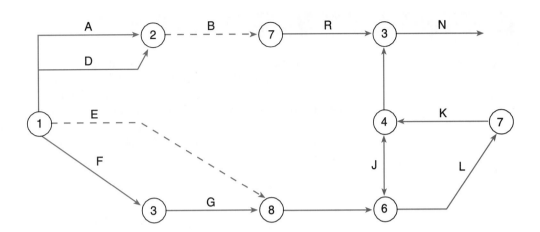

WORLD WIDE WEB EXERCISES

If you have difficulty accessing any of the Web addresses listed here, you can find these exercises (with up-to-date addresses) on the home page of Dr. James P. Clements, co-author of this book, at

www.towson.edu/~clements

1. A very good Web site on project management is maintained by researchers at the University of Umea in Sweden. Visit their home page at

www.hh.umu.se/fek

Scroll through the Swedish text until you reach a link (written in English) for "Research on Temporary Organizations and Project Management." Click on this link.

2. Read about the research activities that are being conducted by these researchers. Describe what you read.

3. List the names of the program director and at least three other researchers.

4. Scroll down until you see a link for IRNOP (International Research Network on Organizing by Projects). Click on this link. What is this research network all about? What countries are involved? Check out some of their Web sites.

5. Return to the IRNOP page. Find information on conferences. List the titles of at least five papers presented at these conferences that relate to topics discussed so far in this book.

6. Check out the link from the IRNOP page to the *Scandinavian Journal of Management.* List the titles of at least three project man-

agement papers in this journal. Which of these relate directly to project planning?

CASE STUDY

Assume that after several years of dating, you and your beloved have finally decided to get married. Your partner wants a fairly elaborate wedding, and you begin to realize that a lot of planning and work need to be done. Noticing your nervousness, your friends and families try to reassure you that everything will be okay, and they even offer to help with the wedding arrangements. Being a perfectionist, you want to make sure that everything goes as smoothly as possible.

Case Questions
1. List your assumptions.
2. Choose an overall project time span.
3. Develop a work breakdown structure.
4. Develop a responsibility matrix.
5. List the activities necessary to accomplish the project.
6. Draw a network diagram—use either format discussed in the chapter.

Group Activity
Form groups of three or four members. Within each group, do items 1 through 6 listed above as a team. Each group must choose one individual to make a five-minute presentation to the class explaining what the group has done.

10 Scheduling

A World-Class Sulphur, Oil, and Gas Mining Project

Main Pass Mine, located in waters over 200 feet deep in the Gulf of Mexico south of the Louisiana coastline, is an $850-million offshore complex for the production of molten sulphur, crude oil, and natural gas. It commenced full operation in April 1992. In order to construct this major complex, a project team was organized and sound project management principles were applied. The application of these principles resulted in the completion of this project on schedule and within cost constraints.

Because of the complexity of the project, a high degree of detail was required in the schedule. The activities that were critical to the successful on-time completion of this project and the interrelationships among the activities were clearly defined. A work breakdown structure (WBS) was developed, incorporating approximately 1,600 activities. Twenty-one thousand jobs were created in support of the design and construction of this offshore complex, and expenditures averaged over $30 million per month during the nearly 2 ½ years that it took to build the mine.

Main Pass Mine represents the first commercially viable source of elemental sulphur found in the United States in twenty-five years, and annual production is expected to meet nearly one-fifth of the total demand in the United States for the next thirty years. In addition, the oil and gas reserves are among the largest discovered in the Gulf of Mexico in recent years.

Source: W. Parr, "Main Pass Mine: A World-Class Sulphur, Oil, and Gas Mining Project," *PM Network*, June 1994.

Turgut Ozal

Turgut Ozal, the late President of Turkey, was a true believer in the democratic system of government and an optimist full of hope for a better world. He rose to worldwide prominence during the Persian Gulf War of 1990–1991, when he became the first leader to apply the United Nations' sanctions against Iraq. He was often seen on CNN speaking on Middle Eastern politics and the need for international cooperation and friendship.

Upon the unfortunate death of Turgut Ozal in 1993, Yapi Merkezi was assigned the job of forming a project team to build, in just a few days, a shrine that could accommodate the millions who would come to visit the resting place of the late president. Once the design had been selected, the project objective was the construction of the highest-quality resting place possible that was in compliance with religious beliefs and that would accommodate the needs of domestic and foreign visitors.

The project was extremely schedule-driven; by the time Merkezi had his project team assembled and the plan ready, only 78.5 hours were left for the project tasks. A complete schedule of 27 different activities—including materials preparation, surveying of the site, excavation, drainage, pouring of concrete, laying of marble work, setup of lighting, installation of flower beds, and cleanup—was developed. Each task was given literally hours hours to be completed. The 15,000-square-meter shrine—consisting of a lower platform, stairs, and an upper platform—was built by 20 engineers and 40 construction workers who worked around the clock. The total cost in U.S. dollars was near $1.5 million, and the shrine stands as a great monument to the much-admired former leader of Turkey.

The highest priority for the project was to meet the strict schedule, with the second-highest priority given to quality. An excellent discussion of this project, including the scheduling constraints and corresponding charts, can be found in an article by Ahmet Taspinar in *PM Network*.

Source: A. Taspinar, "Building the Tomb of the Late Turkish President Turgut Ozal," *PM Network*, April 1994.

Chapter 9 dealt with determining what activities needed to be done and in what sequence they should be done in order to accomplish a project objective. The result was a plan in the form of a network diagram that graphically portrayed activities in the appropriate interdependent sequence to accomplish the project work scope. When network planning techniques are used, the scheduling function depends on the planning function. A schedule is a timetable for a plan and, therefore, cannot be established until the plan has been developed. In this chapter, we will establish a schedule for the plan. You will become familiar with

* estimating the duration for each activity
* establishing the estimated start time and required completion time for the overall project

FIGURE 10.1   Activity Duration Estimate (Activity-in-the-Box Format)

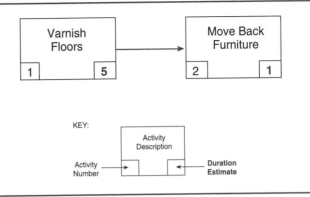

- calculating the earliest times at which each activity can start and finish, based on the project's estimated start time
- calculating the latest times by which each activity must start and finish in order to complete the project by its required completion time
- determining the amount of positive or negative slack between the time each activity *can* start or finish and the time it *must* start or finish
- identifying the critical (longest) path of activities

ACTIVITY DURATION ESTIMATES

The first step in establishing a project schedule is to estimate how long each activity will take, from the time it is started until the time it is finished. This **duration estimate** for each activity must be the *total elapsed time*—the time for the work to be done plus any associated waiting time. In Figure 10.1, for example, the duration estimate for activity 1, "Varnish Floors," is 5 days, which includes both the time to varnish the floors and the waiting time for the varnish to dry.

The activity's duration estimate is usually shown in the lower right-hand corner of the box in the activity-in-the-box format of network diagrams. It's shown below the arrow in the activity-on-the-arrow format (see Figure 10.2).

FIGURE 10.2   Activity Duration Estimate (Activity-on-the-Arrow Format)

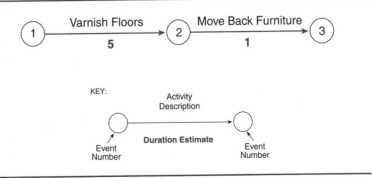

FIGURE 10.3   Network Diagram for Consumer Market Study Project, Showing Duration Estimates (Activity-in-the-Box Format)

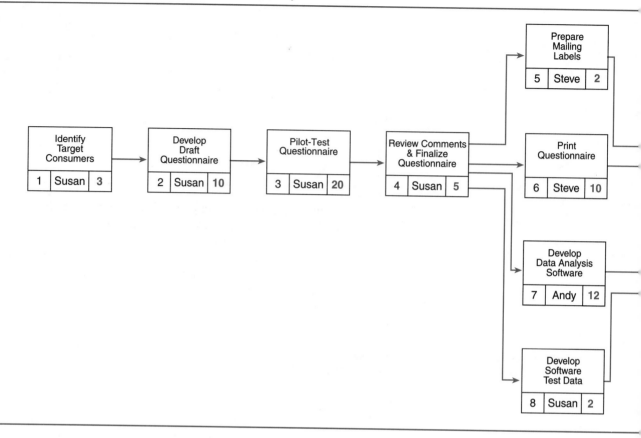

It's a good practice to have the person who will be responsible for performing a particular activity make the duration estimate for that activity. This generates a commitment from that person and avoids any bias that may be introduced by having one person make the duration estimates for all of the activities. In some cases, though—such as for large projects that involve several hundred people performing various activities over several years—it may not be practical to have each person provide activity duration estimates at the beginning of the project. Rather, each organization or subcontractor responsible for a group or type of activities may designate an experienced individual to make the duration estimates for all the activities for which the organization or subcontractor is responsible. If an organization or subcontractor has performed similar projects in the past and has kept records of how long specific activities actually took, these historical data can be used as a guide in estimating activity durations for future projects.

An activity's duration estimate must be based on the quantity of resources expected to be used on the activity. The estimate should be aggressive, yet realistic. It should not include time for a lot of things that could possibly go wrong; nor should it be too optimistically short. It is generally better to be somewhat aggressive and estimate a

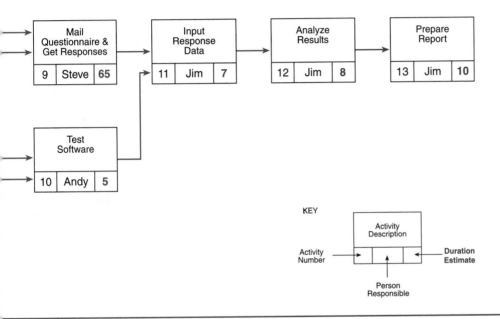

KEY

Activity
Description

Activity
Number

Person
Responsible

Duration
Estimate

duration for an activity at 5 days, say, and then actually finish it in 6 days, than to be overly conservative and estimate a duration at 10 days and then actually take 10 days. People sometimes perform to expectations—if an activity is estimated to take 10 days, their effort will expand to fill the whole 10 days allotted, even if the activity could have been performed in a shorter time.

Playing the game of inflating duration estimates in anticipation of the project manager's negotiating shorter durations is not a good practice. Nor is padding estimates with the vision of becoming a hero when the activities are completed in less time than estimated.

Throughout the performance of the project, some activities will take longer than their estimated duration, others will be done in less time than their estimated duration, and a few may conform to the duration estimates exactly. Over the life of a project that involves many activities, however, such delays and accelerations will tend to cancel one another out. For example, one activity may take two weeks longer than originally estimated, but this delay may be offset by two other activities that are each done a week sooner than originally estimated.

Figures 10.3 and 10.4 show network diagrams for a consumer market study in the AIB and AOA formats, respectively, with the duration estimates in days for each activity. A consistent time base—

REINFORCE YOUR LEARNING

1. True or false: The duration estimate for an activity should include the time required to perform the work plus any associated waiting time.

**FIGURE 10.4   Network Diagram for Consumer Market Study Project,
Showing Duration Estimates (Activity-on-the-Arrow Format)**

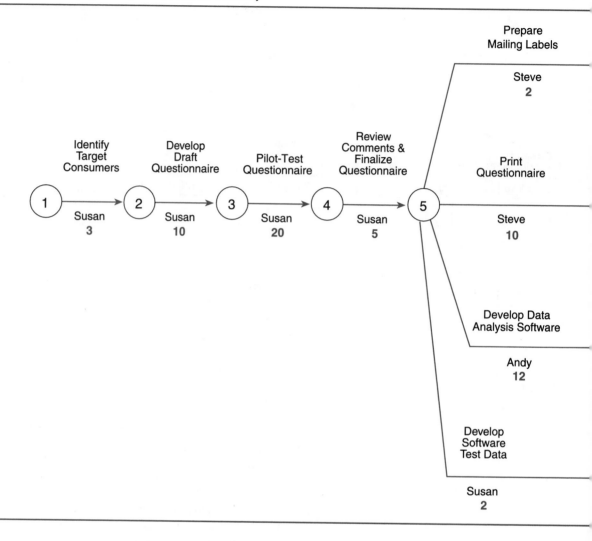

such as hours or days or weeks—should be used for all the activity duration estimates in a network diagram. Note that in the AOA format it is not necessary to give a duration estimate for dummy activities, because by definition their duration is 0.

With projects for which there is a high degree of uncertainty about the activity duration estimates, it is possible to use three duration estimates: an optimistic, a pessimistic, and a most likely estimate. For a discussion of this technique, see the appendix entitled "Probability Considerations" at the end of this chapter.

PROJECT START AND FINISH TIMES

In order to establish a basis from which to calculate a schedule using the duration estimates for the activities, it's necessary to select an **esti-**

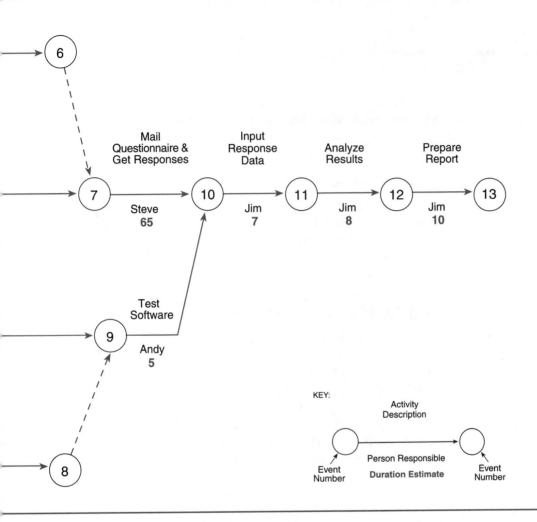

KEY:

Activity
Description

Event
Number

Person Responsible

Duration Estimate

Event
Number

mated start time and a **required completion time** for the overall project. These two times (or dates) define the overall window, or envelope, of time in which the project must be completed.

The project's required completion time is normally part of the project objective and stated in the contract. In some cases, both estimated start time and required completion time are stated, as in "The project will not start before June 1 and must be completed by September 30." In other cases, the customer specifies only the date by which the project must be completed.

The contractor, however, may not want to commit to completing the project by a specific date until the customer has approved the contract. In such cases the contract may state, "The project will be completed within 90 days of the signing of the contract." Here the overall project time is stated in terms of a cycle time (90 days) rather than in terms of specific calendar dates.

Assume that the consumer market study project shown in Figures 10.3 and 10.4 must be completed in 130 working days. If we define the project's estimated start time as 0, its required completion time is day 130.

SCHEDULE CALCULATIONS

Once you have an estimated duration for each activity in the network and an overall window of time in which the project must be completed, you must determine (based on durations and precedential sequence) whether the activities can be done by the required completion time. To determine this, you can calculate a project schedule that provides a timetable for each activity and shows

1. the earliest times (or dates) at which each activity can start and finish, based on the project's estimated start time (or date)
2. the latest times (or dates) by which each activity must start and finish in order to complete the project by its required completion time (or date)

Earliest Start and Finish Times

Given an estimated duration for each activity in the network and using the project's estimated start time as a reference, you can calculate the following two times for each activity:

1. **Earliest start time (ES)** is the earliest time at which a particular activity can begin, calculated on the basis of the project's estimated start time and the duration estimates for preceding activities.

REINFORCE YOUR LEARNING

3. *What is the equation for calculating an activity's earliest finish time?*

2. **Earliest finish time (EF)** is the earliest time by which a particular activity can be completed, calculated by adding the activity's duration estimate to the activity's earliest start time:

$$EF = ES + Duration\ Estimate$$

The ES and EF times are determined by calculating *forward*—that is, by working through the network diagram from the beginning of the project to the end of the project. There is one rule that must be followed in making these forward calculations.

REINFORCE YOUR LEARNING

4. *The earliest start and earliest finish times for activities are determined by calculating _____ through the network diagram.*

Rule 1:   The earliest start time for a particular activity must be the same as or later than the latest of all the earliest finish times of all the activities leading directly into that particular activity.

Figure 10.5 shows three activities leading directly into "Dress Rehearsal." "Practice Skit" has an EF of day 5, "Make Costumes" has an EF of day 10, and "Make Props" has an EF of day 4. "Dress Rehearsal" cannot start until all three of these activities are finished, so the latest of the EFs for these three activities determines the ES for "Dress Rehearsal." The latest of the three EFs is day 10—the earliest finish time for "Make Costumes." Therefore, "Dress Rehearsal" cannot start any earlier than day 10. That is, its ES must be day 10 or later. Even though "Practice Skit" and "Make Props" may finish

FIGURE 10.5   Earliest Start Times

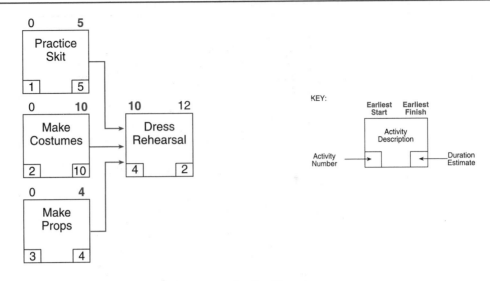

(a) Activity-in-the-Box Format

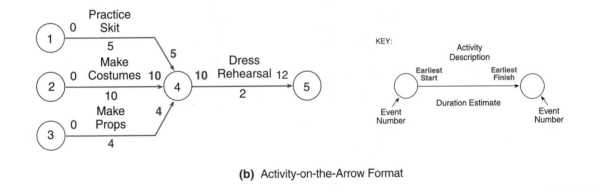

(b) Activity-on-the-Arrow Format

REINFORCE YOUR LEARNING

5. *Refer to Figures 10.6 and 10.7. What are the earliest start and earliest finish times for "Pilot-Test Questionnaire"?*

sooner than "Make Costumes," "Dress Rehearsal" cannot start because the network logic indicates that *all three activities* must be finished before "Dress Rehearsal" can start.

Figures 10.6 and 10.7 show the forward calculations for the consumer market study project. The project's estimated start time is 0. Therefore, the earliest "Identify Target Consumers" can start is time 0, and the earliest it can finish is 3 days later (since its estimated duration is 3 days). When "Identify Target Consumers" is finished on day 3, "Develop Draft Questionnaire" can start. It has a duration of 10 days, so its ES is day 3 and its EF is day 13. The calculations of ES and EF for subsequent activities are done similarly, continuing forward through the network diagram.

Look for a moment at "Test Software." It has an ES of day 50 because, according to Rule 1, it cannot start until the two activities leading directly into it are finished. "Develop Data Analysis Software"

FIGURE 10.6   Network Diagram for Consumer Market Study Project, Showing Earliest Start and Finish Times (Activity-in-the-Box Format)

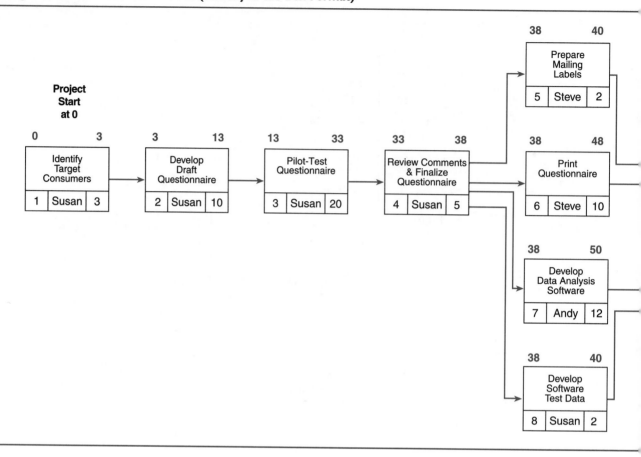

doesn't finish until day 50, and "Develop Software Test Data" doesn't finish until day 40. Since "Test Software" cannot start until both of these are finished, "Test Software" cannot start until day 50.

As a further illustration of Rule 1, refer once more to Figures 10.6 and 10.7. In order to start "Mail Questionnaire & Get Responses," the two activities immediately preceding it, "Prepare Mailing Labels" and "Print Questionnaire," must be finished. The EF of "Prepare Mailing Labels" is day 40, and the EF of "Print Questionnaire" is day 48. According to Rule 1, it is the later of the two EFs, which is day 48, that determines the ES of "Mail Questionnaire & Get Responses."

If you continue calculating the ES and EF for each remaining activity in the network diagram in Figures 10.6 and 10.7, you'll see that the very last activity, "Prepare Final Report," has an EF of day 138. That is 8 days beyond the project's required completion time of 130 days. At this point, we know there's a problem.

It should be noted that although the ES and EF times for each activity are shown on the network diagrams in Figures 10.6 and 10.7, this is *not* normally the case. Rather, the ES and EF times

REINFORCE YOUR LEARNING

6. *What determines a particular activity's earliest start time?*

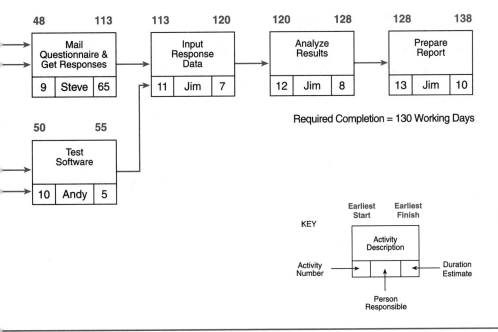

Required Completion = 130 Working Days

KEY

(and the LS and LF times, explained in the following section) are listed in a separate schedule table, like the one in Figure 10.8. Separating the schedule table from the network logic diagram makes it easier to generate revised and updated schedules (perhaps using project management software), without continually making changes to the ES, EF, LS, and LF times on the network diagram itself.

Latest Start and Finish Times

Given a duration estimate for each activity in the network and using the project's required completion time as a reference, you can calculate the following two times for each activity:

1. **Latest finish time (LF)** is the latest time by which a particular activity must be completed in order for the entire project to be finished by its required completion time, calculated on the basis of the project's required completion time and the duration estimates for succeeding activities.

FIGURE 10.7   Network Diagram for Consumer Market Study Project, Showing Earliest Start and Finish Times (Activity-on-the-Arrow Format)

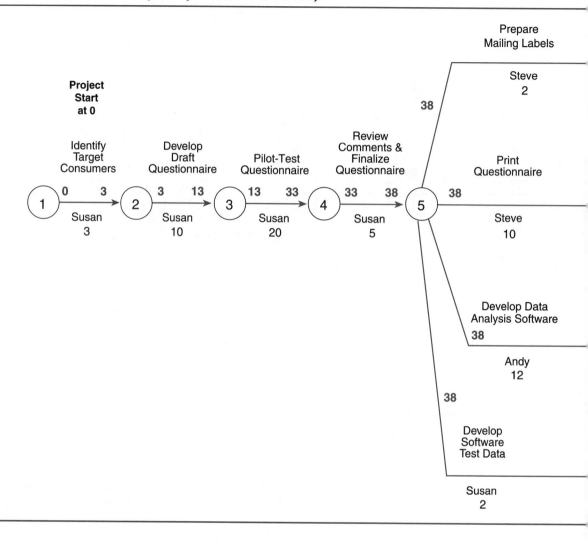

REINFORCE YOUR LEARNING
7. *What is the equation for calculating an activity's latest start time?*

2. **Latest start time (LS)** is the latest time by which a particular activity must be started in order for the entire project to be finished by its required completion time, calculated by subtracting the activity's duration estimate from the activity's latest finish time:

$$LS = LF - \text{Duration Estimate}$$

The LF and LS times are determined by calculating *backward*—that is, by working through the network diagram from the end of the project to the beginning of the project. There is one rule that must be followed in making these backward calculations.

REINFORCE YOUR LEARNING
8. *The latest finish and latest start times are determined by calculating _____ through the network diagram.*

Rule 2:   The latest finish time for a particular activity must be the same as or earlier than the earliest of all the latest start times of all the activities emerging directly from that particular activity.

Figure 10.9 shows two activities emerging directly from "Print Posters & Brochures." This project is required to be completed by day

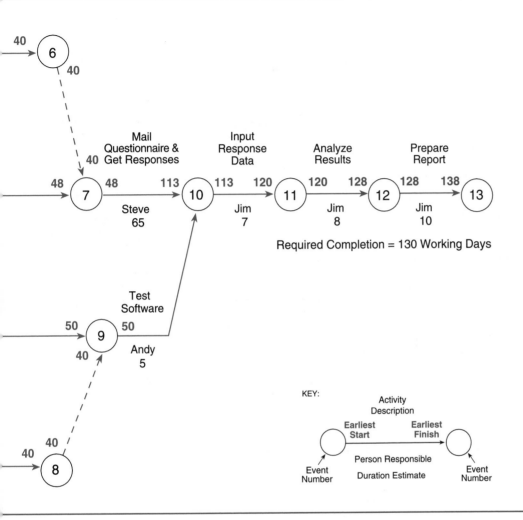

Required Completion = 130 Working Days

KEY:

Activity
Description

Earliest   Earliest
Start   Finish

Person Responsible

Event   Duration Estimate   Event
Number   Number

30. Therefore, "Distribute Posters" must be started by day 20, since it has a duration of 10 days, and "Mail Brochures" must be started by day 25, since it has a duration of 5 days. The earlier of these two LSs is day 20. Therefore, the latest that "Print Posters & Brochures" can finish is day 20, so that "Distribute Posters" can start by day 20. Even though "Mail Brochures" does not have to start until day 25, "Print Posters & Brochures" must finish by day 20, or else the whole project will be delayed. If "Print Posters & Brochures" does not finish until day 25, then "Distribute Brochures" will not be able to start until day 25. Since "Distribute Brochures" has an estimated duration of 10 days, it won't finish until day 35, which is 5 days beyond the project's required completion time.

Figures 10.10 and 10.11 show the backward calculations for the consumer market study project. The required completion time for the project is 130 working days. Therefore, the latest that "Prepare

FIGURE 10.8   Schedule for Consumer Market Study Project, Showing Earliest Start and Finish Times

CONSUMER MARKET STUDY PROJECT

	ACTIVITY	RESPON.	DUR. ESTIM.	EARLIEST START	FINISH			
1	Identify Target Consumers	Susan	3	0	3			
2	Develop Draft Questionnaire	Susan	10	3	13			
3	Pilot-Test Questionnaire	Susan	20	13	33			
4	Review Comments & Finalize Questionnaire	Susan	5	33	38			
5	Prepare Mailing Labels	Steve	2	38	40			
6	Print Questionnaire	Steve	10	38	48			
7	Develop Data Analysis Software	Andy	12	38	50			
8	Develop Software Test Data	Susan	2	38	40			
9	Mail Questionnaire & Get Responses	Steve	65	48	113			
10	Test Software	Andy	5	50	55			
11	Input Response Data	Jim	7	113	120			
12	Analyze Results	Jim	8	120	128			
13	Prepare Report	Jim	10	128	138			

REINFORCE YOUR LEARNING

9. Refer to Figures 10.10 and 10.11. What are the latest finish and latest start times for "Input Response Data"?

Report," that last activity, can finish is day 130, and the latest that it can start is day 120, since its estimated duration is 10 days. In order for "Prepare Report" to start on day 120, the latest that "Analyze Results" can finish is day 120. If the LF for "Analyze Results" is day 120, then its LS is day 112, since its estimated duration is 8 days. The calculations of LF and LS for prior activities are done similarly, continuing backward through the network diagram.

Look at "Review Comments & Finalize Questionnaire." In order for the four activities emerging from this activity to start by their LS times (so that the project can finish by its required completion time of 130 days), "Review Comments & Finalize Questionnaire" must be finished by the earliest LS of all four activities, according to Rule 2. The earliest of the four LSs is day 30, the latest time by which "Print Questionnaire" must start. Therefore, the latest that "Review Comments & Finalize Questionnaire" can finish is day 30.

If you continue calculating the LF and LS for each activity in the network diagram, you'll see that the very first activity, "Identify Target Consumers," has an LS of −8! This means that in order to com-

FIGURE 10.9 Latest Finish Times

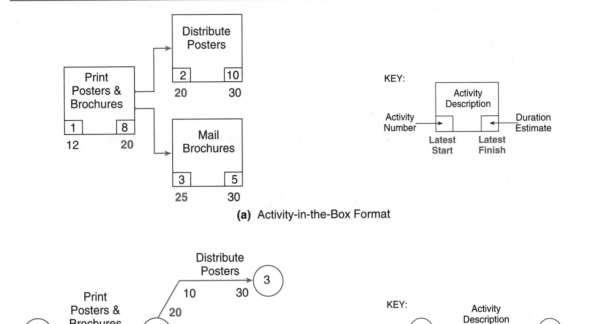

(a) Activity-in-the-Box Format

(b) Activity-on-the-Arrow Format

REINFORCE YOUR LEARNING

10. *What determines a particular activity's latest finish time?*

plete the entire project by its required completion time of 130 days, the project must start 8 days earlier than it is estimated to start. Note that this difference of 8 days is equal to the difference we got when calculating forward through the network diagram to obtain the ES and EF times. In essence, what we have found is that this project may take 138 days to complete, even though its required completion time is 130 days.

Like the earliest start and earliest finish times, the latest start and latest finish times are usually not shown on the network diagram itself, but rather in a separate schedule table (see Figure 10.12).

Total Slack

In the consumer market study project, there is a difference of 8 days between the calculated earliest finish time of the very last activity ("Prepare Report") and the project's required completion time. This difference is the **total slack (TS),** sometimes called **float.** When the total slack is a negative number, as in this example, it indicates a lack of slack over the entire project.

FIGURE 10.10   Network Diagram for Consumer Market Study Project, Showing Latest Start and Finish Times (Activity-in-the-Box Format)

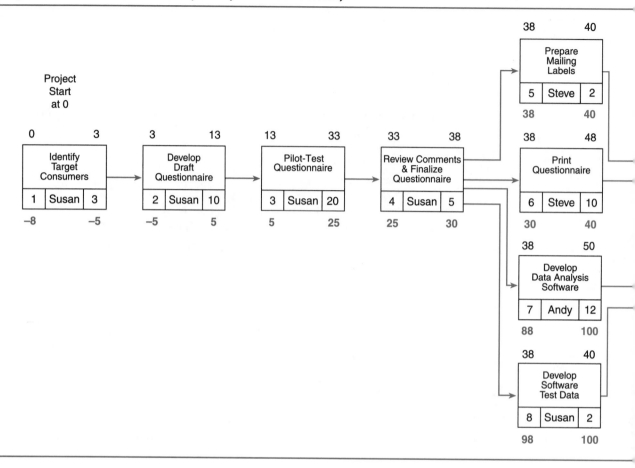

If total slack is positive, it represents the maximum amount of time that the activities on a particular path can be delayed without jeopardizing completion of the project by its required completion time. On the other hand, if total slack is negative, it represents the amount of time that the activities on a particular path must be accelerated in order to complete the project by its required completion time. If total slack is zero, the activities on the path do not need to be accelerated but cannot be delayed.

The total slack for a particular path of activities is common to and shared among all the activities on that path. Consider the project diagrammed below.

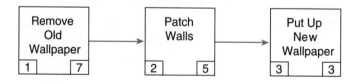

Required Completion = 20 Days

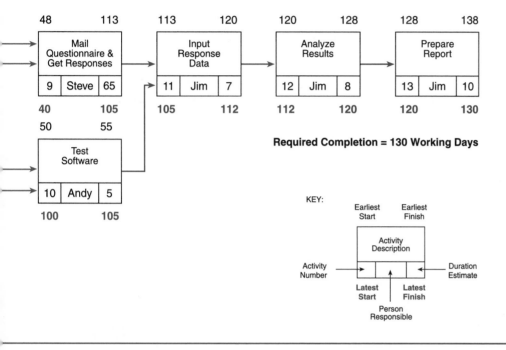

Required Completion = 130 Working Days

KEY:

The earliest the project can finish is day 15 (the sum of the durations of the three activities, $7 + 5 + 3$). However, the required completion time for the project is 20 days. The three activities on this path can therefore be delayed up to 5 days without jeopardizing completion of the project by its required completion time. This does *not* mean that each activity on the path can be delayed 5 days (because this would create a total delay of 15 days); rather, it means that all the activities that make up the path can have a total delay of 5 days among them. For example, if "Remove Old Wallpaper" actually takes 10 days (3 days longer than the estimated 7 days), then it will use up 3 of the 5 days of total slack, and only 2 days of total slack will remain.

Total slack is calculated by subtracting the activity's earliest finish (or start) time from its latest finish (or start) time. That is, the slack is equal to either the latest finish time (LF) minus the earliest finish time (EF) for the activity or the latest start time (LS) minus the earliest start time (ES) for that activity. The two calculations are equivalent.

$$\text{Total Slack} = \text{LF} - \text{EF} \quad \text{or} \quad \text{Total Slack} = \text{LS} - \text{ES}$$

REINFORCE YOUR LEARNING

12. Total slack is the difference between the _____ _____ time and the _____ _____ time.

FIGURE 10.11   Network Diagram for Consumer Market Study Project, Showing Latest Start and Finish Times (Activity-on-the-Arrow Format)

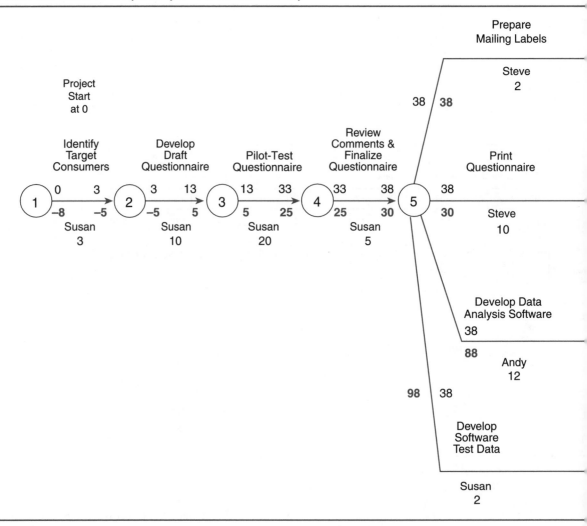

Critical Path

Not all networks are as simple as the three–activity one just used to illustrate total slack. In large network diagrams there may be many paths of activities from the project start to the project completion, just as there are many routes you can follow to get from New York City to Los Angeles. If twenty friends were going to leave at the same time from New York City and each were going to drive a different route to Los Angeles, they couldn't get together for a party in Los Angeles until the last person had arrived—the one who took the longest (most time consuming) route. Similarly, a project cannot be completed until the longest (most time consuming) path of activities is finished. This longest path in the overall network diagram is called the **critical path.**

One way to determine which activities make up the critical path is to find which ones have the least slack. Subtract the earliest finish

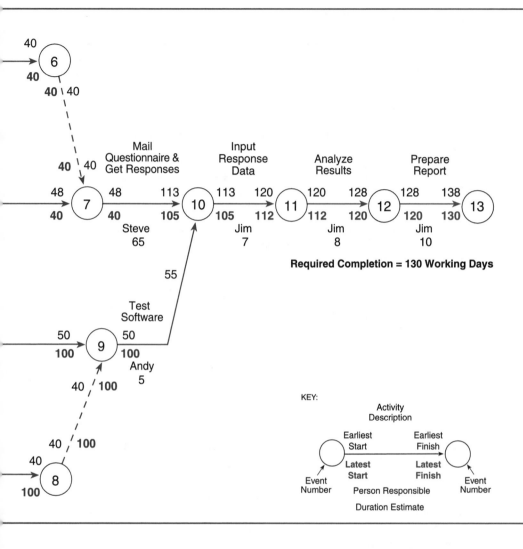

KEY:

Activity
Description

Earliest Start   Earliest Finish

Latest Start   Latest Finish

Event Number   Person Responsible   Event Number

Duration Estimate

Required Completion = 130 Working Days

time from the latest finish time for each activity (or subtract the earliest start time from the latest start time—both calculations will result in the same value) and then look for all the activities that have the lowest value (either least positive or most negative). All the activities with this value are on the critical path of activities.

The values of total slack for the consumer market study project are shown in Figure 10.13. The lowest value is −8 days. The activities that have this same value of total slack make up the path 1−2−3−4−6−9−11−12−13. These nine activities constitute the critical, or most time-consuming, path. The estimated durations of the activities on this path add up to 138 days (3 + 10 + 20 + 5 + 10 + 65 + 7 + 8 + 10). Among them, these activities need to be accelerated 8 days in order to complete the project by its required completion time of 130 days. Figures 10.14 and 10.15 highlight the activities that make up the critical path.

FIGURE 10.12   Schedule for Consumer Market Study Project, Showing Latest Start and Finish Times

CONSUMER MARKET STUDY PROJECT

	ACTIVITY	RESPON.	DUR. ESTIM.	EARLIEST		LATEST			
				START	FINISH	START	FINISH		
1	Identify Target Consumers	Susan	3	0	3	–8	–5		
2	Develop Draft Questionnaire	Susan	10	3	13	–5	5		
3	Pilot-Test Questionnaire	Susan	20	13	33	5	25		
4	Review Comments & Finalize Questionnaire	Susan	5	33	38	25	30		
5	Prepare Mailing Labels	Steve	2	38	40	38	40		
6	Print Questionnaire	Steve	10	38	48	30	40		
7	Develop Data Analysis Software	Andy	12	38	50	88	100		
8	Develop Software Test Data	Susan	2	38	40	98	100		
9	Mail Questionnaire & Get Responses	Steve	65	48	113	40	105		
10	Test Software	Andy	5	50	55	100	105		
11	Input Response Data	Jim	7	113	120	105	112		
12	Analyze Results	Jim	8	120	128	112	120		
13	Prepare Report	Jim	10	128	138	120	130		

To eliminate the −8 days of slack, the estimated durations of one or more activities on this critical path need to be reduced. Suppose we reduce the estimated duration of "Mail Questionnaire & Get Responses" from 65 days to 55 days, by reducing the time respondents are given to return the questionnaire. Since the estimated duration of an activity on the critical path is being reduced by 10 days, the total slack changes from −8 days to +2 days. The revised duration estimate of 55 days can be used to prepare a revised project schedule, as shown in Figure 10.16. This schedule shows that the critical path now has a total slack of +2 days, and the project is now estimated to finish in 128 days, which is 2 days earlier than the required completion time of 130 days.

As stated earlier, a large network diagram can have many paths or routes from its beginning to its end. Some of the paths may have positive values of total slack, and others may have negative values of total slack. Those paths with positive values of total slack are sometimes referred to as **noncritical paths,** while those paths with zero or negative values of total slack are referred to as *critical paths*. In this case the longest path is often referred to as the **most critical path.**

FIGURE 10.13 Schedule for Consumer Market Study Project, Showing Total Slack Values

CONSUMER MARKET STUDY PROJECT

	ACTIVITY	RESPON.	DUR. ESTIM.	EARLIEST		LATEST		TOTAL SLACK	
				START	FINISH	START	FINISH		
1	Identify Target Consumers	Susan	3	0	3	−8	−5	−8	
2	Develop Draft Questionnaire	Susan	10	3	13	−5	5	−8	
3	Pilot-Test Questionnaire	Susan	20	13	33	5	25	−8	
4	Review Comments & Finalize Questionnaire	Susan	5	33	38	25	30	−8	
5	Prepare Mailing Labels	Steve	2	38	40	38	40	0	
6	Print Questionnaire	Steve	10	38	48	30	40	−8	
7	Develop Data Analysis Software	Andy	12	38	50	88	100	50	
8	Develop Software Test Data	Susan	2	38	40	98	100	60	
9	Mail Questionnaire & Get Responses	Steve	65	48	113	40	105	−8	
10	Test Software	Andy	5	50	55	100	105	50	
11	Input Response Data	Jim	7	113	120	105	112	−8	
12	Analyze Results	Jim	8	120	128	112	120	−8	
13	Prepare Report	Jim	10	128	138	120	130	−8	

Free Slack

Another type of slack that is sometimes calculated is **free slack.** It's the amount of time a particular activity can be delayed without delaying the earliest start time of its immediately succeeding activities. It is the *relative difference* between the amounts of total slack for activities entering into the same activity. Free slack is calculated by finding the lowest of the values of total slack for all the activities entering into a particular activity and then subtracting it from the values of total slack for the other activities also entering into that same activity. Since free slack is the relative difference between values of total slack for activities entering into the same activity, it will exist only when two or more activities enter into the same activity. Also, since free slack is a relative difference between values of total slack, *it is always a positive value.*

For an illustration of free slack, consider Figures 10.13 and 10.14. In the network diagram (Figure 10.14), there are three instances where a particular activity has more than one activity entering into it:

- Activity 9, "Mail Questionnaire & Get Responses," has activities 5 and 6 entering into it.

FIGURE 10.14   Network Diagram for Consumer Market Study Project, Showing the Critical Path (Activity-in-the-Box Format)

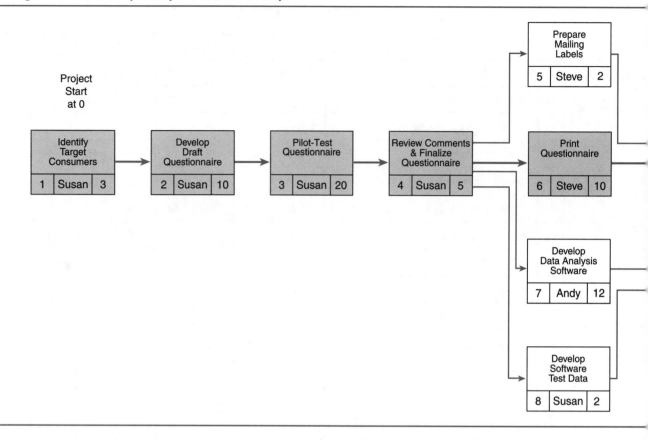

- Activity 10, "Test Software," has activities 7 and 8 entering into it.
- Activity 11, "Input Response Data," has activities 9 and 10 entering into it.

In the schedule (Figure 10.13), the values of total slack for activities 5 and 6 are 0 and −8 days, respectively. The lesser of these two values is −8 days for activity 6. The free slack for activity 5 is the relative difference between its total slack, 0, and −8. This relative difference is 8 days: $0 - (-8) = 8$ days. This means that activity 5, "Prepare Mailing Labels," already has a free slack of 8 days and can slip by up to that amount without delaying the earliest start time of activity 9, "Mail Questionnaire & Get Responses."

Similarly, the values of total slack for activities 7 and 8 are 50 and 60 days, respectively. The lesser of these two values is 50 days. Therefore, activity 8, "Develop Software Test Data," has a free slack of 10 days $(60 - 50 = 10)$ and can slip by up to that amount without delaying the earliest start time of activity 10, "Test Software."

REINFORCE YOUR LEARNING

14. Refer to Figures 10.13 and 10.14. Of the two activities entering into activity 11, "Input Response Data," which activity has free slack? What is its value?

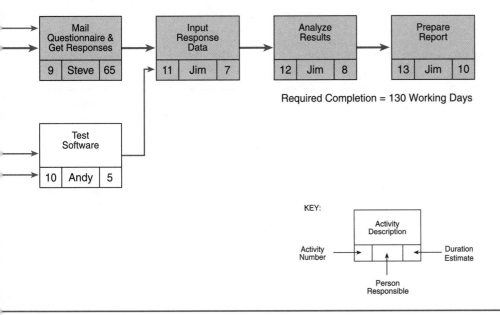

Required Completion = 130 Working Days

KEY:

SCHEDULING FOR INFORMATION
SYSTEMS DEVELOPMENT

Chapter 9 defined an information system (IS) as a computer-based system that accepts data as input, processes the data, and produces information required by users. Scheduling the development of an information system is a challenging process. Unfortunately, such scheduling is often done in a haphazard manner, and thus a large percentage of IS projects are finished much later than originally promised or never finished at all. One of the most important factors in effective scheduling is arriving at activity duration estimates that are as realistic as possible. This is not an easy task; however, it does become easier with experience.

Among the common problems that often push IS development projects beyond their required completion time are the following:

- Failure to identify all user requirements
- Failure to properly identify user requirements

FIGURE 10.15   Network Diagram for Consumer Market Study Project, Showing the Critical Path (Activity-on-the-Arrow Format)

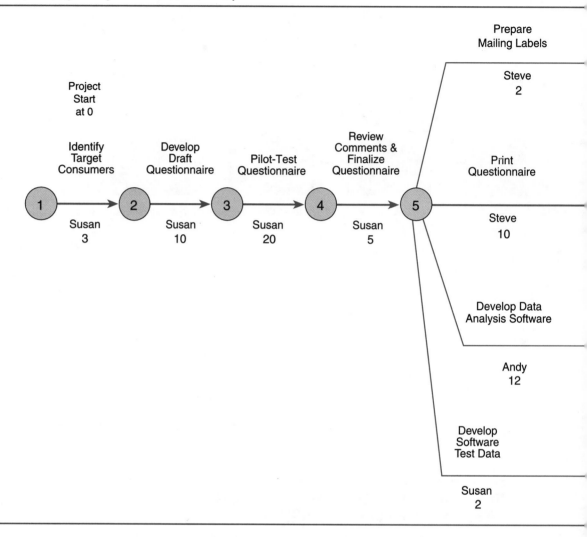

- Continuing growth of project scope
- Underestimating learning curves for new software packages
- Incompatible hardware
- Logical design flaws
- Poor selection of software
- Failure to select the best design strategy
- Data incompatibility issues
- Failure to perform all phases of the SDLC

An IS Example: ABC Office Designs (Continued)

Recall from Chapter 9 that ABC Office Designs has a large number of sales representatives who sell office furniture to major corporations. Each sales representative is assigned to a specific state, and each

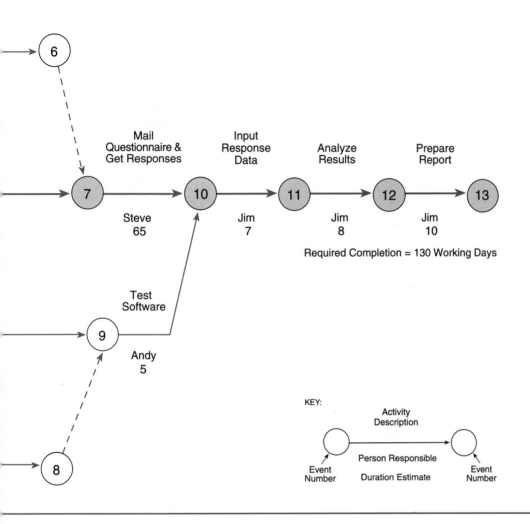

KEY:

Activity
Description

Person Responsible

Event
Number

Duration Estimate

Event
Number

state is part of one of four regions in the country. To enable management to monitor the number and amount of sales for each representative, for each state, and for each region, ABC has decided to build an IS. In addition, the IS needs to be able to track prices, inventory, and the competition.

The IS Department within the corporation assigned Beth Smith to be the project manager of the Sales Reporting System development project. Previously, Beth identified all of the major tasks that need to be accomplished and developed the work breakdown structure, responsibility matrix, and network diagram. Her next step was to come up with activity duration estimates. After consulting extensively with the project team, she derived the estimates shown in Figure 10.17.

Recall from Chapter 9 that 50 weeks have been allotted for this project and the project needs to be started as soon as possible. Given

FIGURE 10.16   Revised Schedule for Consumer Market Study Project

CONSUMER MARKET STUDY PROJECT

	ACTIVITY	RESPON.	DUR. ESTIM.	EARLIEST		LATEST		TOTAL SLACK	
				START	FINISH	START	FINISH		
1	Identify Target Consumers	Susan	3	0	3	2	5	2	
2	Develop Draft Questionnaire	Susan	10	3	13	5	15	2	
3	Pilot-Test Questionnaire	Susan	20	13	33	15	35	2	
4	Review Comments & Finalize Questionnaire	Susan	5	33	38	35	40	2	
5	Prepare Mailing Labels	Steve	2	38	40	48	50	10	
6	Print Questionnaire	Steve	10	38	48	40	50	2	
7	Develop Data Analysis Software	Andy	12	38	50	88	100	50	
8	Develop Software Test Data	Susan	2	38	40	98	100	60	
9	Mail Questionnaire & Get Responses	Steve	55	48	103	50	105	2	
10	Test Software	Andy	5	50	55	100	105	50	
11	Input Response Data	Jim	7	103	110	105	112	2	
12	Analyze Results	Jim	8	110	118	112	120	2	
13	Prepare Report	Jim	10	118	128	120	130	2	

each activity's duration estimate and the project's required start and finish times, Beth was ready to perform the calculations for the earliest start (ES) and earliest finish (EF) times for each activity. These values are shown above each activity in Figure 10.18.

Beth calculated the ES and EF times by going forward through the network. The first tasks, "Gather Data" and "Study Feasibility," have ES times of 0. Since "Gather Data" is expected to take 3 weeks, its EF is $0 + 3 = 3$ weeks. Since "Study Feasibility" is expected to take 4 weeks, its EF is $0 + 4 = 4$ weeks. Beth continued this process, moving forward through the network diagram until all activities had been assigned ES and EF times.

After the ES and EF times were calculated, Beth calculated the LS and LF times. The starting point here is the time by which the project must be completed—50 weeks. The LS and LF times are shown below each activity in Figure 10.19.

Beth calculated the LF and LS times by going backward through the network. The last task, "Prepare Implementation Report," has an

FIGURE 10.17   List of Activities, Immediate Predecessors, and Duration Estimates

SALES REPORTING SYSTEM PROJECT

Activity	Immediate Predecessors	Duration Estimate (wks.)
1. Gather Data	—	3
2. Study Feasibility	—	4
3. Prepare Problem Definition Report	1, 2	1
4. Interview Users	3	5
5. Study Existing System	3	8
6. Define User Requirements	4	5
7. Prepare System Analysis Report	5, 6	1
8. Input & Output	7	8
9. Processing & Database	7	10
10. Evaluation	8, 9	2
11. Prepare System Design Report	10	2
12. Software Development	11	15
13. Hardware Development	11	10
14. Network Development	11	6
15. Prepare System Development Report	12, 13, 14	2
16. Software Testing	15	6
17. Hardware Testing	15	4
18. Network Testing	15	4
19. Prepare Testing Report	16, 17, 18	1
20. Training	19	4
21. System Conversion	19	2
22. Prepare Implementation Report	20, 21	1

LF time of 50—the time by which the project needs to be complete. Since "Prepare Implementation Report" is expected to take 1 week to perform, its LS is $50 - 1 = 49$ weeks. This means that "Prepare Implementation Report" must be started by week 49 at the latest, or else the project will not finish by its required completion time. Beth continued this process, moving backward through the network diagram until all activities had been assigned LF and LS times.

After the ES, EF, LS, and LF times were calculated, Beth calculated the total slack. These values are shown in Figure 10.20. Recall that the total slack is calculated by either subtracting ES from LS or subtracting EF from LF for each activity.

After she calculated the total slack for each activity, Beth had to identify the critical path. For the sales reporting system development project, any activity with a slack of -9 is on the critical path. Figure 10.21 shows the critical path for this development project. At this point Beth and her team must either determine a way to reduce the development time by 9 weeks or request that the project completion date be extended from 50 to 59 weeks, or some compromise.

FIGURE 10.18   Network Diagram for Sales Reporting System Project, Showing Earliest Start and Finish Times (Activity-in-the-Box Format)

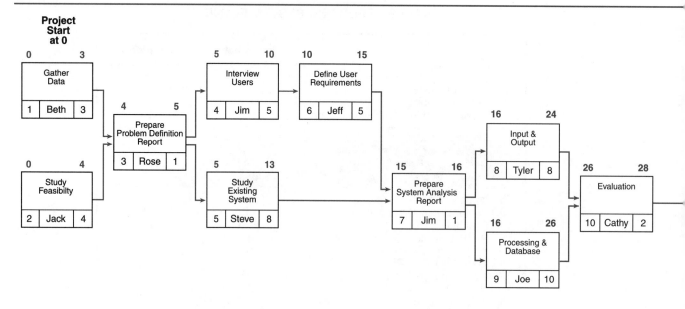

PROJECT MANAGEMENT SOFTWARE

Almost all project management software packages allow you to perform the scheduling functions identified in this chapter. Specifically, activity durations can be estimated in hours, days, weeks, months, or years, and with a click of the mouse, time scales can easily be converted from days to weeks, weeks to days, and so on. The duration estimates can easily be updated and revised. In addition, calendaring systems provide the project manager with the ability to handle weekends, company holidays, and vacation days.

Project start and finish times can be entered as specific calendar dates (for example, June 1, 1998 and December 1, 1998), or an overall number of days (or weeks or months), without specific calendar dates assigned, can be entered (for example, the project needs to finish by week 50). Given the required project completion date and the list of activities with their estimated durations, the software will calculate

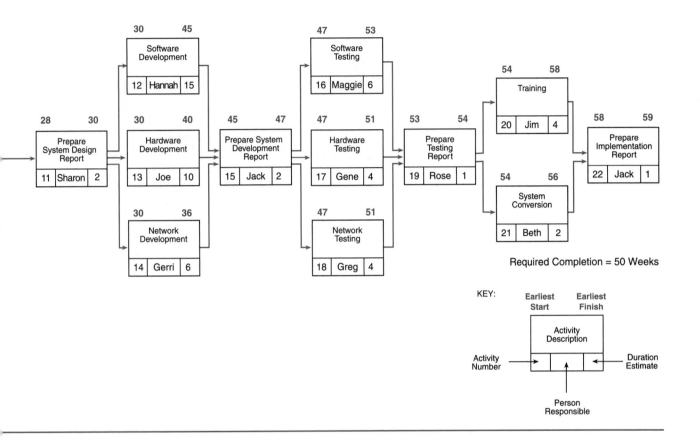

KEY:

	Earliest Start		Earliest Finish
		Activity Description	
Activity Number			Duration Estimate

Person Responsible

Required Completion = 50 Weeks

the date by which a project needs to start. Similarly, it will calculate the earliest project completion date, based on the actual start date and the list of activities with their estimated durations.

The software will also calculate ES, EF, LS, and LF times, total and free slack, and the critical path, all with a click of the mouse. It is important, however, for the project manager to understand what these terms are and what the calculations mean. See Appendix A at the end of the book for a thorough discussion of project management software, including a list of vendors.

SUMMARY

After a plan is developed for a project, the next step is to develop a project schedule. The first step in this process is to estimate how long each activity will take, from the time it is started until the time it is

FIGURE 10.19   Network Diagram for Sales Reporting System Project, Showing Latest Start and Finish Times (Activity-in-the-Box Format)

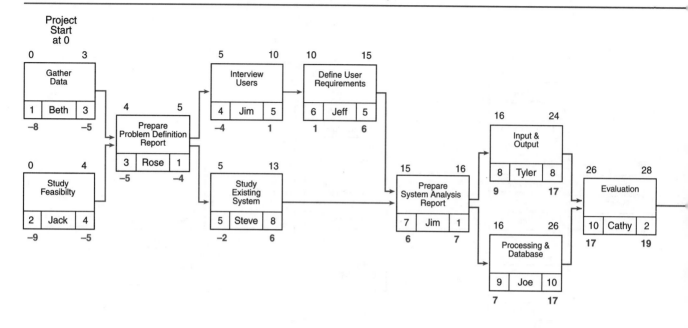

finished. It's a good practice to have the person who will be responsible for an activity estimate its duration; however, with larger projects this is often not possible.

An activity's duration estimate must be based on the quantity of resources expected to be used on the activity. The estimate should be aggressive, yet realistic. A consistent time base—such as hours or days or weeks—should be used for all the activity duration estimates.

The earliest start and earliest finish (ES and EF) times and the latest start and latest finish (LS and LF) times can be calculated for each activity. The ES and EF times are calculated by working forward through the network. The earliest start time for an activity is calculated on the basis of the project's estimated start time and the duration estimates for preceding activities. The earliest finish time for an activity is calculated by adding the activity's duration estimate to the activity's earliest start time. The earliest start time for a particular activity must be the same as or later than the latest of all the earliest finish times of all the activities leading directly into that particular activity.

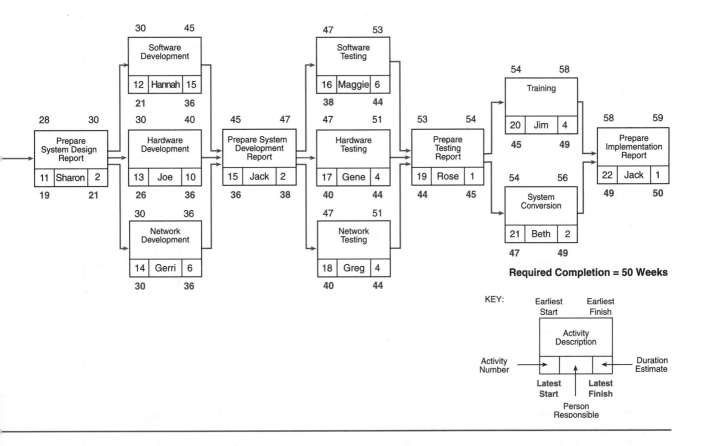

Required Completion = 50 Weeks

KEY:

The LS and LF times are calculated by working backward through the network. The latest finish time for an activity is calculated on the basis of the project's required completion time and the duration estimates for succeeding activities. The latest start time is calculated by subtracting the activity's duration estimate from the activity's latest finish time. The latest finish time for a particular activity must be the same as or earlier than the earliest of all the latest start times of all the activities emerging directly from that particular activity.

The total slack for a particular path through the network is common to and shared among all activities on that path. If it's positive, it represents the maximum amount of time that the activities on a particular path can be delayed without jeopardizing completion of the project by its required completion time. If total slack is negative, it represents the amount of time that the activities on that path must be accelerated in order to complete the project by its required completion time. If it's zero, the activities on that path do not need to be accelerated but cannot be delayed. The critical path is the longest

FIGURE 10.20   Schedule for Sales Reporting System Project

SALES REPORTING SYSTEM PROJECT

	ACTIVITY	RESPON.	DUR. ESTIM.	EARLIEST		LATEST		TOTAL SLACK	
				START	FINISH	START	FINISH		
1	Gather Data	Beth	3	0	3	−8	−5	−8	
2	Study Feasibility	Jack	4	0	4	−9	−5	−9	
3	Prepare Problem Definition Report	Rose	1	4	5	−5	−4	−9	
4	Interview Users	Jim	5	5	10	−4	1	−9	
5	Study Existing System	Steve	8	5	13	−2	6	−7	
6	Define User Requirements	Jeff	5	10	15	1	6	−9	
7	Prepare System Analysis Report	Jim	1	15	16	6	7	−9	
8	Input & Output	Tyler	8	16	24	9	17	−7	
9	Processing & Database	Joe	10	16	26	7	17	−9	
10	Evaluation	Cathy	2	26	28	17	19	−9	
11	Prepare System Design Report	Sharon	2	28	30	19	21	−9	
12	Software Development	Hannah	15	30	45	21	36	−9	
13	Hardware Development	Joe	10	30	40	26	36	−4	
14	Network Development	Gerri	6	30	36	30	36	0	
15	Prepare System Development Report	Jack	2	45	47	36	38	−9	
16	Software Testing	Maggie	6	47	53	38	44	−9	
17	Hardware Testing	Gene	4	47	51	40	44	−7	
18	Network Testing	Greg	4	47	51	40	44	−7	
19	Prepare Testing Report	Rose	1	53	54	44	45	−9	
20	Training	Jim	4	54	58	45	49	−9	
21	System Conversion	Beth	2	54	56	47	49	−7	
22	Prepare Implementation Report	Jack	1	58	59	49	50	−9	

(most time consuming) path of activities in the network diagram and represents a series of activities that cannot be delayed without delaying the entire project.

Scheduling the development of an information system is a challenging process. Unfortunately, such scheduling is often done in a haphazard manner, and thus a large percentage of IS projects are finished much later than originally promised. One of the most important factors in effective scheduling is arriving at activity duration estimates that are as realistic as possible. The project manager should be aware of the common problems that often push IS development projects beyond their scheduled completion dates.

Project management software packages can help with the scheduling process.

QUESTIONS

1. Why does the scheduling function depend on the planning function? Which one must be done first? Why?
2. Describe what an activity duration estimate is. How is it determined?
3. Can an activity have an estimated duration of 0? Why or why not?
4. Think of a project on which you are about to work or have worked. What are the project objective and the project start and finish times?
5. Why might a contractor prefer to state a project completion time in terms of a number of days after the project starts rather than a specific date? Give some examples of instances when this would be appropriate.
6. How do you calculate earliest start and earliest finish times for an activity? What rule must be followed?
7. Refer to Figures 10.6 and 10.7. Why is the earliest start time for "Review Comments & Finalize Questionnaire" day 33? Why is the earliest finish time day 38?
8. How do you calculate latest start and latest finish times for an activity? What rule must be followed?
9. Refer to Figures 10.10 and 10.11. Why is the latest start time for "Mail Questionnaires & Get Responses" day 40? Why is the latest finish time day 105?
10. Why are the ES, EF, LS, and LF times typically displayed in a separate schedule table?
11. What is meant by the term *slack* as applied to a particular activity? What is the difference between positive slack and negative slack? How is it calculated?
12. What is meant by the term *total slack* as applied to a path? When is a path considered to be a critical path?
13. Why is it important to determine the critical path of a project? What happens if activities on this path are delayed? What happens if activities on this path are accelerated?

FIGURE 10.21   Network Diagram for Sales Reporting System Project, Showing the Critical Path (Activity-in-the-Box Format)

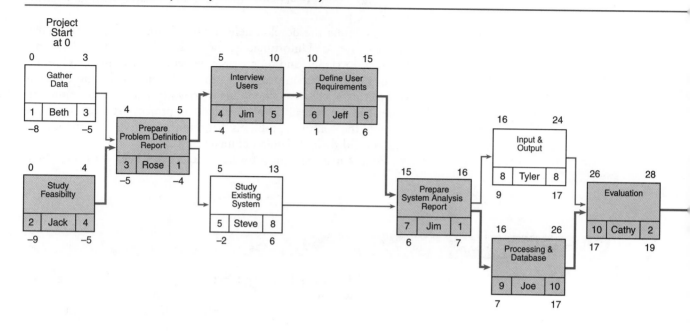

14. Why is the scheduling of IS projects so challenging? What are some of the common problems that push IS projects beyond their due dates?

15. Calculate the ES, EF, LS, and LF times and the slack for each activity in the figure below and identify the critical path for the project. Can the project be completed in 40 weeks?

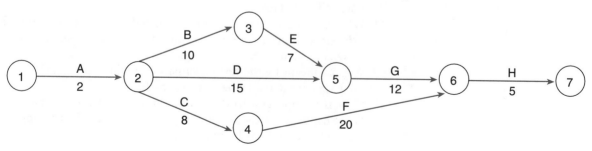

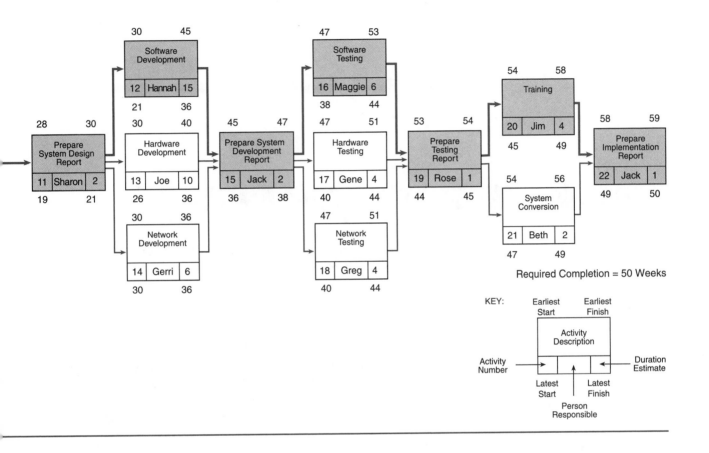

Required Completion = 50 Weeks

16. Calculate the ES, EF, LS, and LF times and the slack for each activity in the figure below and identify the critical path for the project. Can the project be completed in 30 weeks?

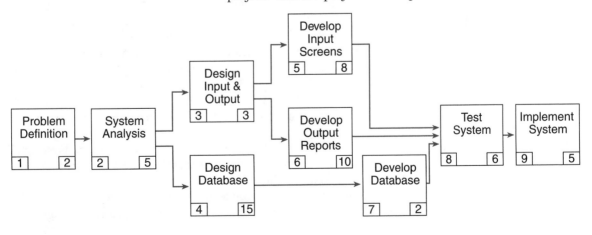

17. Calculate the ES, EF, LS, and LF times and the slack for each activity in the figure below and identify the critical path for the project. Can the project be completed in 30 weeks?

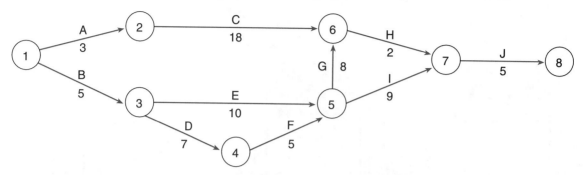

WORLD WIDE WEB EXERCISES

If you have difficulty accessing any of the Web addresses listed here, you can find these exercises (with up-to-date addresses) on the home page of Dr. James P. Clements, co-author of this book, at

www.towson.edu/~clements

1. Revisit the Web site (discussed in Chapter 9) at

www.hh.umu.se/fek

Find the link for "Research on Temporary Organizations and Project Management." From "Research on Temporary Organizations and Project Management," scroll down until you see the link for "WWW Guide to Project Management Research." Explore this link.

2. Name five international research networks and/or journals that are listed at this site. Explore their sites.

3. Return to "WWW Guide to Project Management Research." Name at least five universities worldwide that are doing project management research. Explore their sites.

4. Return to "WWW Guide to Project Management Research." Check out the list of project management indices. Explore at least three of these links, and describe what they contain.

5. Return to "WWW Guide to Project Management Research." Find as many resources for project management planning and scheduling as you can. Describe what you find.

6. Return to "WWW Guide to Project Management Research." Name at least three professional associations that are listed. Explore these links.

7. Return to "WWW Guide to Project Management Research." Name at least five organizations that do project management consulting. Explore these links.

8. Return to "WWW Guide to Project Management Research." Check out the link for the six phases of project management.

Describe these phases. How are they similar to or different from the ones described in this book?

CASE STUDY

This case study is a continuation of the one started in Chapter 9. Recall that after several years of dating, you and your beloved have finally decided to get married. Your partner wants a fairly elaborate wedding, and you have realized that a lot of planning and work need to be done. Noticing your nervousness, your friends and families have tried to reassure you that everything will be okay, and they have even offered to help with the wedding arrangements. Being a perfectionist, you want to make sure that everything goes as smoothly as possible.

Case Questions
1. Review your work from Chapter 9.
2. Make any additions, deletions, or modifications that seem appropriate.
3. Set a duration estimate for each activity.
4. Establish the project start and required completion times.
5. Calculate the ES, EF, LS, and LF times and the slack for each activity.
6. Determine the critical path.
7. Highlight the activities that make up the critical path.

Group Activity
Return to your groups of three or four members. Within each group, do items 1 through 7 listed above as a team. Each group must choose one individual to make a five-minute presentation to the class explaining what the group has done.

A p p e n d i x   Probability Considerations

ACTIVITY DURATION ESTIMATES

Recall that the duration estimate for each activity is the estimated total elapsed time from the time the activity is started until the time it is finished. With projects for which there is a high degree of uncertainty about the activity duration estimates, it is possible to use three estimates for each activity:

1. *Optimistic time* (t_o) is the time in which a particular activity can be completed if everything goes perfectly well and there are no complications. A rule of thumb is that there should be only one chance in ten of completing the activity in less than the optimistic time estimate.
2. *Most likely time* (t_m) is the time in which a particular activity can most frequently be completed under normal conditions. If an activity has been repeated many times, the actual duration that occurs most frequently can be used as the most likely time estimate.
3. *Pessimistic time* (t_p) is the time in which a particular activity can be completed under adverse circumstances, such as in the presence of unusual or unforeseen complications. A rule of thumb is that there should be only one chance in ten of completing the activity in more than the pessimistic time estimate.

Establishing three time estimates makes it possible to take uncertainty into account when estimating how long an activity will take. The most likely time must be longer than or equal to the optimistic time, and the pessimistic time must be longer than or equal to the most likely time.

It is not required that three time estimates be made for each activity. If someone has wide experience or data on how long it took to perform very similar activities in completed projects, it may be preferable to make only one estimate for how long an activity is expected to take (as discussed in the chapter). However, using three time estimates $(t_o, t_m, \text{and } t_p)$ can be helpful when there is a high degree of uncertainty as to how long an activity may take.

THE BETA PROBABILITY DISTRIBUTION

In network planning, when three time estimates are used for each activity, it is assumed that the three estimates follow a **beta probability distribution.** Based on this assumption, it's possible to calculate an expected (also called mean or average) duration, t_e, for each activity from the activity's three time estimates. The expected duration is calculated using the following formula:

$$t_e = \frac{t_o + 4(t_m) + t_p}{6}$$

Assume that the optimistic time for an activity is 1 week, the most likely time is 5 weeks, and the pessimistic time is 15 weeks. The beta probability distribution for this activity is shown in Figure 10.22. The expected duration for this activity is

$$t_e = \frac{1 + 4(5) + 15}{6} = 6 \text{ weeks}$$

Assume that the optimistic time for another activity is 10 weeks, the most likely time is 15 weeks, and the pessimistic time is 20 weeks. The beta probability distribution for this activity is shown in Figure 10.23. The expected duration for this activity is

$$t_e = \frac{10 + 4(15) + 20}{6} = 15 \text{ weeks}$$

Coincidentally, this happens to be the same as the most likely time estimate.

The peaks of the curves in Figures 10.22 and 10.23 represent the most likely times for their respective activities. The expected duration, t_e, divides the total area under the beta probability curve into two equal parts. In other words, 50 percent of the area under any beta probability curve will be to the left of t_e and 50 percent will be to the right. For example, Figure 10.22 shows that 50 percent of the area under the curve is to the left of 6 weeks and 50 percent of the area is to the right of 6 weeks. Thus, there is a 50-50 chance that an activity will actually take more or less time than its expected duration. Stated another way, there is a probability of 0.5 that an activity will take more time than t_e, and a probability of 0.5 that it will take less time than t_e. In Figure 10.22, there is a 50 percent chance that the

FIGURE 10.22   Beta Probability Distribution

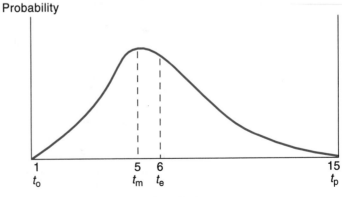

FIGURE 10.23   Beta Probability Distribution

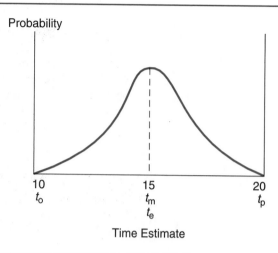

Probability

10   15   20
t_o t_m t_p
            t_e

Time Estimate

REINFORCE YOUR LEARNING
15. *Calculate the expected duration for an activity having the following time estimates: $t_o = 8$, $t_m = 12$, and $t_p = 22$.*

activity will actually take longer than 6 weeks and a 50 percent chance that it will take less than 6 weeks.

It is assumed that, as a project progresses, some activities will take less time than their expected duration and some activities will take more time than their expected duration. It is further assumed that, by the time the entire project is completed, the total net difference between all *expected* durations and all *actual* durations will be minimal.

PROBABILITY FUNDAMENTALS

Network planning in which three time estimates are used for each activity can be considered a *stochastic,* or *probabilistic, technique,* since it allows for uncertainty in activity duration by incorporating three estimates that are assumed to be distributed according to the beta probability distribution. Any technique that uses only one time estimate is considered to be a *deterministic technique.* Since it's assumed that the three time estimates for each activity follow a beta probability distribution, it is possible to calculate the probability, or likelihood, of actually completing the project before its required completion time. If only one time estimate is used for each activity, probability calculations cannot be made.

When three time estimates are used, all of the activities on the critical path of the network diagram can be added together to obtain a total probability distribution. The central limit theorem of probability theory states that this total probability distribution is not a beta probability distribution but a **normal probability distribution,** which is bell-shaped and symmetrical around its mean value. Furthermore, this total probability distribution has an expected duration that is equal to the sum of the expected durations of all of the activities that make up the total distribution. It also has a variance that is equal to the sum of the variances of all of the activities that make up the total distribution.

REINFORCE YOUR LEARNING

16. Compute the expected duration (t_e) and the variance (σ^2) for the following beta probability distribution.

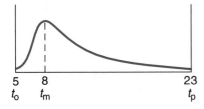

The **variance** for the beta probability distribution of an activity is found with the following formula:

$$\text{Variance} = \sigma^2 = \left(\frac{t_p - t_o}{6}\right)^2$$

Note that the variance of the normal distribution is the sum of the variances of the beta distribution.

Whereas the expected duration—which divides the area under a probability distribution into two equal parts—is a measure of the central tendency of a distribution, the variance is a measure of the dispersion, or spread, of a distribution from its expected value. The **standard deviation, σ,** is another measure of the dispersion of a distribution and *is equal to the square root of the variance.* The standard deviation gives a better visual representation of the spread of a distribution from its mean, or expected value, than does the variance. For a normal distribution (see Figure 10.24), the area within one standard deviation of the mean (to both sides) includes approximately 68 percent of the total area under the curve, the area within two standard deviations includes approximately 95 percent of the total area under the curve, and the area within three standard deviations includes approximately 99 percent of the total area under the curve.

REINFORCE YOUR LEARNING

17. What percentage of the area under this normal curve is shaded?

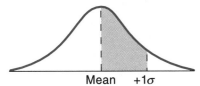

As noted above, the standard deviation is a measure of the dispersion of a distribution. Figure 10.25 shows two normal distributions. The distribution in (a) of Figure 10.25 is more widespread and thus has a larger standard deviation than that in (b). However, for both distributions 68 percent of the area under the curve is included within one standard deviation of the mean.

The total probability distribution of all the activities on the critical path of a network diagram is a normal distribution, with a mean equal to the sum of the individual activity expected durations and a variance equal to the sum of the individual activity variances. Consider the simple network in Figure 10.26. Assume that the project can start at time 0 and must be completed by day 42. The probability distributions for the activities in Figure 10.26 are shown in Figure 10.27.

The expected duration for each activity is as follows.

FIGURE 10.24   Normal Probability Distribution

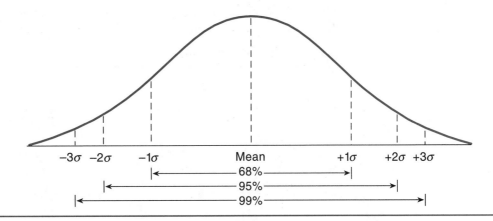

FIGURE 10.25   Normal Probability Distributions

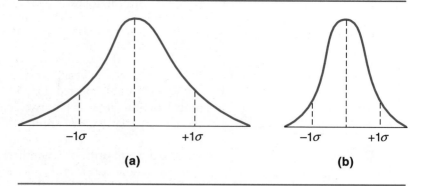

(a)   (b)

REINFORCE YOUR LEARNING
18. *If 95 percent of the area under
the following normal curve is
between the two labeled points,
what is the standard deviation?
What is the variance?*

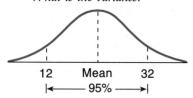

12   Mean   32
|←——— 95% ———→|

Activity A $t_e = \dfrac{2 + 4(4) + 6}{6} = 4$ days

Activity B $t_e = \dfrac{5 + 4(13) + 15}{6} = 12$ days

Activity C $t_e = \dfrac{13 + 4(18) + 35}{6} = 20$ days

Total $= 36$ days

If we sum the three distributions, we obtain a total mean, or total t_e:

Activity	t_o	t_m	t_p
A	2	4	6
B	5	13	15
C	13	18	35
Total	20	35	56

$$\text{Total } t_e = \frac{20 + 4(35) + 56}{6} = 36 \text{ days}$$

This result is the same as the sum of the three individual expected durations calculated previously: $4 + 12 + 20 = 36$ days. The total

FIGURE 10.26   Example Project

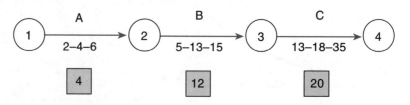

Required Completion = 42 Days

probability distribution is shown in (d) of Figure 10.27. The total expected duration for path 1–2–3–4 is 36 days. Thus, the project has an earliest expected completion time of day 36. As previously stated, the project has a required completion time of day 42.

The total distribution has a mean elapsed time equal to the sum of the three individual means, or expected durations. There is a probability of 0.5 that the project will be completed before day 36 and a probability of 0.5 that it will be completed after day 36.

For the simple example in Figure 10.26, the variances for the beta distributions of the three activities are as follows.

$$\text{Activity A} \qquad \sigma^2 = \left(\frac{6 - 2}{6}\right)^2 = 0.444$$

$$\text{Activity B} \qquad \sigma^2 = \left(\frac{15 - 5}{6}\right)^2 = 2.778$$

$$\text{Activity C} \qquad \sigma^2 = \left(\frac{35 - 13}{6}\right)^2 = 13.444$$

$$\text{Total} = 16.666$$

FIGURE 10.27 Probability Distributions

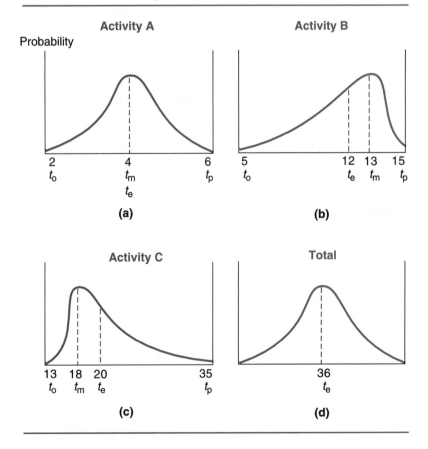

FIGURE 10.28   Normal Probability Distribution for Sample Project

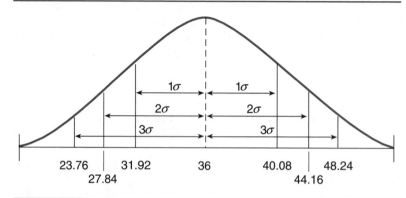

The variance for the total distribution, which is a normal probability distribution, is the sum of the three individual variances, or 16.666. The standard deviation, σ, of the total distribution is

$$\text{Standard deviation} = \sigma = \sqrt{\sigma^2} = \sqrt{16.666} = 4.08 \text{ days}$$

Figure 10.28, like (d) of Figure 10.27, shows the total probability curve, with the addition of the standard deviations.

Figure 10.28 is a normal curve, so 68 percent of its total area is contained within $\pm 1\sigma$ (standard deviation) of t_e, or between 31.92 days and 40.08 days; 95 percent of its area is between 27.84 days and 44.16 days; and 99 percent of its area is between 23.76 days and 48.24 days. This probability distribution can be interpreted as follows:

- There is a 99% chance (0.99 probability) of completing the project in 23.76 to 48.24 days.
- There is a 95% chance (0.95 probability) of completing the project in 27.84 to 44.16 days.
- There is a 47.5% chance (0.475 probability) of completing the project in 27.84 to 36 days.
- There is a 47.5% chance (0.475 probability) of completing the project in 36 to 44.16 days.
- There is a 68% chance (0.68 probability) of completing the project in 31.92 to 40.08 days.
- There is a 34% chance (0.34 probability) of completing the project in 31.92 to 36 days.
- There is a 34% chance (0.34 probability) of completing the project in 36 to 40.08 days.
- There is a 13.5% chance (0.135 probability) of completing the project in 27.84 to 31.92 days.
- There is a 13.5% chance (0.135 probability) of completing the project in 40.08 to 44.16 days.
- There is a 0.5% chance (0.005 probability) of completing the project before 23.76 days.
- There is a 0.5% chance (0.005 probability) of completing the project after 48.24 days.

Thus, it can be stated that the ratio of the area under certain parts of the normal curve to the total area under the curve is related to the probability.

CALCULATING PROBABILITY

The earliest expected finish time for a project is determined by the critical path through the network diagram. It is equal to the scheduled start time of the project plus the sum of the expected durations of the activities on the critical path leading from project start to project completion. As stated previously, the probability of actually completing a project before its earliest expected finish time is 0.5, since half of the area under the normal distribution curve is to the left of this expected time; the probability of actually completing a project after its earliest expected finish time is also 0.5, since half of the area under the normal curve is to the right of this expected time. Knowing the required completion time for a project makes it possible to calculate the probability of actually completing the project before this time.

In order to find the probability of actually completing a project before its required completion time, the following formula is used:

$$Z = \frac{LF - EF}{\sigma_t}$$

The elements in this formula are as follows:

* LF is the required completion time (latest finish) for the project.
* EF is the earliest expected finish time for the project (mean of the normal distribution).
* σ_t is the standard deviation of the total distribution of the activities on the longest (most time consuming) path leading to project completion.

In the above equation, Z measures the number of standard deviations between EF and LF on the normal probability curve. This Z value must be converted into a number that gives the proportion of the area under the normal curve that lies between EF and LF. Since the total area under a normal curve is equal to 1.0, the probability of finishing the project before its required completion time is equal to the proportion of the area under the curve that is to the left of LF.

The earliest expected finish time (EF) for the simple three-activity network in Figure 10.26 was calculated to be 36 days. Recall that the required completion time (LF) for the project is 42 days, or 6 days later than the EF. Figure 10.29 shows the normal curve for the project, with EF = 36 days and LF = 42 days.

The proportion of the area under the curve to the left of LF is equal to the probability of completing the project before 42 days. EF divides the area under the curve into two equal parts, each containing half of the area, so we know that the proportion of the area to the left of EF is 0.5. We must now find the proportion of the area between EF and LF and add this to 0.5 to obtain the proportion of the total area to the left of LF. Using the previous equation to find the proportion of the area between EF and LF, we can calculate Z:

FIGURE 10.29   Normal Probability Distribution for Sample Project

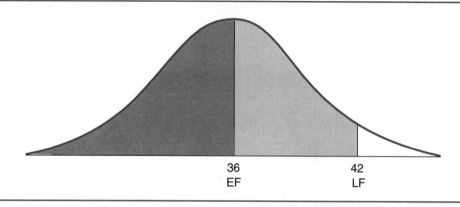

36
EF

42
LF

$$Z = \frac{LF - EF}{\sigma_t} = \frac{42 - 36}{4.08} = \frac{6}{4.08} = 1.47$$

The Z value of 1.47 indicates that there are 1.47 standard deviations (1 standard deviation 4.08 days) between EF and LF. However, the Z value does not directly give the proportion of the area under the curve between EF and LF. In order to find this area, we must convert the Z value to a number that gives the area directly, using a standard conversion table such as Table 10.1.

TABLE 10.1   Table of Areas of the Normal Curve Between the Maximum Ordinate and Values of Z

Z	0.00	0.01	0.02	0.03	0.04	0.05	0.06	0.07	0.08	0.09
0.0	.00000	.00399	.00798	.01197	.01595	.01994	.02392	.02790	.03188	.03586
0.1	.03983	.04380	.04776	.05172	.05567	.05962	.06356	.06749	.07142	.07535
0.2	.07926	.08317	.08706	.09095	.09483	.09871	.10257	.10642	.11026	.11409
0.3	.11791	.12172	.12552	.12930	.13307	.13683	.14058	.14431.	.14803	.15173
0.4	.15542	.15910	.16276	.16640	.17003	.17364	.17724	.18082	.18439	.18793
0.5	.19146	.19497	.19847	.20194	.20540	.20884	.21226	.21566	.21904	.22240
0.6	.22575	.22907	.23237	.23565	.23891	.24215	.24537	.24857	.25175	.25490
0.7	.25804	.26115	.26424	.26730	.27035	.27337	.27637	.27935	.28230	.28524
0.8	.28814	.29103	.29389	.29673	.29955	.30234	.30511	.30785	.31057	.31327
0.9	.31594	.31859	.32121	.32381	.32639	.32894	.33147	.33398	.33646	.33891
1.0	.34134	.34375	.34614	.34850	.35083	.35314	.35543	.35769	.35993	.36214
1.1	.36433	.36650	.36864	.37076	.37286	.37493	.37698	.37900	.38100	.38298
1.2	.38493	.38686	.38877	.39065	.39251	.39435	.39617	.39796	.39973	.40147
1.3	.40320	.40490	.40658	.40824	.40988	.41149	.41309	.41466	.41621	.41774
1.4	.41924	.42073	.42220	.42364	.42507	.42647	.42786	.42922	.43056	.43189

(continued)

TABLE 10.1   Table of Areas of the Normal Curve (continued)

Z	0.00	0.01	0.02	0.03	0.04	0.05	0.06	0.07	0.08	0.09
1.5	.44319	.43448	.43574	.43699	.43822	.43943	.44062	.44179	.44295	.44408
1.6	.44520	.44630	.44738	.44845	.44950	.45053	.45154	.45254	.45352	.45449
1.7	.45543	.45637	.45728	.45818	.45907	.45994	.46080	.46164	.46246	.46327
1.8	.46407	.46485	.46562	.46638	.46712	.46784	.46856	.46926	.46995	.47062
1.9	.47128	.47193	.47257	.47320	.47381	.47441	.47500	.47558	.47615	.47670
2.0	.47725	.47778	.47831	.47882	.47932	.47982	.48030	.48077	.48124	.48169
2.1	.48214	.48257	.48300	.48341	.48382	.48422	.48461	.48500	.48537	.48574
2.2	.48610	.48645	.48679	.48713	.48745	.48778	.48809	.48840	.48870	.48899
2.3	.48928	.48956	.48983	.49010	.49036	.49061	.49086	.49111	.49134	.49158
2.4	.49180	.49202	.49224	.49245	.49266	.49286	.49305	.49324	.49343	.49361
2.5	.49377	.49396	.49413	.49430	.49446	.49461	.49477	.49492	.49506	.49520
2.6	.49534	.49547	.49560	.49573	.49585	.49598	.49609	.49621	.49632	.49643
2.7	.49653	.49664	.49674	.49683	.49693	.49702	.49711	.49720	.49728	.49736
2.8	.49744	.49752	.49760	.49767	.49774	.49781	.49788	.49795	.49801	.49807
2.9	.49813	.49819	.49825	.49831	.49836	.49841	.49846	.49851	.49856	.49861
3.0	.49865	.49869	.49874	.49878	.49882	.49886	.49889	.49893	.49897	.49900
3.1	.49903	.49906	.49910	.49913	.49916	.49918	.49921	.49924	.49926	.49929
3.2	.49931	.49934	.49936	.49938	.49940	.49942	.49944	.49946	.49948	.49950
3.3	.49952	.49953	.49955	.49957	.49958	.49960	.49961	.49962	.49964	.49965
3.4	.49966	.49968	.49969	.49970	.49971	.49972	.49973	.49974	.49975	.49976
3.5	.49977	.49978	.49978	.49979	.49980	.49981	.49981	.49982	.49983	.49983
3.6	.49984	.49985	.49985	.49986	.49986	.49987	.49987	.49988	.49988	.49989
3.7	.49989	.49990	.49990	.49990	.49991	.49991	.49992	.49992	.49992	.49992
3.8	.49993	.49993	.49993	.49994	.49994	.49994	.49994	.49995	.49995	.49995
3.9	.49995	.49995	.49996	.49996	.49996	.49996	.49996	.49996	.49997	.49997
4.0	.49997	.49997	.49997	.49997	.49997	.49997	.49998	.49998	.49998	.49998

The first column and top row of the table are used to find the desired Z value with a significance of 0.01. To find the area for a Z value of 1.47, first go down the column on the far left to 1.4, then go across this row to the 0.07 column. The number there is .42922. This means that for a Z value of 1.47, the proportion of the area under a normal curve is 0.42922. This number tells us that the probability of actually completing the project between EF and LF, or in 36 to 42 days, is 0.42922; thus, there is a 42.922% chance. However, since we are interested in finding the probability of actually completing the project any time before 42 days, we must add the probability of finishing before 36 days. The probability of finishing the project any time before 42 days is equal to the probability of finishing before 36 days plus the probability of finishing between 36 days and 42 days:

$$0.50000 + 0.42922 = 0.92922$$

The probability of actually completing the project before its required completion time of 42 days is 0.92922; there is a 92.922% chance.

SUMMARY

If each activity in the network diagram for a project has three time estimates (optimistic, most likely, and pessimistic), it is possible to calculate the probability of actually completing the project before its required completion time using the methods discussed in this appendix. However, you should be careful in interpreting this probability, especially when there are several paths that are nearly as long as the critical path. If the standard deviations of these alternative paths are substantially different from that of the critical path, the probability of the project's actually being finished before its required completion time may be lower when these paths are used in the probability calculations than when the critical path is used. This discrepancy usually arises only when two or more paths that are equal or nearly equal in length lead to project completion.

QUESTIONS

1. True or false: In order to calculate the probability of finishing a project by its required completion time, it is necessary to have three time estimates for each activity and the required completion time for the project.
2. What are the expected duration, variance, and standard deviation for an activity whose three time estimates are $t_o = 2$, $t_m = 14$, and $t_p = 14$?
3. Which of the following is *not* a measure of the dispersion, or spread, of a distribution: variance, mean, or standard deviation?
4. The earliest expected finish time for a project is 138 days, and its required completion time is 130 days. What is the probability of completing the project before its required time if σ_t (the standard deviation of the total distribution of the activities on the longest path) is 6?

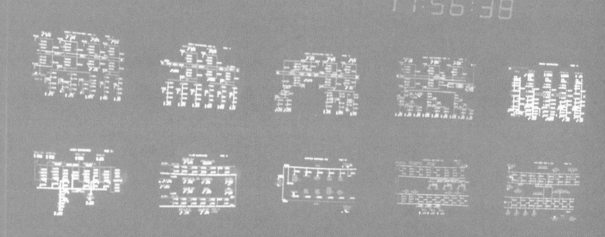

11

Schedule Control

Controlling Project Variables

According to James Ward, a specialist in management of information systems development projects, it is not uncommon for large information systems development consulting firms to have 25 percent of large projects canceled, 60 percent experience significant cost overruns, and 75 percent suffer problems with quality. Just a small percentage of projects actually come in on time and meet all requirements. These problems, he states, can be avoided with proper planning, scheduling, and controlling of the project.

The focus of Ward's research is on controlling work, resources, and time in order to ensure project success. Among the important factors in controlling a project, he suggests, are monitoring actual progress against the plan and schedule on a regular basis, recognizing deviations, and taking appropriate corrective action. The project manager, after all, is the one who is chiefly responsible for making sure that the work meets all quality standards and that it conforms to requirements and specifications, so ongoing monitoring of progress is essential.

The project manager should receive regular, formal status reports from all team members to compare actual progress against the plan. Each team member should state which of his or her tasks are done, when the others will be done, and, if they are behind schedule, why. Each project team should have at least one task (or subtask) due for completion every week and at least one bigger task due every month. Of course, this depends on project size, but the point is that a team should always have a goal and that progress toward that goal should be monitored. The project manager should recognize any deviations as early as possible, properly identify the causes of those deviations, and institute the appropriate corrective measures.

This chapter will focus on these topics in depth.

Source: J. Ward, "Productivity Through Project Management: Controlling the Project Variables," *Information Systems Management,* Winter 1994.

Controlling Technology-Based Projects

According to Hans Thamhain, project management is a powerful competitive tool for world-class companies, crucial for achieving superior business performance. A major aspect of this tool is the effective implementation and use of project management control techniques, which can be critical to the success of any project, especially technology-based projects.

Since the late 1980s the business environment has changed dramatically. New technologies have become and will continue to be a significant factor for almost every business. Computers and communications technology have radically transformed the workplace, and many managers see this new environment as more challenging than the old one. Technology-based projects are often characterized by a high degree of work complexity, evolving solutions, high levels of innovation, and multidisciplinary teamwork. This environment requires a sophisticated management style that relies on group interaction, resource and power sharing, individual accountability, commitment, and a self-directed form of project control. Many project managers fail because they lack an understanding of how to use proper project control techniques.

In order to help overcome this lack, Thamhain provides an excellent in-depth discussion of various project management control techniques. He offers the following recommendations for effective project control: involve the team, make the techniques consistent with the work process, establish standard management practices, anticipate anxieties and conflicts, foster a challenging work environment, and focus on continuous improvement.

Source: H. Thamhain, "Best Practices for Controlling Technology-Based Projects," *Project Management Journal,* December 1996.

Chapters 9 and 10 established a baseline plan and a schedule, respectively, for the consumer market study project. Once a project actually starts, it's necessary to monitor the progress to ensure that everything is going according to schedule. This involves measuring actual progress and comparing it to the schedule. If at any time during the project it is determined that the project is behind schedule, corrective action must be taken to get back on schedule. If a project gets too far behind schedule, it may be very difficult to get back on track.

The key to effective project control is to measure actual progress and compare it to planned progress on a timely and regular basis and to take necessary corrective action immediately. A project manager must not simply hope that a problem will go away without corrective intervention—it won't. Based on actual progress and on consideration of other changes that may occur, it's possible to regularly calculate an updated project schedule and forecast whether the project will finish ahead of or behind its required completion time.

This chapter will cover the details of controlling a project and will focus mainly on the critical role of controlling the scheduling to ensure that the work gets done on time. By mastering the concepts discussed in this chapter, you should be well prepared to help control your projects. You will become familiar with

- performing the steps in the project control process
- determining the effects of actual schedule performance on the project schedule
- incorporating project changes into the schedule
- calculating an updated project schedule
- controlling the project schedule

PROJECT CONTROL PROCESS

The project control process involves regularly gathering data on project performance, comparing actual performance to planned performance, and taking corrective actions if actual performance is behind planned performance. This process must occur regularly throughout the project.

Figure 11.1 illustrates the steps in the project control process. It starts with establishing a baseline plan that shows how the project scope (tasks) will be accomplished on time (schedule) and within budget (resources, costs). Once this baseline plan is agreed upon by the customer and the contractor or project team, the project can start.

A regular **reporting period** should be established for comparing actual progress with planned progress. Reporting may be daily, weekly, bi-weekly, or monthly, depending on the complexity or overall duration of the project. If a project is expected to have an overall duration of a month, the reporting period might be as short as a day. On the other hand, if a project is expected to run five years, the reporting period might be a month.

During each reporting period, two kinds of data or information need to be collected:

1. *Data on actual performance.* This includes
   - the actual time that activities were started and/or finished
   - the actual costs expended and committed

FIGURE 11.1   Project Control Process

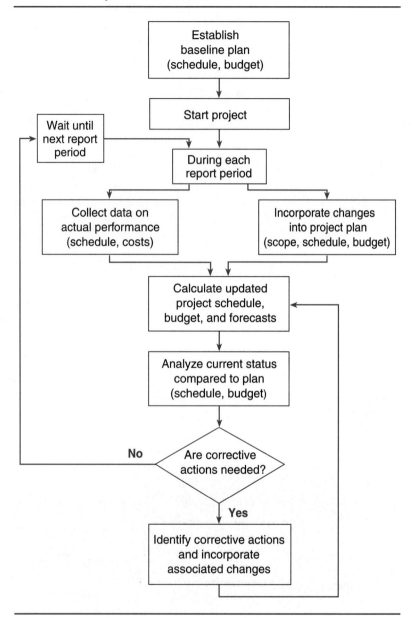

2. *Information on any changes to the project scope, schedule, and budget.*
   These changes could be initiated by the customer or the project
   team, or they could be the result of an unanticipated occurrence
   such as a natural disaster, a labor strike, or the resignation of a key
   project team member.

   It should be noted that once changes are incorporated into the
plan and agreed on by the customer, a new baseline plan has to be

REINFORCE YOUR LEARNING

1. *What are the two kinds of data or information that need to be collected during each reporting period?*

established. The scope, schedule, and budget of the new baseline plan may be different from those of the original baseline plan.

It is crucial that the data and information discussed above be collected in a timely manner and used to calculate an updated project schedule and budget. For example, if project reporting is done monthly, data and information should be obtained as late as possible in that monthly period so that when an updated schedule and budget are calculated, they are based on the latest possible information. In other words, a project manager should not gather data at the beginning of the month and then wait until the end of the month to use it to calculate an updated schedule and budget, because the data will be outdated and may cause incorrect decisions to be made about the project status and corrective actions.

Once an updated schedule and budget have been calculated, they need to be compared to the baseline schedule and budget and analyzed for variances to determine whether a project is ahead of or behind schedule and under or over budget. If the project status is okay, no corrective actions are needed; the status will be analyzed again for the next reporting period.

If it is determined that corrective actions are necessary, however, decisions must be made regarding how to revise the schedule or the budget. These decisions often involve a trade-off of time, cost, and scope. For example, reducing the duration of an activity may require either increasing costs to pay for more resources or reducing the scope of the task (and possibly not meeting the customer's technical requirements). Similarly, reducing project costs may require using materials of a lower quality than originally planned. Once a decision is made on which corrective actions to take, they must be incorporated into the schedule and budget. It is then necessary to calculate a revised schedule and budget to determine whether the planned corrective measures result in an acceptable schedule and budget. If not, further revisions will be needed.

The project control process continues throughout the project. In general, the shorter the reporting period, the better the chances of identifying problems early and taking effective corrective actions. If a project gets too far out of control, it may be difficult to achieve the project objective without sacrificing the scope, budget, schedule, or quality. There may be situations in which it is wise to increase the frequency of reporting until the project is back on track. For example, if a five-year project with monthly reporting is endangered by a slipping schedule or an increasing budget overrun, it may be prudent to reduce the reporting period to one week in order to monitor the project and the impact of corrective actions more closely.

The project control process is an important and necessary part of project management. Just establishing a sound baseline plan is not sufficient, since even the best laid plans don't always work out. *Project management is a proactive approach to controlling a project,* to ensure that the project objective is achieved even when things don't go according to plan.

REINFORCE YOUR LEARNING

2. *True or false: In general, it is better to have a shorter reporting period during a project.*

REINFORCE YOUR LEARNING

3. *In addition to establishing a sound baseline plan, it is also necessary to proactively _____ the project after it has started in order to assure that the project objective is achieved.*

EFFECTS OF ACTUAL SCHEDULE PERFORMANCE

Throughout a project, some activities will be completed on time, some will be finished ahead of schedule, and others will be finished later than scheduled. Actual progress—whether faster or slower than planned—will have an effect on the schedule of the remaining, uncompleted activities of the project. Specifically, the **actual finish times (AF)** of completed activities will determine the earliest start and earliest finish times for the remaining activities in the network diagram, as well as the total slack.

Part (a) of Figure 11.2 is an AIB network diagram for a simple project. It shows that the earliest the project can finish is day 15 (the sum of the durations of the three activities, 7 + 5 + 3). Since the required completion time is day 20, the project has a total slack of +5 days.

Suppose that activity 1, "Remove Old Wallpaper," is *actually* finished on day 10, rather than on day 7 as planned, because it turns out to be more difficult than anticipated. [See part (b) of Figure 11.2.] This means that the earliest start and finish times for activities 2 and 3 will be 3 days later than on the original schedule. Because "Remove Old Wallpaper" is actually finished on day 10, the ES for "Patch Walls" will be day 10 and its EF will be day 15. Following through with the forward calculations, we find that "Put Up New Wallpaper" will have an ES of day 15 and an EF of day 18. Comparing this new EF of the last activity to the required completion time of day 20, we find a difference of 2 days. The total slack got worse—it changed in a negative direction, from +5 days to +2 days. This example illustrates how the actual finish times of activities have a ripple effect, altering the remaining activities' earliest start and finish times and the total slack.

REINFORCE YOUR LEARNING

4. *What three types of values will the actual finish times of completed activities affect?*

FIGURE 11.2 Effect of Actual Finish Times

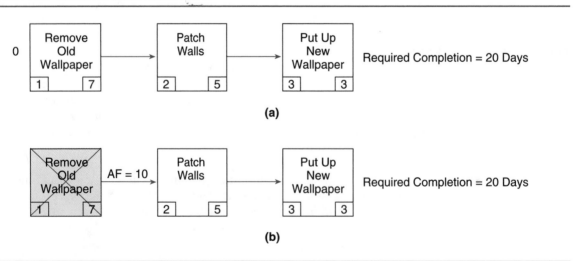

(a)

(b)

It's helpful to indicate on the network diagram, in some manner, which activities have been completed. One method is to shade or crosshatch the activity box, as was done in part (b) of Figure 11.2.

INCORPORATING PROJECT CHANGES INTO THE SCHEDULE

Throughout a project, changes may occur that have an impact on the schedule. As was noted earlier, these changes might be initiated by the customer or the project team, or they might be the result of an unanticipated occurrence.

Here are some examples of changes initiated by the customer:

- A home buyer tells the builder that the family room should be larger and the bedroom windows should be relocated.
- A customer tells the project team developing an information system that the system must have the capability to produce a previously unmentioned set of reports and graphics.

These types of changes represent revisions to the original project scope and will have an impact on the schedule and cost. The degree of impact, however, may depend on when the changes are requested. If they're requested early in the project, they may have less impact on cost and schedule than if they're requested later in the project. For example, changing the size of the family room and relocating the bedroom windows would be relatively easy if the house were still being designed and the drawings being prepared. If the changes were requested after the framing was put up and the windows were installed, however, the impact on costs and schedule would be far greater.

When the customer requests a change, the contractor or project team should estimate the impact on the project budget and schedule and then obtain customer approval before proceeding. If the customer approves the proposed revisions to the project schedule and budget, any additional tasks, revised duration estimates, and material and labor costs should be incorporated.

An example of a change initiated by a project team is the decision by a team planning a town fair to eliminate all amusement rides for adults because of space limitations and insurance costs. The project plan would then have to be revised to delete or modify all those activities involving adult rides. Here is an example of a project manager–initiated change: A contractor, charged with developing an automated invoicing system for a customer, suggests that, rather than incorporate custom-designed software, the system use standard available software in order to reduce costs and accelerate the schedule.

Some changes involve the addition of activities that were overlooked when the original plan was developed. For example, the project team may have forgotten to include activities associated with developing training materials and conducting training for a new information system. Or the customer or contractor may have failed to include the installation of gutters and downspouts in the work scope for the construction of a restaurant.

Other changes become necessary because of unanticipated occurrences, such as a snowstorm that slows down construction of a building, the failure of a new product to pass quality tests, or the untimely death or resignation of a key member of a project team. These events will have an impact on the schedule and/or budget and will require that the project plan be modified.

Still other changes can result from adding more detail to the network diagram as the project moves forward. No matter what level of detail is used in the initial network diagram, there will be some activities that can be broken down further as the project progresses.

Any type of change—whether initiated by the customer, contractor, project manager, a team member, or an unanticipated event—will require a modification to the plan in terms of scope, budget, and/or schedule. When such changes are agreed upon, a new baseline plan is established and used as the benchmark against which actual project performance will be compared.

With respect to the project schedule, changes can result in the addition or deletion of activities, the resequencing of activities, the changing of activities' duration estimates or a new required completion time for the project.

See Chapter 5 and Chapter 8 for further discussion of managing and controlling changes.

REINFORCE YOUR LEARNING

5. What three elements can project changes affect?

UPDATING THE PROJECT SCHEDULE

Network-based planning and scheduling allows project schedules to be dynamic. Because the network plan (diagram) and schedule (tabulation) are separate, they are much easier to update manually than a traditional Gantt chart. However, various project management software packages are available to assist with the automated generation of schedules, network diagrams, budgets, and even network-to-Gantt-chart conversions.

Once data have been collected on the actual finish times of completed activities and the effects of any project changes, an updated project schedule can be calculated. These calculations are based on the methodology explained in Chapter 10:

- The earliest start and finish times for the remaining, uncompleted activities are calculated by working forward through the network, but they're based on the *actual finish times* of completed activities and the estimated durations of the uncompleted activities.
- The latest start and finish times for the uncompleted activities are calculated by working backward through the network.

As an illustration of the calculation of an updated schedule, let's consider the network diagram shown in Figure 11.3 for the consumer market study project. Assume the following:

1. Completed activities:
    a. Activity 1, "Identify Target Consumers," actually finished on day 2.
    b. Activity 2, "Develop Draft Questionnaire," actually finished on day 11.

      c. Activity 3, "Pilot-Test Questionnaire," actually finished on day 30.
2. Project changes:
      a. It was discovered that the database to be used to prepare the mailing labels was not up to date. A new database needs to be purchased before the mailing labels can be prepared. This new database was ordered on day 23. It will take 21 days to get it from the supplier.
      b. A preliminary review of comments from the pilot test of the questionnaire indicates that substantial revisions to the questionnaire are required. Therefore, the duration estimate for activity 4 needs to be increased from 5 days to 15 days.

The network diagram in Figure 11.3 incorporates the above information. Figure 11.4 shows the updated schedule. Note that the total slack for the critical path is now −5 days, instead of the +2 days in the baseline schedule in Figure 10.16 in Chapter 10. The anticipated project completion time is now day 135, which is beyond the required completion time of 130 days.

APPROACHES TO SCHEDULE CONTROL

Schedule control involves four steps:

1. Analyzing the schedule to determine which areas may need corrective action
2. Deciding what specific corrective actions should be taken
3. Revising the plan to incorporate the chosen corrective actions
4. Recalculating the schedule to evaluate the effects of the planned corrective actions

If the planned corrective actions do not result in an acceptable schedule, these steps need to be repeated.

Throughout a project, each time a schedule is recalculated—whether it's after actual data or project changes are incorporated or after corrective actions are planned—it is necessary to analyze the newly calculated schedule to determine whether it needs further attention. The schedule analysis should include identifying the critical path and any paths of activities that have a negative slack, as well as those paths where slippages have occurred (the slack got worse) compared with the previously calculated schedule.

REINFORCE YOUR LEARNING

6. In analyzing a project schedule, it is important to identify all the paths of activities that have a _____ slack.

A concentrated effort to accelerate project progress must be applied to the paths with negative slack. The amount of slack should determine the priority with which these concentrated efforts are applied. For example, the path with the most negative slack should be given top priority.

Corrective actions that will eliminate the negative slack from the project schedule must be identified. These corrective actions must reduce the duration estimates for activities on the negative-slack paths. Remember, the slack for a path of activities is shared among all the activities on that path. Therefore, *a change in the estimated duration*

FIGURE 11.3   Network Diagram for Consumer Market Study Project, Incorporating Actual Progress and Changes

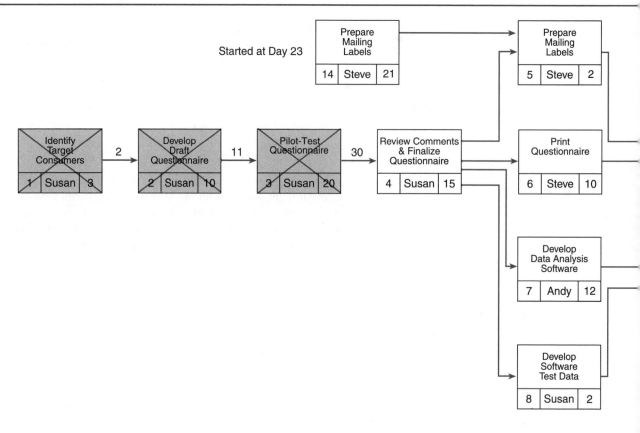

of any activity on that path will cause a corresponding change in the slack for that path.

When analyzing a path of activities that has negative slack, you should focus on two kinds of activities:

1. *Activities that are near term (that is, in progress or to be started in the immediate future).* It's much wiser to take aggressive corrective action to reduce the durations of activities that will be done in the near term than to plan to reduce the durations of activities that are scheduled sometime in the future. If you postpone until the distant future taking corrective action that will reduce the durations of activities, you may find that the negative slack has deteriorated even further by that time. As the project progresses, there is always less time remaining in which corrective action can be taken.

Looking at Figure 11.4, we can see that it would be better to try to reduce the durations of the near-term activities on the critical path, such as "Review Comments & Finalize Questionnaire" or "Print Questionnaire," than to put off corrective action until the last activity, "Prepare Report."

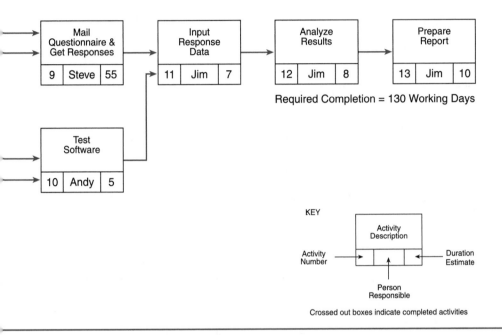

Required Completion = 130 Working Days

KEY

Crossed out boxes indicate completed activities

2. *Activities that have long duration estimates.* Taking corrective measures that will reduce a 20-day activity by 20 percent—that is, by 4 days—has a larger impact than totally eliminating a 1-day activity. Usually, longer-duration activities present the opportunity for larger reductions.

Look again at Figure 11.4: There may be more opportunity to reduce the 55-day duration estimate for "Mail Questionnaire & Get Responses" by 5 days (9 percent) than to reduce the shorter duration estimates of other activities on the critical path.

REINFORCE YOUR LEARNING

7. *When analyzing a path of activities that has negative slack, what two kinds of activities should you look at carefully?*

There are various approaches to reducing the duration estimates of activities. One obvious way is to apply more resources to speed up an activity. This could be done by assigning more people to work on the activity or asking the people working on the activity to work more hours per day or more days per week. Additional appropriate resources might be transferred from concurrent activities that have positive slack. Sometimes, however, adding people to an activity may in fact result in the activity's taking longer, because the people already assigned to the activity are diverted from their work in order to help

FIGURE 11.4 Updated Schedule for Consumer Market Study Project

CONSUMER MARKET STUDY PROJECT

	ACTIVITY	RESPON.	DUR. ESTIM.	EARLIEST		LATEST		TOTAL SLACK	ACTUAL FINISH
				START	FINISH	START	FINISH		
1	Identify Target Consumers	Susan							2
2	Develop Draft Questionnaire	Susan							11
3	Pilot-Test Questionnaire	Susan							30
4	Review Comments & Finalize Questionnaire	Susan	15	30	45	25	40	−5	
5	Prepare Mailing Labels	Steve	2	45	47	48	50	3	
6	Print Questionnaire	Steve	10	45	55	40	50	−5	
7	Develop Data Analysis Software	Andy	12	45	57	88	100	43	
8	Develop Software Test Data	Susan	2	45	47	98	100	53	
9	Mail Questionnaire & Get Responses	Steve	55	55	110	50	105	−5	
10	Test Software	Andy	5	57	62	100	105	43	
11	Input Response Data	Jim	7	110	117	105	112	−5	
12	Analyze Results	Jim	8	117	125	112	120	−5	
13	Prepare Report	Jim	10	125	135	120	130	−5	
14	Order New Database for Labels	Steve	21	23	44	27	48	4	

the new people get up to speed. Another approach is to assign a person with greater expertise or more experience to perform or help with the activity, so as to get it done in a shorter time than was possible with the less experienced people originally assigned to it.

Reducing the scope or requirements for an activity is another way to reduce its duration estimate. For example, it might be acceptable to put only one coat of paint on a room rather than two coats, as originally planned. In an extreme case, it may be decided to totally eliminate some activities, deleting them and their durations from the schedule.

Increasing productivity through improved methods or technology is yet another approach to reducing activities' durations. For example, instead of having people keyboard data from a customer survey into a computer database, optical scanning equipment might be used.

Once specific corrective actions to reduce the negative slack have been decided on, the duration estimates for the appropriate activities must be revised in the network plan. Then a revised schedule needs to be calculated to evaluate whether the planned corrective actions reduce the negative slack as anticipated.

In most cases, eliminating negative slack by reducing durations of activities will involve a trade-off in the form of an increase in costs or a reduction in scope. For a more thorough discussion of this topic, see the appendix on time–cost trade-off at the end of this chapter. If the project is way behind schedule (has substantial negative slack), a substantial increase in costs and/or reduction in work scope or quality may be required to get it back on schedule. This could jeopardize elements of the overall project objective: scope, budget, schedule, and/or quality. In some cases, the customer and contractor or project team may have to acknowledge that one or more of these elements cannot be achieved. Thus, for example, the customer may have to extend the required completion time for the entire project, or there may be a dispute over who should absorb any increased cost to accelerate the schedule—the contractor or the customer.

REINFORCE YOUR LEARNING

8. List four approaches to reducing the estimated durations of activities.

Some contracts include a bonus provision, whereby the customer will pay the contractor a bonus if the project is completed ahead of schedule. Conversely, some contracts include a penalty provision, whereby the customer can reduce the final payment to the contractor if the project is not completed on time. Some of these penalties can be substantial. In either of these situations, effective schedule control is crucial.

The key to effective schedule control is to aggressively address any paths with negative or deteriorating slack values as soon as they are identified, rather than hoping that things will improve as the project goes on. Addressing schedule problems early will minimize the negative impact on cost and scope. If a project gets too far behind, getting back on schedule becomes more difficult, and it doesn't come free. It requires spending more money or reducing the scope or quality.

On projects that don't have negative slack, it's important not to let the slack deteriorate by accepting delays and slippages. If a project is ahead of schedule, a concentrated effort should be made to *keep* it ahead of schedule.

Project meetings are a good forum for addressing schedule control issues. See Chapter 8 for a discussion of project meetings and Chapter 6 for a discussion of problem solving.

SCHEDULE CONTROL FOR INFORMATION SYSTEMS DEVELOPMENT

Controlling the schedule for the development of an information system is a challenge. Numerous unexpected circumstances arise that can push an IS development project beyond its originally scheduled due date. However, just as with any other type of project, the key to effective project control is to measure actual progress and compare it to planned progress on a timely and regular basis and to take necessary corrective action immediately.

Like other forms of schedule control, schedule control for IS development projects is carried out according to the steps discussed earlier in this chapter. A project control process such as the one

FIGURE 11.5   Network Diagram for Sales Reporting System Project, Incorporating Actual Progress and Changes

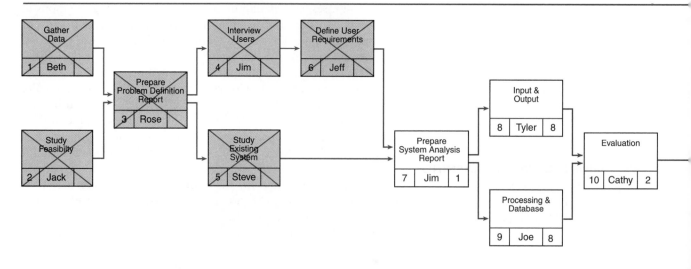

illustrated in Figure 11.1 should be used for comparing actual performance with the schedule. Once the customer and the project team agree on changes, these changes should be recorded and the schedule should be revised.

Among the changes that commonly become necessary during IS development projects are the following:

- *Changes to input screens*—such as added fields, different icons, different colors, different menu structures, or completely new input screens
- *Changes to reports*—such as added fields, different subtotals and totals, different sorts, different selection criteria, different order of fields, or completely new reports
- *Changes to on-line queries*—such as different ad hoc capabilities, access to different fields or databases, different query structures, or additional queries
- *Changes to database structures*—such as additional fields, different data field names, different data storage sizes, different relationships among the data, or completely new databases
- *Changes to software processing routines*—such as different algorithms, different interfaces with other subroutines, different internal logic, or new procedures

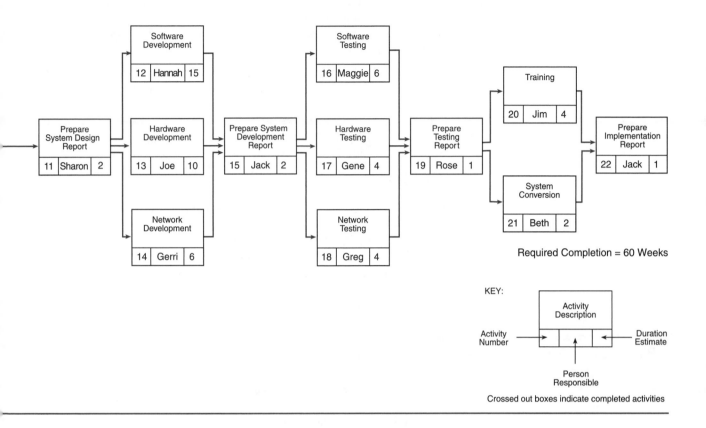

Required Completion = 60 Weeks

KEY:

Activity Number — Activity Description — Duration Estimate

Person Responsible

Crossed out boxes indicate completed activities

- *Changes to processing speeds*—such as higher throughput rates or response times
- *Changes to storage capacities*—such as an increase in the maximum number of data records
- *Changes to business processes*—such as changes in work or data flow, addition of new clients that must have access, or completely new processes that must be supported
- *Changes to software resulting from hardware upgrades* or, conversely, *hardware upgrades resulting from the availability of more powerful software*

An IS Example: ABC Office Designs (Continued)

Recall from Chapters 9 and 10 that ABC Office Designs assigned Beth Smith to be the project manager of the Sales Reporting System development project. Beth identified all of the major tasks that need to be accomplished and developed the work breakdown structure, responsibility matrix, and network diagram. When she calculated the earliest and latest start and finish times for each activity, she discovered that the project would take 59 weeks to complete—9 weeks over the original 50 weeks that was requested. However, after extensive discussions with upper management in which she stressed the importance of developing the system right the first time and not having to rush through some critical phases of the SDLC, Beth convinced her superiors to extend the project completion time to the full 59 weeks required plus an additional week in case anything unexpected happened.

Beth and her team proceeded with the project and completed activities 1 through 6:

Activity 1, "Gather Data," actually finished on day 4.

Activity 2, "Study Feasibility," actually finished on day 4.

Activity 3, "Prepare Problem Definition Report," actually finished on day 5.

Activity 4, "Interview Users," actually finished on day 10.

Activity 5, "Study Existing System," actually finished on day 15.

Activity 6, "Define User Requirements," actually finished on day 18.

They then discovered that, by using some reusable software for the database, they could reduce the estimated duration of activity 9, "Processing & Database," from 10 weeks to 8 weeks.

Figures 11.5 and 11.6 show the updated network diagram and project schedule, respectively, after these changes have been incorporated. Notice that because of the above occurrences, the critical path now has a total slack of 0.

PROJECT MANAGEMENT SOFTWARE

Virtually all project management software packages allow you to perform the control functions identified in this chapter. Specifically, while an activity is in progress or once an activity has been completed, current information can be entered into the system and the software will automatically revise the project schedule. Likewise, if the estimated durations for any future activities change, these changes can be entered into the system and the software will automatically update the schedule. All network diagrams, tables, and reports produced by the software will be updated to reflect the most recent information. See Appendix A at the end of the book for a thorough discussion of project management software, including a list of vendors.

SUMMARY

Once a project actually starts, it's necessary to monitor the progress to ensure that everything is going according to schedule. This involves measuring actual progress and comparing it to the schedule. If at any time during the project it is determined that the project is behind schedule, corrective action must be taken to get back on schedule. The key to effective project control is to measure actual progress and compare it to planned progress on a timely and regular basis and to

FIGURE 11.6   Updated Schedule for Sales Reporting System Project

SALES REPORTING SYSTEM PROJECT

	ACTIVITY	RESPON.	DUR. ESTIM.	EARLIEST		LATEST		TOTAL SLACK	ACTUAL FINISH
				START	FINISH	START	FINISH		
1	Gather Data	Beth							4
2	Study Feasibility	Jack							4
3	Prepare Problem Definition Report	Rose							5
4	Interview Users	Jim							10
5	Study Existing System	Steve							15
6	Define User Requirements	Jeff							18
7	Prepare System Analysis Report	Jim	1	18	19	18	19	0	
8	Input & Output	Tyler	8	19	27	19	27	0	
9	Processing & Database	Joe	8	19	27	19	27	0	
10	Evaluation	Cathy	2	27	29	27	29	0	
11	Prepare System Design Report	Sharon	2	29	31	29	31	0	
12	Software Development	Hannah	15	31	46	31	46	0	
13	Hardware Development	Joe	10	31	41	36	46	5	
14	Network Development	Gerri	6	31	37	40	46	9	
15	Prepare System Development Report	Jack	2	46	48	46	48	0	
16	Software Testing	Maggie	6	48	54	48	54	0	
17	Hardware Testing	Gene	4	48	52	50	54	2	
18	Network Testing	Greg	4	48	52	50	54	2	
19	Prepare Testing Report	Rose	1	54	55	54	55	0	
20	Training	Jim	4	55	59	55	59	0	
21	System Conversion	Beth	2	55	57	57	59	2	
22	Prepare Implementation Report	Jack	1	59	60	59	60	0	

take necessary corrective action immediately. Based on actual progress and on consideration of other changes that may occur, it's possible to regularly calculate an updated project schedule and forecast whether the project will finish ahead of or behind its required completion time.

A regular reporting period should be established for comparing actual progress with planned progress. Reporting may be daily, weekly, bi-weekly, or monthly, depending on the complexity or overall duration of the project. During each reporting period, two kinds of data or information need to be collected: data on actual performance and information on any changes to the project scope, schedule, and budget.

The project control process continues throughout the project. In general, the shorter the reporting period, the better the chances of identifying problems early and taking effective corrective actions. If a project gets too far out of control, it may be difficult to achieve the project objective without sacrificing the scope, budget, schedule, or quality.

Throughout a project, some activities will be completed on time, some will be finished ahead of schedule, and others will be finished later than scheduled. Actual progress—whether faster or slower than planned—will have an effect on the schedule of the remaining, uncompleted activities of the project. Specifically, the actual finish times (AF) of completed activities will determine the earliest start and earliest finish times for the remaining activities in the network diagram, as well as the total slack.

Throughout a project, changes may occur that have an impact on the schedule. These changes might be initiated by the customer or the project team, or they might be the result of an unanticipated occurrence. Any type of change—whether initiated by the customer, contractor, project manager, a team member, or an unanticipated event—will require a modification to the plan in terms of scope, budget, and/or schedule. When such changes are agreed upon, a new baseline plan is established and used as the benchmark against which actual project performance will be compared.

Once data have been collected on the actual finish times of completed activities and the effects of any project changes, an updated project schedule can be calculated. These calculations are based on the methodology explained in Chapter 10.

Schedule control involves four steps: analyzing the schedule to determine which areas may need corrective action, deciding what specific corrective actions should be taken, revising the plan to incorporate the chosen corrective actions, and recalculating the schedule to evaluate the effects of the planned corrective actions. Corrective actions that will eliminate the negative slack from the project schedule must be identified. These corrective actions must reduce the duration estimates for activities on the negative-slack paths. When analyzing a path of activities that has negative slack, you should focus on two kinds of activities: activities that are near term and activities that have long duration estimates.

There are various approaches to reducing the duration estimates of activities. These include applying more resources to speed up an activity, assigning individuals with greater expertise or more experience to work on the activity, reducing the scope or requirements for the activity, and increasing productivity through improved methods or technology.

QUESTIONS

1. Explain why it is important to continually monitor the progress of a project.
2. Describe in your own words what is meant by *the project control process*. Give an example of its use.
3. Why should a project have a regular reporting period? Should all projects have the same reporting period? Explain your answer.
4. Consider a project on which you are currently working or have worked. What is or was the reporting period for that project? Explain why.
5. What types of data should be collected during each reporting period?
6. If a project schedule needs to be adjusted, what trade-offs might have to occur?
7. Who can initiate a change to a project schedule? Why would they do so? When would they do so? Give examples.
8. How are the network diagram and schedule updated after a project is initiated and changes have been requested?
9. Describe the four-step approach to schedule control. Give an example of its use.
10. When a schedule must be accelerated, which activities are likely candidates for adjustment? Why?
11. In what ways can an activity's duration be reduced? Give examples.
12. Why might the use of some slack by one activity affect other activities in a project?
13. Refer to Question 15 at the end of Chapter 10. Assume that task A actually finished at 3 weeks, task B actually finished at 12 weeks, and task C actually finished at 13 weeks. Recalculate the expected project completion time. Which activities would you focus on in order to get the project back on schedule?
14. Refer to Question 16 at the end of Chapter 10. Assume that "Systems Analysis" actually finished at 8 weeks, "Design Input & Output" actually finished at 15 weeks, and "Design Database" actually finished at 19 weeks. Recalculate the expected project completion time. Which activities would you focus on in order to get the project back on schedule?
15. Refer to Question 17 at the end of Chapter 10. Assume that task A actually finished at 5 weeks and task B actually finished at 5 weeks. Recalculate the expected project completion time. Which activities would you focus on in order to get the project back on schedule?

WORLD WIDE WEB EXERCISES

If you have difficulty accessing any of the Web addresses listed here, you can find these exercises (with up-to-date addresses) on the home page of Dr. James P. Clements, co-author of this book, at

www.towson.edu/~clements

1. NASA is a pioneer in developing project management techniques and has successfully used these techniques for many years. NASA maintains an excellent on-line handbook for project management, called *PMDP (The Project Management Development Process),* at

**www.hq.nasa.gov/office/HR-Education/
training/handbook.html**

Visit this site.

2. Explore the link for "PMDP Process Description." What is this process all about?
3. Return to the main page and explore the link for "Benefits of Participation." What are the benefits of this process?
4. Return to the main page and explore the link for "PMDP Structure." What four general levels of accomplishment in project management are described?
5. Using information from this page, describe the five steps of the PMDP process.
6. Return to the main page and explore the link for "Working Your Plan." What tips are given?
7. Explore some of the other links from the main page. Describe at least two of these links.
8. Explain why you think this project management development process is so important to NASA.

CASE STUDY

This case study is a continuation of the one from Chapters 9 and 10. Recall that after several years of dating, you and your beloved have finally decided to get married. Your partner wants a fairly elaborate wedding, and you have realized that a lot of planning and work need to be done. Noticing your nervousness, your friends and families have tried to reassure you that everything will be okay, and they have even offered to help with the wedding arrangements.

Being a perfectionist, you want to make sure that everything goes as smoothly as possible. However, you have just received some very bad news. The facility where you thought you were going to have your reception has been double-booked for the date you requested. Since the other couple booked first and already put down a significant deposit, the manager of the facility has decided that they will get that day. After apologizing profusely, the owner offers you a few other dates and promises a 10 percent discount. However, you know that when you pick a new date, conflicts might arise with some of the other arrangements you have made.

Case Questions
1. Review your work from Chapter 10.
2. Ignoring for a moment what you just found out from the owner of the reception facility, discuss how you would use the project control process to help you prepare for the wedding.
3. Based on the bad news concerning the reception facility, make new arrangements for your special day.
4. Update your network diagram.
5. Recalculate the ES, EF, LS, and LF times and the slack for each activity.
6. Determine the critical path.
7. Highlight the activities that make up the critical path.

Group Activity
Return to your groups of three or four members. Within each group, do items 1 through 7 as a team. Each group must choose one individual to make a five-minute presentation to the class explaining what the group has done.

Appendix

Time–Cost Trade-Off

The time–cost trade-off methodology is used to incrementally reduce the project duration with the smallest associated increase in incremental cost. It is based on the following assumptions:

1. Each activity has two pairs of duration and cost estimates: normal and crash. The **normal time** is the estimated length of time required to perform the activity under normal conditions, according to the plan. The **normal cost** is the estimated cost to complete the activity in the normal time. The **crash time** is the shortest estimated length of time in which the activity can be completed. The **crash cost** is the estimated cost to complete the activity in the crash time. In Figure 11.7, each of the four activities has a pair of normal time and cost estimates and a pair of crash time and cost estimates. The estimated normal time to perform activity A is 7 weeks, and its estimated normal cost is $50,000. The crash time for this activity is 5 weeks, and the cost to complete the activity in this duration is $62,000.

2. An activity's duration can be incrementally accelerated from its normal time to its crash time by applying more resources—assigning more people, working overtime, using more equipment, and so on. Increased costs will be associated with expediting the activity.

3. An activity cannot be completed in less than its crash time, no matter how many additional resources are applied. For example, activity A cannot be completed in less than 5 weeks, no matter how many more resources are used or how much money is spent.

4. The resources necessary to reduce an activity's estimated duration from its normal time to its crash time will be available when needed.

5. Within the range between an activity's normal and crash points, the relationship between time and cost is linear. Each activity has its own *cost per time period* for accelerating the activity's duration from its normal time to its crash time. This acceleration cost per time period is calculated as follows:

$$\frac{\text{Crash Cost} - \text{Normal Cost}}{\text{Normal Time} - \text{Crash Time}}$$

For example, in Figure 11.7, the cost per week to accelerate activity A from its normal time to its crash time is

$$\frac{\$62,000 - \$50,000}{7 \text{ weeks} - 5 \text{ weeks}} = \frac{\$12,000}{2 \text{ weeks}} = \$6,000 \text{ per week}$$

The network diagram in Figure 11.7 has two paths from start to finish: path A–B and path C–D. If we consider only the normal duration estimates, path A–B will take 16 weeks to complete, while path C–D will take 18 weeks to complete. Therefore, the earliest the project can be finished based on these time estimates is 18 weeks—the length of its critical path, made up of activities C and D. The total

REINFORCE YOUR LEARNING

9. *What are the normal and crash times and costs for activities B, C, and D in Figure 11.7?*

	Normal Time	Normal Cost	Crash Time	Crash Cost
Activity B	——	——	——	——
Activity C	——	——	——	——
Activity D	——	——	——	——

REINFORCE YOUR LEARNING

10. *What are the cost-per-week rates to accelerate activities B, C, and D in Figure 11.7?*

FIGURE 11.7   Network with Normal and Crash Times and Their Costs

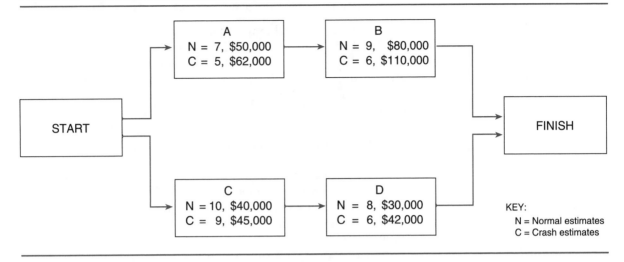

project cost, based on the cost associated with performing each activity in its normal time, is

$$\$50,000 + \$80,000 + \$40,000 + \$30,000 = \$200,000$$

REINFORCE YOUR LEARNING

11. *If all the activities in Figure 11.7 were performed in their crash times, what would be the total project cost?*

If all the activities were performed in their respective crash times, path A–B would take 11 weeks and path C–D would take 15 weeks. The earliest the project can be finished based on the crash time estimates is 15 weeks, which is 3 weeks earlier than if the activities were performed in their normal times.

It is usually not necessary or even constructive to crash all the activities. For example, in Figure 11.7, we want to crash only the appropriate activities by the amount necessary to accelerate project completion from 18 weeks to 15 weeks. Any additional crashing of activities will merely increase total project cost; it will not reduce the total project duration any further because that's determined by the length of the critical path. In other words, expediting activities not on the critical path will not reduce the project completion time but will increase total project cost.

The objective of the time–cost trade-off method is to determine the shortest project completion time based on crashing those activities that result in the smallest increase in total project cost. To accomplish this, it's necessary to shorten the total project duration, one time period at a time, crashing only those activities that are on the critical path(s) and have the lowest acceleration cost per time period. From Figure 11.7, we previously determined that, based on normal time and cost estimates, the earliest the project could be completed is 18 weeks (as determined by the critical path C–D), at a total project cost of $200,000. The cost per week of accelerating each of the activities is

Activity A $6,000 per week
Activity B $10,000 per week

Activity C $5,000 per week
Activity D $6,000 per week

To reduce the total project duration from 18 weeks to 17 weeks requires first identifying the critical path, which is C–D, and then determining which activity on the critical path can be accelerated at the lowest cost per week. Activity C costs $5,000 per week to accelerate, and activity D costs $6,000 per week to accelerate. Therefore, it's less expensive to expedite activity C. If activity C is crashed 1 week (from 10 weeks to 9 weeks), the total project duration is shortened from 18 weeks to 17 weeks, but the total project cost increases by $5,000, to $205,000.

To shorten the total project duration one more time period, from 17 weeks to 16 weeks, we must again identify the critical path. The durations of the two paths are 16 weeks for A–B and 17 weeks for C–D. Therefore, the critical path is still C–D, and it must be reduced again. Looking at path C–D, we see that although activity C has a lower acceleration cost per week than activity D, we cannot accelerate activity C any further since we reached its crash time of 9 weeks when the project was reduced from 18 weeks to 17 weeks. Therefore, the only choice is to accelerate activity D by 1 week, from 8 weeks to 7 weeks. This reduces the duration of critical path C–D to 16 weeks, but the total project cost increases by $6,000 (the cost per week for accelerating activity D), from $205,000 to $211,000.

Once again, let's reduce the project duration another week, from 16 weeks to 15 weeks. If we look at our two paths, we see that they are now of equal duration, 16 weeks, so we now have two critical paths. To reduce the total project duration from 16 weeks to 15 weeks, it's necessary to accelerate each path by 1 week. In looking at path C–D, we see that the only activity with any remaining time to be crashed is activity D. It can be crashed 1 more week, from 7 weeks to 6 weeks, at an additional cost of $6,000. To accelerate path A–B by 1 week, we have a choice of crashing activity A or activity B. Activity A has a $6,000 cost per week to accelerate, compared with a $10,000 per week rate for activity B. Therefore, to reduce the total project duration from 16 weeks to 15 weeks, we need to crash activities D and A 1 week each. This increases the total project cost by $12,000 ($6,000 + $6,000), from $211,000 to $223,000.

Let's try again to shorten the total project duration by 1 week, from 15 weeks to 14 weeks. We again have two critical paths with the same duration, 15 weeks. Therefore, they must both be accelerated by 1 week. However, in looking at path C–D, we see that both activities are already at their crash time—9 weeks and 6 weeks, respectively—and therefore cannot be expedited any further. Accelerating path A–B would thus be of no value, because it would increase the total project cost but not reduce the total project duration. Our ability to reduce the total project duration is limited by the fact that path C–D cannot be reduced any further.

Table 11.1 displays the incremental acceleration in total project completion and the associated incremental increase in total project cost. It indicates that reducing the total project duration by 1 week would

TABLE 11.1   Time–Cost Trade-Off

Project Duration (weeks)	Critical Path(s)	Total Project Cost
18	C–D	**$200,000**
17	C–D	$200,000 + $5,000 = **$205,000**
16	C–D	$205,000 + $6,000 = **$211,000**
15	C–D, A–B	$211,000 + $6,000 + $6,000 = **$223,000**

increase the total project cost by $5,000. To reduce it by 2 weeks would cost $11,000, and to reduce it by 3 weeks would cost $23,000.

If all four activities were crashed, the total cost of the project would be $259,000, but it would still not be completed any earlier than 15 weeks. Using the time–cost trade-off method, we were able to reduce the project duration from 18 weeks to 15 weeks at an additional cost of $23,000 by selectively crashing the critical activities with the lowest acceleration cost per time period. Crashing all the activities would have resulted in a waste of $36,000 because no reduction in total project duration beyond 15 weeks could be achieved.

SUMMARY

The time–cost trade-off methodology is used to incrementally reduce the project duration with the smallest associated increase in incremental cost. It is based on the assumptions that each activity has a normal and a crash duration and cost estimate, that an activity's duration can be incrementally accelerated by applying more resources, and that the relationship between time and cost is linear. Normal time is the estimated length of time required to perform the activity under normal conditions; normal cost is the estimated cost to complete the activity in the normal time. Crash time is the shortest estimated length of time in which the activity can be completed; crash cost is the estimated cost to complete the activity in the crash time.

QUESTIONS

1. What is the time–cost trade-off methodology, and when is it used?
2. Why do you need both normal and crash times and costs for this procedure?
3. Assume that an activity has a normal time of 20 weeks, a normal cost of $72,000, a crash time of 16 weeks, and a crash cost of $100,000. By how many weeks, at most, can this activity's duration be reduced? What is the cost per week to accelerate this activity?
4. Why isn't it appropriate to crash all of the activities in a project to achieve the shortest project schedule?

12   Resource Considerations

Incorporating Resources into the Schedule

The scheduling methods discussed so far in this text generally assume that resources (people, equipment, facilities) have an infinite capacity and availability. However, in reality this is often not the case. Nearly all projects have defined limits on the resources available because of costs, skill levels, hours available, and competing activities. Unfortunately, most discussions of scheduling in the project management arena focus largely on timing issues without taking into account the link between resource availability and capability and the project schedule. The fact that certain resources might not be available at all, might be only partially available, might not have the desired capacity, or might not be available when desired will certainly affect the schedule.

Real-world project delays often occur at critical times because some combination of labor, equipment, and facilities is not available. In addition, if these resources are not managed properly, labor costs can increase because projects are delayed or overtime must be paid and equipment costs can increase because equipment is rented or leased before it is needed or equipment is unavailable when it is needed.

Source: M. Matthews, "Resource Scheduling: Incorporating Capacity into Schedule Construction," *Project Management Journal,* June 1994.

Effectively Utilizing Resources

Once you realize that resources must be taken into account when building the project schedule, you can attempt to minimize fluctuations in the use of those resources. Rather than have all of your people or machines overutilized for a few consecutive days and then sitting idle for the next few, it's better to provide some balance in the process. *Resource leveling,* or *smoothing,* is a technique used to minimize fluctuations in resource utilization. This procedure attempts to utilize resources as uniformly as possible without extending the project schedule beyond the required completion date.

Harvey Levine, who is with the New York State–based Project Knowledge Group and has been a practitioner of project management for over thirty years, discusses many of the factors that can be considered in performing resource leveling, including the preferences of the decision maker, the effect of imposed dates, the use of overtime, and short-term versus long-term considerations. Modern project management software packages have started to incorporate resource leveling, and he provides an overview of the differences in the ways some popular software packages do so.

Sources: H. Levine, "Resource Leveling and Roulette: Games of Chance," *PM Network,* April 1994; H. Levine, "Resource Leveling and Roulette: Games of Chance—Part 2," *PM Network,* July 1994.

In previous chapters, we established schedules based on the time element. We assumed that the resources required to perform the individual activities would be available when they were needed. These resources can include people, equipment, machines, tools, facilities, and space. Among the people there may be many different types, such as painters, designers, cooks, computer programmers, and assembly workers.

The consideration of resources adds another dimension to planning and scheduling. In many projects, the amounts of the various types of resources available to perform the project activities are limited. Several activities may require the same resources at the same time, and there may not be sufficient resources available to satisfy all the demands. In a sense, these activities are *competing* for the use of the same resources. If sufficient resources are not available, some activities may have to be rescheduled for a later time when resources *are* available for them. Therefore, resources can constrain the project schedule. They can also be an obstacle to completing the project within budget if it is determined that additional resources are needed to complete the project on time.

This chapter covers several approaches to incorporating resource considerations into the project plan and schedule. You will become familiar with

- taking resource constraints into account when developing a network diagram

- determining the planned resource utilization for a project
- leveling the use of resources within the required time frame of the project
- determining the shortest project schedule with the limited resources available

RESOURCE-CONSTRAINED PLANNING

One way to consider resources is to take them into account when drawing the logical relationships among activities in the network diagram. At a minimum, network diagrams illustrate the *technical constraints* among activities. Activities are drawn in a serial relationship because, from a technical standpoint, they must be performed in that sequence. For example, Figure 12.1 shows that the three house-building activities—build foundation, build frame, and put on roof—must be done in series. Technically, these activities must be performed in this sequence. The roof cannot be put on before the frame is built!

In addition to showing the technical constraints among activities, the network logic can also take into account *resource constraints*. The sequence of activities can be drawn to reflect the availability of a limited number of resources. Part (a) of Figure 12.2 shows that, technically, three activities—paint living room, paint kitchen, and paint bedroom—could be performed concurrently; that is, there is no technical reason why the start of any one of these activities should depend on the completion of any other one. Suppose, however, that there is only one person available to do all the painting; this limitation introduces a resource constraint on the painting activities. That is, although technically all three activities could be done concurrently, they will have to be performed in series since only one painter is available to do all three. To incorporate this resource constraint, the diagram will have to be drawn as shown in part (b) of Figure 12.2. The exact sequence of these three activities—which particular room gets painted first, second, and third—is another decision that must be made when the network diagram is drawn.

This example illustrates how resource limitations can be considered when a network plan is drawn. This approach of incorporating resource constraints into the logical relationships among activities in the network diagram is feasible for small projects involving few resources. However, it becomes complicated for large projects and for projects in which several different resources are needed for some of the activities.

REINFORCE YOUR LEARNING

1. *At a minimum, network diagrams illustrate the _____ constraints among activities. However, when limited resources are available, the network diagram can be drawn to also reflect _____ constraints.*

FIGURE 12.1   Technically Constrained Activity Sequence

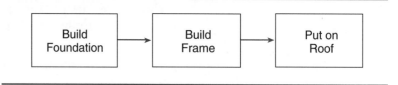

FIGURE 12.2   Resource-Constrained Planning

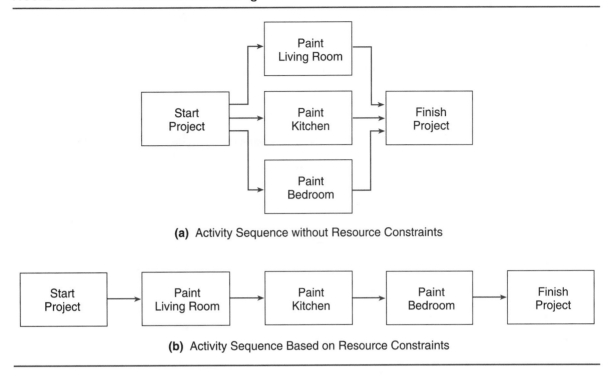

(a) Activity Sequence without Resource Constraints

(b) Activity Sequence Based on Resource Constraints

PLANNED RESOURCE UTILIZATION

If resources are to be considered in planning, it's necessary to indicate the amounts and types of resources needed to perform each activity. Figure 12.3 is a network diagram for a painting project; each activity box shows the estimated activity duration (in days), as well as the number of painters needed to accomplish the activity within its estimated duration.

Using the information in Figure 12.3, we can prepare a resource utilization chart as shown in Figure 12.4, which indicates how many painters are needed each day based on the earliest start and finish times for each activity. The resource utilization chart shows that four painters are needed on days 1 through 4, three painters are needed on days 5 and 6, two painters are needed on days 7 through 10, and only one painter is needed on days 11 and 12. A total of 32 painter-days are needed. The resource profile for painters is illustrated in Figure 12.5. It shows an uneven utilization of painters. A peak of four painters is needed during one portion of the project, and a low of only one painter is needed during another portion of the project.

Resources such as painters cannot usually be hired on a day-to-day basis to meet fluctuating requirements. If the same number of painters must be employed throughout the project, it will be necessary to pay some painters to work overtime during periods of peak demand and to pay some painters to remain idle during periods of

FIGURE 12.3   Painting Project Showing Needed Resources

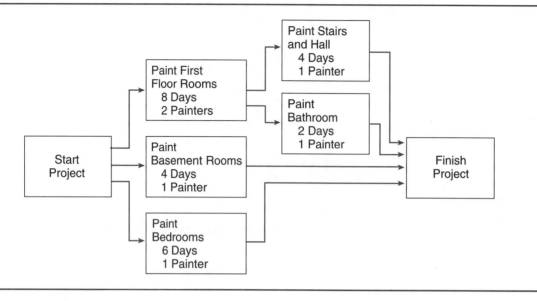

low demand. Thus, it's preferable to have a more uniform, or level, application of resources.

It should be noted that the resource utilization charts shown in Figures 12.4 and 12.5 are based on each activity's earliest start time. Such resource utilization charts are said to be based on an **as-soon-as-possible (ASAP) schedule.** Resource utilization charts based on each activity's latest start time are said to be based on an **as-late-as-possible (ALAP) schedule.**

RESOURCE LEVELING

Resource leveling, or **smoothing,** is a method for developing a schedule that attempts to minimize the fluctuations in requirements for resources. This method levels the resources so that they are applied as uniformly as possible without extending the project schedule beyond the required completion time. It's a trial-and-error method in which noncritical activities (those with positive slack values) are delayed beyond their earliest start times in order to maintain a uniform level of required resources. Activities can be delayed only to the point where all their positive slack is used up, as any further delays would cause the project to extend beyond the project due date. Resource leveling attempts to establish a schedule in which resource use is made as level as possible without extending the project beyond the required completion time.

Let us look at the painting project in Figures 12.3, 12.4, and 12.5 to determine whether resource utilization can be leveled. Figures 12.3 and 12.4 show that the critical path for the project is made up of two activities and is 12 days long (8 days to paint the first floor rooms plus 4 days to paint the stairs and hall). Therefore, these two

FIGURE 12.4   Planned Resource Utilization

	DAY	1	2	3	4	5	6	7	8	9	10	11	12	PAINTER DAYS
First Floor Rooms (2 Painters)														16
Stairs & Hall (1 Painter)														4
Bathroom (1 Painter)														2
Basement Rooms (1 Painter)														4
Bedrooms (1 Painter)														6
PAINTERS		4	4	4	4	3	3	2	2	2	2	1	1	32

activities cannot be delayed without extending the project completion time beyond 12 days. Looking at Figure 12.4, however, we can see that "Bathroom" could be delayed up to 2 days, "Basement Rooms" could be delayed up to 8 days, and "Bedrooms" could be delayed up to 6 days—all without extending the project completion time beyond 12 days. Looking at Figure 12.4, we can see that two alternative actions could be taken to level the daily resource requirements for painters:

Alternative 1. Delay the activity with the most positive slack— "Basement Rooms" (+8 days slack)—by 6 days so that it will start after "Bedrooms" is finished. Rather than have two separate

FIGURE 12.5   Resource Profile for Painters

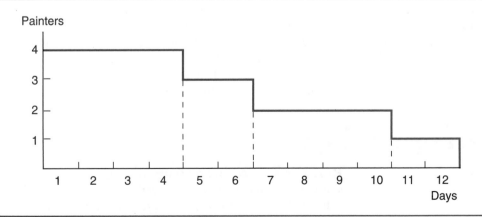

FIGURE 12.6   Resource-Leveled Utilization

	DAY	1	2	3	4	5	6	7	8	9	10	11	12	PAINTER DAYS
First Floor Rooms (2 Painters)														16
Stairs & Hall (1 Painter)														4
Bathroom (1 Painter)														2
Basement Rooms (1 Painter)														4
Bedrooms (1 Painter)														6
	PAINTERS	3	3	3	3	3	3	3	3	3	3	1	1	32

painters paint the basement rooms and bedrooms concurrently, the resource-leveled schedule will use the same painter to first paint the bedrooms and then paint the basement rooms.

Alternative 2. Delay "Bedrooms" so that it will start on day 4, after "Basement Rooms" is completed. This alternative will use the same painter to first paint the basement rooms and then paint the bedrooms (the reverse of alternative 1, achieving the same result).

Figures 12.6 and 12.7 illustrate the resource profile for the resource-leveled schedule if we choose alternative 1. Comparing Figure 12.6 with Figure 12.4, we see that the earliest start time for "Basement Rooms" has been delayed from time 0 to day 6, and its earliest finish time is now day 10 rather than day 4. Figure 12.7 shows a more uniform utilization of painters than Figure 12.5, except for days 11 and 12, which remain the same. In both cases 32 painter-days are required, but in the resource-leveled schedule they're utilized with less fluctuation.

For a large project with many different resources, resource leveling can get very complicated. Various project management software packages are available that will assist in generating a resource-leveled schedule and resource utilization charts and profiles.

REINFORCE YOUR LEARNING
2. *Resource leveling attempts to establish a schedule in which resource use is made as level as possible without extending the project beyond the _____ _____ time.*

RESOURCE-LIMITED SCHEDULING

Resource-limited scheduling is a method for developing the shortest schedule when the number or amount of available resources is fixed. This method is appropriate when the resources available for

FIGURE 12.7   Resource-Leveled Profile for Painters

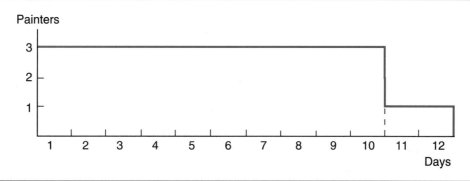

the project are limited and these resource limits cannot be exceeded. This method will extend the project completion time if necessary in order to keep within the resource limits. It is an iterative method in which resources are allocated to activities based on the least slack. When several activities need the same limited resource at the same time, the activities with the least slack have first priority. If resources are left over, the activities with the second least slack have the next priority, and so forth. If other activities need the resource but the resource has been totally allocated to higher-priority activities, the lower-priority activities get delayed; as their slack becomes worse, they eventually move up the priority ladder. This delaying of activities can extend the project completion time.

Figure 12.8 illustrates what would happen if only a limited number of painters—two—were available to do the painting project.

FIGURE 12.8   Effect of Limited Resource Availability

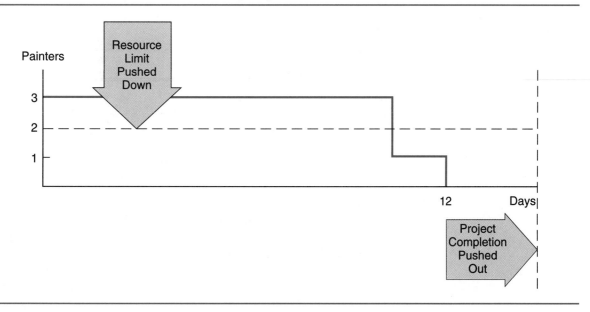

FIGURE 12.9   Original Resource Utilization

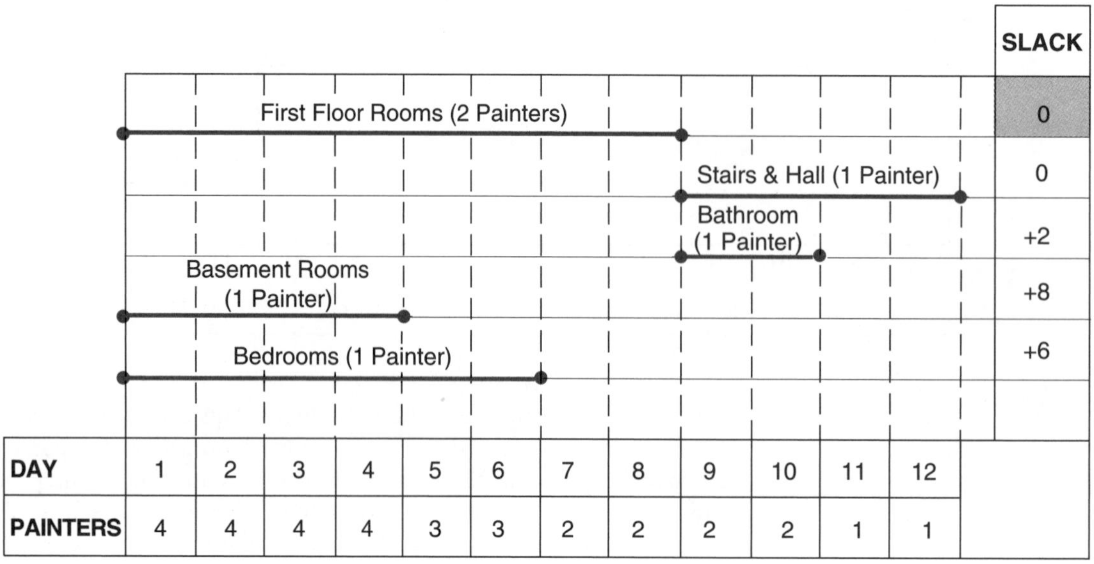

When we push down on the level of resources because no more than two painters can be used, we push out the project completion time. If only two painters are available at any time, the project completion time has to be extended from day 12 to at least day 16, in order to get the 32 painter-days required.

Let us apply resource-limited scheduling to the painting project shown in Figure 12.3. Figure 12.9, which is the same as Figure 12.4, is our original resource utilization; it shows a project completion time of 12 days. Let us now assume, however, that we're limited to only two painters.

Figure 12.9 shows that, as the project starts, three activities require a total of four painters ("First Floor Rooms," "Basement Rooms," and "Bedrooms"). Only two painters are available, though, so they will be allocated to the activities based on a priority determined by slack. "First Floor Rooms" has a slack of 0, while "Basement Rooms" has a slack of +8 days and "Bedrooms" has a slack of +6 days. Therefore, the two painters will be allocated to the first floor rooms and will continue to be assigned to that activity until it is finished. (In this example, it's assumed that, once an activity starts, it continues until it's finished and cannot be stopped and restarted.) Since all the available resources are assigned to "First Floor Rooms" from time 0 through day 8, the other two activities ("Basement Rooms" and "Bedrooms") will have their starts delayed until after day 8. This first resource allocation is shown in Figure 12.10.

The result of this first iteration of allocating the painters is extension of project completion from day 12 to day 14 because of the delay of "Bedrooms." Additionally, there is still a problem on days 9

FIGURE 12.10   First Resource Allocation

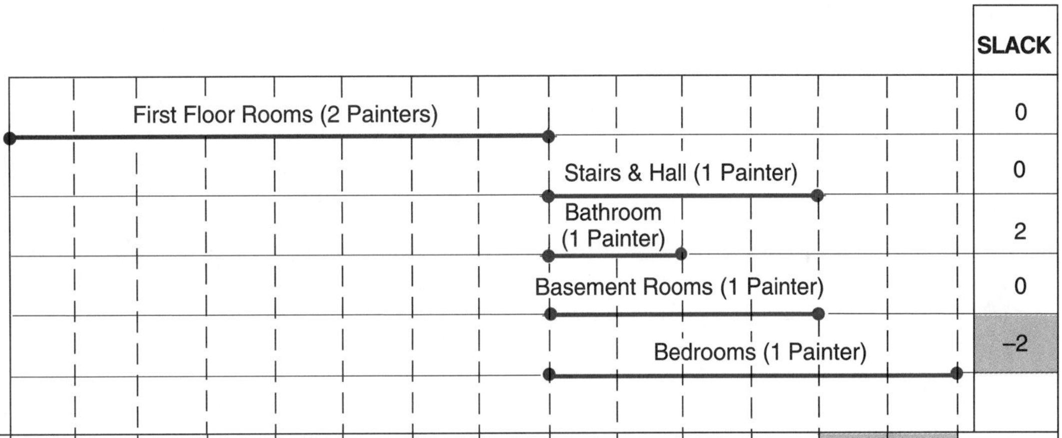

DAY	1	2	3	4	5	6	7	8	9	10	11	12	13	14
PAINTERS	2	2	2	2	2	2	2	2	4	4	3	3	1	1

through 12 because the resource requirements exceed the limit of two painters. So it's now necessary to do a second allocation of painters on day 9. "Bedrooms" has the least slack, with −2 days; its earliest expected finish time is now day 14, and the required project completion time is 12 days. "Bedrooms" requires one painter, so one of the two available painters is allocated to it. One painter is still to be allocated. Two activities, "Stairs and Hall" and "Basement Rooms," have the same next lowest value of slack (0). One way to choose between these two is to determine which has been critical for a longer time. Looking back, we see that "Stairs and Hall" was more critical (0 slack) than "Basement Rooms" (+8 days slack) in Figure 12.9. Therefore, the remaining painter should be allocated to "Stairs and Hall." "Bedrooms" will start after day 8 and will continue through day 14. "Stairs and Hall" will also start after day 8 and will continue through day 12. The next time a painter will become available is after "Stairs and Hall" is finished on day 12. Therefore, the remaining two activities, "Basement Rooms" and "Bathrooms," will have their starts delayed until after day 12. This second resource allocation is shown in Figure 12.11.

The result of this second iteration of allocating the painters is another extension of project completion, this time from day 14 to day 16, because of the delay of "Basement Rooms." And there is still a problem on days 13 and 14 because the resource requirements exceed the limit of two painters. So it's now necessary to do a third allocation of painters on day 13, when one painter becomes available after finishing "Stairs and Hall." (Remember that the second painter is still working on "Bedrooms.") Two activities, "Bathrooms" and "Basement

FIGURE 12.11   Second Resource Allocation

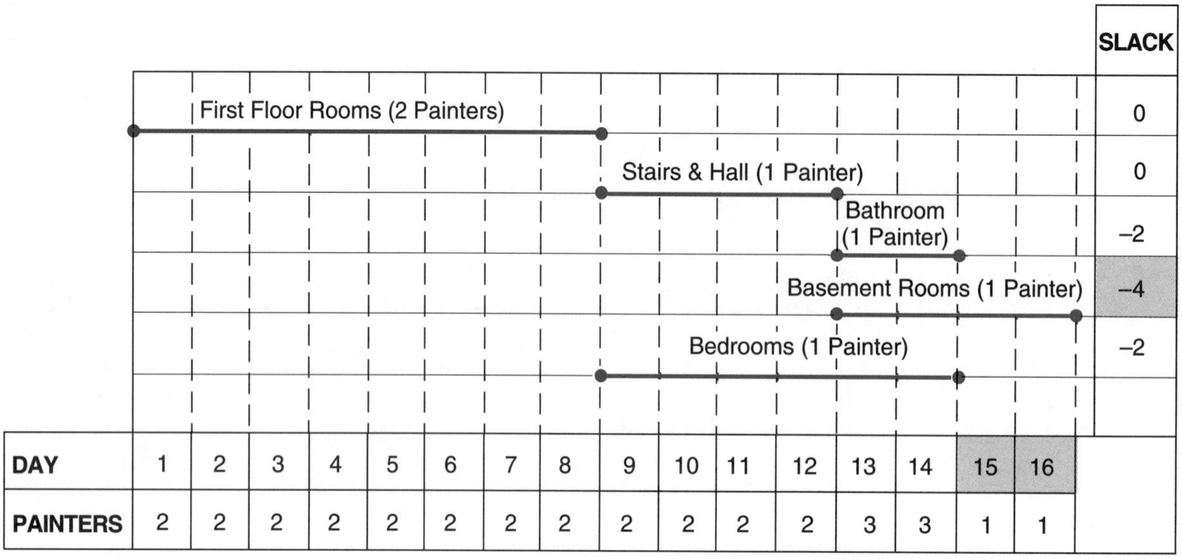

Rooms," need a painter on day 13. "Basement Rooms" has less slack (−4 days) than the other activity, so the available painter will be allocated to it. "Basement Rooms" will start after day 12 and will continue through day 16. The next time a painter will become available is after "Bedrooms" is finished on day 14. Therefore, "Bathroom" will have its start delayed until after day 14. This third resource allocation is shown in Figure 12.12.

As a result of this third iteration of allocating the painters, the project completion time is still 4 days beyond the required project completion time, but all the activities have been scheduled to start and finish so as to stay within the limit of two painters. No further iterations are needed.

In order to accelerate the schedule to complete the project by day 12, it would be necessary to implement one or more of the approaches to schedule control mentioned in Chapter 11, such as adding more painters, working overtime, reducing the scope of work or the requirements for some of the activities, or increasing productivity.

For a large project that requires many different resources, each of which has a different limit of availability, resource-limited scheduling can get very complicated. Various project management software packages are available that will perform resource-limited scheduling.

REINFORCE YOUR LEARNING

3. *Resource-limited scheduling develops the _____ schedule when the number or amount of available resources is fixed. This method will _____ the project completion time if necessary in order to keep within the _____ limits.*

PROJECT MANAGEMENT SOFTWARE

Project management software provides excellent features for handling resource considerations within a project. Most software packages

FIGURE 12.12   Third Resource Allocation

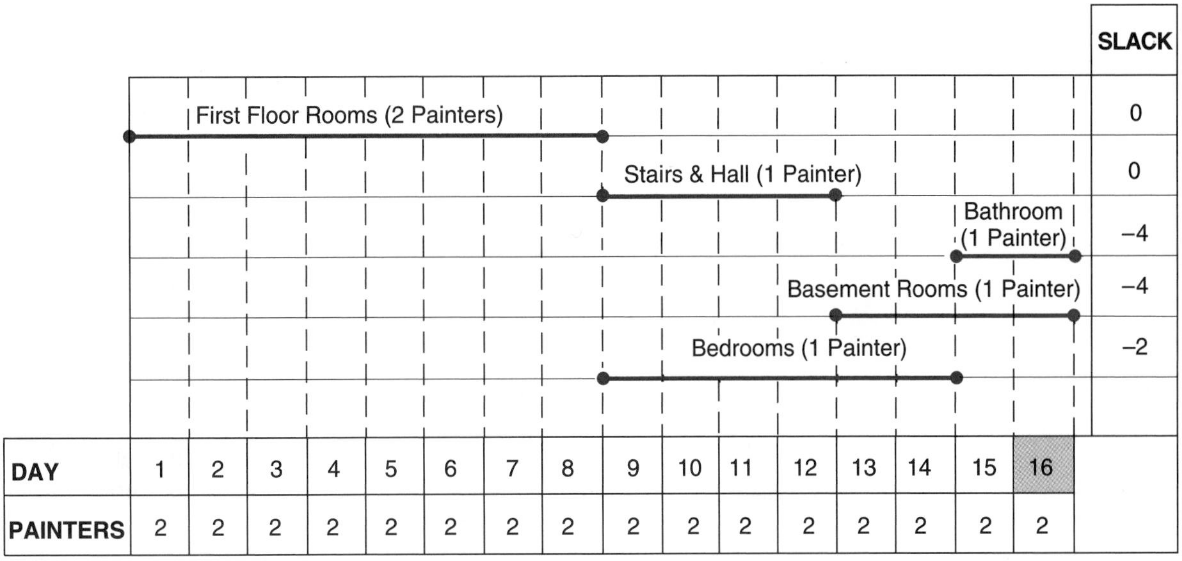

	SLACK
First Floor Rooms (2 Painters)	0
Stairs & Hall (1 Painter)	0
Bathroom (1 Painter)	−4
Basement Rooms (1 Painter)	−4
Bedrooms (1 Painter)	−2

DAY	1	2	3	4	5	6	7	8	9	10	11	12	13	14	15	16
PAINTERS	2	2	2	2	2	2	2	2	2	2	2	2	2	2	2	2

allow you to create and maintain a list of resources that can be accessed by all of the tasks within a project. The list typically allows you to store the resource name, maximum number of units available, standard and overtime rates, and costs. In addition, because the expenses for resources can be accrued at different times throughout a project, most software systems allow you to create charges for a resource at the beginning of its use, at fixed intervals, or at the end of the project. Each resource can also be assigned a calendar of availability.

The software will typically inform the user if any resources have time conflicts or if any resources are overallocated within a project or among concurrent projects. Tables and graphs of resource usage are often available.

To resolve any conflicts or to level, or smooth, the resources, the software typically provides two options. The first is to correct the situation manually. With this option, the user modifies the task information and requirements and/or the resource list and then sees whether the situation has been resolved. The second option is to allow the software to perform this process automatically. If the automatic process is selected, the software typically asks the user whether the deadline can be extended if that's the only way to resolve the conflict or smooth the resources.

As with the other features of project management software that have been discussed, all of this can be done with simple point-and-click commands. See Appendix A for a thorough discussion of project management software and a list of project management software vendors.

SUMMARY

Resources can include people, equipment, machines, tools, facilities, and space. Among the people may be many different types, such as painters, designers, cooks, computer programmers, and assembly workers.

The consideration of resources adds another dimension (beyond the element of time) to planning and scheduling. In many projects, the amounts of the various types of resources available to perform the project activities are limited. Several activities may require the same resources at the same time, and there may not be sufficient resources available to satisfy all the demands. If sufficient resources are not available, some activities may have to be rescheduled for a later time when resources *are* available for them.

One way to consider resources is to take them into account when drawing the logical relationships among activities in the network diagram. In addition to showing the technical constraints among activities, the network logic can also take into account resource constraints. The sequence of activities can be drawn to reflect the availability of a limited number of resources. If resources are to be considered in planning, it's necessary to indicate the amounts and types of resources needed to perform each activity. For this reason, a resource profile is often developed.

Resource leveling, or smoothing, is a method for developing a schedule that attempts to minimize the fluctuations in requirements for resources. This method levels the resources so that they are applied as uniformly as possible without extending the project schedule beyond the required completion time. Resource leveling attempts to establish a schedule in which resource use is made as level as possible without extending the project beyond the required completion time. In resource leveling, the required project completion time is fixed, and the resources are varied in an attempt to eliminate fluctuation.

Resource-limited scheduling is a method for developing the shortest schedule when the number or amount of available resources is fixed. This method is appropriate when the resources available for

FIGURE 12.13   Fixed and Variable Elements for Resource Leveling and Resource-Limited Scheduling

	Fixed	Variable
Resource Leveling	Project Required Completion Time	Resources
Resources-Limited Scheduling	Resources	Project Required Completion Time

the project are limited and these resource limits cannot be exceeded. This method will extend the project completion time if necessary in order to keep within the resource limits. It is an iterative method in which resources are allocated to activities based on the least slack. The steps are repeated until all resource constraints have been satisfied. In resource-limited scheduling, the resources are fixed, and the project completion time is varied (extended) in order not to exceed the resource limits.

Figure 12.13 shows the differences between resource leveling and resource-limited scheduling.

For a large project that requires many different resources, each of which has a different limit of availability, resource-limited scheduling can get very complicated. Various project management software packages are available that will assist with this process.

QUESTIONS

1. Give at least ten examples of resources.
2. Think about a project that you are currently working on or have worked on. List all of the resources used in this project.
3. Discuss why resources need to be considered when developing a schedule.
4. Describe how resources can be considered when drawing a network diagram.
5. What are technical constraints? Give some examples.
6. What are resource constraints? Give some examples.
7. Describe what is meant by *resource leveling* or *smoothing*. Why is it used? When is it used?
8. Does resource leveling keep a project on schedule? If so, how?
9. Describe what is meant by *resource-limited scheduling*. Why is it used? When is it used?
10. Does resource-limited scheduling keep a project on schedule? If so, how?
11. Using the figure below, perform resource leveling. Assume that each task can be performed independently of the other tasks.

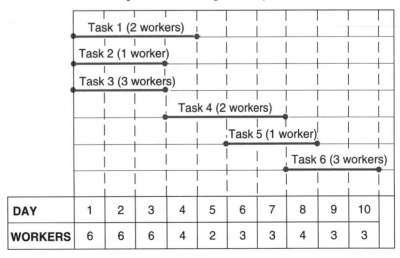

DAY	1	2	3	4	5	6	7	8	9	10
WORKERS	6	6	6	4	2	3	3	4	3	3

12. Using the figure in Question 11, perform resource-limited scheduling. Assume that you have only three workers available at any given time. What is the new completion date for the project?

WIDE WORLD WEB EXERCISES

If you have difficulty accessing any of the Web addresses listed here, you can find these exercises (with up-to-date addresses) on the home page of Dr. James P. Clements, co-author of this book, at

www.towson.edu/~clements

1. Revisit the Project Management Forum home page (discussed in Chapter 8) at

www.pmforum.org

2. Check out the site map, which provides an extensive list of resources.
3. From the site map, visit and describe at least four links in the Professional Directory, such as Careers, Certification, Education, and Standards.
4. From the site map, visit and describe at least three links in the Commercial Directory, such as Consulting, Software Vendors, and Technology.
5. From the site map, visit and describe at least three links in the Library, such as Bookstore, Journals, and Newsletters.
6. From the site map, visit and describe what you find in the links for Communications and Cyberia.

CASE STUDY

You and some friends recently spent a week vacationing at one of New York State's beautiful Finger Lakes. After a week of swimming, fishing, water skiing, and golfing in this picturesque setting, you and your friends have decided to build a vacation house on the shore of the lake. This is to be a joint project, but because you have a knowledge of project management, your friends have asked you to lead the effort, to ensure that all goes well.

Case Questions
1. List your assumptions.
2. List the activities necessary to accomplish the project.
3. List the resources required. Which of these resources might be constraints on the project?
4. Taking those constrained resources into account, choose an overall project time span.
5. Draw a network diagram that takes into account all available resources.
6. Make a duration estimate for each activity.

7. Determine the critical path.
8. Highlight the activities that make up the critical path.

Group Activity

Form groups of three or four members to carry out items 1 through 8 above as a team. Have one individual from each group make a 5-minute presentation to the class explaining what the group has done.

13

Cost Planning and Performance

On Time and On Budget

According to Marie Scotto, project management is the only tested, cohesive management approach we have that allows us to pull together a team of experts, focus them on a specific job, disband them when they have finished, and start all over again as soon as a new need is detected. Effective project management enables project teams to deliver high-quality products in the shortest time and at the lowest cost. However, she notes that projects sometimes fail because of poor budgeting and cost-control techniques that lead to problems such as low-quality products, poorly motivated work groups, and runaway project costs.

First, to calculate budget requirements successfully, Scotto suggests the following process:

1. Get a clear understanding of what the client wants.
2. Identify all of the work that will have to be done.
3. Identify the personnel available to do the work.
4. Try to identify all of the risks involved with doing the work.
5. Have each person give you her or his best estimate of the time and resources that she or he will need.
6. Try to anticipate any problems that could interrupt the project once it has started.
7. Calculate and publish project time and cost targets.

Second, Scotto suggests that the project manager make estimators responsible for continuously fine-tuning their estimates, that team members report actual hours expended, and that project managers institute a standard method of analysis to identify problems and to allow for continuous improvement. Finally, she stresses that to really manage costs effectively, there must be consistent monitoring of the amount of money spent on the project and consistent comparison of that amount to the amount of work produced.

Source: M. Scotto, "Project Budgeting: The Key to Bringing Business Projects in On Time and On Budget," *Project Management Journal,* March 1994.

Why Do Some Projects Overrun the Budget?

According to Arild Sigurdsen, a project management consultant in Norway who has more than twenty years of experience working with large development projects, poor cost control is what often puts a project in danger of exceeding the budget. Sigurdsen believes that we still have a long way to go before the largest pitfalls in cost control are removed. However, he offers the following insights into why these pitfalls occur:

1. Many cost overruns stem from poor cost estimates.
2. In many companies there is no standardization or common set of rules for developing cost estimates and cost-control techniques, and neither is given very much importance.
3. Many people believe that because of the huge number of variables in a project, overruns are simply unavoidable—a devastating way of thinking, especially since it is not true.
4. Project plans and controls often don't take into account probabilistic measures, such as those in the appendix at the end of Chapter 10.

Source: A. Sigurdsen, "Project Control: Why Do Budget Overruns Occur?" *PM Network,* April 1995.

In addition to establishing a baseline schedule for a project, it's also necessary to develop a baseline budget. Project costs are estimated when a proposal is prepared for the project. Once a decision is made to go forward with the proposed project, it's necessary to prepare a budget, or plan, for how and when funds will be spent over the duration of the project. Once the project starts, it's important to monitor actual costs and work performance to ensure that everything is within budget. At regular intervals during the project, the following cost-related parameters should be monitored:

- cumulative actual amount spent since the start of the project
- cumulative earned value of the work performed since the start of the project

- cumulative budgeted amount planned to be spent, based on the project schedule, from the start of the project

Comparisons must be made among these three parameters to evaluate whether the project is being accomplished within budget and whether the value of the work performed is in line with the actual amount expended.

If at any time during the project it is determined that the project is overrunning the budget or the value of the work performed isn't keeping up with the actual amount expended, corrective action must be taken. Once project costs get out of control, it will be very difficult to complete the project within budget. As you will see in this chapter, the key to effective cost control is to analyze cost performance on a timely and regular basis. Early identification of cost variances allows corrective action to be taken before the situation gets worse. In this chapter, you will learn how to regularly forecast, based on the actual amount spent and the value of the work performed, whether the entire project will be completed within budget. You will become familiar with

- items to be considered when estimating project cost
- preparation of a baseline budget, or plan, for how and when funds will be spent over the duration of the project
- cumulating actual costs
- determining the earned value of the work performed
- analyzing cost performance
- forecasting project cost at completion
- controlling project costs
- managing cash flow

PROJECT COST ESTIMATES

Cost planning starts with the proposal for the project. It is during the development of the proposal by the contractor or project team that project costs are estimated. In some cases, the proposal will indicate only the total bottom-line cost for the proposed project. In other cases, the customer may request a detailed breakdown of various costs. The cost section of a proposal may consist of tabulations of the contractor's estimated costs for such elements as the following:

1. *Labor.* This portion gives the estimated costs for the various classifications of people who are expected to work on the project, such as painters, designers, and computer programmers. It might include the estimated hours and hourly rate for each person or classification.
2. *Materials.* This portion gives the cost of materials the contractor or project team needs to purchase for the project, such as paint, lumber, wallpaper, shrubbery, carpeting, paper, art supplies, food, computers, or software packages.
3. *Subcontractors and consultants.* When contractors or project teams do not have the expertise or resources to do certain project tasks, they may hire subcontractors or consultants to perform those tasks.

Examples of such tasks include designing a brochure, developing a training manual, developing software, and catering a reception.

4. *Equipment and facilities rental.* Sometimes the contractor may need special equipment, tools, or facilities solely for the project. The equipment may be too expensive to purchase if it's going to be used on only one or a few projects. In such cases, the contractor may decide to rent the equipment for as long as it is needed on the project.

5. *Travel.* If travel (other than local travel) is required during the project, the costs for travel (such as air fare), hotel rooms, and meals need to be included.

In addition to the above items, the contractor or project team may include an amount for contingencies, to cover unexpected situations that may come up during the project. For example, items may have been overlooked when the project cost estimates were prepared, tasks may have to be redone because they did not work the first time, or the costs of labor (wages, salaries) or materials may escalate during a multi-year project.

It is good practice to have the person who will be responsible for the costs associated with the work make the cost estimates. This generates a commitment from the responsible person and prevents any bias that might result from having one person make all the cost estimates for the entire project. In large projects involving several hundred people, it is not practical to have every person provide cost estimates. In such cases, each organization or subcontractor involved may designate an experienced individual to make the cost estimates for which that organization or subcontractor will be responsible. If a contractor or organization has performed similar projects in the past and has kept records of the actual costs for various items, these historical data can be used as guides in estimating costs on the current project.

Cost estimates should be aggressive yet realistic. They should not be so heavily "padded" that they include contingency funds for every conceivable thing that might come up or go wrong. If cost estimates are overly conservative, the total estimated cost for the project is likely to be more than the customer is willing to pay—and higher than that of competing contractors. On the other hand, if cost estimates are overly optimistic and some unexpected expenditures need to be made, the contractor is likely to either lose money (on a fixed-price contract) or have to suffer the embarrassment of going back to the customer to request additional funds to cover cost overruns.

REINFORCE YOUR LEARNING

1. List the items for which costs should be estimated.

PROJECT BUDGETING

The project budgeting process involves two steps. First, the project cost estimate is allocated to the various work packages in the project work breakdown structure (see Chapter 9). Second, the budget for each work package is distributed over the duration of the work package so that it's possible to determine how much of its budget should have been spent at any point in time.

Allocating the Total Budgeted Cost

Allocating total project costs for the various elements—such as labor, materials, and subcontractors—to the appropriate work packages in the work breakdown structure will establish a **total budgeted cost (TBC)** for each work package. There are two approaches to establishing the TBC for each work package. One is a top-down approach, in which total project costs (for labor, materials, and so forth) are reviewed in relation to the work scope for each work package, and a proportion of the total project cost is allocated to each work package. The other is a bottom-up approach, which is based on an estimate of the costs for the detailed activities associated with each work package. The project cost is usually estimated when the proposal for the project is prepared, but detailed plans are not usually prepared at that time. At the start of the project, however, detailed activities are defined and a network plan is developed. Once detailed activities have been defined, time, resource, and cost estimates can be made for each activity. The TBC for each work package will be the sum of the costs of all the activities that make up that work package.

Figure 13.1 illustrates the allocation of costs to individual work packages in the work breakdown structure for a $600,000 project.

FIGURE 13.1   Work Breakdown Structure with Allocated Budgets

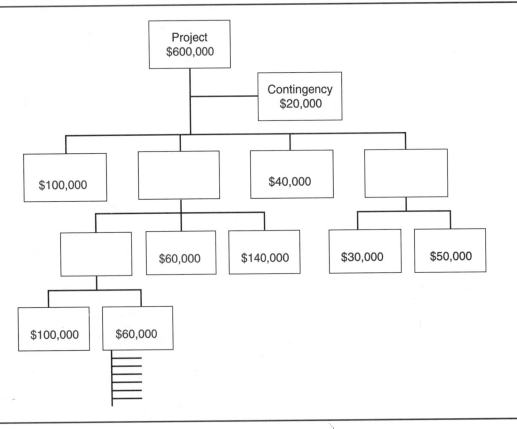

FIGURE 13.2 Network Diagram for the Packaging Machine Project

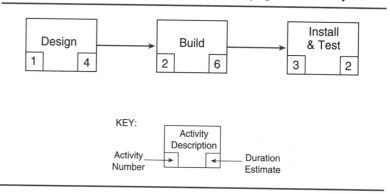

The amount allocated to each work package represents the TBC for completing all the activities associated with the work package. Whether the top-down or the bottom-up approach is used to establish the total budgeted cost for each work package, *when the budgets for all the work packages are summed, they cannot exceed the total project budgeted cost.*

Figure 13.2 is a network diagram for a project to make a specialized automated packaging machine and install it at the customer's factory. The machine will insert the customer's product into boxes rolling by at high speed on a conveyor. *This project will be used as an example throughout the remainder of this chapter, so it has been kept simple.* The project consists of three activities, and the network diagram shows the duration (in weeks) for each activity. Figure 13.3 shows the work breakdown structure with the total budgeted cost for each work package.

Developing the Cumulative Budgeted Cost

Once a total budgeted cost has been established for each work package, the second step in the project budgeting process is to distribute each TBC over the duration of its work package. A cost is determined

FIGURE 13.3 Work Breakdown Structure for the Packaging Machine Project

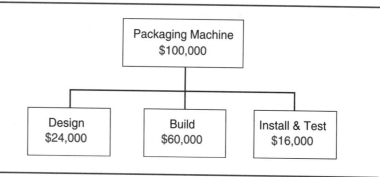

FIGURE 13.4 Budgeted Cost by Period for the Packaging Machine Project

	TBC	1	2	3	4	5	6	7	8	9	10	11	12
							Week						
Design	24	4	4	8	8								
Build	60					8	8	12	12	10	10		
Install & Test	16											8	8
Total	100	4	4	8	8	8	8	12	12	10	10	8	8
Cumulative		4	8	16	24	32	40	52	64	74	84	92	100

Amounts are in thousands of dollars.

for each period, based on when the activities that make up the work package are scheduled to be performed. When the TBC for each work package is spread out by time period, it can be determined how much of the budget should have been spent at any point in time. This amount is calculated by adding up the budgeted costs for each time period up to that point in time. This total amount, known as the **cumulative budgeted cost (CBC),** is the amount that was budgeted to accomplish the work that was scheduled to be performed up to that point in time. The CBC is the *baseline* that will be used in analyzing the cost performance of the project.

For the packaging machine project, Figure 13.4 shows how the TBC for each work package is spread over the time periods, based on the estimated durations shown in Figure 13.2. Also shown is the period-by-period budgeted cost for the entire project, as well as its cumulative budgeted cost (CBC). Figure 13.4 indicates that $32,000 was budgeted to accomplish the work that was scheduled to be performed through week 5. The periods over which budgeted costs are spread usually are determined by the earliest start and finish times for the activities in the baseline project schedule (adjusted to take into account resource leveling or resource-limited scheduling).

With the CBC values, it's possible to draw a cumulative budgeted cost curve to illustrate budgeted expenditures over the duration of the project. Figure 13.5 shows the cumulative budgeted cost curve for the packaging machine project. Although the table in Figure 13.4 and the cost curve in Figure 13.5 display cumulative budgeted cost for the total project, a similar cumulative table and curve can be made for each work package, if desired.

The CBC for the entire project or each work package provides a baseline against which actual cost and work performance can be compared at any time during the project. It would be misleading to merely compare actual amounts expended to the total budgeted cost

FIGURE 13.5   Cumulative Budgeted Cost Curve for the Packaging Machine Project

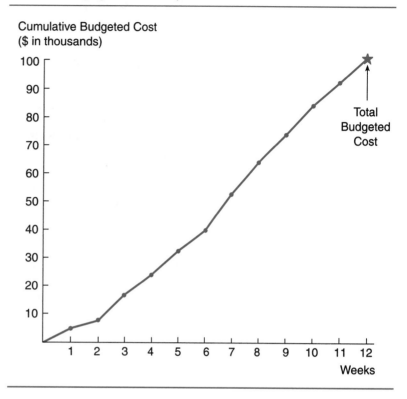

for the project or work package, as cost performance will always look good as long as actual costs are below the TBC. In the packaging machine example, we would think that the project cost was under control as long as the total actual cost was below $100,000. But what happens when one day the total actual cost exceeds the $100,000 TBC, and the project isn't finished? It's too late to control the project so as to complete it within budget—the project budget has been exceeded and work remains to be done, so more costs have to be incurred to complete the project!

To avoid such nightmares, it's important to use the cumulative budgeted cost, rather than the total budgeted cost, as the standard against which actual cost is compared. This way, if actual cost begins to exceed the CBC, corrective action can be taken before it's too late.

For large projects involving many work packages or activities, project management software is available that will assist with project budgeting.

DETERMINING ACTUAL COST

Once the project starts, it's necessary to keep track of actual cost and committed cost so that they can be compared to the CBC.

Actual Cost

To keep track of **actual cost** on a project, it's necessary to set up a system to collect, on a regular and timely basis, data on funds actually expended. Such a system might include procedures and forms for gathering data. An accounting structure should be established based on the work breakdown structure numbering system so that each item of actual cost can be charged to the appropriate work package. Each work package's actual cost can then be totaled and compared to its CBC.

Weekly timesheets are often used to collect actual labor costs. Individuals working on the project indicate the numbers of the work packages on which they worked and the number of hours they spent on each work package. These hours are then multiplied by the hourly cost rate for each individual to determine the actual dollar cost. In companies using a matrix organization structure, individuals may be assigned to several projects concurrently. In such cases, the individual has to indicate the proper project number as well as the work package number on the timesheet to ensure that the actual labor costs are charged to the appropriate project. When invoices are received for materials or services that were purchased for use on the project, they, too, have to be charged to the proper work package number.

Committed Cost

In many projects, large dollar amounts are expended for materials or services (subcontractors, consultants) that are used over a period of time longer than one cost reporting period. These **committed costs** need to be treated in a special way so that the system periodically assigns a portion of their total cost to actual cost, rather than waiting until the materials or services are finished to charge to the total actual costs.

Committed costs are also known as *commitments* or *encumbered costs*. Costs are committed when an item (material, subcontractor) is ordered, usually by means of a purchase order, even though actual payment may take place at some later time—when the material or service has been completed, delivered, and invoiced. When a purchase order is issued to a supplier or subcontractor for an item, the funds for that purchase order are committed and are no longer available to be spent on other project activities. The committed amount must be considered as encumbered, or set aside, since funds will be needed to pay the supplier or subcontractor at some time in the future, when the material or service is delivered and an invoice is received. For example, if you hire a contractor to paint your home for $5,000, you have committed $5,000, even though you may not actually pay the contractor until the work is finished.

To permit a realistic comparison of actual cost to total budgeted cost, portions of the committed amount should be assigned to actual cost while the work is being performed. In some cases, the supplier or subcontractor may require progress payments, rather than waiting until all the work is finished before being paid. In such situations, when an invoice is received from the supplier or subcontractor for a partial or progress payment, the amount of that invoice should be charged to the actual cost for the proper work package. Suppose a project to develop a computerized inventory control system includes a subcontract with a consultant to develop six different software modules for $12,000. As each module is completed and delivered, the consultant submits an invoice for $2,000. When the invoice is received, the $2,000 should be considered an actual cost.

Now let's consider a different scenario, in which the subcontractor or supplier does not issue invoices for partial or progress payments, but rather waits until all the work is finished and delivered and then submits an invoice for the total amount. Even in such a case, a portion of the total committed amount should be periodically assigned as an actual cost, since work is actually being performed. For example, suppose a project to remodel an office building includes a subcontract with a heating contractor to install new heating units in each office throughout the building over four months for $80,000. Even though the subcontractor will submit only one invoice for $80,000 when all the work has been completed, $20,000 should be assigned to actual cost each month, since work is actually being performed.

Comparing Actual Cost to Budgeted Cost

As data are collected on actual cost, including portions of any committed cost, they need to be totaled by work package so that they can be compared to the cumulative budgeted cost. For the packaging machine project, Figure 13.6 shows actual cost by time period for each work package through week 8. Also shown is the period-by-period actual cost for the entire project, as well as the **cumulative actual cost (CAC).**

Figure 13.6 indicates that at the end of week 8, $68,000 has actually been expended on this project. The CBC in Figure 13.4 reveals that only $64,000 was budgeted to have been spent by the end of week 8. There is a variance of $4,000—the project is overrunning its budget.

FIGURE 13.6   Actual Cost by Period for the Packaging Machine Project

	Week								Total Expended
	1	2	3	4	5	6	7	8	
Design	2	5	9	5	1				22
Build				2	8	10	14	12	46
Install & Test									0
Total	2	5	9	7	9	10	14	12	**68**
Cumulative	2	7	16	23	32	42	56	68	**68**

Amounts are in thousands of dollars.

FIGURE 13.7   Cumulative Budgeted and Actual Cost for the Packaging Machine Project

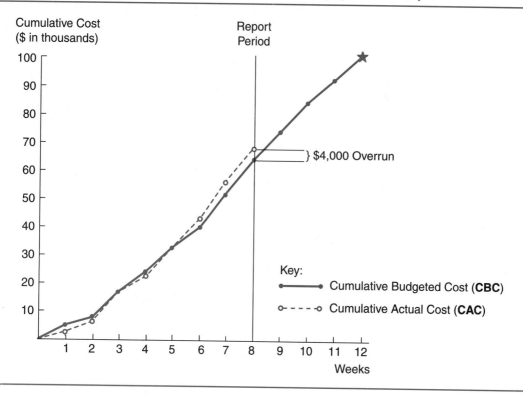

With the CAC values, it's possible to draw a cumulative actual cost curve. Drawing this curve on the same axes as the cumulative budgeted cost curve, as shown in Figure 13.7, provides a good visual comparison.

Although the table in Figure 13.6 and the cost curves in Figure 13.7 display data for the total project, similar cumulative tables and curves can be made for each work package, if desired. Generating individual curves will help pinpoint the particular work packages that are contributing to the overrun.

DETERMINING THE VALUE OF WORK PERFORMED

Consider a project that involves painting ten similar rooms over ten days (one room per day) for a total budgeted cost of $2,000. The budget is $200 per room. At of the end of day 5, you determine that $1,000 has actually been spent. When you compare expenditures to the cumulative budgeted cost of $1,000 for five days, it looks as if actual costs are tracking the budget. But that's only part of the story.

What if, at the end of day 5, only three rooms have been painted? That wouldn't be very good, since half of the budget has been spent on only three of the ten rooms that need to be painted. On the other hand, what if, at the end of day 5, six rooms have been painted? That would be excellent, since only half of the budget has been spent and six of the ten rooms have been painted. This example introduces the concept of *earned value* of the work performed. The fact that half the budget was actually expended doesn't necessarily mean that half the work was performed. If the work performed isn't keeping up with the actual cost, there's trouble, even if the actual cost is in line with the CBC.

Earned value, the value of the work actually performed, is a key parameter that must be determined throughout the project. Comparing the cumulative actual cost to the cumulative budgeted cost tells only part of the story and can lead to wrong conclusions about the status of the project.

Just as it's important to track actual cost for a project, it's also necessary to set up a companion system to collect data on a regular and timely basis regarding the earned value of the work performed on each work package. Determining the earned value involves collecting data on the **percent complete** for each work package and then converting this percentage to a dollar amount by multiplying the TBC of the work package by the percent complete.

The percent complete data usually are obtained each period from the individual responsible for the work package. In many cases, the estimate is subjective. It's extremely important that the person who comes up with the percent complete estimate make an honest assessment of the work performed relative to the entire work scope for the work package. There often seems to be an inclination to be overly optimistic and make a high percent complete estimate too soon. For example, suppose the team leader of a work package with a 20-week duration reports, at the end of week 10, that the work is 90 percent complete. If this report is unrealistic, it will create a false sense of security that work performance is outpacing actual cost. An unrealistic report will lead the project manager to conclude that project performance is better than it actually is and keep her or him from taking any corrective action. As the percent complete begins to stretch out while the actual cost continues to pile up, it will appear that project performance is deteriorating over the last weeks. By week 20, the percent complete may be only 96 percent and the actual cost may have exceeded the cumulative budgeted cost. If corrective action had been taken earlier, though, maybe problems could have been prevented. One way to prevent premature inflated percent complete estimates is to keep the work packages or activities small in terms of scope and duration. It's important that the person estimating the percent complete not only assess how much work has been performed but also consider what work remains to be done.

Once the percent complete data have been gathered, the earned value can be calculated. This is done by multiplying the total budgeted cost for the work package by its percent complete. For example, in the project involving painting ten rooms for $2,000, if three rooms were completed, it's safe to say that 30 percent of the work has been performed. The earned value is

$$0.30 \times \$2,000 = \$600$$

FIGURE 13.8   Cumulative Percent Complete by Period for the Packaging Machine Project

	Week							
	1	2	3	4	5	6	7	8
Design	10	25	80	90	100	100	100	100
Build	0	0	0	5	15	25	40	50
Install & Test	0	0	0	0	0	0	0	0

Amounts are cumulative percentages complete.

Let us now return to the example of the packaging machine project. At the end of week 8, the "Build" work package is the only one in progress, and it's estimated to be 50 percent complete. The "Design" work package had previously been finished, so it's 100 percent complete; and the "Install & Test" work package hasn't yet started, so it's 0 percent complete. Figure 13.8 shows the cumulative percent complete estimates reported during each of the first 8 weeks for each work package. Figure 13.9 shows the associated **cumulative earned value (CEV)** for each work package, calculated by multiplying each percent complete by the TBC for the work package. Figure 13.9 indicates that, at the end of week 8, the earned value of the work performed on this project is $54,000.

With the CEV values, it's possible to draw a cumulative earned value curve. Drawing this curve on the same axes as the cumulative budgeted cost and cumulative actual cost curves, as shown in Figure 13.10, provides an excellent visual comparison. Although the cost curves in Figure 13.10 illustrate the CBC, CAC, and CEV for the entire project, similar curves can be made for each work package, if

REINFORCE YOUR LEARNING

6. *Cumulative earned value is calculated by first determining the* _____ _____ *for each work package and then multiplying it by the* _____ _____ _____ *for the work package.*

FIGURE 13.9   Cumulative Earned Value by Period for the Packaging Machine Project

	TBC	Week							
		1	2	3	4	5	6	7	8
Design	24	2.4	6	19.2	21.6	24	24	24	24
Build	60				3	9	15	24	30
Install & Test	16								
Cumulative	100	2.4	6	19.2	24.6	33	39	48	54

Amounts are in thousands of dollars.

FIGURE 13.10   Cumulative Budgeted, Actual, and Earned Value for the Packaging Machine Project

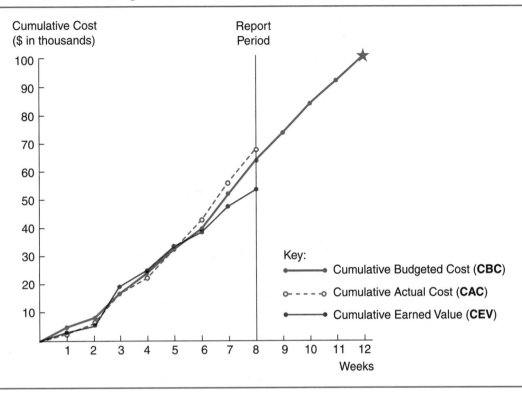

desired. Generating individual curves will help identify how much each work package is affecting project cost performance.

COST PERFORMANCE ANALYSIS

The following four cost-related measures are used to analyze project cost performance:

- TBC   (total budgeted cost)
- CBC   (cumulative budgeted cost)
- CAC   (cumulative actual cost)
- CEV   (cumulative earned value)

They are used to determine whether the project is being performed within budget and whether the value of the work performed is in line with the actual cost.

In analyzing the tables in Figures 13.4, 13.6, and 13.9 for the packaging machine project at the end of week 8, we see that

- $64,000 was budgeted through the end of week 8 to perform all the work scheduled to be performed during the first 8 weeks
- $68,000 was actually expended by the end of week 8
- $54,000 was the earned value of work actually performed by the end of week 8

A quick analysis indicates that the actual cost is exceeding the budgeted cost. Aggravating the situation further is the fact that the value of the work performed isn't keeping up with the actual cost.

It is a good idea to plot CBC, CAC, and CEV curves on the same axes, as shown in Figure 13.10, at the end of each report period. This will reveal any trends toward improving or deteriorating the cost performance.

Another way to approach the situation is to analyze progress in terms of percentages of the total budgeted cost of $100,000 for the project. Using the format in Figure 13.11, we could say that, at the end of week 8,

- 64 percent of the total budget for the project was to have been spent to perform all the work scheduled to be performed during the first 8 weeks
- 68 percent of the total budget was actually expended by the end of week 8
- 54 percent of the total project work was actually performed by the end of week 8

REINFORCE YOUR LEARNING

7. *List the four cost-related measures used to analyze project cost performance.*

In addition to plotting the CBC, CAC, and CEV curves on the same axes, it may be useful to tabulate or draw curves for the percentages. This, too, will indicate any trends toward improving or deteriorating cost performance.

Cost Performance Index

Another indicator of cost performance is the **cost performance index (CPI),** which is a measure of the cost efficiency with which the project is being performed. The formula for determining the CPI is

$$\text{Cost performance index} = \frac{\text{Cumulative earned value}}{\text{Cumulative actual cost}}$$

$$\text{CPI} = \frac{\text{CEV}}{\text{CAC}}$$

In the packaging machine project, the CPI as of week 8 is given by

REINFORCE YOUR LEARNING

8. *What is the cost performance index for the "Design" work package in the packaging machine project at the end of week 5?*

$$\text{CPI} = \frac{\$54,000}{\$68,000} = 0.79$$

This ratio indicates that for every $1.00 actually expended, only $0.79 of earned value was received. Trends in the CPI should be watched carefully. When the CPI goes below 1.0 or gradually gets smaller, corrective action should be taken.

Cost Variance

Another indicator of cost performance is **cost variance (CV),** which is the difference between the cumulative earned value of the work performed and the cumulative actual cost. The formula for determining the cost variance is

$$\text{Cost variance} = \text{Cumulative earned value} - \text{Cumulative actual cost}$$
$$\text{CV} = \text{CEV} - \text{CAC}$$

FIGURE 13.11   Packaging Machine Project Status as of Week 8

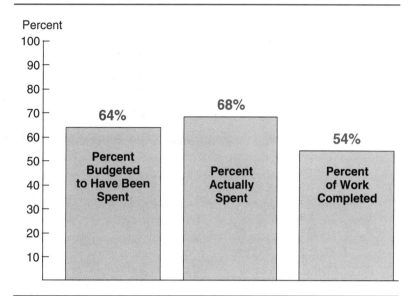

Like the CPI, this indicator shows the gap between the value of the work performed and the actual cost, but the CV is expressed in terms of dollars.

In the packaging machine project, the cost variance as of week 8 is given by

$$CV = \$54,000 - \$68,000 = -\$14,000$$

This calculation indicates that the value of the work performed through week 8 is $14,000 less than the amount actually expended. It's another indication that the work performed is not keeping pace with the actual cost.

For analyzing cost performance, it's important that the data collected all be as current as possible and all be based on the same reporting period. For example, if the costs are collected as of the 30th of each month, then the percent complete estimates for the work packages should be based on work performed through the 30th of the month.

REINFORCE YOUR LEARNING

9. What is the cost variance for the "Build" work package in the packaging machine project at the end of week 8?

COST FORECASTING

Based on analysis of *actual* cost performance throughout the project, it's possible to forecast what the total costs will be at the completion of the project or work package. There are three different methods for determining the **forecasted cost at completion (FCAC)**.

The first method assumes that the work to be performed on the remaining portion of the project or work package will be done at the same rate of efficiency as the work performed so far. The formula for calculating the FCAC using this first method is

$$\text{Forecasted cost at completion} = \frac{\text{Total budgeted cost}}{\text{Cost performance index}}$$

$$\text{FCAC} = \frac{\text{TBC}}{\text{CPI}}$$

For the packaging machine project, the forecasted cost at completion is given by

$$\text{FCAC} = \frac{\$100,000}{0.79} = \$126,582$$

REINFORCE YOUR LEARNING

10. Using the first forecasting method described, calculate the forecasted cost at completion for the "Build" work package in the packaging machine project.

As of week 8, the project has a cost efficiency, or CPI, of 0.79, and if the remainder of the project continues to be performed at this same efficiency rate, then the entire project will actually cost $126,582. If this forecast is correct, there will be an overrun of $26,582 beyond the total budgeted cost for the project of $100,000.

A second method for determining the forecasted cost at completion assumes that, regardless of the efficiency rate the project or work package has experienced in the past, the work to be performed on the remaining portion of the project or work package will be done according to budget. The formula for calculating the FCAC using this method is

$$\begin{array}{ccccc} \text{Forecasted} & & \text{Cumulative} & & \left(\begin{array}{c}\text{Total} \\ \text{budgeted} \\ \text{cost}\end{array} \quad - \quad \begin{array}{c}\text{Cumulative} \\ \text{earned} \\ \text{value}\end{array}\right) \\ \text{cost at} & = & \text{actual} & + & \\ \text{completion} & & \text{cost} & & \end{array}$$

$$\text{FCAC} = \text{CAC} + (\text{TBC} - \text{CEV})$$

For the packaging machine project, the forecasted cost at completion is given by

$$\text{FCAC} = \$68,000 + (\$100,000 - \$54,000)$$
$$= \$68,000 + \$46,000$$
$$= \$114,000$$

REINFORCE YOUR LEARNING

11. Using the second forecasting method described, calculate the forecasted cost at completion for the "Build" work package in the packaging machine project.

As of week 8, the cumulative actual cost was $68,000, but the cumulative earned value of the work performed was only $54,000. Therefore, work with an earned value of $46,000 needs to be performed to complete the project. This method assumes that the remaining work will be performed at an efficiency rate of 1.0, even though the project has been experiencing an efficiency rate of 0.79 as of the end of week 8. This method results in a forecasted cost at completion of $114,000, a forecasted overrun of $14,000 beyond the total budgeted cost for the project.

A third method for determining the forecasted cost at completion is to re-estimate the costs for all the remaining work to be performed and then add this re-estimate to the cumulative actual cost. The formula for determining the FCAC using this third method is

$$\text{FCAC} = \text{CAC} + \text{Re-estimate of remaining work to be performed}$$

This approach can be time consuming, but it may be necessary if the project experiences persistent deviations from the plan or if there are extensive changes.

As part of the regular cost performance analysis, the FCAC for the project should be calculated, using the first or second method described above. The forecasted overrun or underrun can then be determined. When cost is forecasted to the completion of the project or work package, a small variance in a given reporting period can expand to a much greater overrun, signaling the need for corrective action.

COST CONTROL

The key to effective cost control is to analyze cost performance on a regular and timely basis. It's crucial that cost variances and inefficiencies be identified early so that corrective action can be taken before the situation gets worse. Once project costs get out of control, it may be very difficult to complete the project within budget.

Cost control involves the following:

1. Analyzing cost performance to determine which work packages may require corrective action
2. Deciding what specific corrective action should be taken
3. Revising the project plan—including time and cost estimates—to incorporate the planned corrective action

The cost performance analysis should include identifying those work packages that have a negative cost variance or a cost performance index of less than 1.0. Also, those work packages for which the CV or CPI has deteriorated since the prior reporting period should be identified. A concentrated effort must be applied to the work packages with negative variances, to reduce cost or improve the efficiency of the work performed. The amount of CV should determine the priority for applying these concentrated efforts; that is, the work package with the largest negative CV should be given top priority.

When evaluating work packages that have a negative cost variance, you should focus on taking corrective actions to reduce the costs of two types of activities:

1. *Activities that will be performed in the near term.* Don't plan to reduce the costs of activities that are scheduled sometime in the distant future. You'll get more timely feedback on the effects of corrective actions if they are done in the near term. If you put off corrective actions until some point in the distant future, the negative cost variance may deteriorate even further before the corrective actions are ever implemented. As the project progresses, less and less time remains in which corrective actions can be taken.
2. *Activities that have a large cost estimate.* Taking corrective measures that reduce the cost of a $20,000 activity by 10 percent will have a larger impact than totally eliminating a $300 activity. Usually, the larger the estimated cost for an activity, the greater the opportunity for a large cost reduction.

There are various ways to reduce the costs of activities. One way is to substitute less expensive materials that meet the required specifications. Maybe another supplier can be found who can supply the same material but at a lower cost. Another approach is to assign a person with greater expertise or more experience to perform or help with the activity so as to get it done more efficiently.

Reducing the scope or requirements for the work package or specific activities is another way to reduce costs. For example, a contractor might decide to put only one coat of paint on a room rather than two coats, as originally planned. Increasing productivity through improved methods or technology is yet another approach to reducing costs. For example, by renting automatic paint spraying equipment, a contractor may substantially reduce the cost and time of painting a room below what it would be for painters working with rollers and brushes.

In many cases, there will be a trade-off—reducing cost variances will involve a reduction in project scope or a delay in the project schedule. If the negative cost variance is very large, a substantial reduction in the work scope or quality may be required to get the project back within budget. The scope, budget, schedule, or quality of the overall project could be in jeopardy. In some cases, the customer and contractor or project team may have to acknowledge that one or more of these elements cannot be achieved. This could result in the customer's providing additional funds to cover the forecasted overrun, or it could result in a contract dispute over who caused the cost overrun and who should pay for it—the customer or the contractor.

The key to effective cost control is aggressively addressing negative cost variances and cost inefficiencies as soon as they are identified, rather than hoping that things will get better as the project goes on. Cost problems that are addressed early will have less impact on scope and schedule. Once costs get out of control, getting back within budget is likely to require reducing the project scope or extending the project schedule.

Even when projects have only positive cost variances, it's important not to let the cost variances deteriorate. If a project's cost performance is positive, a concentrated effort should be made to keep it that way. Once a project gets in trouble with cost performance, it becomes difficult to get back on track.

MANAGING CASH FLOW

It is important to manage the cash flow on a project. Managing cash flow involves making sure that sufficient payments are received from the customer in time so that you have enough money to cover the costs of performing the project—employee payroll, charges for materials, invoices from subcontractors, and travel expenses, for example. *The key to managing cash flow is to ensure that cash comes in faster than it goes out.* If sufficient cash isn't available to meet expenses, money must be borrowed. Borrowing increases project cost because any money borrowed must be paid back to the lender, along with a charge for borrowing the money—the interest.

The flow of cash coming in from the customer can be controlled by the terms of payment in the contract. From the contractor's point of view, it's desirable to receive payments from the customer early in the project rather than later. The contractor might try to negotiate payment terms that require the customer to do one or more of the following:

- Provide a down payment at the start of the project. This requirement is reasonable when the contractor needs to purchase a significant amount of materials and supplies during the early stages of the project.
- Make equal monthly payments based on the expected duration of the project. Cash outflow usually is smaller in the early stages of a project. If more cash is coming in than is going out during the early part of the project, the contractor may be able to invest some of the excess cash and earn interest. The saved funds can then be withdrawn to meet the greater cash outflow requirements later in the project.
- Provide frequent payments, such as weekly or monthly payments rather than quarterly payments.

The worst scenario from the contractor's point of view is to have the customer make only one payment at the end of the project. In this situation, the contractor will need to borrow money to have cash available to meet expenses throughout the project.

The contractor's outflow of cash can also be controlled by the terms of payment, in this case in contracts with suppliers. The contractor wants to delay payments (cash outflow) as long as possible. For example, a contractor who has ordered $100,000 worth of material would want to wait until it has all been delivered before paying the supplier. If the supplier's invoice states that it must be paid within thirty days, the contractor would probably hold off until about the 27th day before making the payment.

PROJECT MANAGEMENT SOFTWARE

Project management software makes it fairly easy to handle the cost considerations of a project. All costs associated with each resource in a project can be stored, and the software will calculate the budget for each work package and for the entire project. It will calculate the actual costs as the project proceeds and will forecast the final costs, as well. Because various resources have different rate structures and charge their rates at various points in the project, project management software usually allows the user to define different rate structures for each resource and when charges for those resources will actually be accrued. At any time during a project, cost estimates, allocated total budgeted cost, cumulative budgeted cost, actual cost, earned value, committed costs, a cost performance index, cost variance, and a cost forecast can be calculated for each task, each work package, or the entire project, with a click of the mouse. Cost tables and graphs are often available to help analyze cost performance. See Appendix A for a thorough discussion of project management software and a list of project management software vendors.

SUMMARY

Project costs are estimated when a proposal is prepared for the project. Once a decision is made to go forward with the proposed project, it's necessary to prepare a budget, or plan, for how and when funds will be spent over the duration of the project. Once the project starts, it's important to monitor actual costs and work performance to ensure that everything is within budget. Several parameters should be monitored at regular intervals during the project: cumulative actual amount spent since the start of the project, cumulative earned value of the work performed since the start of the project, and cumulative budgeted amount planned to be spent, based on the project schedule, from the start of the project.

Cost planning starts with the proposal for the project. The cost section of a proposal may consist of tabulations of the contractor's estimated costs for such elements as labor, materials, subcontractors and consultants, equipment and facilities rental, and travel. In addition, the proposal might also include an amount for contingencies, to cover unplanned expenses.

The project budgeting process involves two steps. First, the project cost estimate is allocated to the various work packages in the project work breakdown structure. Second, the budget for each work package is distributed over the duration of the work package so that it's possible to determine how much of its budget should have been spent at any point in time.

Allocating total project costs for the various elements—such as labor, materials, and subcontractors—to the appropriate work packages in the work breakdown structure will establish a total budgeted cost (TBC) for each work package. Once a total budgeted cost has been established for each work package, the second step in the project budgeting process is to distribute each TBC over the duration of its work package in order to determine how much of the budget should have been spent at any point in time. This amount is calculated by adding up the budgeted costs for each time period up to that point in time. This total amount, known as the cumulative budgeted cost (CBC), will be used in analyzing the cost performance of the project. The CBC for the entire project or each work package provides a baseline against which actual cost and work performance can be compared at any time during the project.

Once the project starts, it's necessary to keep track of actual cost and committed cost so that they can be compared to the CBC. In addition, it is also necessary to monitor the earned value of the work that has been performed. Determining the earned value involves collecting data on the percent complete for each work package and then converting this percentage to a dollar amount by multiplying the TBC of the work package by the percent complete. This figure can then be compared to the cumulative budgeted cost and the cumulative actual cost.

After this has been done, the project cost performance can be analyzed by looking at the total budgeted cost, the cumulative budgeted cost, the cumulative actual cost, and the cumulative earned value. They are used to determine whether the project is being performed within budget and whether the value of the work performed is in line with the actual cost.

Another indicator of cost performance is the cost performance index (CPI), which is a measure of the cost efficiency with which the project is being performed. The CPI is calculated by dividing the cumulative earned value by the cumulative actual cost. Another indicator of cost performance is cost variance (CV), which is the difference between the cumulative earned value of the work performed and the cumulative actual cost.

Based on analysis of actual cost performance throughout the project, it's possible to forecast what the total costs will be at the completion of the project or work package. There are three different methods for determining the forecasted cost at completion (FCAC). The first method assumes that the work to be performed on the remaining portion of the project or work package will be done at the same rate of efficiency as the work performed so far. The second method assumes that, regardless of what efficiency rate the project or work package has experienced in the past, the work to be performed on the remaining portion of the project or work package will be done according to budget. The third method for determining the forecasted cost at completion is to re-estimate the costs for all the remaining work to be performed and then add this re-estimate to the cumulative actual cost.

The key to effective cost control is to analyze cost performance on a regular and timely basis. It's crucial that cost variances and inefficiencies be identified early so that corrective action can be taken before the situation gets worse. Cost control involves analyzing cost performance to determine which work packages may require corrective action, deciding what specific corrective action should be taken, and revising the project plan—including time and cost estimates—to incorporate the planned corrective action.

It is important to manage the cash flow on a project. Managing cash flow involves making sure that sufficient payments are received from the customer in time so that you have enough money to cover the costs of performing the project—employee payroll, charges for materials, invoices from subcontractors, and travel expenses, for example. The key to managing cash flow is to ensure that cash comes in faster than it goes out.

QUESTIONS

1. Describe why it is necessary to develop a baseline budget for a project.
2. List and describe the cost parameters that should be monitored throughout a project. To what should these parameters be compared?
3. A proposal for a project often includes a cost section. List and describe the items that should be included in that section.
4. What does the term *contingencies* mean? Should contingency costs be included in a project proposal? Explain your answer.
5. What is the problem with making cost estimates conservative or aggressive?
6. Describe the project budgeting process.
7. Define the following: TBC, CBC, CAC, CEV, CPI, CV, and FCAC. How is each calculated?
8. Why is it necessary to track actual and committed costs once a project starts?
9. Why is it necessary to calculate the earned value of work performed? How is this done?
10. How is a cost performance index calculated? What does it mean when it's below 1.0? What does it mean when it's above 1.0?
11. How is cost variance calculated? What does it mean when it's negative? What does it mean when it's positive?
12. What is the FCAC? Describe three ways to calculate it.
13. When evaluating a work package with a negative cost variance, on what two types of activities should you focus? Why?
14. What is the key to managing cash flow? How can this goal be accomplished?
15. Refer to the table below. What is the cumulative budgeted cost at the end of week 6?

		Week									
	TBC	1	2	3	4	5	6	7	8	9	10
Task 1	30	10	15	5							
Task 2	70		10	10	10	20	10	10			
Task 3	40				5	5	25	5			
Task 4	30							5	5	20	
Total	170	10	25	15	10	25	15	35	10	5	20
Cumulative											

Amounts are in thousands of dollars.

16. Below is a table of actual costs for the project introduced in question 15. What is the cumulative actual cost at the end of week 6?

Referring to the cumulative budgeted cost shown in the table in question 15, determine whether there is a cost overrun or underrun. What is causing it?

	Week					
	1	2	3	4	5	6
Task 1	10	16	8			
Task 2		10	10	12	24	12
Task 3					5	5
Task 4						
Total	10	26	18	12	29	17
Cumulative						

Amounts are in thousands of dollars.

17. Below is a table of the cumulative percentages of work completed by the end of week 6 for the project introduced in question 15. What is the cumulative earned value of the project at the end of week 6? Is it good?

	Week					
	1	2	3	4	5	6
Task 1	30	80	100			
Task 2		10	25	35	55	65
Task 3					10	20
Task 4						

Amounts are cumulative percentages complete.

18. Refer to questions 15–17. What is the CPI at the end of week 6? What is the CV?
19. Refer to questions 15–17. Calculate the FCAC using the first two methods described in the chapter.

WORLD WIDE WEB EXERCISES

If you have difficulty accessing any of the Web addresses listed here, you can find these exercises (with up-to-date addresses) on the home page of Dr. James P. Clements, co-author of this book, at

www.towson.edu/~clements

1. As stated in Chapter 11, NASA is one of the pioneers of project management techniques and has successfully used these techniques for many years. NASA maintains an excellent resource list for program and project management, which covers many of the topics presented in this book. Check out this site at

   www.hq.nasa.gov/office/hqlibrary/ppm/ppmbib.htm

2. Check out the link to "Creating the Empowered Organization." Describe the types of resources listed, and list at least three resources on this topic.
3. Check out the link to "Creating the High-Performance Organizations." Describe the types of resources listed, and list at least three resources on this topic.
4. Check out the link to "Creative Problem Solving." Describe the types of resources listed, and list at least three resources on this topic.
5. Check out the link to "Developing Leadership Skills." Describe the types of resources listed, and list at least three resources on this topic.
6. Check out the link to "Group Dynamics and Decision Making for Project Success." Describe the types of resources listed, and list at least three resources on this topic.
7. Check out the link to "Management Communication." Describe the types of resources listed, and list at least three resources on this topic.
8. Check out the link to "Program Control." Describe the types of resources listed, and list at least three resources on this topic.
9. Check out the link to "Project Budgeting and Cost Control." Describe the types of resources listed, and list at least three resources on this topic.
10. Check out at least three other links to topics that interest you.

CASE STUDY

This case study is a continuation of the one presented in Chapter 12. Recall that you and some friends recently spent a week vacationing at one of New York State's beautiful Finger Lakes. After a week of swimming, fishing, water skiing, and golfing in this picturesque setting, you and your friends decided to build a vacation house on the shore of the lake. This is to be a joint project, but because you have a knowledge of project management, your friends asked you to lead the effort, to ensure that all goes well.

A few unexpected circumstances have arisen. First, the builder doesn't seem to be progressing as quickly as you had expected, and, to make matters worse, a week of heavy rain is forecasted. Second, the builder has informed you that, because of a recent labor strike, the cost of lumber has jumped by 20 percent and he has only enough lumber to finish 25 percent of the house. Third, you have inquired about having several trees removed from the shore so that you and your friends can have a perfect view of the lake, but the builder has informed you that he would have to subcontract the task out to another company because certain regulations have to be followed.

Case Questions
Be creative in approaching this case study. You will have to make several assumptions to answer the following questions. Make sure that you describe all assumptions made.

1. Develop a project cost estimate for the original project.
2. Assume that you are several weeks or months into the project. Develop a chart showing the total budgeted cost, cumulative budgeted cost, and actual cost.
3. List any committed costs.
4. Compare actual cost to budgeted cost.
5. Determine the value of work performed.
6. Perform a cost performance analysis using the cost performance index and the cost variance.
7. Forecast the new expected cost at the completion of the project.

Group Activity
Return to your groups of three or four members and do items 1 through 7 as a team. One individual from each group should then make a five-minute presentation to the class, explaining what the group has done.

Appendix A

Project Management Software

Project management software has been around nearly as long as the computer itself. In the early days, however, project management software ran only on big mainframe computers and was used only for very large projects. These early systems were limited in their capabilities and, by today's standards, were hard to use.

Today, numerous PC-based project management software packages exist, and they are finding their way into almost every type of business. These systems, which often have an easy-to-use graphical user interface, can help you plan activities, schedule work to be performed, view the relationships among tasks, manage resources, and monitor the progress of the project.

This appendix provides

- a discussion of the common features available in most project management software packages
- sample printouts from a popular project management software package for the consumer market study discussed throughout Part 3 of this book
- a review of a few popular project management software packages
- criteria for selecting a project management software system
- a discussion of some advantages of using project management software

> • a discussion of some concerns about project management software
> • a list of vendors offering project management software

PROJECT MANAGEMENT SOFTWARE FEATURES

Following is a list of features offered by most of today's project management software. This list, though by no means complete, gives a general overview of the types of features available. It should be noted, however, that different project management software packages provide different features, and some of the features listed are not found in every project management package. In addition, some products do a much better job than other products at providing software support for some of these features.

1. *Budgeting and cost control.* With most project management systems, it's possible to associate cost information with each activity and each resource in a project. Individuals' pay can usually be defined in hourly rates, overtime rates, or one-time-only rates. Dates when payments are due can also be specified. For materials, one-time-only or ongoing costs can be defined, and accounting and budgeting codes can be set up that are associated with each type of material. In addition, user-defined formulas can be developed to handle cost functions. Most packages use this information to help calculate projected costs of the project and track costs during the project. At any time during the project, actual costs can be compared with budgeted costs for individual resources, for groups of resources, or for the entire project. This information can be used not only for planning purposes but also for reporting purposes. Most packages allow you to display and print the costs for each task, for each resource (person, machine, etc.), or for the entire project, at any time during the project.

2. *Calendars.* Base calendars typically can be used to define working days and hours for each individual resource or group of resources on a project. These calendars are used in calculating the schedule for the project. Most systems provide a default for the standard working period, such as Monday through Friday from 8:00 a.m. to 5:00 p.m., with an hour for lunch. These calendars can be modified for each individual resource or group of resources. For example, work hours can be modified, company holidays can be entered as nonworking days, various shifts (daytime, nighttime) can be entered, and vacation days can be included, as well as variable scales (hour, day, week). The calendars can be used for reporting purposes and can often be printed by day, week, or month for each individual resource or in the form of a full, possibly wall-sized, complete project calendar.

3. *Email.* The ability to send project information through email is a feature of several project management software packages. This

option allows the user to direct project information to email instead of to the screen or printer. Project team members can be notified of important changes such as updated project plans or schedules, can be informed about the current project status, and can be sent various charts, all through email.

4. *Graphics.* For projects that involve a large number of activities, manually drawing a Gantt chart or network diagram is a tedious and error-prone task, as is redrawing the chart by hand to incorporate any modifications. One of the greatest features of modern project management software is the ability to easily and quickly generate a variety of charts, including Gantt charts and network diagrams, based on current data. Once the baseline plan has been created, any modifications to the plan can easily be entered into the system, and the charts will automatically reflect those changes. Project management software allows tasks in Gantt charts to be linked together so that the precedence activities can be shown. Typically, the user can jump back and forth between Gantt chart and network diagram displays with a single command. Furthermore, graphic and charting capabilities often allow the user to

   • perform interactive manipulations of tasks and relationships, such as changing precedence relationships by graphically linking tasks together or changing activity durations by stretching out the activity duration display
   • customize formats, such as column sizes, headings, colors, fonts, and the placement of text
   • show baseline-versus-actual charts for tasks or costs
   • highlight the critical path and show the slack for any activity
   • zoom in and out of (reduce or magnify) displays

5. *Importing/exporting data.* Many project management software packages allow the user to bring in information from other applications, such as word processing, spreadsheet, and database applications. The process of bringing information into the project management software is called *importing*. For example, instead of retyping cost-related information on people or machines from a spreadsheet into your project management software package and possibly entering conflicting or erroneous data, you can simply import that spreadsheet information when it's needed. Similarly, it's often possible to send information from your project management software to those applications. The process of sending out information is called *exporting*. For example, a schedule report for a specific subcontractor might be exported to a word processing memo.

   Most project management software packages allow the transfer of information in standard ASCII text, from the Windows Clipboard, and to SQL databases, Lotus, Excel, Microsoft Project Exchange, OLE client/server, DDE client/server, and several other systems.

6. *Handling multiple projects and subprojects.* Some projects are so large that they need to be divided into smaller subsets of tasks or sub-

projects. In other situations, experienced project managers are overseeing several projects simultaneously, and team members are assigned to more than one project simultaneously, with their time divided between the projects. Most project management software packages provide support for these situations. They often can store multiple projects in separate files with connecting links between the files, store multiple projects in the same file, handle several hundred or even several thousand projects at the same time, and create Gantt charts and network diagrams for multiple projects.

7. *Report generation.* When project management software packages first became available, they typically contained only a small set of reports, often tabular, that summarized the schedule, the resources, or the budget. Most of today's project management software packages have more extensive reporting capabilities. Among the reports they can generate are the following:

- reports on the project as a whole
- reports on the major steps (milestones) of a project
- reports that provide a variety of information with respect to a date range, such as tasks that have been completed within that range, tasks that are in progress, and tasks that will start within that range
- financial reports that show a full range of information, including budgets for all tasks as well as the entire project, tasks and resources that are over budget, cumulative budgeted costs, actual costs, and committed costs
- C/SCSC (Cost/Schedule Control System Criteria) reports, generally required by the U.S. Department of Defense for defense projects
- resource allocation reports for each resource or group of resources involved in a project
- customizable standard reports, cross-tabs, and baseline-to-actual variance reports

Most systems will automatically adjust the size of the type to fit the report to the page and will allow the user to view the page (page preview) before printing.

8. *Resource management.* Modern project management software can maintain a resource list consisting of resource names, the maximum amount of time resources are available, standard and overtime rates for resources, accrual methods, and textual descriptions of the resources. Each resource can have a code assigned to it, as well as an individual personalized calendar. Constraints can be assigned to each resource, such as the number of hours or times that it is available. Users can also assign resources to a percentage of a task, set priority levels for resource assignments, assign more than one resource to the same task, and keep memos or notes on each resource. The system will highlight and help correct overallocation and perform resource leveling and resource smoothing. Most software packages allow the user to handle several thousand resources for a project.

9. *Planning.* All project management software packages allow the user to define the activities that need to be performed. Just as the software typically allows a resource list to be maintained, it allows an activity or task list to be maintained. For each task, the user can provide a title, a start date, a finish date, comments, and estimated durations (including optimistic, most likely, and pessimistic estimates in various time scales) and can specify any precedential relationships with other tasks, as well as the person(s) responsible. Typically, project management software allows several thousand tasks to be associated with a project. In addition, most packages allow you to create a work breakdown structure (WBS) (see Chapter 9) to aid in the planning process.

10. *Project monitoring and tracking.* Tracking progress, actual costs, and actual resource use is a fundamental component of project management. Most project management software packages allow the user to define a baseline plan and compare actual progress and costs with those in the baseline plan. Most packages can track tasks in progress, completed tasks, associated costs, time expended, start and finish dates, actual dollars committed or spent, and resources used, as well as remaining durations, resources, and expenses. There are numerous report formats associated with these monitoring and tracking features.

11. *Scheduling.* Real-world projects are often very large. Scheduling activities manually can be an extremely complex process. Project management software packages provide extensive, and often automatic, support for scheduling. Most systems will build Gantt charts and network diagrams based on the task and resource lists and all of their associated information. Any changes to those lists will automatically be reflected in the schedules. In addition, users can schedule recurring tasks, set priorities for scheduled tasks, perform reverse scheduling (from the end date backward to the beginning), define work shifts, schedule elapsed time, schedule tasks to start as late as possible or as soon as possible, and specify a must-start-by or must-finish-by date or a no-earlier-than or no-later-than date.

12. *Security.* A relatively new feature in project management software is security. Some systems provide password access to the project management program itself, password access to individual project files, and password access to specific data within a project file (such as pay rates).

13. *Sorting and filtering.* Sorting allows the user to view information in a desired order, such as pay rates from highest to lowest, resource names in alphabetical order, or task names in alphabetical order. Most programs allow multiple levels of sorting (for example, by last name and then by first name). Filtering enables the user to select only certain data that meet some specified criteria. For example, if the user wants information on just the tasks that require a certain resource, a simple request tells the software to ignore tasks that don't use that resource and display just tasks that do use that resource.

14. *What-if analysis*. One very helpful feature of project management software is the ability to perform what-if analysis. This feature allows the user to explore the effects of various scenarios. At some point in a project, the user might ask the system "What if _____ were delayed by a week?" The effects of the delay on the entire project would automatically be calculated, and the results would be presented. For example, to explore what would happen if lumber rates went up by 1.5 percent during a construction project, a contractor could enter this change into the computer, and all associated costs would be projected. Almost any variable (people, pay rates, costs) in a project can be tested to see the effects of certain occurrences. This type of analysis enables the manager to better control any risks associated with the project.

SAMPLE PRINTOUTS

The following pages contain sample printouts from Microsoft Project for the consumer market study discussed in Part 3 of this text:

Figure A.1—a network diagram

Figure A.2—a Gantt chart

Figure A.3—a calendar of activities for a given month

Figure A.4—a resource allocation graph for one team member for a specific time frame

Figure A.5—a resource usage chart for all team members for a specific time frame

Figure A.6—a task list with estimated durations, start and end dates, predecessors, and resource names

Figure A.7—an assignment report, showing which resource is assigned to which tasks and when

Figure A.8—another view of who does which tasks and when

Figure A.9—a task list with the names of the team members working on each task

Figure A.10—a resource list that gives each person's name, lists the tasks, and notes the amount of time devoted to each task during a given time frame

FIGURE A.1   Network Diagram for the Consumer Market Study

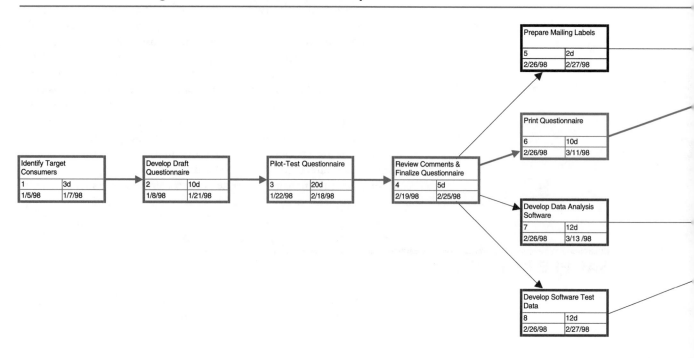

Project: Consumer Market Study
Date: 1/1/98

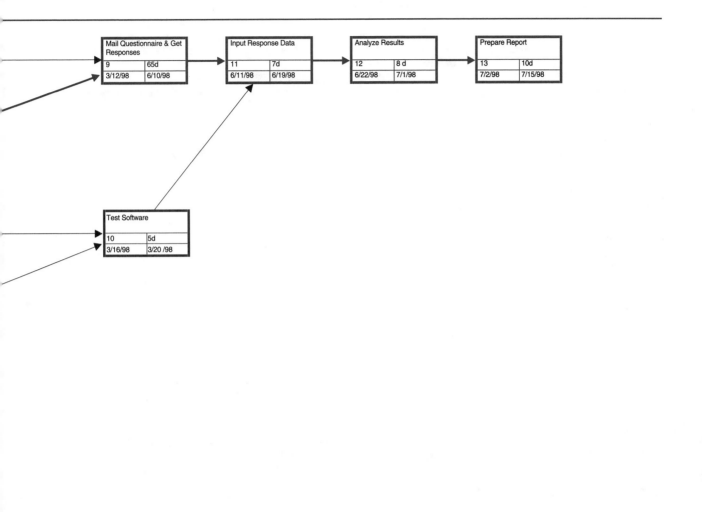

FIGURE A.2 Gantt Chart for the Consumer Market Study

ID	Task Name	Duration
1	Identify Target Consumers	3d
2	Develop Draft Questionnaire	10d
3	Pilot-Test Questionnaire	20d
4	Review Comments & Finalize	5d
5	Prepare Mailing Labels	2d
6	Print Questionnaire	10d
7	Develop Data Analysis Soft.	12d
8	Develop Software Test Data	2d
9	Mail Questionnaire & Get Res.	65d
10	Test Software	5d
11	Input Response Data	7d
12	Analyze Results	8d
13	Prepare Report	10d

Project: Consumer Market Study
Date: 1/1/98

Task	Milestone	Rolled Up Critical Task
Critical Task	Summary	Rolled Up Milestone
Progress	Rolled Up Task	Rolled Up Progress

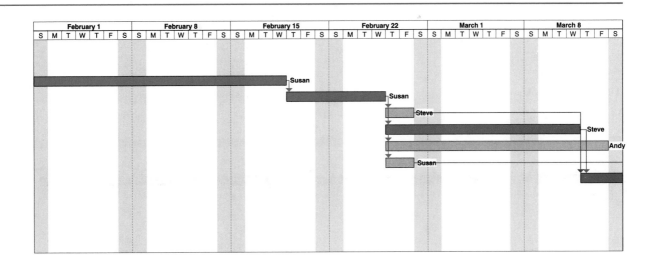

February 1	**February 8**	**February 15**	**February 22**	**March 1**	**March 8**
S M T W T F S	S M T W T F S	S M T W T F S	S M T W T F S	S M T W T F S	S M T W T F S

Project: Consumer Market Study
Date: 1/1/98

Task	Milestone ◆	Rolled Up Critical Task
Critical Task	Summary	Rolled Up Milestone ◇
Progress	Rolled Up Task	Rolled Up Progress

FIGURE A.2   Gantt Chart for the Consumer Market Study (continued)

Project: Consumer Market Study
Date: 1/1/98

Task	Milestone	Rolled Up Critical Task
Critical Task	Summary	Rolled Up Milestone
Progress	Rolled Up Task	Rolled Up Progress

	April 26							May 3							May 10							May 17							May 24							May 31					
S	M	T	W	T	F	S	S	M	T	W	T	F	S	S	M	T	W	T	F	S	S	M	T	W	T	F	S	S	M	T	W	T	F	S	S	M	T	W	T	F	S

Project: Consumer Market Study Date: 1/1/98	Task		Milestone	◆	Rolled Up Critical Task	
	Critical Task		Summary		Rolled Up Milestone	◇
	Progress		Rolled Up Task		Rolled Up Progress	

FIGURE A.2   Gantt Chart for the Consumer Market Study (continued)

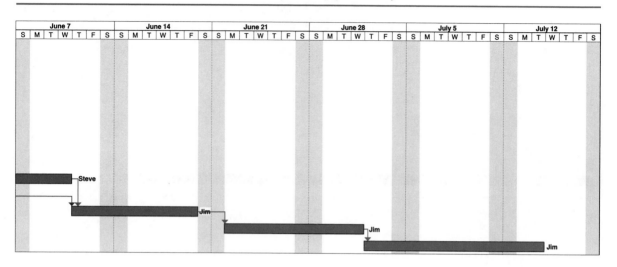

FIGURE A.3 Calendar for the Consumer Market Study

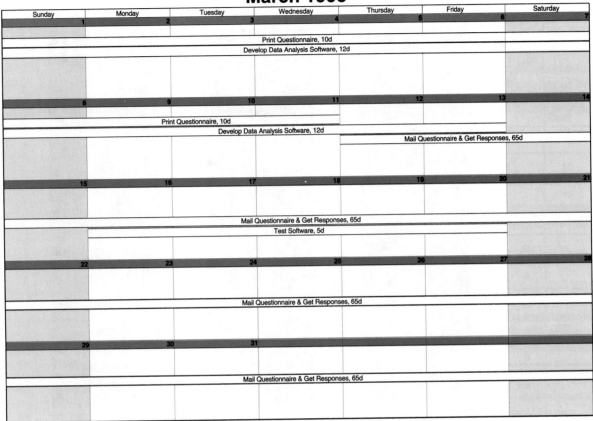

FIGURE A.4   Resource Allocation Graph for the Consumer Market Study

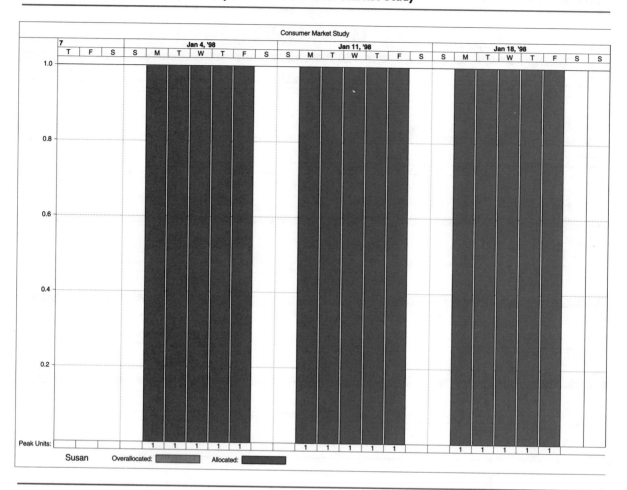

FIGURE A.5   Resource Usage Chart for the Consumer Market Study

			7				Jan 4, '98									Jan 11, '98			
ID	**Resource Name**	**Work**	T	F	S	S	M	T	W	T	F	S	S	M	T	W	T
1	Susan	320h					8h	8h	8h	8h	8h			8h	8h	8h	8h
2	**Steve**	**616h**															
3	Andy	136h															
4	Jim	200h															

FIGURE A.6   Task List for the Consumer Market Study

			Consumer Market Study			
ID	**Task Name**	**Duration**	**Start**	**Finish**	**Predecessors**	**Resource Names**
1	Identify Target Consumers	3d	1/5/98	1/7/98		Susan
2	Develop Draft Questionnaire	10d	1/8/98	1/21/98	1	Susan
3	Pilot-Test Questionnaire	20d	1/22/98	2/18/98	2	Susan
4	Review Comments & Finalize	5d	2/19/98	2/25/98	3	Susan
5	Prepare Mailing Labels	2d	2/26/98	2/27/98	4	Steve
6	Print Questionnaire	10d	2/26/98	3/11/98	4	Steve
7	Develop Data Analysis Soft.	12d	2/26/98	3/13/98	4	Andy
8	Develop Software Test Data	2d	2/26/98	2/27/98	4	Susan
9	Mail Questionnaire & Get Res.	65d	3/12/98	6/10/98	5,6	Steve
10	Test Software	5d	3/16/98	3/20/98	7,8	Andy
11	Input Response Data	7d	6/11/98	6/19/98	9,10	Jim
12	Analyze Results	8d	6/22/98	7/1/98	11	Jim
13	Prepare Report	10d	7/2/98	7/15/98	12	Jim

FIGURE A.7   Assignment Report for the Consumer Market Study

Who Does What as of 1/1/98
Consumer Market Study

ID	Resource Name	Work
1	Susan	320h

ID	Task Name	Units	Work	Delay	Start	Finish
1	Identify Target Consumers	1	24h	0h	1/5/98	1/7/98
2	Develop Draft Questionnaire	1	80h	0h	1/8/98	1/21/98
3	Pilot-Test Questionnaire	1	160h	0h	1/22/98	2/18/98
4	Review Comments & Finalize	1	40h	0h	2/19/98	2/25/98
8	Develop Software Test Data	1	16h	0h	2/26/98	2/27/98

ID	Resource Name	Work
2	Steve	616h

ID	Task Name	Units	Work	Delay	Start	Finish
5	Prepare Mailing Labels	1	16h	0h	2/26/98	2/27/98
6	Print Questionnaire	1	80h	0h	2/26/98	3/11/98
9	Mail Questionnaire & Get Responses	1	520h	0h	3/12/98	6/10/98

ID	Resource Name	Work
3	Andy	136h

ID	Task Name	Units	Work	Delay	Start	Finish
7	Develop Data Analysis Software	1	96h	0h	2/26/98	3/13/98
10	Test Software	1	40h	0h	3/16/98	3/20/98

ID	Resource Name	Work
4	Jim	200h

ID	Task Name	Units	Work	Delay	Start	Finish
11	Input Response Data	1	56h	0h	6/11/98	6/19/98
12	Analyze Results	1	64h	0h	6/22/98	7/1/98
13	Prepare Report	1	80h	0h	7/2/98	7/15/98

FIGURE A.8   Another Assignment Report for the Consumer Market Study

Who Does What When as of 1/1/98
Consumer Market Study

	2/2	2/3	2/4	2/5	2/6	2/7	2/8	2/9
Susan	8h	8h	8h	8h	8h			8h
Identify Target Consumers								
Develop Draft Questionnaire								
Pilot-Test Questionnaire	8h	8h	8h	8h	8h			8h
Review Comments & Finalize								
Develop Software Test Data								
Steve								
Prepare Mailing Labels								
Print Questionnaire								
Mail Questionnaire & Get Responses								
Andy								
Develop Data Analysis Software								
Test Software								
Jim								
Input Response Data								
Analyze Results								
Prepare Report								

FIGURE A.9 Task Usage Report for the Consumer Market Study

Task Usage as of 1/1/98
Consumer Market Study

	12/28/97	1/4/98	1/11/98	1/18/98	1/25/98	2/1/98	2/8/98	2/15/98
Identify Target Consumers		24h						
Susan		24h						
Develop Draft Questionnaire		16h	40h	24h				
Susan		16h	40h	24h				
Pilot-Test Questionnaire				16h	40h	40h	40h	24h
Susan				16h	40h	40h	40h	24h
Review Comments & Finalize								16h
Susan								16h
Prepare Mailing Labels								
Steve								
Print Questionnaire								
Steve								
Develop Data Analysis Software								
Andy								
Develop Software Test Data								
Susan								
Mail Questionnaire & Get Responses								
Steve								
Test Software								
Andy								
Input Response Data								
Jim								
Analyze Results								
Jim								
Prepare Report								
Jim								
Total		40h	40h	40h	40h	40h	40h	40h

FIGURE A.10   Resource Usage Table for the Consumer Market Study

Resource Usage as of 1/1/98
Consumer Market Study

	2/22/98	3/1/98	3/8/98	3/15/98	3/22/98	3/29/98	4/5/98	4/12/98
Susan	40h							
Identify Target Consumers								
Develop Draft Questionnaire								
Pilot-Test Questionnaire								
Review Comments & Finalize	24h							
Develop Software Test Data	16h							
Steve	32h	40h	40h	40h	40h	40h	40h	40h
Prepare Mailing Labels	16h							
Print Questionnaire	16h	40h	24h					
Mail Questionnaire & Get Responses			16h	40h	40h	40h	40h	40h
Andy	16h	40h	40h	40h				
Develop Data Analysis Software	16h	40h	40h					
Test Software				40h				
Jim								
Input Response Data								
Analyze Results								
Prepare Report								
Total	88h	80h	80h	80h	40h	40h	40h	40h

POPULAR PROJECT MANAGEMENT SOFTWARE PACKAGES

Following are brief descriptions of some of today's most popular project management software packages. Most of these packages are available for a personal computer at a cost of between $400 and $700. For more detailed information, contact each company. The company will probably provide you a demo disk and some additional documentation. In addition, about every two years, *PC Magazine* provides an excellent review of the most popular project management software packages. (Reviews of the following software packages can be found in Carey, 1995, and King, 1995; see the References.)

CA-SuperProject

CA-SuperProject, by Computer Associates International, Inc., is a popular package, especially among those who manage an enterprisewide network of projects, those working in a Unix or Windows environment, and those needing advanced features. The package supports up to 16,000 tasks per project, and many reviewers rate it excellent for large-scale projects as well as small-scale projects. It can create and consolidate multiple project files, provide multiple-level password entry for networked users, and conduct PERT probability analysis, and it contains a resource-leveling algorithm that allows higher-priority tasks to take precedence when necessary. Its principal weakness, which should be resolved in future versions, is its user interface, which is not as user friendly as those of some other packages.

Microsoft Project

As you might expect, Microsoft Project, being part of the Microsoft family, has captured a large share of the market for project management software packages. Microsoft Project's primary strength is that it looks and feels just like the other Microsoft products (Access, Excel, PowerPoint, and Word). The menu bar is nearly identical, and the customized toolbars work exactly the same way. In addition, the user can easily move information back and forth between applications. For example, cost information can easily be moved from an Excel resource table into Microsoft Project, and a Microsoft Project Gantt chart can easily be moved into a Word document, via dragging and dropping or linking. Tips of the day, cue cards, and numerous help Wizards make the package extremely easy to use. The interactive calendaring system is very powerful, as are the email and distribution facilities. Visual Basic for Applications is now included, allowing the advanced user to tailor the interface or automate repetitive tasks. Microsoft Project's weaknesses are its handling of the critical path (not always easy to see) and its inability to handle multiple projects and subprojects as well as some other packages do.

Project Scheduler

Sold by Scitor Corp., Project Scheduler is an easy-to-use Windows-based project management software package that won an Editors' Choice Award from *PC Magazine*. It provides all of the traditional project management features with a well-designed graphical interface. The reporting features are strong, and so are its charts, such as the Gantt chart, which uses various colors to distinguish critical tasks, positive and negative slack, completed tasks, and tasks in progress. Links between tasks can easily be added graphically, as can modifications to task durations. Priority settings for resources and resource-leveling algorithms are very effective. Multiple projects and large-scale projects are easy to handle, and the links to external databases are superior. Some weaknesses of Project Scheduler are its limited on-line help and documentation and its limited email features; however, these should be improved in future releases.

SureTrak Project Manager

SureTrak Project Manager is produced by Primavera Systems, Inc., which also produces an excellent high-end project management software package called Project Planner. SureTrak is a very visually oriented program and provides excellent zooming, compressing, and dragging-and-dropping features. Its standard structures—such as column sizes, tables, colors, and data organizations—are easily modifiable, and customized templates can easily be created. Its work breakdown structure (WBS) features are excellent and easy to use. Recurring activities can be handled easily, and activity network charts can be cut into fragments, saved on disk, and loaded into other programs. Sure-Trak's weaknesses include its on-line help and documentation, which should be improved in future releases.

Time Line

Time Line, sold by Symantec Corp., is another winner of a *PC Magazine* Editors' Choice Award. Although sometimes a little hard for beginners to use, Time Line is first-rate for experienced project managers. Its reports facilities are excellent, as are its links to SQL databases. Its calendars, email features, sorting and filtering capabilities, and handling of multiple projects are also well designed. In addition, it contains a feature called the Co-Pilot, which is an effective pop-up help facility. The user interface is good and fairly easy to use. However, many reviewers believe that Time Line is best suited for large projects and/or multiple projects and is not as easy for beginners to use as some of the other packages.

High-End Project Management Software

When the PC-based software packages discussed above don't have the power to manage your large-scale or enterprisewide projects, high-end project management software packages should be considered. These systems—which include Artemis by Lucas Management Systems, Open Plan by Welcom Software Technology, Project Planner by Primavera, and Project/2 by PSDI—can share data in a distributed database environment; handle multiple projects easily; provide links to other business information systems such as accounting, purchasing, and procurement systems; and often contain highly sophisticated algorithms for scheduling and resource allocation. These systems cost anywhere from several thousand dollars to $75,000, but expect the price of these systems to drop and the power of the PC-based systems to continue to increase.

CRITERIA FOR SELECTING PROJECT MANAGEMENT SOFTWARE

Following is a list of factors to consider before purchasing a project management software package. Depending on your individual needs, certain factors listed below may be more important or less important to you than they are to other people.

1. *Capacity.* Here the main concern is whether or not the system can handle the number of tasks you expect to perform, the number of resources you expect to need, and the number of projects you expect to be managing simultaneously.
2. *Documentation and on-line help facilities.* The quality of documenta-

tion and on-line help facilities varies greatly among project management software packages. Consideration should be given to the readability of the user's manual, the logical presentation of ideas in the user's manual, the level of detail of the manual and on-line help, the number and quality of examples provided, and the level of the discussion of advanced features.

3. *Ease of use.* This is often an important factor in the selection of any type of software package. Consideration should be given to the "look" and "feel" of the system, the menu structures, available short-cut keys, color displays, the amount of information in each display, the ease with which data can be entered, the ease with which existing data can be modified, the ease with which reports can be generated, the quality of the printouts that are produced, the consistency among screens, and the amount of learning required to become proficient with the system.

4. *Features available.* Here consideration must be given to whether or not the system provides the features that are required for your organization. For example, does the package include work breakdown structures and both Gantt charts and network diagrams? How good are the resource-leveling and smoothing algorithms? Can the system sort and filter information, monitor the budget, produce customized calendars, and help with tracking and control? Does it have the capability to check for and help resolve overallocation of resources?

5. *Integration with other systems.* More and more in today's digital world there is a convergence of numerous electronic systems. If you are working in an environment where pertinent data are stored in various places, such as databases and spreadsheets, then special attention should be given to the integration capabilities of the project management software. Some systems allow very basic integration with a few popular software packages, whereas others provide sophisticated integration with distributed databases and even object-oriented databases. In addition, the ability of the project management software to export information to word processing and graphics packages and through email may affect your decision.

6. *Installation requirements.* The considerations here are the hardware and software required to run the project management software: the memory required, the amount of hard disk space required, the processing speed and power required, the type of graphics display needed, printer requirements, and operating system requirements.

7. *Reporting capabilities.* Current project management systems vary in the number and types of reports they can provide. Some support just the basic planning, scheduling, and cost reports, whereas others have extensive facilities for providing reports on individual tasks, resources, actual costs, committed costs, progress, and so on. In addition, some systems are easier to customize than others. Reporting capabilities should be given a fairly high priority, because the ability to produce extensive and powerful reports is a feature that most users rate very high.

8. *Security.* Some project management software packages provide greater levels of security than others. If security is important, then

special attention should be given to the methods of restricting access to the project management software system itself, to each project file, and to the data within each file.

9. *Vendor support.* Special attention should be given to whether or not the vendor or dealer provides technical support, the price of that support, and the reputation of the vendor.

ADVANTAGES OF USING PROJECT MANAGEMENT SOFTWARE

There are numerous advantages of using project management software. Some of these are as follows:

1. *Accuracy.* A major benefit of using project management software is that accuracy is greatly improved. For large projects, manually drawing network diagrams, calculating start and finish times, and monitoring resource usage are very difficult. Project management software packages have accurate algorithms for calculating project information and contain numerous built-in routines that check for user errors.

2. *Affordability.* Excellent PC-based project management software can be purchased for between $400 and $700. This price might be high for an individual, but for most businesses such software is well worth the money.

3. *Ease of use.* Over the past few years, project management software packages have become extremely easy to use. They can often be mastered with only a minimal amount of training. This fact and the fact that most packages are affordable have led to a significant increase in the number of users of project management software.

4. *Ability to handle complexity.* It's obvious that software can handle certain aspects (especially numeric aspects) of large-scale projects more easily than a person can manually. For projects that have just a few activities and span a short period of time, a manual approach may be feasible. But for projects that have thousands of activities and thousands of resources and span a few years' time, project management software provides indispensable assistance with the level of complexity.

5. *Maintainability and modifiability.* With manual systems it's often difficult to maintain and modify project information. For example, if a project is being managed without computer support, the network diagrams must be manually redrawn and costs must be recalculated every time there's a change. With project management software, any change in the data will automatically be reflected in all the project documents, such as the diagrams, the cost tables, and the resource allocation charts. This is a handy feature because, no matter how well your plans are laid, chances are that something along the way is going to change (at least a little).

6. *Record keeping.* A major benefit of project management software is its ability to keep excellent records. For instance, data can be kept on individual team members' schedules, each task, costs, and

resources used. These data can be used to produce high-quality reports and can be helpful in planning future projects. However, record-keeping benefits will exist only as long as the user continues to update the files.

7. *Speed.* Once input data have been collected and entered, almost every imaginable calculation can be done very rapidly by the software. Manually creating or revising plans, schedules, and budgets can take hours, days, or weeks. However, revisions can typically be performed in minutes or seconds with today's systems. The savings in time are usually enough to pay for the software itself.

8. *What-if analysis.* One further feature of project management software that's a great benefit is the ability to perform what-if analysis. What-if analysis, as discussed earlier, allows the user to see the effects of various scenarios on a project. These different scenarios can be run on the software, and their effects can be evaluated. This allows the project manager to prepare and plan for certain contingencies and to assess consequences. Conducting what-if analysis without the software is not nearly as easy—and is sometimes impossible.

CONCERNS ABOUT USING PROJECT MANAGEMENT SOFTWARE

Although there are numerous benefits to using project management software, there are also a few concerns to be considered and pitfalls to be avoided, if possible.

1. *Becoming distracted by the software.* In some cases, for some project managers, project management software can be something of a distraction. A manager can spend too much time playing with and focusing on the software, with all of its reports and features, and forget about the most important part of a project: the people.

2. *A false sense of security.* The software can sometimes lull project managers into a false sense of security. This can happen in several ways. First, project managers might believe that, because they have powerful software, they can manage and accomplish more than is actually feasible. Second, managers might think that, although a project is slipping, the software will be able to figure out a way to get it back on track. Third, if the software is not used properly, it might report that the project is doing fine, when in reality it's not. Just because the software says everything is all right doesn't necessarily make it so.

3. *Information overload.* Project management software packages provide a great number of features and a huge amount of information. At times the sheer quantity can be overwhelming. Only needed features of the software should be used. Project managers have to resist the temptation to use features that produce more reports or more data without contributing to the successful completion of the project.

4. *The learning curve.* It does take a certain amount of time to become proficient in the use of project management software packages.

The amount of time required varies, depending on the individual's background. For those not currently using computers and business software, there can be a significant learning curve. However, the amount of training typically required to master the software has been decreasing over the past few years as the packages have become easier and easier to use.

5. *Overreliance on software.* Because project management software has become so easy (and even fun) to use and because it provides so many appealing features, project managers have started relying heavily on it. Individuals with little or no knowledge of the fundamentals of project management sometimes use the software without really understanding what they're doing. If the basic concepts of project management have not been mastered, the software won't make much of a difference. Stated simply, the software is just a tool to help you do your job more effectively and efficiently—the software itself cannot manage a project. You must manage the project, relying mainly on your skills and the skills of your team.

PROJECT MANAGEMENT SOFTWARE VENDORS

Table A.1 lists some project management software packages and the vendors that produce them. Most of these vendors have home pages on the World Wide Web. In addition, the Project Management Institute has a Web site at

www.pmi.org/mem_prod/venalpha.htm

that lists project management software vendors. This is an excellent Web site, containing addresses, phone numbers, and direct links to most vendors' home pages, as well as links to their email. Synapse also maintains a Web site that provides a list of consultants and vendors of several popular project management software packages, along with their mailing addresses, email addresses, and Web sites. The list maintained by Synapse can be found at

www.synapse.net/~loday/PMForum/vsoftwar.htm

SUMMARY

This appendix discusses several features that are typically found in project management software. Among the most common are budgeting and cost control, calendars, email, graphics, importing and exporting data, handling multiple projects and subprojects, report generation, resource management, planning, project monitoring and tracking, scheduling, security, sorting and filtering, and what-if analysis.

Criteria are given for selecting a project management software package, including capacity, documentation and on-line help facilities, ease of use, features available, integration with other systems,

TABLE A.1   Software Packages and Vendors

Software Package	Vendor Name
Artemis	Lucas Management Systems
CA-Super Project	Computer Associates International, Inc.
Harvard Project Manager	Software Publishing Corp.
InstaPlan	InstaPlan Corp.
Micro-Frame Program Manager	Micro-Frame Technologies, Inc.
Micro Planner	Micro Planning Software
Micro Trak	Softrak Systems
Microfusion	Integrated Management Concepts
MicroMan	Poc-It Management Systems
Microsoft Project	Microsoft Corp.
Milestones, Etc.	Kidasa
Multitrak	Multisystems, Inc.
Open Plan	Welcom Software Technology
PAC Micro	AGS Management Systems
PERT Master	PERT Master International
Plan View	Plan View, Inc.
Plantrac	Computer Line, Inc.
Plot Trek	Softrak Systems
PMS	North America Mica
Power Planner	Sphygmic Software, Ltd.
PowerProject	ASTA Development, Inc.
PREMIS	K&H Professional Management Services
Project/2	PSDI, Inc.
Project Alert	CRI, Inc.
Project Outlook	Strategic Software, Inc.
Project Planner	Primavera Systems, Inc.
Project Scheduler	Scitor Corp.
Project Workbench	Applied Business Technologies
PROMIS	Strategic Software
Prothos	New Technology Association
Quick Plan	Mitchell Management
Qwiknet Professional	Project Software & Development Corp.
Skyline	Applitech Software
SureTrak Project Manager	Primavera Systems, Inc.
Task Monitor	Monitor Software
Texim Project	Welcom Software Technology
Time Line	Symantec Corp.
Top Down Project Planner	Ajida Technologies
ViewPoint	Computer Aided Management, Inc.
VISIONmicro	Systonetics, Inc.
Vue	National Information Systems

installation requirements, reporting capabilities, security, and vendor support. Several popular project management software packages are reviewed, and a vendor list is provided.

Finally, a list is provided of advantages of and concerns about using project management software. The benefits include accuracy, affordability, ease of use, ability to handle complexity, maintainability and modifiability, record keeping, speed, and what-if analysis. Concerns include becoming distracted by the software, a false sense of security, information overload, the learning curve, and overreliance on software.

QUESTIONS

1. Discuss at least ten common features of project management software. In your opinion, which of these are the most important?
2. Look at the printouts in this appendix. Describe at least three others that would be useful.
3. Discuss the criteria that should be considered when purchasing project management software. If you had to rank these in order of importance, how would you rank them?
4. What are some of the advantages of using project management software?
5. What are some of the concerns about using project management software? Do the advantages outweigh the concerns? Explain your answer.

WORLD WIDE WEB EXERCISES

1. Visit the Project Management Institute's Web site for project management software vendors at

   www.pmi.org/mem_prod/venalpha.htm

   Discuss what you find.

2. Visit the WWW Project Management Forum's Vendor's Market Square at

   www.pmforum.org/vsoftwar.htm

   Discuss what you find.

3. By either phone or email, contact some of the companies you found in the above two exercises, and find out whether they can send you a free demo package.
4. Search for and visit the sites of at least three other project management software vendors. Give their addresses and discuss their sites.

Appendix B   Project Management Organizations

Association Française des Ingénieurs et Techniciens d'Estimation, de Planification et de Projets (AFITEP)
3, rue Francaise
75001 Paris, France
Telephone: 33 42 36 36 37
Fax: 33 42 36 36 35

Association of Project Managers (APM)
85 Oxford Road
High Wycombe
Bucks, England HP11 2DX
Telephone: 44 14 94 44 00 90
Fax: 44 14 94 52 89 37

International Project Management Association (IPMA)
Pia Dyhr, DiEU
Dr Neegarrds Vej3
DK-2970
Hoersholm, Denmark
   or
IPMA
International Secretariat
Tödistrasse 47
Postbox 656 CH-8027
Zürich, Switzerland
Telephone: 41 01 249 31 98
Fax: 41 01 249 30 64

International Research Network on Organizing by Projects (IRNOP)
Professor Rolf A. Lundin
Umeå Business School, FEK
Umeå University
S-901 87 Umeå, Sweden
Telephone: 46 90 16 61 53
Fax: 46 90 16 66 74

Project Management Institute (PMI)
130 South State Road
Upper Darby, PA 19082
Telephone: (610) 734-3330
Fax: (610) 734-3266

Swedish Project Academy/
Svenska Projekt Akademien
Anna Hagberg
Norrmälarstrand 20
112 40 Stockholm, Sweden
Telephone: 08 653 56 35
Fax: 08 651 51 98

Appendix C

Project Management World Wide Web Sites

Following is a list of some excellent World Wide Web sites on project management. Many of these can be reached directly from the home page of Dr. James P. Clements, co-author of this book. His home page address is

www.towson.edu/~clements

Association for Project Management (APM)
www.asterisk.co.uk/project/Pmgen.html

Department of Defense (DOD) Software Program Managers Network
www.spmn.com

International Project Management Association (IPMA)
www.oslonett.no/html/adv/INTERNET

International Research Network on Organizing by Projects (IRNOP)
www.hh.umu.se/fek/irnop

NASA—One Hundred Rules for NASA Project Managers
**pscinfo.pscni.nasa.gov/online/msfc/project_mgmt/
100_Rules.html**

NASA—The Project Management Development Process Handbook
**www.hq.nasa.gov/office/HR-Education/training/
handbook.html**

NASA—Resource list for program and project management
www.hq.nasa.gov/office/hqlibrary/ppm/ppmbib.htm

Project Management Insight
www.infoser.com/infocons/pmi/insight.html

Project Management Institute
www.pmi.org

Project Management Institute—Canada
www.pmicanada.org

Project Manager
www.projectmanager.com

Project Manager's Palette
www.4pm.com/frmain.html

ProjectNet
www.projectnet.co.uk

Research on Temporary Organizations and Project Management
www.hh.umu.se/fek/irnop/umea.html

WWW Guide to Project Management Research
www.hh.umu.se/fek/irnop/projweb.html

WWW Project Management Forum
www.pmforum.org

Appendix D   Abbreviations

AF	Actual finish time	EV	Earned value
AIB	Activity in the box	FCAC	Forecasted cost at completion
ALAP	As late as possible	FS	Free slack
AOA	Activity on the arrow	LF	Latest finish time
ASAP	As soon as possible	LS	Latest start time
CAC	Cumulative actual cost	MIS	Management information system
CBC	Cumulative budgeted cost	PERT	Program evaluation and review technique
CEV	Cumulative earned value	RFP	Request for proposal
CPI	Cost performance index	SDLC	Systems development life cycle
CPM	Critical path method	SOW	Statement of work
CV	Cost variance	TBC	Total budgeted cost
EF	Earliest finish time	TS	Total slack
ES	Earliest start time	WBS	Work breakdown structure

REFERENCES

Chapter 1

Adams, J., and Kirchof, N. (Eds.). *A Decade of Project Management: Selected Readings from the Project Management Quarterly, 1970 Through 1980.* Project Management Institute, 1981.

Archibald, R. *Managing High-Technology Programs and Projects,* 2nd ed. John Wiley, 1992.

Badiru, A. *Project Management in Manufacturing and High Technology Operations.* John Wiley, 1988.

Barkley, B., and Saylor, J. *Customer-Driven Project Management: A New Paradigm in Total Quality Management.* McGraw Hill, 1994.

Bentley, T. "Project Management 1: A Methodology," *Management Accounting* (March 1992).

Cleland, D., and King, W. (Eds.). *Project Management Handbook,* 2nd ed. Van Nostrand Reinhold, 1988.

Darnall, R. *Achieving TQM on Projects: A Journey of Continuous Improvement.* Project Management Institute, 1994.

Dinsmore, P. *Human Factors in Project Management,* rev. ed. Amacom Books, 1990.

Dinsmore, P. (Ed.), *The AMA Handbook of Project Management.* Amacom Books, 1993.

Flippo, C. "Seventh Farm Aid Benefit," *Billboard* (September 30, 1995).

Hutchinson, C. *Vitality and Renewal: A Manager's Guide for the 21st Century.* Praeger, 1995.

Ireland, L. *Quality Management for Projects and Programs.* Project Management Institute, 1991.

Johannsen, H., and Page, G. *International Dictionary of Management,* 5th ed. Nichols, 1994.

Kerzner, H. "The Growth of Modern Project Management," *Project Management Journal* (June 1994).

Kezsbom, D., et al. *Dynamic Project Management.* John Wiley, 1989.

Kharbanda, O., and Stallworthy, E. *Lessons from Project Disasters.* MCB University Press, 1992.

Kimmons, R. *Project Management Basics: A Step by Step Approach.* Marcel Dekker, 1990.

Kliem, R. *The Noah Project.* Gower, 1993.

Leavitt, J., and Nunn, P. *Total Quality Through Project Management.* McGraw Hill, 1994.

Levine, H. "The Future of Project Management: Implications for Organizations, Practices and Tools," *PM Network* (May 1994).

Lewis, J. *Fundamentals of Project Management.* Amacom Books, 1995.

Lientz, B., and Ross, K. *Project Management for the 21st Century.* Academic Press, 1995.

Lock, D. *Project Management,* 5th ed. Gower, 1992.

Lock, D. *Project Management Handbook.* Gower, 1987.

Mattus, T. "Why Project Management? Why Now?" *PM Network* (April 1993).

Meredith, J., and Mantel, S. *Project Management: A Managerial Approach,* 3rd ed. John Wiley, 1995.

Murphy, P., Brelin, H., Jennings, L., and Davenport, K. *Focused Quality: Managing for Results.* St. Lucie Press, 1994.

Newcombe, T. "Project Management at Ground Zero," *Government Technology* (March 1996).

Nicholas, J. *Managing Business and Engineering Projects: Concepts and Implementation.* Prentice Hall, 1990.

The PMI Standards Committee. *Guide to the Project Management Body of Knowledge (PMBOK).* Project Management Institute, 1995.

Ross, J. *Total Quality Management: Text, Cases and Readings,* 2nd ed. St. Lucie Press, 1995.

Shtub, A., Bard, J., and Globerson, S. *Project Management: Engineering, Technology, and Implementation.* Prentice Hall, 1994.

Swanson, R. *The Quality Improvement Handbook: Team Guide to Tools and Techniques.* St. Lucie Press, 1995.

Turner, J. "Project Management: A Managerial Approach," *International Journal of Project Management* (June 1996).

Waddell, R. "Another Farm Aid Hit," *Amusement Business* (October 21, 1996).

Wearne, S. "The Management of Projects," *International Journal of Project Management* (June 1996).

Weiss, J., and Wysocki, R. *5-Phase Project Management.* Addison-Wesley, 1992.

Westley, F. "Bob Geldof and Live Aid: The Affective Side of Global Social Innovation," *Human Relations* (October 1991).

Wilker, D. "Hurriedly Arranged Hurricane Event Is a Hit," *Billboard* (October 12, 1992).

Barakat, R. "Writing to Win New Business," *PM Network* (November 1991).

Burnett, J., and Finch, J. "Effective Bid Pricing for Unit Price Contracts," *Engineering Economist* (Summer 1994).

Cavendish, P., and Martin, M. *Negotiating and Contracting for Project Management.* Project Management Institute, 1982.

Cleland, D., and King, W. (Eds.). *Project Management Handbook,* 2nd ed. Van Nostrand Reinhold, 1988.

Downey, J., Gilbert, R., and Gilbert, P. *Successful Interior Projects Through Effective Contract Documents.* R. S. Means, 1995.

Foster, N., Trauner, T., Vespe, R., and Chapman, W. *Construction Estimates from Take-Off to Bid,* 3rd ed. McGraw Hill, 1995.

Fraser, J. *Professional Project Proposals.* Gower, 1995.

Goff, L. "Method to Madness: Developing Request for Proposals," *Computerworld* (January 16, 1995).

Humphreys, K., and English, L. *Project and Cost Engineers' Handbook,* 3rd ed. Marcel Dekker, 1993.

Martin, M., Teagarden, C., and Lambreth, C. *Contract Administration for the Project Manager.* Project Management Institute, 1983.

O'Brien, T. "'Everything in Place' for Minnesota Indy Midway," *Amusement Business* (May 15, 1995).

The PMI Standards Committee. *Guide to the Project Management Body of Knowledge (PMBOK).* Project Management Institute, 1995.

Schuyler, J. *Decision Analysis in Projects.* Project Management Institute, 1996.

Scotto, M. "Project Budgeting: The Key to Bringing Business Projects in On Time and On Budget," *Project Management Journal* (March 1994).

Stewart, R., Wyskida, R., and Johannes, J. (Eds.). *Cost Estimator's Reference Manual,* 2nd ed. John Wiley, 1995.

Waddell, R. "Minnesota Midway Grosses $4.4 Million," *Amusement Business* (September 18, 1995).

Wideman, R. (Ed.). *Project and Program Risk Management: A Guide to Managing Project Risks and Opportunities.* Project Management Institute, 1991.

Chapter 2

Acuff, F. *How to Negotiate with Anyone Anywhere Around the World.* Amacom Books, 1994.

Chapter 3

Barakat, R. "Writing to Win New Business," *PM Network* (November, 1991).

Burnett, J., and Finch, J. "Effective Bid Pricing for Unit Price Contracts," *Engineering Economist* (Summer 1994).

Cavendish, P., and Martin, M. *Negotiating and Contracting for Project Management.* Project Management Institute, 1982.

Chatzoglou, P., and Macaulay, L. "A Review of Existing Models for Project Planning and Estimation and the Need for a New Approach," *International Journal of Project Management* (June 1996).

Cleland, D., and King, W. (Eds.). *Project Management Handbook,* 2nd ed. Van Nostrand Reinhold, 1988.

Downey, J., Gilbert, R., and Gilbert, P. *Successful Interior Projects Through Effective Contract Documents.* R. S. Means, 1995.

The Florida High Speed Rail Office. "Five Bidders, Five Contrasting Scenarios," *Railway Age* (December 1995).

Foster, N., Trauner, T., Vespe, R., and Chapman, W. *Construction Estimates from Take-Off to Bid,* 3rd ed. McGraw Hill, Inc., 1995.

Fraser, J. *Professional Project Proposals.* Gower, 1995.

Humphreys, K., and English, L. *Project and Cost Engineers' Handbook,* 3rd ed. Marcel Dekker, 1993.

Martin, M., Teagarden, C., and Lambreth, C. *Contract Administration for the Project Manager.* Project Management Institute, 1983.

The PMI Standards Committee. *Guide to the Project Management Body of Knowledge (PMBOK).* Project Management Institute, 1995.

Schuyler, J. *Decision Analysis in Projects.* Project Management Institute, 1996.

Scotto, M. "Project Budgeting: The Key to Bringing Business Projects in On Time and On Budget," *Project Management Journal* (March 1994).

Stewart, R., Wyskida, R., and Johannes, J. (Eds.). *Cost Estimator's Reference Manual,* 2nd ed. John Wiley, 1995.

Wideman, R. (Ed.). *Project and Program Risk Management: A Guide to Managing Project Risks and Opportunities.* Project Management Institute, 1991.

Chapter 4

Barkley, B., and Saylor, J. *Customer-Driven Project Management: A New Paradigm in Total Quality Management.* McGraw Hill, 1994.

Belassi, W., and Tukel, O. "A New Framework for Determining Critical Success/Failure Factors in Projects," *International Journal of Project Management* (June 1996).

Berg, P. "Making Affordable Housing Attainable Through Modern Project Management," *PM Network* (August 1994).

Burke, R. *Project Management: Planning and Control,* 2nd ed. John Wiley, 1992.

Christopher, W. *Management Master Series, Set 2: Total Quality.* Productivity Press, 1995.

Cleland, D. *Project Management: Strategic Design and Implementation,* 2nd ed. McGraw Hill, 1994.

Darnall, R. *Achieving TQM on Projects: A Journey of Continuous Improvement.* Project Management Institute, 1994.

Dinsmore, P. *Human Factors in Project Management,* rev. ed. Amacom Books, 1990.

Dinsmore, P. (Ed.). *The AMA Handbook of Project Management.* Amacom Books, 1993.

Fleming, Q., and Koppelman, J. *Earned Value Project Management Systems.* Project Management Institute, 1996.

Gannon, A. "Project Management: An Approach to Accomplishing Things," *Records Management Quarterly* (vol. 28, no. 3, 1994).

Ireland, L. *Quality Management for Projects and Programs.* Project Management Institute, 1991.

Jiang, J., Klein, G., and Balloun, J. "Ranking of System Implementation Success Factors," *Project Management Journal* (December 1996).

Kharbanda, O., and Stallworthy, E. *Lessons from Project Disasters.* MCB University Press, 1992.

Kliem, R. *The Noah Project.* Gower, 1993.

Leavitt, J., and Nunn, P. *Total Quality Through Project Management.* McGraw Hill, 1994.

Lewis, J. *Fundamentals of Project Management.* Amacom Books, 1995.

Meredith, J., and Mantel, S. *Project Management: A Managerial Approach,* 3rd ed. John Wiley, 1995.

Morris, P. *The Management of Projects.* Thomas Telford, 1994.

Munns, A., and Bjeirmi, B. "The Role of Project Management in Achieving Project Success," *International Journal of Project Management* (April 1996).

Newcombe, T. "Turning Fuzzy Ideas into Reality," *Government Technology* (March 1996).

Nicholas, J. *Managing Business and Engineering Projects: Concepts and Implementation.* Prentice Hall, 1990.

Ouellette, T. "Project Management Helps Airline Stick to Schedule," *Computerworld* (November 7, 1994).

Pinto, J. *Successful Information Systems Implementation: The Human Side.* Project Management Institute, 1994.

Pinto, J., and Mantel, S. "The Causes of Project Failure," *IEEE Transactions on Engineering Management,* 1990, pp. 269–276.

Pinto, J., and Slevin, D. "Critical Factors in Successful Project Implementation," *IEEE Transactions on Engineering Management,* 1987, pp. 22–27.

Pinto, J., and Slevin, D. "Critical Success Factors Across the Project Life Cycle," *Project Management Journal* (vol. 19, no. 3, 1988).

Pinto, J., and Slevin, D. *Project Implementation Profile.* Xicom, 1992.

The PMI Standards Committee. *Guide to the Project Management Body of Knowledge (PMBOK).* Project Management Institute, 1995.

Rafferty, J. *Risk Analysis in Project Management.* Chapman & Hall, 1994.

Schuyler, J. *Decision Analysis in Projects.* Project Management Institute, 1996.

Shtub, A., Bard, J., and Globerson, S. *Project Management: Engineering, Technology, and Implementation.* Prentice Hall, 1994.

Stuckenbruck, L. (Ed.). *The Implementation of Project Management: The Professional's Handbook.* Project Management Institute, 1981.

Woldring, R. "Learning Lessons of Project Management," *Computing Canada* (vol. 22, no. 2, 1996).

Chapter 5

Adams, J., and Campbell, B. *Roles and Responsibilities of the Project Manager.* Project Management Institute, 1982.

Armstrong, M. *How to Be an Even Better Manager,* 3rd ed. Nichols, 1994.

Badawy, M. *Developing Managerial Skills in Engineers and Scientists: Succeeding as a Technical Manager,* 2nd ed. Van Nostrand Reinhold, 1995.

Bentley, T. "Project Management 2: The Skills Needed," *Management Accounting* (April 1992).

Blanchard, C., and Parisi, C. *The One Minute Manager Builds High Performing Teams.* Morrow, 1990.

Blank, W. *The Nine Natural Laws of Leadership.* Amacom Books, 1995.

Bolman, L., and Deal, T. *Leading with Soul: An Uncommon Journey of Spirit.* Jossey-Bass, 1995.

Brinkman, R., and Kirschner, R. *Dealing with People You Can't Stand: Bringing Out the Best in People at Their Worst.* McGraw Hill, 1994.

Christopher, W. *Management Master Series, Set 2: Total Quality.* Productivity Press, 1995.

Davies, J. "Defining the Responsibilities of the Project Manager," *Plant Engineering* (July 1994).

Deep, S., and Sussman, L. *Smart Moves for People in Charge.* Addison-Wesley, 1995.

Dickinson, J. "Leadership in a World of Change," *PM Network* (March 1994).

Dinsmore, P., Martin, M., and Huettel, G. *The Project Manager's Work Environment: Coping with Time and Stress.* Project Management Institute, 1985.

Geddes, M., Hastings, C., and Briner, W. *Project Leadership.* Gower, 1993.

Guzzo, R., and Salas, E. *Team Effectiveness and Decision Making in Organizations.* Jossey-Bass, 1995.

Hildebrand, C. "Loud and Clear," *CIO* (April 15, 1996).

Hutchinson, C. *Vitality and Renewal: A Manager's Guide for the 21st Century.* Praeger, 1995.

Kerzner, H. "The Growth of Modern Project Management," *Project Management Journal* (June 1994).

Kliem, R., and Ludin, I. *The People Side of Project Management.* Gower, 1992.

Kouzes, J., and Posner, B. *Credibility: How Leaders Gain and Lose It, Why People Demand It.* Jossey-Bass, 1993.

Losoncy, L. *The Motivating Team Leader.* St. Lucie Press, 1995.

Maucher, H. *Leadership in Action: Tough-Minded Strategies from the Global Giant.* McGraw Hill, 1994.

Newman, J. *How to Stay Cool, Calm and Collected When the Pressure's On: A Stress-Control Plan for Business People.* Amacom Books, 1992.

Parkin, J. "Organizational Decision Making and the Project Manager," *International Journal of Project Management* (October 1996).

Pedler, M., Boydell, T., and Burgoyne, J. *A Manager's Guide to Self Development,* 3rd ed. McGraw Hill, 1994.

Peters, L., and Homer, J. "Learning to Lead, to Create Quality, to Influence Change in Projects," *Project Management Journal* (March 1996).

Pinto, J. *Power and Politics in Project Management.* Project Management Institute, 1996.

Pinto, J., and Kharbanda, O. "Lessons for an Accidental Profession." *Business Horizons* (March–April 1995).

Pinto, J., and Kharbanda, O. *Successful Project Managers: Leading Your Team to Success.* Van Nostrand Reinhold, 1995.

Posner, B. "What It Takes to Be a Good Project Manager," *Project Management Journal* (January 1987).

Price, J., and Valentine, M. "The Leadership Attributes and Strengths of Female Project Managers," *PM Network* (March 1994).

Randolph, W., and Posner, B. "What Every Manager Should Know About Project Management," *Sloan Management Review* (vol. 29, no. 4, 1989).

Rees, D. "The New Leaders," *International Journal of Project Management* (October 1996).

Ruskin, A., and Estes, W. *What Every Engineer Should Know About Project Management,* 2nd ed. Marcel Dekker, 1995.

Salisbury, F. *Developing Managers as Coaches: A Trainer's Guide.* McGraw Hill, 1994.

Stewart, T. "The Corporate Jungle Spawns a New Species: The Project Manager," *Fortune* (July 10, 1995).

Thamhain, H. "Developing Project Management Skills," *Project Management Journal* (September 1991).

Verma, V. *Human Resource Skills for the Project Manager.* Project Management Institute, 1996.

Ward, M. *50 Essential Management Techniques.* Gower, 1995.

Winch, G. "Renaissance of Project Management," *The Financial Times* (August 9, 1996).

Chapter 6

Blake, R. R., and Mouton, J. S. *The Managerial Grid.* Gulf, 1964.

Blanchard, C., and Parisi, C. *The One Minute Manager Builds High Performing Teams.* Morrow, 1990.

Blank, R., and Slipp, S. *Voices of Diversity.* Amacom Books, 1994.

Bowsky, P. "Teamwork Works: Two Tales of Top Teams," *The Journal of Quality and Participation* (September 1996).

Boyle, D. *Secrets of a Successful Employee Recognition System.* Productivity Press, 1995.

Brinkman, R., and Kirschner, R. *Dealing with People You Can't Stand: Bringing Out the Best in People at Their Worst.* McGraw Hill, 1994.

Carroll, B. "The Power of Empowerment Teams," *National Productivity Review* (Autumn 1996).

Couillard, J. "The Role of Project Risk in Determining Project Management Approach: Project Management and Conflict Resolution," *Project Management Journal* (December 1995).

Daniels, A. *Bringing Out the Best in People.* McGraw Hill, 1994.

Dinsmore, P., Martin, M., and Huettel, G. *The Project Manager's Work Environment: Coping with Time and Stress.* Project Management Institute, 1985.

Frame, J. *Managing Projects in Organizations: How to Make the Best Use of Time, Techniques, and People,* 2nd ed. Jossey-Bass, 1995.

Gross, S. *Compensation for Teams: How to Design and Implement Team-Based Reward Programs.* Amacom Books, 1995.

Guzzo, R., and Salas, E. *Team Effectiveness and Decision Making in Organizations.* Jossey-Bass, 1995.

Hupp, T., Polak, C., and Westgaard, O. *Designing Work Groups, Jobs, and Work Flow.* Jossey-Bass, 1995.

Johns, T. "Managing the Behavior of People Working in Teams: Applying the Project-Management Method," *International Journal of Project Management* (February 1995).

Katzenbach, J., and Smith, D. *The Wisdom of Teams: Creating the High-Performance Organization.* McGraw Hill, 1993.

Kezsbom, D. "Making a Team Work: Techniques for Building Successful Teams," *Industrial Engineer* (January 1995).

Kilmann, R. *Conflict Mode Instrument.* Xicom, 1974.

Kinlaw, D. *The Practice of Empowerment.* Gower, 1995.

Kirchof, N., and Adams, J. *Conflict Management for Project Managers.* Project Management Institute, 1982.

Kliem, R., and Ludin, I. *The People Side of Project Management.* Gower, 1992.

Kostner, J., and Strubiak, C. "How to Get Breakthrough Performance with Teamwork," *PM Network* (May 1993).

Lewis, J. *How to Build and Manage a Winning Project Team.* Amacom Books, 1993.

Lews, J. *Project Manager's Desk Reference.* Irwin Professional Publishing, 1993.

Losoncy, L. *The Motivating Team Leader.* St. Lucie Press, 1995.

MacLennan, N. *Coaching and Mentoring.* Gower, 1995.

Mears, P. *Team Building: A Structured Learning Approach.* St. Lucie Press, 1995.

Mohrman, S., Cohen, S., and Mohrman, A. *Designing Team-Based Organizations: New Forms for Knowledge Work.* Jossey-Bass, 1995.

Parker, G. *Parker Team Player Survey.* Xicom, 1991.

Parker, G. *Team Development Survey.* Xicom, 1992.

Pinto, J., and Kharbanda, O. "Project Management and Conflict Resolution," *Project Management Journal* (December 1995).

Pinto, J., and Kharbanda, O. *Successful Project Managers: Leading Your Team to Success.* Van Nostrand Reinhold, 1995.

The PMI Standards Committee. *Guide to the Project Management Body of Knowledge (PMBOK).* Project Management Institute, 1995.

Posner, B. "What's All the Fighting About? Conflicts in Project Management," *IEEE Transactions on Engineering Management,* 1986, pp. 207–211.

Ray, D., and Bronstein, H. *Teaming Up.* McGraw Hill, 1994.

Rees, D. "Managing Cultural Diversity at Work," *International Journal of Project Management* (October 1996).

Robbins, H., and Finley, M. *Why Teams Don't Work: What Went Wrong and How to Make It Right.* Peterson's, 1995.

Rossy, G., and Archibald, R. "Building Commitment in Project Teams," *Project Management Journal* (June 1992).

Rowe, M. "The Trials of Teamwork," *Lodging Hospitality* (February 1996).

Sprague, D., and Greenwell, R. "Project Management: Are Employees Trained to Work in Project Teams?" *Project Management Journal* (March 1992).

Stuckenbruck, L., and Marshall, D. *Team Building for Project Managers.* Project Management Institute, 1985.

Thamhain, H., and Wilemon, D. "Building High Performance Engineering Project Teams," *IEEE Transactions on Engineering Management,* 1987, pp. 130–137.

Thomas, K., and Kilmann, R. *Thomas-Kilmann Conflict Mode.* Xicom, 1974.

Tippett, D., and Peters, J. "Team Building: How Are We Doing?" *Project Management Journal* (December 1995).

Tuckman, B. W. "Developmental Sequence in Small Groups," *Psychological Bulletin* (vol. 63, 1965), pp. 384–399.

Verma, V. *Managing the Project Team.* Project Management Institute, 1996.

Wellins, R., et al. *Empowered Teams: Creating Self-Directed Work Groups That Improve Quality, Productivity, and Participation.* Jossey-Bass, 1993.

Whitten, N. *Becoming an Indispensable Employee in a Disposable World.* The Neal Whitten Group, 1995.

Wilemon, D., and Thamhain, H. "Team Building in Project Management," *Project Management Quarterly* (vol. 14, 1983, pp. 21–33).

Williams, M. "From Zero to Teamwork: A Manufacturing Journey," *Hospital Material Management Quarterly* (February 1996).

Chapter 7

Adams, J., Bilbro, C., and Stockert, T. *An Organization Development Approach to Project Management.* Project Management Institute, 1986.

Anderson, Richard E. "Matrix Redux," *Business Horizons* (November–December 1994).

Cable, D., and Adams, J. *Organizing for Project Management.* Project Management Institute, 1982.

Cleland, D., and King, W. (Eds.). *Project Management Handbook,* 2nd ed. Van Nostrand Reinhold, 1988.

Connor, P., and Lake, L. *Managing Organizational Change,* 2nd ed. Praeger, 1994.

Dangot-Simpkin, G. "Making Matrix Management a Success," *Supervisory Management* (November 1991).

Frame, J. *Managing Projects in Organizations: How to Make the Best Use of Time, Techniques, and People,* 2nd ed. Jossey-Bass, 1995.

Galbraith, J. *Designing Organizations: An Executive Briefing on Strategy, Structure, and Process.* Jossey-Bass, 1995.

Gogin, William C. "How the Multidimensional Structure Works at Dow Corning," *Harvard Business Review* (January–February 1974).

Huddleston, K. *Back on the Quality Track: How Organizations Derailed and Recovered.* Amacom Books, 1995.

Johann, B. *Designing Cross-Functional Business Processes.* Jossey-Bass, 1995.

Katzenbach, J., and Smith, D. *The Wisdom of Teams:*

Creating the High-Performance Organization. McGraw Hill, 1993.

Larson, E., and Gobeli, D. "Significance of Project Management Structure on Development Success," *IEEE Transactions on Engineering Management,* 1989, pp. 119–125.

Levine, H. "The Future of Project Management: Implications for Organizations, Practices and Tools," *PM Network* (May 1994).

Martinsons, A. "In Search of Structural Excellence," *Leadership & Organization Development Journal* (March 1994).

McCollum, J., and Sherman, J. "The Matrix Structure: Bane or Benefit to High Tech Organizations?" *Project Management Journal* (June 1993).

Mohrman, S., Cohen, S., and Mohrman, A. *Designing Team-Based Organizations: New Forms for Knowledge Work.* Jossey-Bass, 1995.

Parkin, J. "Organizational Decision Making and the Project Manager," *International Journal of Project Management* (October 1996).

Partington, D. "The Project Management of Organizational Change," *International Journal of Project Management* (February 1996).

Payne, H. "Introducing Formal Project Management into a Traditionally Structured Organization," *International Journal of Project Management* (November 1993).

The PMI Standards Committee. *Guide to the Project Management Body of Knowledge (PMBOK).* Project Management Institute, 1995.

The Price Waterhouse Change Integration Team. *Better Change: Best Practices for Transforming Your Organization.* Irwin Professional Publishing, 1995.

Smith, D. *Taking Charge of Change: Ten Principles for Managing Today's Most Urgent Organizational Challenge.* Addison-Wesley, 1995.

Teplitz, C., and Worley, C. "Project Managers Are Gaining Power Within Matrix Organizations," *PM Network* (February 1992).

Turner, J., and Peymai, R. "Process Management in the Versatile Approach to Achieving Quality in Project Based Organizations," *Journal of General Management* (Autumn 1995).

Turner, R. *Handbook of Project-Based Management.* McGraw Hill, 1993.

Verma, V. *Organizing Projects for Success.* Project Management Institute, 1995.

Yuval, A. "The Matrix Approach to Information System Development," *Computers in Industry* (June 1996).

Chapter 8

Acuff, F. *How to Negotiate with Anyone Anywhere Around the World.* Amacom Books, 1994.

Alessandra, A., and Hunsaker, P. *Communicating at Work.* Simon & Schuster, 1993.

Barakat, R. "Writing to Win New Business," *PM Network* (November 1991).

Bentley, T. "Project Management 2: The Skills Needed," *Management Accounting* (April 1992).

Blake, R. *Quick Tips for Better Business Writing.* McGraw Hill, 1995.

Blank, R., and Slipp, S. *Voices of Diversity.* Amacom Books, 1994.

Booher, D. *Communicate with Confidence! How to Say It Right the First Time and Every Time.* McGraw Hill, 1994.

Burley-Allen, M. *Listening—The Forgotten Skill.* John Wiley, 1982.

Drummond, H. "Talking and Listening," *International Journal of Bank Marketing* (October 1993).

Dupre, L. *Bugs in Writing.* Addison-Wesley, 1995.

Glaser, R. "Good Communication Aids Project Success," *PM Network* (May 1994).

Hildebrand, C. "Loud and Clear," *CIO* (April 15, 1996).

Huyler, G., and Crosby, K. "The Best Investment a Project Manager Can Make . . . Improve Meetings!" *PM Network* (June 1993).

Juliano, W. "External Communication as an Integral Part of Project Planning," *PM Network* (February 1995).

Kurtz, P. *The Global Speaker: An English Speaker's Guide to Making Presentations Around the World.* Amacom Books, 1995.

Mauss, S. "Communication: The Key to Effective Project Management," *PM Network* (August 1993).

Miller, M. "The Great Communicator," *PM Network* (February 1995).

O'Brian, J. "How You Say It Does Make a Difference," *Supervisory Management* (April 1994).

Ramsey, R. "The Role of Communication in Global Business," *Bulletin of the Association for Business Communication* (March 1994).

Rees, D. "Managing Cultural Diversity at Work," *International Journal of Project Management* (October 1996).

Tepper, R. *The Only 250 Letters and Memos Managers Will Ever Need*. John Wiley, 1993.

The 3M Meeting Management Team. *Mastering Meetings: Discovering the Hidden Potential of Effective Business Meetings*. McGraw Hill, 1994.

Tittel, E., and Robbins, M. *E-Mail Essentials*. Academic Press, 1994.

Chapter 9

Andersen, E. "Warning: Activity Planning Is Hazardous to Your Project's Health!" *International Journal of Project Management* (April 1996).

Archibald, R. *Managing High-Technology Programs and Projects,* 2nd ed. John Wiley, 1992.

Belanger, T. *How to Plan Any Project: A Guide for Teams and Individuals,* 2nd ed. Sterling Planning Group, 1995.

Burke, R. *Project Management: Planning and Control,* 2nd ed. John Wiley, 1992.

Burton, C., and Michael, N. *A Practical Guide to Project Planning*. Nichols, 1994.

Cable, D., and Adams, J. *Organizing for Project Management*. Project Management Institute, 1982.

Chatzoglou, P., and Macaulay, L. "A Review of Existing Models for Project Planning and Estimation and the Need for a New Approach," *International Journal of Project Management* (June 1996).

Davies, J. "Planning for a Successful Project," *Plant Engineering* (September 1995).

Down, A., Coleman, M., and Absolan, P. *Risk Management for Software Projects*. McGraw Hill, 1994.

Gido, J. *An Introduction to Project Planning,* 2nd ed. Industrial Press, 1985.

Goodman, L. *Project Planning and Management: An Integrated System for Improving Productivity*. Chapman & Hall, 1988.

Harrell, W. "Breaking the Communication Barrier with a WBS," *PM Network* (August 1994).

Jensen, C. "Effective Project Planning Techniques," *Civil Engineering* (February 1994).

Juliano, W. "External Communication as an Integral Part of Project Planning," *PM Network* (February 1995).

Kelley, R. *Planning Techniques: Basic and Advanced*. Kel-

ley Communication Development, 1988.

Kempfer, L. "Planning for Success," *Computer-Aided Engineering* (vol. 13, no. 4, 1994).

Kerzner, H. *Project Management: A Systems Approach to Planning, Scheduling, and Controlling,* 5th ed. Van Nostrand Reinhold, 1994.

Knutson, J., and Bitz, I. *Project Management: How to Plan and Manage a Successful Project*. Amacom Books, 1991.

Levine, H. "The Future of Project Management: Implications for Organizations, Practices and Tools," *PM Network* (May 1994).

Levine, H. "Project Planning Methods and Tools for Manufacturing," *PM Network* (August 1995).

Lewis, J. *Project Planning, Scheduling and Control,* rev. ed. Irwin Professional Publishing, 1995.

Luby, R., Peel, D., and Swahl, W. "Component-Based Work Breakdown Structure," *Project Management Journal* (December 1995).

Mar, W. "New Paradigms for Project Plans," *PM Network* (June 1993).

Mars, L. "If It's Not Scheduled . . . It's Not Going to Happen," *PM Network* (October 1993).

Miller, D. *Visual Project Planning and Scheduling: A Personal Approach to Project Management*. The 15th Street Press, 1994.

Moder, J., Phillips, C., and Davis, E. *Project Management with CPM, PERT and Precedence Diagramming,* 3rd ed. Blitz, 1995.

The PMI Standards Committee. *Guide to the Project Management Body of Knowledge (PMBOK)*. Project Management Institute, 1995.

Reiss, G. *Project Management Demystified: Today's Tools and Techniques*. Chapman & Hall, 1995.

Rolstadas, A. "Planning and Control of Concurrent Engineering Projects," *International Journal of Production Economics* (March 1995).

Smith, A. "A Personal Philosophy of Planning," *PM Network* (June 1995).

Tulip, A. Book review. "Project Management Demystified: Today's Tools and Techniques," *International Journal of Project Management* (October 1996).

Vandersluis, C. "Poor Planning Can Sabotage Implementation," *Computing Canada* (May 25, 1994).

Williams, P. *Getting a Project Done on Time: Managing*

People, Time and Results. Amacom Books, 1995.

Youker, R. "A Look at the WBS: Project Work Breakdown Structure," *PM Network* (November 1991).

Chapter 10

Burke, R. *Project Management: Planning and Control,* 2nd ed. John Wiley, 1992.

Burton, C., and Michael, N. *A Practical Guide to Project Planning.* Nichols, 1994.

Davies, J. "Planning for a Successful Project," *Plant Engineering* (September 1995).

Gannon, A. "Project Management: An Approach to Accomplishing Things," *Records Management Quarterly* (vol. 28, no. 3, 1994).

Gido, J. *An Introduction to Project Planning,* 2nd ed. Industrial Press, 1985.

Jaafari, A. "Time and Priority Allocation Scheduling Technique for Projects," *International Journal of Project Management* (October 1996).

Jensen, C. "Effective Project Planning Techniques," *Civil Engineering* (February 1994).

Kelley, R. *Planning Techniques: Basic and Advanced.* Kelley Communication Development, 1988.

Kerzner, H. *Project Management: A Systems Approach to Planning, Scheduling, and Controlling,* 5th ed. Van Nostrand Reinhold, 1994.

Knutson, J., and Bitz, I. *Project Management: How to Plan and Manage a Successful Project.* Amacom Books, 1991.

Levine, H. "Project Planning Methods and Tools for Manufacturing," *PM Network* (August 1995).

Lewis, J. *Project Planning, Scheduling and Control,* rev. ed. Irwin Professional Publishing, 1995.

Mar, W. "New Paradigms for Project Plans," *PM Network* (June 1993).

Mars, L. "If It's Not Scheduled . . . It's Not Going to Happen," *PM Network* (October 1993).

Matthews, M. "Resource Scheduling: Incorporating Capacity into Schedule Construction," *Project Management Journal* (June 1994).

McSpedon, E. "Los Angeles Metro Rail: A World-Class Rail System," *PM Network* (January 1994).

Miller, D. *Visual Project Planning and Scheduling: A Personal Approach to Project Management.* The 15th Street Press, 1994.

Moder, J., Phillips, C., and Davis, E. *Project Management with CPM, PERT and Precedence Diagramming,* 3rd ed. Blitz, 1995.

Ouellette, T. "Project Management Helps Airline Stick to Schedule," *Computerworld* (November 7, 1994).

Parr, W. "Main Pass Mine: A World-Class Sulphur, Oil, and Gas Mining Project," *PM Network* (June 1994).

Reiss, G. *Project Management Demystified: Today's Tools and Techniques.* Chapman & Hall, 1995.

Rolstadas, A. "Planning and Control of Concurrent Engineering Projects," *International Journal of Production Economics* (March 1995).

Smith, A. "A Personal Philosophy of Planning," *PM Network* (June 1995).

Taspinar, A. "Building the Tomb of the Late Turkish President Turgut Ozal," *PM Network* (April 1994).

Tulip, A. Book review. "Project Management Demystified: Today's Tools and Techniques," *International Journal of Project Management* (October 1996).

Vandersluis, C. "Poor Planning Can Sabotage Implementation," *Computing Canada* (May 25, 1994).

Williams, P. *Getting a Project Done on Time: Managing People, Time and Results.* Amacom Books, 1995.

Chapter 11

Babu, A., and Suresh, N. "Project Management with Time, Cost, and Quality Considerations," *European Journal of Operational Research* (January 1996).

Burke, R. *Project Management: Planning and Control,* 2nd ed. John Wiley, 1992.

Christensen, D. "A Review of Cost/Schedule Control Systems Criteria Literature," *Project Management Journal* (September 1994).

Gido, J. *An Introduction to Project Planning,* 2nd ed. Industrial Press, 1985.

Jaafari, A. "Time and Priority Allocation Scheduling Technique for Projects," *International Journal of Project Management* (October 1996).

Kerzner, H. *Project Management: A Systems Approach to Planning, Scheduling, and Controlling,* 5th ed. Van Nostrand Reinhold, 1994.

Knutson, J., and Bitz, I. *Project Management: How to Plan*

and Manage a Successful Project. Amacom Books, 1991.

Levine, H. "Project Planning Methods and Tools for Manufacturing," *PM Network* (August 1995).

Lewis, J. *Project Planning, Scheduling and Control,* rev. ed. Irwin Professional Publishing, 1995.

MacLeod, K., and Petersen, P. "Estimating the Tradeoff Between Resource Allocation and Probability of On-Time Completion in Project Management," *Project Management Journal* (March 1996).

Matthews, M. "Resource Scheduling: Incorporating Capacity into Schedule Construction," *Project Management Journal* (June 1994).

Miller, D. *Visual Project Planning and Scheduling: A Personal Approach to Project Management.* The 15th Street Press, 1994.

Moder, J., Phillips, C., and Davis, E. *Project Management with CPM, PERT and Precedence Diagramming,* 3rd ed. Blitz, 1995.

Pinto, J., and Slevin, D. "Critical Success Factors Across the Project Life Cycle," *Project Management Journal* (vol. 19, no. 3, 1988).

Rolstadas, A. "Planning and Control of Concurrent Engineering Projects," *International Journal of Production Economics* (March 1995).

Sigurdsen, A. "Project Control: Why Do Budget Overruns Occur?" *PM Network* (April 1995).

Sunde, L., and Lichtenberg, S. "Net-Present-Value Cost/Time Tradeoff," *International Journal of Project Management* (February 1995).

Thamhain, H. "Best Practices for Controlling Technology-Based Projects," *Project Management Journal* (December 1996).

Tulip, A. Book review. "Project Management Demystified: Today's Tools and Techniques," *International Journal of Project Management* (October 1996).

Ward, J. "Productivity Through Project Management: Controlling the Project Variables," *Information Systems Management* (Winter 1994).

Chapter 12

Christensen, D. "A Review of Cost/Schedule Control Systems Criteria Literature," *Project Management Journal* (September 1994).

Gannon, A. "Project Management: An Approach to Accomplishing Things," *Records Management Quarterly* (vol. 28, no. 3, 1994).

Gido, J. *An Introduction to Project Planning,* 2nd ed. Industrial Press, 1985.

Goodman, L. *Project Planning and Management: An Integrated System for Improving Productivity.* Chapman & Hall, 1988.

Jaafari, A. "Time and Priority Allocation Scheduling Technique for Projects," *International Journal of Project Management* (October 1996).

Kerzner, H. *Project Management: A Systems Approach to Planning, Scheduling, and Controlling,* 5th ed. Van Nostrand Reinhold, 1994.

Knutson, J., and Bitz, I. *Project Management: How to Plan and Manage a Successful Project.* Amacom Books, 1991.

Levine, H. "The Future of Project Management: Implications for Organizations, Practices and Tools," *PM Network* (May 1994).

Levine, H. "Project Planning Methods and Tools for Manufacturing," *PM Network* (August 1995).

Levine, H. "Resource Leveling and Roulette: Games of Chance," *PM Network* (April 1994).

Levine, H. "Resource Leveling and Roulette: Games of Chance—Part 2," *PM Network* (July 1994).

Lewis, J. *Project Planning, Scheduling and Control,* rev. ed. Irwin Professional Publishing, 1995.

MacLeod, K., and Petersen, P. "Estimating the Tradeoff Between Resource Allocation and Probability of On-Time Completion in Project Management," *Project Management Journal* (March 1996).

Matthews, M. "Resource Scheduling: Incorporating Capacity into Schedule Construction," *Project Management Journal* (June 1994).

Meredith, J., and Mantel, S. *Project Management: A Managerial Approach,* 3rd ed. John Wiley, 1995.

Miller, R. "Marshal Your Resources with Project Management Software," *Today's Office* (vol. 24, no. 8, 1990).

Moder, J., Phillips, C., and Davis, E. *Project Management with CPM, PERT and Precedence Diagramming,* 3rd ed. Blitz, 1995.

Raz, T., and Marshall, B. "Effect of Resource Constraints on Float Calculations in Project Networks," *International Journal of Project Management* (August 1996).

Reiss, G. *Project Management Demystified: Today's Tools and Techniques.* Chapman & Hall, 1995.

Rolstadas, A. "Planning and Control of Concurrent Engineering Projects," *International Journal of Production Economics* (March 1995).

Sigurdsen, A. "Project Control: Why Do Budget Over-runs Occur?" *PM Network* (April 1995).

Thamhain, H. "Best Practices for Controlling Technology-Based Projects," *Project Management Journal* (December 1996).

Tulip, A. Book review. "Project Management Demystified: Today's Tools and Techniques," *International Journal of Project Management* (October 1996).

Chapter 13

Babu, A., and Suresh, N. "Project Management with Time, Cost, and Quality Considerations," *European Journal of Operational Research* (January 1996).

Christensen, D. "A Review of Cost/Schedule Control Systems Criteria Literature," *Project Management Journal* (September 1994).

Kimmons, R. *Project Management Basics: A Step by Step Approach.* Marcel Dekker, 1990.

King, N. "On Time and On Budget," *PC Magazine* (April 11, 1995).

Levine, H. "Project Planning Methods and Tools for Manufacturing," *PM Network* (August 1995).

Lewis, J. *Project Planning, Scheduling and Control,* rev. ed. Irwin Professional Publishing, 1995.

Lock, D. *Project Management Handbook.* Gower, 1987.

MacLeod, K., and Petersen, P. "Estimating the Tradeoff Between Resource Allocation and Probability of On-Time Completion in Project Management," *Project Management Journal* (March 1996).

Matthews, M. "Resource Scheduling: Incorporating Capacity into Schedule Construction," *Project Management Journal* (June 1994).

Meredith, J., and Mantel, S. *Project Management: A Managerial Approach,* 3rd ed. John Wiley, 1995.

Moder, J., Phillips, C., and Davis, E. *Project Management with CPM, PERT and Precedence Diagramming,* 3rd ed. Blitz, 1995.

The PMI Standards Committee. *Guide to the Project Management Body of Knowledge (PMBOK).* Project Management Institute, 1995.

Rafferty, J. *Risk Analysis in Project Management.* Chapman & Hall, 1994.

Reiss, G. *Project Management Demystified: Today's Tools and Techniques.* Chapman & Hall, 1995.

Riggs, H. *Financial and Cost Analysis for Engineering and Technology Management.* John Wiley, 1994.

Rolstadas, A. "Planning and Control of Concurrent Engineering Projects," *International Journal of Production Economics* (March 1995).

Scotto, M. "Project Budgeting: The Key to Bringing Business Projects in On Time and On Budget," *Project Management Journal* (March 1994).

Sigurdsen, A. "Project Control: Why Do Budget Over-runs Occur?" *PM Network* (April 1995).

Stewart, R., Wyskida, R., and Johannes, J. (Eds.). *Cost Estimator's Reference Manual,* 2nd ed. John Wiley, 1995.

Sunde, L., and Lichtenberg, S. "Net-Present-Value Cost/Time Tradeoff," *International Journal of Project Management* (February 1995).

Thamhain, H. "Best Practices for Controlling Technology-Based Projects," *Project Management Journal* (December 1996).

Tulip, A. Book review. "Project Management Demystified: Today's Tools and Techniques," *International Journal of Project Management* (October 1996).

Wipper, L. "Oregon Department of Transportation Steers Improvement with Performance Measurement," *National Productivity Review* (vol. 13, no. 3, 1994).

Appendix A

Archibald, R. *Managing High-Technology Programs and Projects,* 2nd ed. John Wiley, 1992.

Badiru, A. *Project Management in Manufacturing and High Technology Operations.* John Wiley, 1988.

Buckholtz, T. *Information Proficiency: Your Key to the Information Age.* Van Nostrand Reinhold, 1995.

Carey, T. "Take It to the Limit: High-End Project Management Software," *PC Magazine* (April 11, 1995).

Down, A., Coleman, M., and Absolan, P. *Risk Management for Software Projects.* McGraw Hill, 1994.

Ford, R., and McLaughlin, F. "Ten Questions and Answers on Managing MIS Projects," *Project Management Journal* (September 1992).

Frame, J. *The New Project Management: Tools for an Age of Rapid Change, Corporate Reengineering, and Other Business Realities.* Jossey-Bass, 1994.

Heindel, L., and Kasten, V. "Next Generation PC-Based Project Management Systems: Implementation Considerations," *International Journal of Project Management* (October 1996).

Heindel, L., and Kasten, V. "Next Generation PC-Based

Project Management Systems: The Path Forward," *International Journal of Project Management* (August 1996).

King, N. "On Time and On Budget," *PC Magazine* (April 11, 1995).

Levine, H. "One More Time: How to Choose Project Management Software," *PM Network* (July 1991).

Levine, H. "Using Project Management Software: A Reality Check," *PM Network* (April 1995).

Logical Operations Corp. *Microsoft Project for Windows: Advanced, Training Manual.* 1996.

Logical Operations Corp. *Microsoft Project for Windows: Introduction, Training Manual.* 1996.

Lowery, G. *Managing Projects with Microsoft Project: Version 4.0 for Windows and the Macintosh,* 3rd ed. Van Nostrand Reinhold, 1994.

Meredith, J., and Mantel, S. *Project Management: A Managerial Approach,* 3rd ed. John Wiley, 1995.

Miller, R. "Marshal Your Resources with Project Management Software," *Today's Office* (vol. 24, no. 8, 1990).

Nicholas, J. *Managing Business and Engineering Projects: Concepts and Implementation.* Prentice Hall, 1990.

Shtub, A., Bard, J., and Globerson, S. *Project Management: Engineering, Technology, and Implementation.* Prentice Hall, 1994.

Waterridge, J. "IT Projects: A Basis for Success," *International Journal of Project Management* (June 1995).

Whitten, N. *Managing Software Development Projects,* 2nd ed. John Wiley, 1994.

Woldring, R. "Learning Lessons of Project Management," *Computing Canada* (vol. 22, no. 2, 1996).

REINFORCE YOUR LEARNING ANSWERS

Chapter 1

1. What are some attributes of a project?
   - A well-defined objective
   - Interdependent tasks
   - Use of various resources
   - A specific time frame
   - A unique or one-time endeavor
   - A customer
   - Degree of uncertainty

3. What are four factors that constrain the achievement of a project objective?
   - Scope
   - Cost
   - Schedule
   - Customer satisfaction

4. Match the phases of the project life cycle, in the column on the left, with the descriptions, in the column on the right:

C	First phase	A. Developing the proposed solution
A	Second phase	B. Implementing the proposed solution
B	Third phase	C. Identifying the need or problem
D	Fourth phase	D. Terminating the project

5. The front-end effort of managing a project involves establishing a *baseline plan*.

6. Implementing the baseline plan for a project involves *performing* the work according to the plan and *controlling* the work so that the project scope is achieved within the *budget* and *schedule*.

Chapter 2

1. The initial phase of the project life cycle is *needs identification*. It starts with the recognition of a need or opportunity and ends with the issuance of a *request for proposal*.

2. What is the purpose of a request for proposal?
An RFP states, comprehensively and in detail, what is required, from the customer's point of view, to address the identified need.

3. What are some elements that may be included in a request for proposal?
   - Statement of work
   - Customer requirements
   - Deliverables
   - Customer-supplied items
   - Approvals required
   - Type of contract
   - Payment terms
   - Required schedule
   - Instructions for the format and content of contractor proposals
   - Due date
   - Proposal evaluation criteria
   - Funds available

Chapter 3

1. What is the outcome of a successful pre-RFP/proposal marketing effort?
The outcome is eventually winning a contract from the customer to perform the project.

2. What are some factors that a contractor should consider when deciding whether to respond to an RFP?
   - Competition
   - Risk
   - Consistency with business mission
   - Opportunity to extend and enhance capabilities
   - Reputation with the customer
   - Availability of customer funds
   - Availability of resources to prepare a quality proposal
   - Availability of resources to perform the project

3. The proposal process is a *competitive* process. A proposal is a *selling* document.

4. A proposal should address three topics or contain three sections. What are they?
   - Technical section
   - Management section
   - Cost section

5. What is the objective of the technical section of a proposal?
The objective is to convince the customer that the contractor understands the need or problem and can provide the least risky and most beneficial solution.

6. What is the objective of the management section of a proposal?
The objective is to convince the customer that the contractor can do the proposed work and achieve the intended results.

7. What is the objective of the cost section of a proposal?
The objective is to convince the customer that the contractor's price for the proposed project is realistic and reasonable.

8. What elements might each of the three sections of a proposal contain?
Technical section
   • Understanding of the problem
   • Proposed approach or solution
   • Benefits to the customer
Management section
   • Description of work tasks
   • Deliverables
   • Project schedule
   • Project organization
   • Related experience
   • Equipment and facilities
Cost section
   • Labor
   • Materials
   • Subcontractors and consultants
   • Equipment and facilities rental
   • Travel
   • Documentation
   • Overhead or indirect costs
   • Escalation
   • Contingency or management reserve
   • Fee or profit

9. What are some items a contractor needs to consider when determining a price for a proposed project?
   • Reliability of the cost estimates
   • Risk
   • Value of the project to the contractor
   • Customer's budget
   • Competition

10. Write the word *low* or *high* in each box, depending on the degree of risk for the customer and contractor associated with each type of contract.

	Customer	**Contractor**
Fixed price	*Low*	*High*
Cost reimbursement	*High*	*Low*

Chapter 4

1. What are the two parts of the project phase of the life cycle?
The two parts are planning and then implementing the plan to accomplish the project objective.

2. The first part of the project phase of the life cycle involves establishing a *baseline plan*.

3. What are the two kinds of data or information that need to be collected during each reporting period?
   • Data on actual performance
   • Information on any changes to the project scope, schedule, and budget

4. In addition to establishing a baseline plan, it is also necessary to proactively *control* the project to ensure that the project *objective* is achieved and the customer is *satisfied*.

5. What is the purpose of properly terminating a project?
The purpose is to learn from the experience in order to improve the performance on future projects.

6. What are the two types of internal post-project evaluation meetings the project manager should have?
   • An individual meeting with each team member
   • A group meeting with the entire project team

7. List three reasons to have a post-project evaluation meeting with the customer.
   • To determine whether the project provided the customer with the anticipated benefits
   • To assess the level of customer satisfaction
   • To obtain feedback

8. For a contractor, what are two potential consequences of having a project terminated early by a dissatisfied customer?
   • The contractor may suffer a financial loss.
   • The contractor's reputation will be tarnished.

Chapter 5

1. What two benefits does the project manager realize by involving the team in developing the plan?
The project manager assures a more comprehensive plan and gains the commitment of the team to achieve the plan.

2. The project manager secures the *appropriate resources* to perform the work and then assigns *responsibility* and delegates *authority* to specific individuals for the various tasks.

3. The project manager implements a project management information system to serve what two functions?
The two functions are to track actual progress and compare it with planned progress.

4. The project manager has primary responsibility for providing leadership for what three management functions?
   • Planning
   • Organizing
   • Controlling

5. Project leadership involves *inspiring* the people assigned to the project to work as a team to successfully implement the *plan* and achieve the *project objective*.

6. Project leadership requires *involvement* and *empowerment* of the project team.

7. The capable project manager understands what *motivates* team members and creates a *supportive* environment in which individuals work as part of a high-performing team.

8. People want to feel that they are making a *contribution* to the project and need to be *recognized*.

9. A project manager sets the tone for the project team by establishing an environment of *trust,* high *expectations,* and *enjoyment*.

10. People working on projects look for *affiliation* and *socialization;* they don't want to work in *isolation*.

11. Leadership requires that the project manager be highly *motivated* and set a *positive example* for the project team.

12. A good project manager believes that all individuals are *valuable* to the organization and that they can make greater contributions through *continuous learning*.

13. Rather than create a fear of *failure,* the project manager acknowledges that mistakes are part of the *learning* and *growth* experience.

14. A good project manager values and expects continuous *self-improvement*.

15. List five reasons it is important for the project manager to have frequent communication.
   • To keep the project moving
   • To identify potential problems
   • To solicit suggestions for improving project performance
   • To keep abreast of customer satisfaction
   • To avoid surprises

16. A high level of communication is especially important early in the project to help build a good *working relationship* with the project team and to establish clear *expectations* with the customer.

17. What are three ways in which a project manager communicates?
   • Meetings
   • Informal conversations
   • Written reports

18. Good project managers spend more time *listening* than *talking*.

19. Give three reasons the project manager should establish ongoing communication with the customer.
   • To keep the customer informed
   • To determine whether there are any changes in expectations
   • To keep abreast of the degree of customer satisfaction

20. Why does communication by project managers need to be timely, honest, and unambiguous?
Such communication establishes credibility, builds trust, and prevents rumors.

21. The project manager should have an informal *conversation* with each person on the project team and with each key individual in the *customer* organization.

22. The project manager should use *open-ended* questions and do a lot of *listening*.

23. The project manager needs to have a good sense of *humor* and needs to stay *physically* fit.

24. In solving problems, the project manager needs to be able to see the *big picture* and how potential solutions might affect other parts of the project.

25. What skills do effective project managers have?
  - Leadership ability
  - Ability to develop people
  - Communication skills
  - Interpersonal skills
  - Ability to handle stress
  - Problem-solving skills
  - Time management skills

27. Delegation involves *empowering* the project team to achieve the *project objective* and each team member to accomplish the *expected results* for his or her area of responsibility.

28. Project managers should not tell individuals *how* to do the assigned tasks.

29. When assigning individuals to specific tasks, the project manager needs to take into consideration the person's *capabilities, potential,* and *workload.*

30. Effective delegation requires that the project manager have *confidence* in each member of the project team.

31. Delegation requires that individuals be *accountable* for achieving the expected results.

32. Changes may be initiated by the *customer* or by the *project team* or may be caused by *unanticipated occurrences* during the performance of the project.

33. The project manager's job is to *manage* and *control* changes in order to *minimize* any negative impact on the successful accomplishment of the project objective.

34. At the start of the project, the project manager needs to establish *procedures* regarding how changes will be *documented* and *authorized.*

Chapter 6

1. A team is a group of individuals working *interdependently* to achieve a common *goal.*

2. Teamwork is a *cooperative* effort by members of a team to achieve a common goal.

3. During the forming stage, little actual work is accomplished because of the *high* level of anxiety individuals have.

4. In the forming stage, individuals do a lot of *questioning.*

5. During the forming stage, the project manager must provide *direction* and *structure* for the project team.

6. During the storming stage, *conflict* emerges and *tension* increases.

7. During the storming stage, team members wonder how much *control* and *authority* they have.

8. During the storming stage, the project manager needs to provide *guidance* and foster *conflict resolution.*

9. In the norming stage, *conflict* and *dissatisfaction* are reduced, *cohesion* begins to develop, and there is a sense of *team*.

10. During the norming stage, *trust* begins to develop. There is a greater sharing of *information, ideas,* and *feelings; cooperation* increases.

11. In the norming stage, *work performance* accelerates and *productivity* increases.

12. During the performing stage, there is a great degree of *interdependency*—members frequently *collaborate* and willingly *help* each other with work beyond their own assigned tasks.

13. During the performing stage, the project manager fully *delegates* responsibility and authority, thereby empowering the project team.

14. What are the four stages of team development and growth?
- Forming
- Storming
- Norming
- Performing

15. An effective project team has a clear *understanding* of the *project objective* and clear expectations of each person's *role* and *responsibilities*.

16. Effective project teams have a *results* orientation; each person has a strong commitment to achieving the *project objective*. There is a high degree of *cooperation* and *collaboration*.

17. Effective project teams have a high level of *trust*. They are able to resolve conflict through constructive and timely *feedback* and positive *confrontation* of the issues.

18. The project manager needs to articulate the project *objective* frequently. At periodic meetings, he or she should always ask whether anyone has any *questions* about what must be accomplished.

19. The project manager should meet individually with each team member, to tell the member why she or he was *selected* for the project and describe her or his expected *role* and *responsibilities*.

20. The project manager needs to establish preliminary operating *procedures* at the beginning of the project, but be open to suggestions for *eliminating* or *streamlining* them when they no longer *contribute* to the effective and efficient performance of the project.

21. The project manager should try to determine what *motivates* each individual and then create a project *environment* where these motivators are available.

22. It's important for the project manager to have regular project *status review* meetings with a published agenda. *Participation* and *questions* should be encouraged during such meetings.

23. A project manager should periodically solicit others' suggestions for improving her or his *leadership* skills.

24. A project team made up of a *small* number of individuals with *long*-term assignments will be more efficient than a project team composed of a *large* number of individuals with *short*-term assignments.

25. What are some barriers to team effectiveness?
    - Unclear goals
    - Unclear definition of roles and responsibilities
    - Lack of project structure
    - Lack of commitment
    - Poor communication
    - Poor leadership
    - Turnover of project team members
    - Dysfunctional behavior

26. Effective team members plan, control, and feel *accountable* for their individual work efforts. They have high *expectations* of themselves.

27. Effective team members *participate* and *communicate*. They are not only problem identifiers, but also *problem solvers*.

29. Team building is the responsibility of both the *project manager* and the *project team*.

30. *Socializing* among team members supports team building. Individual members need to *communicate* with one another frequently.

31. What are common sources of conflict on projects?
    - Work scope
    - Resource assignments
    - Schedule
    - Cost
    - Priorities
    - Organizational issues
    - Personal differences

32. Handled properly, conflict can be *beneficial*.

33. What are five approaches to handling conflict?
    - Avoiding or withdrawing
    - Competing or forcing
    - Accommodating or smoothing
    - Compromising
    - Collaborating, confronting or problem solving

34. What are the nine steps involved in problem solving?
    - Develop a problem statement.
    - Identify potential causes of the problem.
    - Gather data and verify the most likely causes.
    - Identify possible solutions.
    - Evaluate the alternative solutions.
    - Determine the best solution.
    - Revise the project plan.
    - Implement the solution.
    - Determine whether the problem has been solved.

35. In brainstorming, the *quantity* of ideas generated is more important than the *quality* of the ideas.

36. What are some things you can do to effectively manage your time?
    - Identify weekly goals.
    - Make a to-do list each day.
    - Focus on accomplishing your daily to-do list.
    - Control interruptions.

- Learn to say "no."
- Make effective use of waiting time.
- Handle paperwork only once.
- Reward yourself.

Chapter 7

1. The functional organization emphasizes the importance of the contribution of each functional component's *expertise* to the company's products.

2. True or false: In a functional organization, individuals continue to perform their regular functional jobs while they serve part-time on a project task force.
True

3. A company with a functional structure may periodically form project task forces to work on *internal* projects, but will seldom perform projects involving *external* customers.

4. In a project-type organization, all resources are assigned *full-time* to work on a particular project. The project manager has complete *project* and *administrative* authority over the project team.

5. A project-type organization can be cost-*inefficient*.

6. Project-type organization structures are found primarily in companies that are involved in very *large* projects.

7. The matrix organization structure provides the project and customer focus of the *project* structure, but it retains the functional expertise of the *functional* structure.

8. In a matrix organization, the *functional* components provide a pool of *expertise* to support ongoing projects.

9. The matrix organization structure results in effective utilization of *resources* and minimizes overall costs because it allows for the *sharing* of individuals' time among several *projects*.

10. In a matrix-type organization, each member of a *project team* has a dual reporting relationship—to the temporary *project* manager and to a permanent *functional* manager.

11. In a matrix organization, the project manager defines *what* has to be done, by *when,* and for how much *money* to meet the project *objective* and satisfy the customer.

12. In a matrix organization, each functional manager is responsible for *how* the work will be accomplished and *who* will do each task.

13. The matrix organization structure allows for fast response upon problem identification because it has both a *horizontal* and a *vertical* path for the flow of *information.*

14. List three common types of structures that can be used to organize people to work on projects.
- Functional
- Project
- Matrix

15. What are some advantages and disadvantages of the functional organization structure?

Advantages:
  • No duplication of activities
  • Functional excellence

Disadvantages:
  • Insularity
  • Slow response time
  • Lack of customer focus

16. What are some advantages and disadvantages of the project organization structure?

Advantages:
  • Control over resources
  • Responsiveness to customers

Disadvantages:
  • Cost-inefficiency
  • Low level of knowledge transfer among projects

17. What are some advantages and disadvantages of the matrix organization structure?

Advantages:
  • Efficient utilization of resources
  • Functional expertise available to all projects
  • Increased learning and knowledge transfer
  • Responsiveness
  • Customer focus

Disadvantages:
  • Dual reporting relationships
  • Need for balance of power

Chapter 8

1. Identify two types of personal oral communication.
  • Face-to-face communication
  • Telephone conversations

2. Body language can be used not only by the person *talking,* but also by the *listener,* as a way of providing *feedback* to the person talking.

3. In personal communication, people need to be sensitive to body language reflective of the *cultural diversity* of the participants.

4. Project team members need to be *proactive* in initiating timely communication to *get* and *give* information.

5. Identify two methods you can use to generate feedback during oral communication.
  • Ask the other person to state her or his understanding of what you said.
  • Paraphrase what you think the other person said.

6. What are two forms of personal written communication?
  • Internal memos
  • External letters

7. Failure to *listen* can cause a *breakdown* in communication between people.

8. List some common barriers to effective listening.
  • Pretending to listen
  • Distractions

- Bias and closed-mindedness
- Impatience
- Jumping to conclusions

9. What are some things you can do to improve your listening skills?
- Focus on the person talking.
- Engage in active listening.
- Ask questions.
- Don't interrupt.

10. What are the primary purposes of a status review meeting?
- Inform
- Identify problems
- Identify action items

11. True or false: When members of the project team identify problems or potential problems, they should wait until the next scheduled status review meeting to bring them up for discussion.
False; they should immediately initiate a problem-solving meeting with the appropriate team members.

12. On technical projects there are often two design review meetings: a *preliminary* design review meeting and a *final* design review meeting.

13. To ensure that a meeting is effective, what are some steps that the person calling or conducting the meeting should take before the meeting?
- Determine whether a meeting is really necessary.
- Determine the purpose of the meeting.
- Determine who needs to participate.
- Distribute an agenda.
- Prepare visual aids or handouts.
- Make meeting room arrangements.

14. True or false: It's always a good idea to wait for everyone to arrive before starting a meeting, even if it's beyond the scheduled start time.
False; if the meeting leader waits for latecomers, people will get in the habit of showing up late because they know the meeting won't start on time anyway.

15. What are some important things to do in preparing a presentation?
- Determine the purpose of the presentation.
- Know the audience.
- Make an outline.
- Use simple language.
- Prepare notes.
- Practice.
- Prepare visual aids.
- Make copies of handout materials.
- Request audiovisual equipment.
- Go into the meeting room and get a "feel" for the surroundings.

16. What are some important things to keep in mind when delivering a presentation?
- Expect a bit of nervousness.
- Know your opening lines.
- Use the 3-T approach.
- Talk to the audience, not at it.
- Speak clearly and confidently.
- Use appropriate animation.
- Do not stand in front of your visual aids.

- Build interest by developing your story.
- Don't digress.
- State why key points are important to the audience.
- Sum up each point before moving on.
- Know your closing lines.
- Allow time for questions from the audience.
- Be sincere, candid, and confident in responding to questions.

17. Project reports should be written to address what is of interest to the *readers*, not what is of interest to the person *writing* the report.

18. The primary purpose of progress reports is to report on project *accomplishments* rather than what *activities* the project team was busy on.

19. True or false: A project final report is an accumulation of the progress reports prepared during the project.
False; it's a summary of the project.

20. What are some important guidelines to keep in mind when preparing a report?
- Make it concise.
- Write as you would speak.
- Put the most important points first.
- Use graphics.
- Make format inviting and easy to read.

21. Revisions to project documents can result from changes initiated by the *customer* or by the *project team*.

22. Early in the project, agreement should be reached regarding the way changes will be *documented* and *authorized*.

Chapter 9

1. For a project, the objective is usually defined in terms of *scope, schedule,* and *cost*.

3. What is a work breakdown structure?
A work breakdown structure is a hierarchical tree of end items that will be accomplished or produced by the project team during the project.

4. The lowest-level work item for any given branch of the work breakdown structure is called a *work package*.

5. A responsibility matrix shows which individual is responsible for accomplishing each *work item* in the work breakdown structure.

6. Identify two formats for drawing a network diagram.
Activity in the box
Activity on the arrow

7. Activities are linked in a *precedential* order to show which activities must be *finished* before others can be *started*.

8. In the activity-on-the-arrow format for drawing a network diagram, activities are linked together by circles called *events*.

9. Dummy activities are used only when the *activity-on-the-arrow* format is used for drawing a network diagram. Dummy activities are shown using a *dashed arrow.*

10. Refer to Figure 9.8.
    a. When "Prepare Mailing Labels" and "Print Questionnaire" are finished, what activity can be started?
    "Mail Questionnaire & Get Responses"
    b. In order to start "Input Response Data," which activities must have been finished immediately beforehand?
    "Mail Questionnaire & Get Responses" and "Test Software"

11. Refer to Figure 9.9.
    a. In order to start "Test Software," which activities must have been completed immediately beforehand?
    "Develop Data Analysis Software" and "Develop Software Test Data"
    b. True or false: Once "Print Questionnaire" is finished, "Mail Questionnaire & Get Responses" can start immediately.
    False; "Prepare Mailing Labels" must also be finished in order for "Mail Questionnaire" to start.

Chapter 10

1. True or false: The duration estimate for an activity should include the time required to perform the work plus any associated waiting time.
True

2. The overall window of time in which a project must be completed is defined by its *estimated start* time and *required completion* time.

3. What is the equation for calculating an activity's earliest finish time?

$$EF = ES + \text{Duration Estimate}$$

4. The earliest start and earliest finish times for activities are determined by calculating *forward* through the network diagram.

5. Refer to Figures 10.6 and 10.7. What are the earliest start and earliest finish times for "Pilot-Test Questionnaire"?

$$ES = \text{Day } 13, EF = \text{Day } 33$$

6. What determines a particular activity's earliest start time?
It is determined by the latest of all the earliest finish times of all the activities leading directly into that particular activity.

7. What is the equation for calculating an activity's latest start time?

$$LS = LF - \text{Duration Estimate}$$

8. The latest finish and latest start times are determined by calculating *backward* through the network diagram.

9. Refer to Figures 10.10 and 10.11. What are the latest finish and latest start times for "Input Response Data"?

$$LF = \text{Day } 112, LS = \text{Day } 105$$

10. What determines a particular activity's finish time?
It is determined by the earliest of all the latest start times of all the activities emerging directly from that particular activity.

11. When a project has a positive total slack, some activities can be *delayed* without jeopardizing completion of the project by its required completion time. When a project has negative total slack, some activities need to be *accelerated* in order to complete the project by its required completion time.

12. Total slack is the difference between the *latest* time and the *earliest* time.

13. The longest path of activities from the beginning to the end of a project is called the *critical* path.

14. Refer to Figures 10.13 and 10.14. Of the two activities entering into activity 11, "Input Response Data," which activity has free slack? What is its value?

$$\text{Activity 10, "Test Software"; } 50 - (-8) = 58 \text{ days}$$

15. Calculate the expected duration for an activity having the following time estimates: $t_o = 8$, $t_m = 12$, and $t_p = 22$.

$$t_e = \frac{8 + 4(12) + 22}{6} = 13$$

16. Compute the expected duration (t_e) and the variance (σ^2) for the following beta probability distribution.

$$t_e = \frac{5 + 4(8) + 23}{6} = 10$$

$$\sigma^2 = \left(\frac{23 - 5}{6}\right)^2 = 9$$

17. What percentage of the area under this normal curve is shaded?
34 percent

18. If 95 percent of the area under the following normal curve is between the two labeled points, what is the standard deviation? What is the variance? Since there are a total of four standard deviations ($+2$ and -2) between 12 and 32, $4\sigma = 32 - 12 = 20$, and thus $1\sigma = 5$. Variance $= \sigma^2 = (5)^2 = 25$.

Chapter 11

1. What are the two kinds of data or information that need to be collected during each reporting period?
   • Data on actual performance
   • Information on any changes to the project scope, schedule, and budget

2. True or false: In general, it is better to have a shorter reporting period during a project.
True

3. In addition to establishing a sound baseline plan, it is also necessary to proactively *control* the project after it has started in order to assure that the project objective is achieved.

4. What three types of values will the actual finish times of completed activities affect?
The actual finish times will affect the earliest start times and the earliest finish times of the remaining activities and the total slack.

5. What three elements can project changes affect?
Project changes can affect the scope, the budget, and the schedule of the project.

6. In analyzing a project schedule, it is important to identify all the paths of activities that have a *negative* slack.

7. When analyzing a path of activities that has negative slack, what two kinds of activities should you look at carefully?
   • Activities that are in progress or to be started in the immediate future
   • Activities that have long duration estimates

8. List four approaches to reducing the estimated durations of activities.
   • Apply more resources.
   • Assign a person with greater expertise or more experience.
   • Reduce the scope or requirements.
   • Increase productivity through improved methods or technology.

9. What are the normal and crash times and costs for activities B, C, and D in Figure 11.7?

	Normal Time	Normal Cost	Crash Time	Crash Cost
Activity B	9 weeks	$80,000	6 weeks	$110,000
Activity C	10 weeks	$40,000	9 weeks	$45,000
Activity D	8 weeks	$30,000	6 weeks	$42,000

10. What are the cost-per-week rates to accelerate activities B, C, and D in Figure 11.7?
B, $10,000 per week; C, $5,000 per week; D, $6,000 per week

11. If all the activities in Figure 11.7 were performed in their crash times, what would be the total project cost?
$259,000

Chapter 12

1. At a minimum, network diagrams illustrate the *technical* constraints among activities. However, when limited resources are available, the network diagram can also be drawn to reflect *resource* constraints.

2. Resource leveling attempts to establish a schedule in which resource use is made as level as possible without extending the project beyond the *required completion* time.

3. Resource-limited scheduling develops the *shortest* schedule when the number or amount of available resources is fixed. This method will *extend* the project completion time if necessary in order to keep within the *resource* limits.

Chapter 13

1. List the items for which costs should be estimated.
   • Labor
   • Materials
   • Subcontractors and consultants
   • Equipment and facilities rental
   • Travel

2. The first step in the project budgeting process is to allocate the total project costs to each *work package* in the work breakdown structure, thereby establishing a *total budgeted cost* for each work package.

3. Once a total budgeted cost has been established for each work package, the second step in the project budgeting process is to *distribute* each TBC over the *duration* of its work package.

4. The *cumulative budgeted cost* is the amount that was budgeted to accomplish the *work* that was scheduled to be performed up to that point in time.

5. Look at Figures 13.4 and 13.6. How much did the "Design" work package and the "Build" work package each contribute to the $4,000 cost overrun at the end of week 8?

	Amount	Overrun or Underrun?
Design	$ 2,000	*underrun*
Build	$ 6,000	*overrun*

6. Cumulative earned value is calculated by first determining the *percent complete* for each work package and then multiplying it by the *total budgeted cost* for the work package.

7. List the four cost-related measures used to analyze project cost performance.
- TBC   (total budgeted cost)
- CBC   (cumulative budgeted cost)
- CAC   (cumulative actual cost)
- CEV   (cumulative earned value)

8. What is the cost performance index for the "Design" work package in the packaging machine project at the end of week 5?

$$CPI = \frac{\$24,000}{\$22,000} = 1.09$$

9. What is the cost variance for the "Build" work package in the packaging machine project at the end of week 8?

$$CV = \$30,000 - \$46,000 = -\$16,000$$

10. Using the first forecasting method described, calculate the forecasted cost at completion for the "Build" work package in the packaging machine project.

$$FCAC = \frac{\$60,000}{0.65} = \$92,300 \quad (\textit{Note:} \ CPI = \frac{\$30,000}{\$46,000} = 0.65)$$

11. Using the second forecasting method described, calculate the forecasted cost at completion for the "Build" work package in the packaging machine project.

$$FCAC = \$46,000 + (\$60,000 - \$30,000) = \$76,000$$

12. In analyzing cost performance, it's important to identify all of the work packages that have a *negative* cost variance or a cost performance index of less than *1.0*.

13. When evaluating work packages that have a negative cost variance, you should focus on taking corrective actions to reduce the costs of activities that will be performed in the *near* term and those that have a *large* cost estimate.

14. The key to managing cash flow is to ensure that cash *comes in* faster than it *goes out*.

15. If sufficient funds are not available to meet expenses, a contractor may need to *borrow* money. This adds to the cost of the project, because the contractor then has to pay *interest* also.

GLOSSARY

A

Activity   A defined piece of work that consumes time; task.

Activity in the box (AIB)   A form of network diagramming in which activities are represented by boxes.

Activity on the arrow (AOA)   A form of network diagramming in which activities are represented by arrows.

Actual cost   The amount that has actually been expended.

Actual finish time (AF)   The time at which a particular activity is actually completed.

As-late-as-possible (ALAP) schedule   A schedule based on the latest start time of each activity in the project.

As-soon-as-possible (ASAP) schedule   A schedule based on the earliest start time of each activity in the project.

B

Bar chart   *See* Gantt chart.

Baseline plan   The original plan, or roadmap, laying out the way in which the project scope will be accomplished on time and within budget.

Best and final offer (BAFO)   A final price for a project, submitted by a contractor at the request of a customer who is considering proposals from several contractors for the same project.

Beta probability distribution   A distribution that is frequently used to calculate the expected duration and variance for an activity based on the activity's optimistic, most likely, and pessimistic time estimates.

Bid/no-bid decision   An evaluation by a contractor of whether to go ahead with the preparation of a proposal in response to a customer's request for proposal.

C

Commitment   *See* Committed cost.

Committed cost   The funds that are unavailable to be spent elsewhere because they will be needed at some later time to pay for an item, such as material, that has been ordered; commitment; encumbered cost.

Contingency   An amount a contractor may include in a proposal to cover unexpected costs that may arise during a project; management reserve.

Contract   An agreement between a contractor, who agrees to provide a product or service (deliverables), and a customer, who agrees to pay the contractor a certain amount of money in return.

Cost   The amount the customer has agreed to pay for acceptable project deliverables.

Cost performance index (CPI)   A measure of the cost efficiency with which the project is being performed; the cumulative earned value divided by the cumulative actual cost.

Cost reimbursement contract   A contract in which a customer agrees to pay a contractor for all actual costs incurred during a project, plus some agreed-upon profit.

Cost variance (CV)   An indicator of cost performance; the cumulative earned value minus the cumulative actual cost.

Crash cost   The estimated cost of completing an activity in the shortest possible time (the crash time).

Crash time   The shortest estimated length of time in which an activity can be completed.

Critical path   In a network diagram, any path of activities with zero or negative total slack. *See also* Most critical path.

Critical path method (CPM)   A network planning technique.

Cumulative actual cost (CAC)   The amount that has actually been expended to accomplish all the work performed up to a specific point in time.

Cumulative budgeted cost (CBC)   The amount budgeted to accomplish all the work scheduled to be performed up to a specific point in time.

Cumulative earned value (CEV)   The value of the work actually performed up to a specific point in time; total budgeted cost multiplied by the percent of the work estimated to be complete.

Customer   The entity that provides the funds necessary to accomplish a project. A customer may be a person, an organization, or a group of people or organizations.

Customer requirements   Specifications for a project and/or attributes of a deliverable specified by a customer in a request for proposal. Requirements may include size, quantity, color, speed, and other physical or operational parameters that a contractor's proposed solution must satisfy.

D

Deliverables   The tangible items or products that the customer expects the contractor to provide during performance of the project.

Due date   The date, specified in a request for proposal, by which a customer expects potential contractors to submit proposals.

Dummy activity   A special type of activity, used in the activity-on-the-arrow form of network diagramming, that consumes no time. A dummy activity is represented by a dashed arrow.

Duration estimate   The estimated total time an activity will take from start to finish, including associated waiting time; time estimate.

E

Earliest finish time (EF)   The earliest time by which a particular activity can be completed; the activity's earliest start time plus the activity's estimated duration.

Earliest start time (ES)   The earliest time at which a particular activity can begin; the project's estimated start time plus the estimated duration of preceding activities.

Earned value (EV)   The value of the work actually performed.

Encumbered cost   *See* Committed cost.

Estimated start time   The time or date when a project is expected to begin.

Evaluation criteria   The standards, specified in a request for proposal, that a customer will use to evaluate proposals from competing contractors.

Events   Interconnecting points that link activities in the activity-on-the-arrow form of network diagramming. An event is represented by a circle.

Exception   A variation from a customer's specified requirements, stated by a contractor in a proposal.

Expected duration (t_e)   Also called the mean or average duration. The expected duration for an activity, calculated from the activity's optimistic, most likely, and pessimistic time estimates, as follows:

$$t_e = \frac{t_o + 4(t_m) + t_p}{6}$$

F

Finish event   *See* Successor event.

Fixed price contract   A contract in which a customer and a contractor agree on a price that will not change no matter how much the project actually costs the contractor.

Float   *See* Total slack.

Forecasted cost at completion (FCAC)   The projected total cost of all the work required to complete a project.

Free slack (FS)   The amount of time that a particular activity can be delayed without delaying the earliest start time of its immediately succeeding activities; the relative difference between the amounts of total slack for activities entering into that same activity. It's always a positive value.

Functional organization structure   An organizational structure in which groups are made up of individuals who perform the same function, such as engineering or manufacturing, or have the same expertise or skills, such as electronics engineering or testing.

G

Gantt chart   A planning and scheduling tool that displays project activities along a time scale; bar chart.

Graphical evaluation and review technique (GERT) A type of network planning technique.

I

Indirect costs *See* Overhead.

Information system (IS) A computer-based system that accepts data as input, processes the data, and produces information for users.

L

Laddering A method of showing the logical precedential relationship of a set of activities that is repeated several times consecutively.

Latest finish time (LF) The latest time by which a particular activity must be completed in order for the entire project to be finished by its required completion time.

Latest start time (LS) The latest time by which a particular activity must be started in order for the entire project to be finished by its required completion time; the activity's latest finish time minus the activity's estimated duration.

M

Management reserve *See* Contingency.

Matrix organization structure A hybrid of the functional and project organizational structures, in which resources from appropriate functional components of a company are temporarily assigned to particular projects.

Most critical path In a network diagram, the most time-consuming (longest) path of activities; the path of activities that has the lowest value—either least positive or most negative—for total slack.

Most likely time estimate (t_m) The time in which an activity can most frequently be completed under normal conditions.

N

Network diagram A graphic display of the activities to be performed to achieve the overall project work scope, showing their sequence and interdependencies.

Noncritical path In a network diagram, any path of activities with a positive value of total slack.

Normal cost The estimated cost of completing an activity under normal conditions, according to the plan.

Normal probability distribution A bell-shaped distribution of values that is symmetrical around its mean value.

Normal time The estimated length of time required to perform an activity under normal conditions, according to the plan.

O

Objective The expected result or product of a project, usually defined in terms of scope, schedule, and cost.

Optimistic time estimate (t_o) The time in which an activity can be completed if everything goes perfectly well and there are no complications.

Overhead A percentage of the direct costs of a particular project, added to a contractor's proposal to cover costs of doing business, such as insurance, depreciation, general management, and human resources; indirect costs.

P

Percent complete An estimate, in percentage form, of the proportion of the work involved in a particular work package that has been completed.

Pessimistic time estimate (t_p) The time in which an activity can be completed under adverse conditions, such as in the presence of unusual or unforeseen complications.

Planning The systematic arrangement of tasks to accomplish an objective; determining what needs to be done, who will do it, how long it will take, and how much it will cost.

Precedence diagramming method (PDM) A type of network planning technique.

Precedential relationship The order in which activities must be finished before other activities can start.

Predecessor event The event at the beginning of an activity (tail of the arrow) in the activity-on-the-arrow form of network diagramming; start event.

Program evaluation and review technique (PERT) A network planning technique.

Project An endeavor to accomplish a specific objective through a unique set of interrelated tasks and the effective utilization of resources.

Project control Regularly gathering data on actual project performance, comparing actual performance to planned performance, and taking corrective measures if actual performance is behind planned performance.

Project life cycle The four phases through which a project moves—identification of a need, problem, or opportunity, development of a proposed solution, implementation of the proposed solution, and termination of the project.

Project organization structure An organization structure in which each project has its own project manager and project team and all the resources needed to accomplish an individual project are assigned full-time to that project.

Project scope All the work that must be done to accomplish the project's objective to the customer's satisfaction; scope of the project; work scope.

Proposal A document, usually prepared by a contractor, that outlines an approach to meeting a need or solving a problem for a potential customer.

R

Reporting period The time interval at which actual project performance will be compared to planned performance.

Request for proposal (RFP) A document, usually prepared by the customer, that defines a need or problem, requirements, and expectations.

Required completion time The time or date by which a project must be completed.

Resource leveling A method for developing a schedule that attempts to minimize the fluctuations in requirements for resources without extending the project schedule beyond the required completion time; resource smoothing

Resource-limited scheduling A method for developing the shortest schedule when the number or amount of available resources is limited. This method will extend the project completion time if necessary in order to keep within the resource limits.

Resource smoothing *See* Resource leveling.

Responsibility matrix A table that lists the individuals or organizational units responsible for accomplishing each work item in a work breakdown structure.

S

Schedule A timetable for a project plan.

Scope of the project *See* Project scope.

Slack *See* Total slack.

Standard deviation A measure of the dispersion, or spread, of a distribution from its expected value; the square root of the variance.

Start event *See* Predecessor event.

Statement of work (SOW) A document outlining the tasks, or work elements, the customer wants the contractor to perform.

Successor event The event at the end of an activity (head of the arrow) in the activity-on-the-arrow form of network diagramming; finish event.

Systems development life cycle (SDLC) A project management planning tool consisting of a set of phases or steps to be completed over the course of development of an information system.

T

Task *See* Activity.

Time estimate *See* Duration estimate.

Total budgeted cost (TBC) The portion of the entire project budget that is allocated to complete all of the activities and work associated with a particular work package.

Total slack (TS) Float. If it's a positive value, it's the amount of time that the activities on a particular path can be delayed without jeopardizing completion of the project by its required completion time. If it's a negative value, it's the amount of time that the activities on a particular path must be accelerated in order to complete the project by its required completion time.

V

Variance A measure of the dispersion, or spread, of a distribution from its expected value.

W

Work breakdown structure (WBS) A hierarchical tree of work elements or items that will be accomplished or produced by the project team during the project.

Work items Individual pieces of a project in a work breakdown structure.

Work package The lowest-level item of any branch of a work breakdown structure.

Work scope *See* Project scope.

INDEX